Birth by Design

Birth
by Design

PREGNANCY, MATERNITY CARE,
AND MIDWIFERY IN
NORTH AMERICA AND EUROPE

EDITED BY
Raymond De Vries, Cecilia Benoit,
Edwin R. van Teijlingen,
and Sirpa Wrede

Routledge
NEW YORK LONDON

Published in 2001 by
Routledge
29 West 35th Street
New York, NY 10001

Published in Great Britain by
Routledge
11 New Fetter Lane
London EC4P 4EE

Copyright © 2001 by Routledge
Routledge is an imprint of the Taylor & Francis Group.

Printed in the United States of America on acid-free paper.

10 9 8 7 6 5 4 3 2 1

Library of Congress Cataloging-in-Publication Data

Birth by design : pregnancy, maternity care, and midwifery in North America and Europe / edited by Raymond DeVries . . . [et al.].
       p. cm.
    Includes bibliographical references and index.
    ISBN 0-415-92337-9—ISBN 0-415-92338-7 (pbk.)
    1. Maternal health services—North America. 2. Maternal Health services—Europe. I.
DeVries, Raymond G.

RG963.A1 B57 2001
362.1'982—dc21
                                                                    00-055327

Contents

Foreword

Robbie Davis-Floyd

The title for this book was chosen at a Midwifery Today[1] conference held in Salem, Massachusetts. Three of the contributors to this book—Raymond DeVries, Eugene Declercq, and I—were conference speakers. Our talks on that sunshiny day in the fall of 1997 fit well with the conference theme of counteracting negative stereotypes of midwives. Ray described his extensive research on the Dutch obstetrical system, which American midwives have long regarded with awe, envying the central place held by midwives in Dutch maternity care, the extensive governmental support they receive, and the 30 percent home birth rate they maintain (DeVries 1996, xiv–xix). Gene eloquently told the story of Hannah Porn, a professionally trained Finnish midwife whose life work was attending the births of the women of her immigrant community in Massachusetts in the early 1900s. Through extensive historical research, Gene had discovered that Hannah Porn had been repeatedly arrested and persecuted by the physicians in her area as they sought to cement their monopoly over childbirth, but had nevertheless continued to attend births, literally, until the day she died (Declercq 1994). And I gave a talk about the development of direct-entry midwifery in the United States, focusing on the challenges American midwives have faced and transcended during their process of professionalization (Davis-Floyd 1998). As it turned out, these topics foreshadowed many of the issues addressed in the book you now hold in your hands: the history of midwifery and the tension between the spiritual calling and the professional agenda that many midwives experience, the medicalization of reproduction and the dilemmas this has posed for midwives and for women, the diversity of cultural approaches to birth, and the embeddedness of birth practitioners in larger political and gender struggles over the question, "Whose knowledge counts?"[2]

In the evening, Ray, Gene, and I sat down to discuss these larger issues and their relationship to this volume, the creation of which was but barely begun. Soon our discussion moved into a search for the right book title. We began with *The Social Shaping of Maternity Care in Euroamerica*. It was descriptive and accurate, but too long and too boring to serve as the actual title. We tried several variations, but none of them seemed quite right. We had just gotten to a point of total frustration when mid-wife Elizabeth Davis, renowned author of the midwifery textbook *Heart and Hands* (1983, 1987), joined us. Hoping she could help, we explained that we were stuck try-ing to find the right title for an international collection that would compare birthways in Western, industrialized countries—those that could, by way of strong financial resources and shared access to information and technology, be expected to share equal access to obstetrical information and technology. We told Elizabeth that the driving question behind this project was, "Given a shared knowledge base and equal access to resources, why are there such extreme differences among these countries in the cultural management of birth?"

So what, we asked, should we call the book? Elizabeth thought for a moment, wrote something on a napkin, and handed it to Ray, whose face brightened as he read, "Birth by Design." We were delighted, we had our title. And of course, it is no acci-dent that it was an American direct-entry midwife who conceived it. Elizabeth Davis is one of the pioneers of the American home birth and midwifery movements; she has been practicing and teaching out-of-hospital midwifery for over twenty-five years, during which she has bumped up against the dominant culture thousands of times. Thus she has had ample opportunity to observe the extreme effects that cultural notions about birth can have on its medical management and social treatment and to perceive the cultural design behind Western birthways. And for our part, the twenty years or more that Ray, Gene, and I have each spent researching and writing about both alternative and hegemonic ways of conceptualizing and attending births made us instantly responsive to Elizabeth's keenly perceptive title.

What is "birth by design"? These three words, with brevity and elegance, encapsu-late everything the authors of this volume have tried to accomplish. A point that will emerge repeatedly from these pages is that birth does not just happen: although human parturition may have started out as a process designed by nature over millions of years of human evolution, for millennia it has been consciously and intentionally designed by humans in ways that reflect core aspects of their cultures. This book is about the sociocultural design of childbirth, which means that it is also about the extraordinary cross-cultural variation in that sociocultural design. No human culture is the same as any other, and neither are the birthways human cultures create.

Birth, a physiological process with certain universal characteristics, is at the same time an individual experience totally unique to each woman who experiences it and a profoundly significant cultural event, as the future of a society (still) depends on women giving birth to babies who will grow up to perpetuate that society. Thus, all human cultures take an interest in birth, stamping this physiological and individual experience with a distinct cultural imprint. Identifying the distinctiveness of these myriad cultural stamps is a particularly intriguing enterprise for the countries of the industrialized West, as the obstetrical systems of every such nation insist that their management of childbirth is science-based. If that were so, then there should be *no* significant differences in the management of birth among the countries addressed in this volume, for science, presumably, sets clear standards that are universally applic-able. But, as the chapters in this volume show, there is in fact extreme variation in the cultural treatment of birth among these developed nations. Thus the comparative study of their birthways is particularly revealing, for it demonstrates not only the cul-tural differences among Western nations but also the discrepancy between the scientific rationale claimed by Western medicine and the reality of its actual practice. The chapters that follow reveal the obstetric systems of the developed West as concatenations of thought, practice, and belief that reflect cultural bias and influence as much as they reflect the science on which they purportedly depend.

The authors who have carried out this comparison have studied childbirth in nine different countries (Finland, Norway, Sweden, Germany, the Netherlands, France, the United Kingdom, the United States, and Canada) and represent a variety of academic disciplines, including sociology, anthropology, history, political science, medicine, and midwifery. In the Introduction to this volume, the editors describe the intensely collaborative process that went into its making, which included face-to-face meetings in three countries and a blizzard of e-mail messages accompanied by chapter attachments. What they do not fully address is the special pleasure the members of this group took in this intensive interaction. During the twentieth century, reproductive studies were not central to the concerns of many of the disciplines we represent; it took the feminist movement in the West to bring them into the light as subjects worthy of serious academic investigation. As a result, reproductive studies are less developed and remain more marginalized in academia than do other, longer-established areas of research. Some of the scholars in this book are alone in their cities or countries in their focus on reproductive research. Thus we experienced great joy in finding each other and in the many in-depth discussions we shared on issues of mutual interest.

In addition, we quickly discovered that incorporating many scholars in one project, while a logistical nightmare, is also a cross-cultural researcher's dream. No one scholar has the energy or resources to become an expert on the deep intricacies of reproduction in more than a few cultures in one lifetime. How then to achieve the excellence in analysis that comes from looking deep into the microlevel of people's day-to day-lives and reproductive decisions in a given group, in combination with the broader understandings gained when a variety of larger cultural systems are compared? In this endeavor, it has been abundantly apparent that thirty heads are far better than one.

But that "one" still matters a great deal, and I wish here to acknowledge that this book primarily owes its existence to Raymond DeVries, who conceived the idea for it, obtained funding for the first two meetings, and saw it through copyediting and page proofs to publication. In these endeavors he was ably assisted by his three coeditors, Edwin van Teijlingen, who lives in the United Kingdom but hails from the Netherlands, Sirpa Wrede from Finland, and Cecilia Benoit from Canada. This international editorial team tapped its full resource base of the best scholars studying childbirth and reproduction in the countries in question to create the group that, with the publication of this groundbreaking book, fulfills Ray's vision of a truly transnational and collaborative work that is at once deeply specific and broadly comparative.

Birth tends to bring out the best in people. The intensity of the mother's effort, the magic of the baby's emergence, the thrill generated by the appearance of a tiny new life, and the creation of a new family have an effect on all involved. Around the world, many midwives experience a strong spiritual calling to practice midwifery, to be "with woman" through the intense and agonizing hours of labor to the hard work, mystery, and joy of birth. Midwives' passion for their work is paralleled by the passion many of us who study childbirth feel for our research. We can never forget that our subjects include real women carrying and giving birth to real babies and that this process will be life-transforming in either intensely positive or intensely negative ways. Thus an equal intensity seems to characterize the academic study of childbirth and reproduction. We *care* about the process and the outcomes of birth, about the practitioners who dedicate their lives to facilitating this process and ensuring its safety, and about the effects its social shaping has on mothers, babies, and families. This caring permeates our research, our collaboration, and our writing; it is my hope that you will feel its depth as you peruse these pages.

Notes

1. Midwifery Today is a U.S.-based organization.
2. See Jordan 1997; Davis-Floyd and Sargent 1997.

References

Davis, Elizabeth. 1997 (1983). *Heart and Hands: A Midwife's Guide to Pregnancy and Birth,* 3rd ed. Berkeley, CA: Celestial Arts.

Davis-Floyd, Robbie. 1998. "The Ups, Downs, and Interlinkages of Nurse- and Direct-Entry Midwifery." In *Paths to Becoming a Midwife: Getting an Education,* eds. Jan Tritten and Joel Southern. Eugene, OR: Midwifery Today.

Davis-Floyd, Robbie, and Carolyn Sargent. 1997. *Childbirth and Authoritative Knowledge: Cross-Cultural Perspectives.* Berkeley: University of California Press.

Declercq, Eugene. 1994. The Trials of Hanna Porn: The Campaign to Abolish Midwifery in Massachusetts, *American Journal of Public Health,* 84:1022–1028.

DeVries, Raymond. 1996. *Making Midwives Legal.* Columbus, Ohio: Ohio State University Press.

Jordan, Brigitte. 1997. Authoritative knowledge and its construction. In *Childbirth and Authoritative knowledge: Cross-Cultural Perspectives,* eds. Robbie Davis-Floyd and Carolyn Sargent. Berkeley: University of California Press, pp. 55–79.

Introduction: Why Maternity Care Is *Not* Medical Care

Several years ago, the distinguished Dutch obstetrician-gynecologist, Professor Gerrit-Jan Kloosterman was invited to London to give a lecture to an international association of obstetricians and gynecologists. Kloosterman, Chair of Obstetrics at the University of Amsterdam, was well respected and well known for his support of the maternity care system in the Netherlands, a system that relies heavily on midwife-assisted births at home. He was in the middle of his lecture—an analysis of the Dutch system that showed the continued use of midwife-attended home birth posed no danger to mothers and babies—when a strange thing happened. While he was talking, several members of the audience got up and left the room, noisily, in an obvious display of displeasure with his presentation.

After he finished the lecture, Kloosterman and the president of the association discussed the small "protest." They asked themselves, "Why doesn't this happen in other specialties?" They agreed it would be unheard of for physicians to walk out in the middle of a lecture about cardiology, even if they thought the data were suspect. Protocol in the science of medicine dictates that disagreements about data are hashed out in collegial exchanges: One does not "protest" against data; one challenges the data on the basis of methodology or analytic technique. Kloosterman and the president concluded that obstetrics does not really belong in the field of medicine. Perhaps, they conjectured, obstetrics is better located in the field of physiology. After all, it is the only discipline in medicine where something happens by itself, and, in most cases, with no intervention, everything ends well. Thinking about this incident, Kloosterman concluded: "Obstetrics is wider and broader than pure medicine. It has to do with the whole of life, the way you look at life, making objective discussion difficult. You are almost unable to split the problem off into pure science; always your outlook on life is involved."[1]

Kloosterman has it right. One need not look too far into the world of maternity care to find the wide gap between scientific evidence and clinical practice. For example, consider this: In May 1998 the U.S. National Center for Health Statistics released a report on the comparative infant mortality rates for midwives and physicians in the United States (NCHS, 1998). The study included all single vaginal births in the United States in 1991 delivered between thirty-five and forty-three weeks gestation. Controlling for risk factors[2] the study found that midwives had significantly lower rates of infant mortality and better outcomes with regard to birthweight:

- 19 percent lower infant mortality (death of the child in the first year after birth)
- 33 percent lower neonatal mortality (death of the child in the first twenty-eight days after birth)
- 31 percent lower risk of low birthweight
- 37 grams heavier mean birthweight

The report notes that, in general, midwives' practices include higher numbers of poor and minority women who are at greater risk of poor birth outcome. The report concludes:

> The differences in birth outcomes between certified nurse midwife and physician attended births may be explained in part by difference in prenatal, labor and delivery care practices. Other studies have shown certified nurse midwives generally spend more time with patients during prenatal visits and put more emphasis on patient counseling and education, and providing emotional support. Most certified nurse midwives are with their patients on a one-to-one basis during the entire labor and delivery process providing patient care and emotional support, in contrast with physician's care which is more episodic.

The data are persuasive, but—consistent with Kloosterman's observations—this study has had almost no effect on health policy and the delivery of care in the United States. Although they provide less expensive, more satisfying, and more effective care, certified nurse midwives attended less than 7 percent of all births in the United States in 1997 (Curtin and Park, 1999).

Taken together, these two stories highlight the fact that—more than any other area of medical practice—the organization and provision of maternity care is a highly charged mix of medical science, cultural ideas, and structural forces. Maternity care can be distinguished from other forms of medical care because:

- What is at stake in care at birth is not the survival of one patient but the reproduction of society.
- Latent in the care given to women at birth are ideas about sexuality, about women, and about families.
- While all other medical specialties (with the possible exception of pediatrics) begin with a focus on disease, the essential task here is the supervision of normal, healthy, physical growth.
- The quality of maternity care—in both senses of that word, its nature and its outcomes—is often used as a measure for the quality of an entire health care system. Infant mortality rates have become a shorthand measure for the adequacy of a society's health system and its overall quality of life.

Other medical specialties are marked by a technical uniformity that crosses national borders, but—as this volume shows—the design of care at birth varies widely and clearly bears the marks of the society in which it is found. This complicates clinical practice, but it also affords social scientists a wonderful opportunity to examine the many factors that shape the delivery of care at birth and other medical services. In important ways, birth is to the study of health care as chromosome 22 is to the study of the human genome. Scientists chose chromosome 22—the smallest and simplest of human chromosomes—as the first to be mapped in its entirety. Scientists were convinced that the lessons learned here could be applied to the other, more complex chromosomes. Maternity care plays the same role for researchers interested in health care systems—not because it is "simple" but because, unlike other medical specialties, the influence of culture and society is not masked by uniformity in technology and practice. Study of the various ways care at birth is offered gives us the chance to map out the way medical practice is produced by social situations.

Unfortunately, we social scientists have overlooked this distinctive characteristic of maternity care. We have done too few comparative studies, and when we *have* done comparative research, more often than not we have done single-country studies supplemented with limited observations in a second or third country, observations intended to support, not complicate, the original analysis. The result of our parochial approach to maternity care research has been overreliance on professional and gender rivalries as explanatory variables. Without a sense of how social, political, and cultural factors and differences have shaped care practices, it has been easy for us to see gender and professional power as *the* driving forces in current policies and the organization of care. In reality, the cause of current practices is far more complicated than our single-society studies suggest.

Birth by Design provides a remedy for this social scientific ethnocentrism. The pages that follow are filled with rich descriptions of maternity care in several countries. Our goal is to "decenter" the study of maternity care from particular national contexts, to move it analytically in a direction in which *any and all* contexts are perceived as problematic. As you read these pages we would like you to ask yourself how care at birth has been shaped by:

- Political systems
- State intervention
- The organization of the professions
- Educational systems
- Stratification systems and inequality
- Attitudes about, and uses of, technology

In reflecting on these questions, you will begin to appreciate the great variation in maternity care and the many ways society shapes clinical practices—at birth and elsewhere. Further reflection will lead you to consider the role of culture in the organization of care: As you begin to appreciate varied attitudes about technology or the proper role of the state, you must ask yourself why different societies generate such different ideas. You will see that each of the countries represented here has distinctive cultural values that play an important role in the design of maternity care. The Nordic countries are marked by a thoroughgoing pragmatism that seeks to combine cost-effectiveness with best results. This same attitude is found in the United Kingdom—with its strong emphasis on randomized clinical trials—and in the Netherlands—where the government has invested much money in researching and supporting midwife-assisted home birth. Both the United States and Canada place a high value on technology, but the United States allows the market to determine many aspects of health care delivery, while Canada exhibits a more European concern with social welfare.

Why These Countries?

A researcher who does cross-national comparisons must be ready to explain the selection of countries involved. Often, the choice of subjects in social research has more to do with convenience than with careful prospective consideration of the variables involved: For example, a researcher may choose to do an ethnography of a hospital, *not* because it represents some particularly interesting organizational form but because her brother-in-law is on staff there. The case studies included here represent a combination of convenience and methodological choice. The number of social scientists working in the area of maternity care is not that large. Most of us know each other's work, if not each other. In putting this project together it was logical to work with this core group of scholars: In that sense, *Birth by Design* uses a "convenience sample." But there is a method to our (convenience) madness. The countries studied here all come from Western Europe and North America. In the early stages of this project we *did* consider including countries in Latin America, South America, and Southern and Eastern Europe (we know researchers working in these parts of the world as well), but we decided that inclusion of countries from these regions would introduce a flood of variables that would limit our ability to compare. In restricting our comparisons to the countries of Western Europe and North America we seek to control some intercountry variation: All of the maternity care systems described in these pages are found in high-income, technologically sophisticated countries.

Certain of the several countries described here—in particular, Canada, the United Kingdom, the Netherlands, and the United States—are covered more extensively than others. These countries are oversampled for a number of reasons. First, a great deal of published research on maternity care has been done in these countries. Social scientists and historians turned their attention to maternity care in these four countries in the 1970s and 1980s; in the other countries of Western Europe research of this type did not get underway until the 1990s. Second, peculiar events or conditions in these countries make them attractive models for analysis. In recent years the governments of the United Kingdom and Canada have challenged traditional understandings of birth and maternity care with legislation that lends strong support for an autonomous profession of midwifery. In the United States efforts to revive home birth and midwifery are played out against a system with extremely high use of technology at birth. And the Netherlands remains an obstetric anachronism with extraordinarily high rates of midwife-attended home birth. Finally, these four countries represent the range of approaches to state funding of health care, from socialized systems (in Canada and the United Kingdom), to a mix of public control with private markets (in the Netherlands) to a market-based system (in the United States).

The Framework of Birth by Design

When we began this project, there were no clear frameworks for the organization of comparative studies of maternity care. We did see some similarities between the care systems of the countries of North America and Western Europe—such as the twentieth-century movement of birth from home to hospital and the public provision of maternity services—but we were also confronted with an enormous diversity of designs. Even the two trends just mentioned need to be qualified: In the Netherlands home birth is still quite common, and in the United States there is no system allowing universal access to maternity services. The more we talked together, the more we became aware of numerous differences in how services are provided, in the maternity care division of labor, in the use of obstetrical technology, and in women's wishes and expectations regarding care at birth.

To manage this diversity we created a framework that separates the macro, meso, and micro levels of analysis. Our analysis shows that maternity care is designed at different levels of society. At the macro level we find birth being shaped by the arrangements of national states and political party systems, the *polity*. Moving to the meso level, we see the system of the professions—including relationships between the professional groups that provide maternity care—exerting its influence on how care is delivered. And on the micro level we note how the face-to-face interaction between clients and caregivers determines the experience of birth. The three parts of *Birth by Design* represent these three levels of analysis, although—just as in the real world where these categories intermingle and overlap—some chapters explore more than one level of influence.

Birth by Design offers a nuanced analysis of the differences and similarities in the organization of maternity care in a sample of high-income countries. Using a multi-country, multilevel method we are able to show that maternal health care arrangements have *not* followed the same "evolutionary paths" in all countries; furthermore, our analysis convinces us that a diversity of maternity care designs will survive in the future. The social and cultural diversity of societies cannot be separated from the organizational arrangement of maternity care.

On Collaboration

Birth by Design began as a project entitled *The Evolution of Obstetric Care in North America and Northern Europe,* funded by the Council for European Studies at Columbia University. The primary goal of that project was to bring together a group of researchers from Europe and North America, all of whom had done studies on maternity care. The intent was to allow these researchers to collaborate, using the work they had originally done, to tease out certain themes in the social organization of maternity care. Rather than generating a book of parallel readings ("Maternity Care in France," "Maternity Care in Germany," "Maternity Care in the United Kingdom"), we hoped to produce a book that used existing work to illuminate transnational patterns in maternity care: the influence of the state, the role of attitudes about gender, the effect of educational systems, and so on.

Editing an anthology is widely seen as an easy way to produce a book; only those who have actually served as editors know how time-consuming, patience-testing, and frustrating the task can be. The production of *Birth by Design* suffered all the ordinary problems of anthologies, and then some. We violated nearly every guideline for creating a collection of readings. We did not start with papers prepared for a conference. Each chapter was to have at least two authors, and each author was to come from a different country. When we described this project to our colleagues, most thought that we had lost our minds. It is true we live in the Internet age, where e-mail makes it possible to cooperate with colleagues living miles and countries away. But we were starting each chapter from scratch, we were asking our authors to move between cultures (both academic and national) and to find comfortable ways of working together, and we were creating the additional problem of multiple-author chapters. Is it any wonder our colleagues thought us daft?

We *were* made slightly crazy by the task, but in the end we are delighted with the product. Not only have we transcended the disjointed nature of most anthologies, we have also (we believe) created a new model for cross-national research.

With its authors and editors scattered across two continents, this book represents one of the first efforts at *cyber-teamwork*. However, the project would have been impossible without a few face-to-face meetings. Funding from the Council for European Studies and from the (government-funded) Academy of Finland allowed us to meet on three separate occasions. In November 1997 a group of us met in Washington, D.C., where we worked out the original design of the book. This initial group included a number of people who eventually left the project, but whose help was invaluable for getting this project going, including Hilary Marland, Signild Vallgårda, Robbie Pfeufer Kahn, Marsden Wagner, Marcia Maust, Lisa Vanderlinden, Harald Abrahamse, Rudi Bakker, and Ken Johnson. A second meeting took place in Bilthoven, the Netherlands, in April 1999, hosted by the Royal Dutch Organization of Midwives. At this meeting we presented working drafts of the papers and revised the content and organization of the book. Our final meeting took place in December 1999 at the Åbo Akademi University in Turku, Finland. Final drafts of the chapters were presented, and we editors amended, deleted, and rearranged text. Between these meetings, thousands of e-mail messages carrying comments and versions of the chapters traveled among authors and editors. Together we worked out ways of using technology to generate a truly collaborative social science. We suffered all the problems and misunderstandings of communicating in a medium that does not allow nods, winks, and voice inflection. More than once feathers were ruffled by misunderstood messages.

In the end, we discovered ourselves to be, to greater or lesser degrees, parochial. We fancied ourselves quite cosmopolitan, open to cultural variations, but, as we proceeded with our collaborative work, we discovered that our ideas, our theories, and our methods were culturally bound. One example will illustrate. At our first meeting our group got into a frustrating debate about what should be included in a chapter examining the role of the state in maternity care. The more we talked, the more confused and frustrated we became. In an effort to clear the air, someone asked: "What is the main task of the state?" The Americans in the group replied: "To ensure that individual women have freedom of choice" and "to make choices available for childbearing women." The Europeans in the group had a different response: "To ensure that the poorest women in society have access to a reasonable quality of maternity care" and "to ensure that all women have access to good maternity care." We thought we were all being good open-minded scholars, but, in fact, we were talking from our own culturally colored perspectives.

If your experience as a reader is anything like ours as editors, you too will discover the boundaries of your understanding as you move through this book. If nothing else, we hope that, like us, you will see how theories about the operation of health care systems or professions are limited by a single-society approach.

What Is Not Here

Even a book with as broad a focus as *Birth by Design* cannot do everything. In the interest of "truth in advertising" we wish to point out what we have *not* done in this book. This book is not an attempt to support one design for maternity care over another. Although we discuss empirical research that offers evidence about the safety and/or danger of certain practices, it is not our intent to make a case for a particular system of care. We are interested in how empirical evidence is marshaled and used to support policy decisions, not in offering advice to policymakers.

This is not to say that this work is of no use to those who seek to change childbirth practices. Because we are *not* involving ourselves in making an "evidence-based" case for maternity care practices, we are free to explore the conditions that allow and promote effective reform. Our work highlights the features of the state, the society, and the culture that alter the design of birth. Those who wish to change the way maternity care is organized in their country—be they clients, obstetricians, mid-wives, or legislators—must pay attention to forces that combine to create care systems. Indeed, it is our hope that readers of this book will use our insights to find the most effective ways to promote policies that diminish inequality, poverty, and ill health.

Our focus here is restricted to maternity care during the prepartum, intrapartum, and postpartum periods. We do make occasional references to family policies—including parental leave and childcare—but only in the context of their relation to decisions about care in pregnancy and at birth.

A Few Last Words

In the course of doing our collaborative work we were struck by the great variation in the roles played by midwives. Definitions of the profession of midwifery and of the duties assigned to midwives are *so* varied that it might be fair to say that the "idea" of a midwife is all that is shared between countries. This variation makes it difficult for midwives from different countries to collaborate, but it is a social scientist's dream. When we see variation we see the perfect opportunity to better understand society: Having described different outcomes, we can go to work identifying the sources of that variation. It should be no surprise, then, that midwives are a predominant subject of *Birth by Design*. In examining the varied roles they play we discern much about how birth is regarded and how care is organized.

It should also be no surprise that gender analysis is an important part of this book. Because birth is central to the lives of women and is often regarded as women's work, social scientific studies of maternity care must emphasize gender. A strength of *Birth by Design* is that it locates the gender issues associated with birth in the larger social and cultural system.

The data for the case studies in *Birth by Design* come, for the most part, from the original work of the authors. In some cases these data are supplemented by secondary data and by information from published studies and government reports.

Birth by Design marks an important stride forward in our understanding of maternity care and in the presentation of a new model for scholarly collaboration. We editors would not have been able to do this work were it not for the financial and social support we have been given. The Council for European Studies (Columbia University) provided major funding for this project; the Academy of Finland, the Finnish private foundation *Stiftelsens för Åbo Akademi forskningsinstitut*, and the Royal Dutch Organization of Midwives provided additional funding. De Vries's research on maternity care was funded by the U.S. National Institutes of Health (Grant number F06-TWO1954), the Netherlands Institute for Health Care Research (NIVEL), the *Catharina Schrader Stichting*, and a number of faculty development grants from St. Olaf College. Wrede's research on maternity care is funded through a Ph.D. program supported by the Finnish Ministry of Education and by a grant for work with *Birth by Design* from the private foundation *Stiftelsens för Åbo Akademi forskningsinstitut*. Van Teijlingen's research on maternity care is funded by the University of Aberdeen through its health and health services research theme. Benoit's research on midwifery and maternal health systems is funded by the National Network on Environments and Women's Health (Health Canada).

A community of colleagues, co-workers, and family members offered equally important social support. Our family members tolerated long absences of their mothers, fathers, wives, and husbands; co-workers lent many needed hands for organizational tasks. Steven Polansky offered helpful and needed editorial advice. Eileen Shimota was particularly supportive in the scheduling and organizing of our first two meetings. Our third meeting would not have been possible without the support of Professor Elianne Riska; Lea Henriksson and Lena Marander-Eklund offered kind and enormous assistance in the organization of that meeting.

This book is dedicated to the health and happiness of mothers, babies, and fathers around the world.

Notes

1. Fieldnotes, Raymond DeVries.
2. Controlling for risk eliminates the argument that poorer outcomes for physicians are a consequence of the fact that they see patients at higher-risk. It *is* true that higher risk women are referred to physician care, but these comparisons are made *within* risk categories, so we are looking at outcomes when physicians and midwives care for women at the *same level* of risk.

References

Curtin, S., and M. Park. 1999. *Trends in the Attendant, Place and Timing of Births, and in the Use of Obstetric Interventions: United States, 1989–97* (National Vital Statistics Reports, Vol. 47, No. 27). Hyattsville, MD: National Center for Health Statistics.

NCHS (U.S. National Center for Health Statistics.) 1998. New study shows lower mortality rates for infants delivered by certified nurse midwives. www.cdc.gov/nchswww/releases/98news/98news/midwife.htm, accessed March 27, 2000.

PART I:

The Politics of Maternity Care

Introduction to Part I

Sirpa Wrede

For feminist writers of the 1970s, maternity care, with its medicalized and alienating approach to birth, was an apt illustration of women's oppression by patriarchal social structures. Their critical assessment of the treatment of women at birth led to a blossoming of academic interest in maternity care. Numerous studies were generated, first in Anglo America and somewhat later in other high-income countries. The majority of this early work examined the power relations between physicians, pregnant women, and midwives. As the field developed, research began to present a more complex picture of maternity services, and yet in most studies medical science and the medical profession remained central. Medical science was seen as *the* source of power for maternity care professionals, allowing hospitals and medical specialists to assume control of the conduct of birth.

This single-minded focus on power relations in maternity care was driven by the close links between researchers and the campaigns to reform birth practices that populated the social landscape when the academic study of maternity care was in its infancy. But the field is maturing. Thirty years after the first feminist exposés of the mistreatment of women at birth, maternity care research is becoming more closely linked to academic disciplines and to ongoing scholarly debates. As a result, new perspectives and new areas of inquiry are emerging. One of the more promising of these is comparative research on the politics of maternity care.

The chapters in this part represent some of the best new work in this area. These studies of the comparative politics of maternity care services present a more complicated, but more accurate, understanding of the way maternal health services emerge and are designed. The comparative data presented here show medical science to be just one among several important actors that influence the form and content of maternity care.

The five chapters in this section approach the politics of maternity care from different angles, but taken together they allow us to draw a shared conclusion: The organization of maternal health services is a contested domain where negotiations and struggles constantly occur. Maternal health services in the present-day societies of

North America and Europe result from purposeful designs and are shaped by the actions of multiple groups. No one party, not even the state, has the sole authority to design maternal health services.

The first chapter discusses the issue most central to the organization of maternity services in the twentieth century, the location of birth. Although much discussed in the literature, the topic has not been exhausted and is sorely in need of a perspective drawn from the comparison of developments in different countries. Declercq and his colleagues examine five case studies—the United States, Britain, Finland, the Netherlands, and Norway. The cases exemplify different logics for the organization of birth. The authors show that even though birth in high-income countries generally takes place in large, specialized hospitals, the policy processes that led to this outcome were quite different. Their work also calls attention to maternity policies that run counter to the trend toward centralization. Home birth remains part of the care system in the Netherlands and is being encouraged again in the United Kingdom, while in Norway policymakers are defending small maternity hospitals in rural areas. The variation presented in this chapter—in policy and in the roles of birth attendants and technology—makes clear that it is too early to argue for convergence in the organization of birth in high-income countries. We need more nuanced information about the way care at birth is shaped by different national settings and by different hospitals.

The second chapter focuses on the role of the state in generating variation in maternal health designs. Wrede and her colleagues focus on "critical moments" in maternity health policy. The chapter shows that maternity care has only rarely been at the center of the political arena in the three countries studied (Britain, Canada, and Finland). The authors conclude that state interest in maternity care services generally centers on the same pragmatic interests found in policy questions about other health services. Of course, political currents can, and have, shaped maternity care policy. The British and Finnish cases show how maternity care policies emerged from political concerns about population. In the United Kingdom and Canada we see policymakers responding to the call for "woman-centered" care, and in Finland policymakers have adopted a family-centered approach in an effort to promote, among other things, more equally shared parenthood. In general, however, the organization and transformation of maternal health services have been linked to *overall* policymaking concerning health care systems.

In Chapter 3 Bourgeault and her colleagues look at the influence of consumer interest groups on maternity care policy. Drawing on research in three countries—Canada, the United Kingdom, and the United States—the authors examine the factors that allow consumers to affect maternity policy. Their data suggest that well-organized pressure can make a difference in policy decisions, but they are careful to note the problems and limitations of consumer involvement in policy. Recent events in Canada and the United Kingdom show that effective consumer action requires both access to policymaking arenas *and* a measure of good luck concerning timing. Furthermore, the authors remind us that consumer groups are not democratic: Like all social organizations, these groups come to develop their own expertise and agendas.

Drawing on ethnographic data from Canada and the United States, Chapter 4 offers another perspective on collective action in maternity care reform. Daviss—an apprentice-trained midwife and a long-time activist in the Canadian alternative birth movement (ABM)—writes a passionate defense of the efforts of the ABM to transform the deeper cultural context of birth. She does not necessarily agree that the introduction of midwifery to the health system in Canada (discussed in Chapter 3) has been a success for the ABM. She fears that insiders in maternal health service policy in Canada—some of whom were members of the ABM—have been co-opted and forced to give up their original goals.

The contrast between the ABM described by Daviss and the pressure groups discussed in Chapter 3 is instructive. Supporters of movements like the ABM are drawn from policy outsiders who are often less interested in influencing public policy than in creating alternative solutions that promote great individual freedom. This (voluntarily chosen) position outside the policy system is possible only for people who can afford—economically and/or culturally—to ignore official services. For the majority of childbearing women and their partners it is difficult, if not impossible, to opt out of the existing system of care.

Interestingly, the stories of the ABM and other consumer pressure groups reveal that collaboration between maternity care providers and users is necessary to promote change in maternity services. In fact, maternity care providers—midwives and obstetrician-gynecologists—often play a central role in this type of social action. Most childbearing women and their partners are only temporarily active in issues surrounding birth, giving providers a chance to become the spokespersons for pressure groups. This provider/user collaboration is striking because the interests of providers and users are often in conflict.

In the last chapter of Part I, Nelson and Popenoe look within countries to examine effects of different policy styles. They show that there is significant *intracountry* variation in women's access to maternal health services in high-income countries. The authors illustrate how social categories of class, race/ethnicity, and immigrant status shape women's access to care in the United States and Sweden. In the United States, these categories play a significant role in the quality of care received, while in Sweden women's access to maternal health services is barely affected by social identity. Availability of a national maternity service (in Sweden but not in the United States) goes a long way toward explaining these intracountry differences. Universal care is not an unmixed blessing, however. The authors conclude their chapter by examining how the uniformity of maternity care in Sweden poses limits for new immigrants.

These studies of the political and social organization of birth show maternity care systems to be products of a complex of factors. They correct and complicate earlier views of the field and promote a richer understanding of the forces responsible for the delivery of care at birth.

CHAPTER 1

Where to Give Birth?

POLITICS AND THE PLACE OF BIRTH

*Eugene Declercq, Raymond DeVries, Kirsi Viisainen,
Helga B. Salvesen, and Sirpa Wrede*

Introduction

The most significant change in twentieth-century maternity care was the movement of the place of birth from the home to large hospitals. At the beginning of the last century virtually all births occurred at home; by the end of the century almost every woman who gave birth in an industrialized country (with the odd exception of the Netherlands) did so in a hospital. All the other major trends in maternity care that you will read about in this book—the changing status and role of midwives, the increasing use of technological interventions, the developments in maternity care policy, the redefinition of birth—are intimately related to this move from home to hospital. But the most interesting thing about this change in maternity care is that the end result— the (nearly) complete move of birth to the hospital—was achieved in a number of different ways. The decision to hospitalize birth in Finland was made for different reasons than the decision in the United Kingdom or the United States. This variation between countries offers us the perfect opportunity to isolate and examine societal and cultural differences in maternity care policies and practices.

Why should it matter where a baby is born? Simply stated, the place of birth shapes the experience, determining who is in control and the technologies to be employed. In a home birth, those attending are visitors in the family's domain, and midwives and doctors must rely on the family for an understanding of local customs and practices. The reverse is true for a mother in a hospital. In a hospital birth a

mother is placed in a dependent condition reinforced by the use of unfamiliar language and machinery. The place of birth also determines the way care is organized.
Birth at home is patterned around the values of the family. In hospitals—where
hundreds, or even thousands, of births occur each year—birth is a routine event,
accomplished with speed and efficiency.

The hospitalization of birth encourages the use of technologies that can only feasi-
bly be applied in a hospital. As the twentieth century progressed, hospitals became
centers where new technologies could be easily tested and then applied to large numbers of women. The concentration of women in one place made the training and
staffing needed to maintain the technologies clinically safer and economically feasible; the presence of the latest scientific technologies (e.g., fetal monitors and epidural
anesthesia) in hospitals served to enhance their prestige as centers of science.

Hospitalization of birth also has a variety of economic and social consequences. It
makes feasible a larger client base for providers, a particularly important issue in
those countries whose funding system rewards physicians for the size of their practice. It also eases the demands on providers and allows health planners to make care
more "efficient." Bringing large numbers of patients to a central location is much
more economical—for providers and planners—than providing care in homes or in a
series of small "cottage hospitals." If one considers birthing mothers to be economic
units, the larger the site, the greater the potential for economies of scale. The irony of
this approach is that it often leads to large birthing hospitals also becoming centers of
elaborate, and very expensive, technology, the use of which make birth more costly.

Our analysis of this most important change in twentieth-century maternity care
continues with a detailed look at five countries: the United States, Finland, the Netherlands, the United Kingdom, and Norway. After an overview of the general trend
toward hospital births in these countries, we move to in-depth case studies of each.

The Movement of Birth from the Home to the Hospital

The movement of birth from home to hospital in the twentieth century follows similar
patterns in many industrialized countries, although the change occurs at different times
in different places. The United States made the earliest and most rapid shift to hospitalization, with the biggest changes in the late 1930s. By 1954—when data are available
for the four countries shown in Figure 1–1—the United States was down to 6 percent
non-hospital births; Finland was at 25 percent, the United Kingdom was at 36 percent
and the Netherlands was at 77 percent. The pattern in the United Kingdom clearly parallels that in the Netherlands, with the changes occurring at the same time; the Dutch
out-of-hospital birth rate from the mid-1950s to the present, however, is approximately
35 percent higher than that of the United Kingdom. Universal (99 percent or more) hospitalization of birth occurred in Finland and the United States by the late 1960s and in
all the countries studied in this book (except the Netherlands) by the early 1980s.

The hospitalization of birth parallels the broader movement of health care out of
the home and the (more recent) centralization of health services in large medical centers. As hospitals grew—in number and in size—many procedures once done at
home were relocated to the hospital (Blom 1988). In the context of this larger move
toward the hospitalization of medical ministrations there were several peculiar fac-

FIGURE 1–1.
Finland, Netherlands, U.K. and U.S.
Out-of-Hospital Births, 1935–1997.

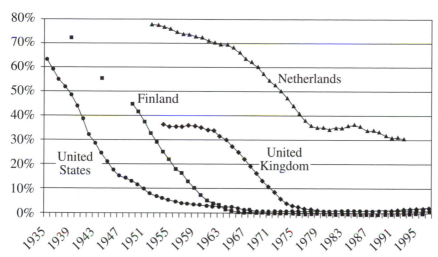

SOURCES: Finnish Data: The official statistics of Finland (Helsinki: National Board of Health); Isterland et al. 1978. *Perinataalistatus 1975* (Helsinki); Medical Birth Registry (Helsinki: STAKES). U.K. Data: 2000. *British Counts: Statistics of Pregnancy and Childbirth,* 2nd ed., vol. 2, tables by A. MacFarlane, M. Mugford, J. Henderson, A. Furtado, J. Stevens, and A. Dunn (London: The Stationary Office). U.S. Data: 1979. Devitt N. Hospital birth vs. home birth: The scientific facts past and present. In *Compulsory Hospitalization or Freedom of Choice in Childbirth?,* vol. 2, ed. D. Stewart and L. Stewart (Marble Hill, Missouri: NAPSAC):

tors that encouraged women to quit their homes to give birth. The move to hospital birth initially also required a redefinition of hospitals. At the opening of the nineteenth century, "Hospitals [in the United States] were regarded with dread and rightly so. They were dangerous places; when sick, people were safer at home" (Starr 1982, p. 72). In the second half of the nineteenth century, hospitals became the focus of successful reform efforts by both local elites and physician groups.

A third factor that helped to move maternity care into hospitals was a redefinition of birth as illness. In the early part of the twentieth century, childbirth was increasingly described as a dangerous malady requiring specialized care that could only be provided in the now "safe" hospital. Abetting this process was the development of anesthetics that were best administered in a hospital.

Finally, the movement of birth to the hospital served the campaign of physicians to undercut the status of midwives. Physician groups saw midwives as a threat to their status, especially in those countries where an attempt was being made to develop obstetrics as a specialty. This professional clash took alternative forms in different countries, but in all cases the hospitalization of birth served the purpose of physicians.

How were these general factors manifested in different countries? Existing studies offer some illustrations. In their comparison of the institutionalization of birth in the

United Kingdom and the Netherlands, Torres and Reich (1989) point to several elements that slowed the move to hospital birth in the Netherlands. Compared to the United Kingdom, they found that in the Netherlands: (1) midwives were in a stronger position relative to physicians, (2) safety was one of several goals in the birth process, and (3) the financing system supported home birth. Vallgarda (1996) offers an instructive comparison of the hospitalization of birth in Sweden and Denmark. Sweden hospitalized birth about twenty-five years earlier than Denmark, a puzzling fact given that the organization of the health care system and the number and scope of practice of midwives did not vary substantially between the two countries. After analyzing several variables she concludes that Sweden's faster adoption of hospital birth was largely a function of societal and economic changes, a greater commitment in Sweden to new technology, and a higher degree of state intervention.

Our case studies extend this earlier work. We begin with the United States and Finland, where the hospitalization of birth came earliest, although under very different circumstances. We follow that with the case of the Netherlands, where 30 percent of births still occur at home, an exception to the trend toward complete hospitalization of birth. We conclude with a look at recent developments in the United Kingdom, a country where home birth is making a comeback.

United States: Hospital Birth in the Private Sector

In 1998, 23,232 home births represented 0.59 percent of the almost 3.9 million births in the United States, a figure that has remained essentially stable over the past two decades (Ventura 2000). At the turn of the century almost all U.S. births were at home; by 1930 two-thirds of U.S. births were still at home. By 1960, however, 97 percent of U.S. births were in the hospital, with the largest change occurring between 1935 and 1944, when the proportion of hospital births more than doubled from 36.9 percent to 75.6 percent (Devitt 1979).

What led to this transformation? How well do the general points described above apply to the U.S. context? The U.S. experience with the lying-in hospital was more limited than it was in Europe, although as centers for birth, these hospitals promoted the education of physicians and the development of new birth technologies. However, hospital birth was still relatively rare as the new century began, gaining ground only in a few major urban areas (notably Boston, New York, and Philadelphia) where there had been concerted efforts to bring birth to the hospital. Hospitals consciously appealed to upper social class women by improving their facilities and providing a level of care not available at home. This was part of the general restructuring of the hospital that, as Starr (1982, pp. 147–148) notes, "involved its redefinition as an institution of medical science rather than of social welfare, its reorganization on the lines of a business rather than a charity, and its reorientation to professionals and their patients rather than to patrons and the poor."

The growth in hospitalization of birth in the period between 1930 and 1960 parallels the growth in hospital beds in the United States and the development of hospital insurance. Between 1935 and 1945 the proportion of hospitalized births in the United States grew from 36.9 percent to 78.8 percent. In the same decade, the United States experienced the fastest growth (163 percent) in the number of hospital beds in its history, with an increase from slightly more than 660,000 beds to 1,738, 944 (Arestad & McGovern 1950). The existence of all those hospital beds satisfied what might have been a latent demand for hospital birth and added to the pressure on physicians to bring births into the hospital. While the funding mechanisms for health care profoundly influence the place of birth in all countries, the reliance in the United States on private funding made its role there especially critical. Hospital insurance began in the United States in the late 1920s, but did not really begin growing until just prior to World War II, a period that coincides with the most rapid growth of hospitalized birth. The public, subsidized by their insurers, became more accustomed to using the local hospital, and, with some of the costs of a hospital birth now covered, the incentive to give birth in a hospital grew substantially.

Hospitalization of birth in the United States was aided in part by the development of new technologies, most notably, Twilight Sleep. Developed in Germany in 1902, Twilight Sleep soon came to the United States and became the focus of a small but vocal women's movement that actively promoted its use. Following the introduction of Twilight Sleep, a spate of books were published with titles like "Painless Childbirth," "The Sleeping Car Twilight," and "The Truth about Twilight Sleep." These books proclaimed that women, particularly upper-class women, were finally to be freed from the pain of childbirth. The fight was taken up by a number of Twilight Sleep societies in different parts of the United States, and a Twilight Sleep Maternity Hospital was opened in Boston (Wertz & Wertz 1977, p. 151). Since Twilight Sleep had to be administered in a hospital, women who sought it could not give birth at home. There is little evidence that Twilight Sleep had as much effect on hospitalization in the other countries studied here, but it crystallized a desire among U.S. women to minimize or eliminate pain in childbirth.

Hospitals came to be seen as the place for "proper women" to have their babies. Immigrant mothers recognized hospital birth as a wholly American practice, a mark of assimilation into a new society (Borst 1995). It is easy to think of the hospitalization of birth as solely a battle among professionals, but the Twilight Sleep campaign serves as a reminder of the important and ironic role played by elements of the early twentieth-century women's movement in the United States. In seeking to free women of childbirth pain, they also contributed to the hospitalization of birth.

The virtual elimination of midwifery in the United States also contributed to the demise of home births. Seeking to elevate the nascent specialty of obstetrics, physicians led the campaign against midwifery. The presence of midwives, many of them immigrants, significantly complicated efforts to promote the obstetric specialty. Joseph De Lee, founder of the Chicago Lying-in Hospital, noted: "Do you wonder that a young man will not adopt this field as his special work? If a delivery requires so little brains and skill that a midwife can conduct it, there is no place for him" (quoted in Litoff 1978, p. 67). Hospitalization of birth was not the primary objective of this effort, but it did mightily serve its cause. With a few exceptions U.S. midwives did not attend a significant number of hospital births, at least not until the rise of nurse-midwives in the 1980s. It was not until 1978 that midwives attended even 1 percent of hospital births in the United States. Therefore moving birth to hospitals, advocated as a goal in itself, was also a powerful weapon in the campaign to eliminate midwives. Equally important, midwives, divided by ethnic differences and lacking a sense of profession, failed to work together to protect their own interests.

Many of these efforts would have been impossible without the redefinition of birth from a natural event to one of "imposing pathologic dignity" (Litoff 1978, p. 67). In addition to the transformation of the hospital, the redefinition of birth was actively going on in the United States as well. The popular press succeeded in portraying birth as unnatural and dangerous for mother and baby. The solution was simple—rely on the new science of birth, which was obstetrics as practiced in those new temples of science, hospitals.

The movement of birth from home to hospital in the United States took half a century, and it was not the result of any *single* factor. Consider the combined impact of the influences just described. In the 1940s and 1950s a woman having her baby at home would be going against the suggestion of her family doctor. She would have difficulty finding a midwife trained to attend a home birth and would be foregoing the use of the new local hospital with its gleaming technology. She would be turning her back on her husband's insurance plan and refusing the use of drugs (deemed safe by physicians and female opinion leaders). Finally, she would be putting herself and her baby at unnecessary health risk. Given the combined impact of these factors, it is surprising *any* women made a free choice for home birth. In fact, it is likely that most women having home births in the 1940s and 1950s were rural and nonwhite and were doing so because of a lack of hospitals or because racial segregation closed local facilities to them

It was not until the late 1960s, in part as an outgrowth of the women's movement and the natural childbirth movement, that home birth was again openly discussed as a birth option. In the 1970s and early 1980s a cohort of white, well-educated mothers chose to give birth at home attended by independent midwives. Great attention was paid to these cases, which in several instances resulted in open conflicts with the medical and legal authorities (DeVries 1996). Nonetheless, the proportion of home births in the United States remained very small, and, as in most industrialized countries, the figures have changed little in recent years. The United States—the most private sector–oriented of the countries discussed here—achieved universal hospital birth with little direct government intervention. It was wider social forces such as the movement to hospitalization in general and the efforts to establish obstetrics as a profession that pushed birth into the hospital. In a consumer-oriented culture, the desire of women to be free of childbirth pain also aided the process. Finally, the tremendous emphasis in the United States on new medical technology made hospitalization of birth a requisite for quality care.

We turn now to Finland, a Nordic country that achieved universal hospitalization of birth by different means.

Finland: Hospital Birth as Social Policy

In Finland the transition from home to hospital occurred about twenty years later than in the United States, but with similar speed: The transition from 30 to 90 percent hospital births took place between 1940 and 1960 (Figure 1–1). Although the statistical change may look straightforward, the transition to hospital birth was gradual and, as in the United States, occurred at different speeds in urban and rural areas. Several major periods in the transition can be identified. The first, from the 1920s to 1950s, was the transition of home births from the hands of lay assistants to trained municipal midwives. Midwives continued to give care in the second period—from the 1940s to 1960s—but that care was delivered in hospitals rather than homes. The third phase—beginning in the 1960s and continuing until today—brought further central-ization of care in larger and better equipped units where medical specialists, includ-ing gynecologists, anesthesiologists, and perinatologists, have taken a more prominent role in birth.

The first maternity hospital (with eight beds) in Finland was established in 1816 as a teaching hospital for midwives assisting in home births in rural areas. The hospital-ization of births in rural areas began in 1861 under an order from the Russian Czar to establish three maternity beds in every county hospital to be used for free maternity care of the poor. The goal was to prevent poor, unwed mothers from committing infanticide. The Finnish health authorities fulfilled the order but decided to establish the maternity beds in separate locations from the hospitals to prevent puerperal fever. In the 1880s maternity beds were made available to married women for a fee, but at the turn of the century, hospitals were still only for poor people.

Finland gained independence from Russia in 1917, and during the first decades as an independent nation, no major changes in maternity care policy were made. In 1927 all rural municipalities were required to hire a trained midwife to assist in home births, yet by the late 1930s almost half of all home births were still assisted by lay midwives or relatives. The law of municipal midwives was intended to lower maternal mortality by abolishing lay birth attendance. The trained municipal midwives were salaried but were to cover a part of their salary with fees from their nonpoor customers. Women in many remote areas, however, resisted trained assistance because the traditional lay birth attendants had a respected mystical and religious role in the rural communities. At the end of 1930s, prenatal care was, by decree, included in municipal midwives' work, and its impact was profound, raising mothers' prenatal care rates from 11 per-cent in 1939 to 95 percent in 1950 (Pitkänen 1960). This development was promoted by a 1944 law that made the organization of free prenatal care for all an obligation for municipalities and a 1949 decree that made the maternity benefit (given in the form of baby clothing and accessories for birth or one-time monetary payment) available to all women, but tied it to early attendance in prenatal care. Women who did not begin pre-natal care before the end of the fourth month of pregnancy could lose their benefit. The growing influence of trained municipal midwives gradually led to the displacement of lay attendants from the birth care scene, and by 1958 lay attendants assisted at only 0.2 percent of all births in the country (Pitkänen 1960).

In 1928 there were forty-seven maternity units: Twenty-two were private, four were run by the state, fifteen by towns, and six by rural municipalities. Only five had more than twenty beds (Chydenius 1931). In most public maternity units midwives assisted at birth. Physicians were called upon only when felt necessary by the midwife. In the 1930s, physicians began seeking, in the name of reducing high maternal mortality, the merging of separate maternity bed units with gynecology departments in hospitals into larger specialist-led units. These larger units would have enough patients to enable specialists to work full-time in maternity hospitals. Midwives were not to be elimi-nated. Rather, a network of prenatal care centers in which municipal midwives would attend pregnant women and assist them in home births in rural areas was seen as the answer to the threat of declining birth rates as well as the high maternal and perinatal mortality rates in home births with lay attendants (Leppo 1943). It was believed that the resources of physicians would be better used in specialized hospital care.

The most rapid transition to hospitals occurred in the 1940s and 1950s. The era was characterized by strong, centrally led planning, gradual urbanization, pronatalist social policies, and high postwar birth rates. As described earlier, many social benefits, including extra food rations, were tied to the use of the recently established prenatal care system in which the municipal midwives played a pivotal role. The flow of population to newly industrialized cities and the resettlement of nearly 10 percent of the population after the peace treaty with the Soviet Union placed a considerable pressure on both urban and rural housing. Pronatalist government also encouraged high fertility rates. The housing conditions were therefore not suitable for hygienic births, nor did they provide privacy or guarantee rest for birthing women. Women turned to hospitals for care at birth, and hospitals could not accommodate the demand. Obstetricians began to discuss ways to prioritize those who should receive hospitalized care and promoted the building of new specialist-led maternity hospitals. Obstetricians argued for larger maternity units, citing the more favorable mortality rates in cesarean sections and other interventions in larger rather than smaller units. Midwives did not appear to resist the change of their jobs from homes to hospitals. In the 1950s, there was a shortage of midwives, and new graduates generally sought employment in modern central hospitals rather than municipalities (Vuorjoki 1958). Hospital midwives had regular hours and were still quite independent in practice.

In the 1960s and 1970s a further centralization of births into larger units occurred. In the 1950s a centralized plan to build a regional network of secondary-level hospitals with specialist care began and continued until the last central hospital was completed in 1976 (Alestalo & Uusitalo 1986). At the same time, maternity units in small general practitioner (GP)–led municipal hospitals and the small private maternity homes were closed. The stated policy was to regionalize hospital care and organize hospitals into referral chains that would make all levels of care widely available, (according to medically defined need), within the publicly funded health care system.

The system was not built on individual choice, but rather on the principle of equal access for all. In this system midwives had one of two roles: They worked either in prenatal care centers in primary health care or in hospital wards assisting births. In both locations physicians oversaw midwives' work. In prenatal care centers GPs were in charge, and in hospitals midwives delivered babies under the authority of obstetricians. The midwives had a pivotal role, but they were not independent practitioners. The midwives' role as home birth assistants ceased gradually in the 1960s; by 1965, 99.9 percent of births were in hospitals. Under the 1972 Public Health Act, municipalities no longer had the obligation to provide midwifery assistance for home births.

The movement of birth into larger settings continued, and by 1975, 70 percent of all births took place in central or university hospitals. The process of centralization was characterized by the development of obstetric technology and involvement of other specialists beyond midwives and obstetricians in maternity care. The focus was no longer on reducing maternal mortality but on preventing perinatal mortality and providing pain relief in labor. After 1975, changes between levels of care were small but continued in the direction of centralization; by 1995, 76 percent of all births occurred in tertiary and secondary hospitals. The most drastic change was in the status of small GP-led primary care birth units. In 1975 there were still twelve such units in the country; by 1995 there was only one left, and it closed in 1999.

Current changes are happening *within* institutions rather than by shifting the site of birth. Reliance on technologies has become much more prominent in birth care at all hospital levels, and women have participated in this development. In 1976 a public controversy was begun by a female physician who claimed that women had a right to demand pain relief in birth. The women's movement and activist groups supported the idea, and, as a result, a group of female members of the parliament started a parliamentary inquiry about women's right to have pain relief in birth. The minister of health assigned a task force to examine the issue, and a set of recommendations about the organization of care were made in 1977 (STM 1977). The association of anesthesiologists actively promoted the petition of the parliamentary women, and the final recommendation was to increase the number of anesthesiologists in maternity hospitals to make epidural analgesia available in secondary hospitals. At the same time, the report suggested the further centralization of births into larger units to make the increased need for on-call specialists cost-effective. In the 1990s virtually all births occurred in publicly funded hospitals, and women had very little freedom over which hospital to choose. The network of maternity hospitals has been decreasing so that in vast areas there is only one secondary or tertiary level hospital available within a range of 100 kilometers. The five tertiary-level hospitals have divided their catchment areas in the country and increasingly serve normal, low-risk births. There is no difference in perinatal outcomes between geographical areas in the country (Viisainen et al. 1994). The main policy question now seems to be how to more economically provide maternity services. Choice for women is advocated mainly by a small but vocal women's consumer organization that promotes women's active involvement in birth care. There is a small fraction in the movement advocating home birth as a choice; however, less than 0.001 percent of births were planned home births in 1991–1995 (Viisainen et al. 1999). Like the United States, although in a different context, the transition of births into hospitals in Finland was swift, peaking in the postwar years of rapid urbanization, industrialization, and modernization. The change in living setting and the postwar belief in modernization created a demand for hospital care. Women flooded the hospitals at the time when few technologies were used there, but the few cesarean sections, blood transfusions, and antibiotics were saving lives. Even without complications, women got bed rest and care for ten days, which for them was seen as a deserved right. Physicians promoted hospitalization of complicated cases, and, later, the development of larger specialized units had already been institutionalized into small local units.

Finland's transition to hospital birth was not accompanied by an attack on midwifery as in the United States. At no point of the transition was there a discussion of transferring normal births from the hands of midwives to the hands of physicians, and normal hospital births today remain in the hands of midwives. The midwives did not voice resistance to the transition of their jobs into hospitals. The hospitalization of births seemed to occur in an atmosphere of collaboration, rather than competition between physicians and midwives, both of whom are employed by the public sector.

The Netherlands: Home Birth as a Viable Option in a
Modern Health Care System

The Dutch system of maternity care differs in profound ways from those described in the preceding sections. The medical system in the Netherlands equals any in its level of technological sophistication, and yet, when it comes to normal birth, there is little reliance on this technology. Nearly one-half of the women who give birth in the Netherlands do so without once seeing a doctor, and over 30 percent of all births occur at home. Although the rates of infant mortality and morbidity in the Netherlands are among the lowest in the world, the Netherlands remains an inconvenient exception in sociological and epidemiological discussions of the hospitalization of birth in industrialized nations.

The Dutch case is especially important to our analysis because it permits us to explore the conditions that allow home birth to survive as a viable option in a modern health care system. It could be argued that patterns in the location of birth in the Netherlands mirror trends in other industrialized nations: Perhaps it is just that the sharp decline in home births came much later and has (temporarily?) leveled off at a much higher rate. Note that in the fifteen years between 1965 and 1980 the percentage of births at home fell precipitously, from nearly 70 percent in 1965 to 35 percent in 1980 (see Figure 1–1). Dutch society is somewhat famous for its "quaintness." The German poet Heinrich Heine is alleged to have said, "If the world should perish, I will move to the Netherlands because everything there occurs fifty years later." But even if Heine's observation about the Netherlands is correct and the rate of home birth in the Netherlands eventually drops below 5 percent, the "quaintness" of the Dutch system explanation does not contribute to our understanding of comparative maternity practices. We need to better understand how this so-called quaintness came to affect health care policy.

Others explain the continued use of home birth by pointing to the geography of the Netherlands. The Netherlands is a small, flat, densely populated country where one is never far from a hospital. Home birth is feasible in this landscape in a way it cannot be viable in the vast expanses of the United States or in the rugged terrain of Norway. But when we look at other industrialized nations we are forced to conclude that geography might be a *necessary,* but hardly a *sufficient,* cause for of the preservation of home birth. Having "conducive" geography—or ways of overcoming geographic problems—is not enough to prevent birth from moving to the hospital. Other small countries—for example, Belgium, the Netherlands's neighbor to the south—have eschewed birth at home.

The persistence of birth at home in the Netherlands is best understood as a product of the organization of health care, Dutch politics, and Dutch cultural ideas about home, women, family, medicine, and science. Taken alone, none of these elements can explain the uniqueness of obstetrics in the Netherlands, but examined together they help us understand Dutch decisions about the location of birth.

Hingstman (1994) calls our attention to three structural features of Dutch health care that support home birth: (1) the special position of the midwife, (2) a screening system for high-risk pregnancies, and (3) a well-organized program of maternity home care. Midwives—the primary attendants at domiciliary deliveries—have a well-established and "protected" place in Dutch health care. Education and certification began early for Dutch midwives. Beginning in the second half of the seventeenth century, local medical societies set up training programs and methods of examination and approval for midwives. In 1818, the first national law regulating midwives was passed, affirming the place of midwives as legitimate and appropriate providers of care at birth; in 1865 a law defining the practice of medicine established midwives as independent medical practitioners (Marland 1993, pp. 26–29). The 1941 law that created the health care system that exists in the Netherlands today gave midwives the so-called *primaat,* referred to by some as a "monopoly over normal obstetrics" (Abraham-Van der Mark 1993, p. 4). The law recognizes a distinction between normal ("physiological") and high-risk ("pathological") births and stipulates that when pregnancy and birth proceed normally, insurance will pay only for the services of a midwife. In locations where midwives are unavailable, a general practitioner (GP) may be employed. Recently, GPs mounted a legal challenge to the *primaat,* but regardless of the decision of the court in this case, the organization of Dutch obstetrics shows a clear preference for domiciliary care offered by midwives and GPs over the high-tech ministrations of specialists in hospitals.

This preference for primary care rests on a generally accepted screening system for identifying physiological and pathological pregnancies. The Obstetric Indications List (sometimes referred to as the Kloosterman List, after its developer, Gerrit-Jan Kloosterman)—first used in an informal way in the late 1950s and revised by a government commission in 1987 and again in 1999 (see *Ziekenfondsraad* 1999)—defines the conditions that require midwives and GPs to refer their clients to specialists. The list allows the Dutch to avoid the assumption made in most other industrialized countries that all births are potentially high risk, and therefore must be monitored by specialists. (See Chapter 6 for a more complete discussion of the Obstetric Indications List.)

The Dutch also have a well-organized system of maternity home care. Women whose pregnancies are defined as physiological may choose to give birth at home or in a polyclinic. Polyclinic births occur in designated rooms in a hospital, are attended by midwives or general practitioners, and are "short-stay" (i.e., less than twenty-four hours). Postpartum care at home is available to those who have their baby at home and those who have a *poliklinische* (polyclincal) birth. Under the current insurance system a new mother is entitled to up to one week of care by a *kraamverzorgster* (postpartum caregiver). *Kraamverzorgsters* follow a three-year training program and offer a range of services, including newborn care, help initiating and sustaining breastfeeding, health advice for mother and child, and help with housework (Van Teijlingen 1990).

These structural features of Dutch health care are just the beginning of our explanation of the continued use of home birth in the Netherlands. We must also look at the political and professional dimensions of health care. Interestingly, some of the harshest critics of home birth in the Netherlands are Dutch gynecologists. Not only have these specialists criticized their obstetric system on the pages of international journals, but, for several years, their professional organization, the *Nederlandse Vereniging voor Obstetrie en Gynaecologie* (NVOG) refused to formally ratify the revised Obstetric Indications List, believing it gave too much power to midwives and GPs. Students of the professions in the United States will find it odd that a prestigious group of medical specialists lacks the power to shape government decisions in a way that favors their interests. Of course the relative weakness of medical specialists as an interest group in health policy is not a unique feature of the Netherlands; this is also the case in many other European countries. What *is* of peculiar importance in the

Netherlands is the use of structured negotiation in health policy decisions. In the Netherlands, government agencies that create health policies are carefully organized to give representation to all parties with a vested interest in health care.

This observation leads us to further questions: Why do the Dutch favor negotiation and compromise? Why is home birth a practice that some sectors of Dutch society—including the government—feel is worth preserving? The answers to these questions lie in a variety of cultural ideas that distinguish the Netherlands from neighboring lands, ideas that have important consequences for the Dutch view of the appropriate way of accomplishing birth.

The distinctive Dutch views of the "family" and of the role of women in the family help shape the process. The Dutch were the first among modern nations to experience the "nuclearization" of the family. According to van Daalen (1988), the Dutch family nuclearized in the late seventeenth and early eighteenth centuries, earlier than the other nations of continental Europe. Furthermore, as the wives of farmers, fishers, and traders—the primary occupations in the Netherlands—Dutch women have played an important and strong role in the family, a fact reflected in their historically high fertility rates and low rates of participation in paid labor. For example in 1990, 41 percent of Dutch married women participated in the labor force, compared to 79 percent of Swedish, 72 percent of Danish, and 60 percent of Belgian married women (see Pott-Buter 1993). These unique features of the Dutch family create and maintain a preference for home birth.

Domestic confinements also fit well with Dutch ideas about home. According to Rybcincski (1986), the Dutch are responsible for our current notions of "home" as a place of retreat for the nuclear family. The Dutch were the first to develop single-family residences—small, tidy, well-lit homes. The importance of the nuclear family, coupled with the domestic role of women and the tidiness of their homes, made home the logical place for birth.

Home birth is further supported by Dutch ideas about medicine, science, and notions of "thriftiness." The Dutch are not quick to seek medical solutions to bodily problems (Van Andel & Brinkman 1997) and have very rational ideas about the use of science in the formation of public policy, experimenting with new approaches and testing their efficacy and efficiency. The government has funded many studies (e.g., Wiegers 1997) to examine the safety, cost, and desirability of home births and has made policy decisions based on those studies. The most recent of these studies openly acknowledges that the study was initiated because of a concern that "the steadily decreasing number of home births . . . threatened to diminish the home birth rate to a level where home birth would no longer be a viable option [and that] the increasing number of hospital births would lead to unnecessary medicalisation of pregnancy and childbirth" (Wiegers 1997, p. 1).

Recent developments suggest that the cultural conditions that have helped home birth survive in the Netherlands are changing. Whether the ethnically more heterogeneous and culturally more fragmented Dutch society of the new millennium will support the continued existence of home birth remains to be seen. Interviews with expectant parents show that Dutch attitudes toward birth are becoming more like those in other countries. When asked why they chose a *polikliniek,* parents expressed an attitude toward home and technology more like those in surrounding lands. The most common reasons for not staying home for birth are "too much mess" and the desire to have emergency equipment readily available (see Wiegers 1997).

These developments suggest there may be further decline in home birth. However, working against these trends are campaigns sponsored by the government, by Dutch midwives, and by consumer groups. The government and health insurance companies fear that the shift to short-stay hospital births will drive up the cost of maternity care with no consequent improvement in outcomes. Midwives are concerned that the disappearance of home birth will diminish the autonomy of their profession. Organizations representing the users of maternity care fear that the choices offered Dutch women will be limited. This active support for birth at home has prevented a faster and more complete turn toward hospital birth. The story of home and hospital birth in the Netherlands reminds us how the delivery of maternity care is shaped by the combination of ideas about birth and the structure of the health care system.

The United Kingdom: The Modest Return of Home Birth

> *On the basis of what we have heard, this committee must draw the conclusion that the policy of encouraging all women to give birth in hospitals cannot be justified on the grounds of safety.*
> (House of Commons Health Committee 1992, p. xciv)

This statement from a British government body signals a unique stance in modern maternity care—that home birth should be a state-supported option for pregnant women. Up until recently the United Kingdom followed the pattern found in its neighboring countries, with a steady decline in home births. Researchers, most notably Campbell and MacFarlane (1994), have analyzed the reasons for this decline. High infant mortality at the turn of the century lead to the establishment of maternity and child welfare systems and to the hospitalization of high-risk births. There was a general movement toward the institutionalization of birth in Britain in the early twentieth century, but the emphasis was on maternity homes with less than twenty beds. A 1920 memorandum from the Ministry of Health called for these maternity homes to provide for normal confinements, while in larger communities maternity hospitals with up to fifty beds would serve higher-risk cases. The redefinition of birth as pathological occurred in Britain, but more slowly than elsewhere. Note this 1936 statement from the British Medical Association (supported by the Royal College of Obstetricians and Gynecologists [RCOG]): "[A]ll the available evidence demonstrates that normal confinements, and those which show only a minor departure from normal, can be more safely conducted at home than in hospital" (Campbell & MacFarlane 1994, p. 14).

As in other countries, growth in the number of hospital beds prompted increased demand for hospitalized birth. Demand intensified with the establishment of the National Health Service in 1946. The RCOG proposed sufficient accommodations be built to allow 70 percent of all births to occur in hospitals, and a 1959 government study concurred with that recommendation. Some of the impetus for hospitalization was a concern with the safety of housing conditions. As in Finland, calls for bringing birth into the hospital were accompanied by plans for long postpartum stays. A minimum of ten days was recommended in 1952.

In 1970 the government took the final step in hospitalizing birth, recommending "that sufficient facilities should be provided to allow for 100 percent hospital delivery. The greater safety of hospital confinement for mother and child justifies this objective" (Campbell & MacFarlane 1994, p. 21). This statement was made at the end of a period in which growth in maternity beds coincided with a falling fertility rate, thus allowing sufficient facilities to accommodate the 100 percent hospitalization of birth. While more than 90 percent of all births occurred in hospitals by the early 1970s, many still took place in small "isolated GP maternity units," the successors to the maternity homes of the 1920s and 1930s. The term "isolated" indicated that they were freestanding and not part of a larger hospital. Concern arose about the safety of births in these units, and there was increasing pressure to close them and move births to large hospitals. This effort culminated in the 1980 recommendation by a House of Commons committee that, "[a]n increasing number of mothers be delivered in large units; . . . and that home delivery is phased out further" (Campbell & MacFarlane 1994, p. 23). At this point 98.5 percent of births were already in the hospital; it seems clear that the complete elimination of home birth was the goal of the government.

HOME BIRTH RETURNS TO BRITAIN, SORT OF

Throughout the 1980s the rate of home births in the United Kingdom remained steady at about 1 percent, but as Figure 1–2 illustrates, in 1989 it began to slowly rise; between 1987 and 1997 the rate of home births increased by 1.53 percent to 2.23 percent of all births. It is easy to associate that growth with reports by government bodies like the one quoted at the beginning of this section, but Figure 1–2 shows that the growth began several years *prior to* what became known as the "Changing Childbirth" initiative. In the early 1980s, demands for more choice in childbirth were growing in Britain, supported by a network of maternity consumer groups that sought change (Declercq 1998). In conjunction with the social movement, the creation of the Association of Radical Midwives pressed for more independent practice for midwives, including training for attendance at home births. These factors likely helped account for the initial growth we see in home births in the late 1980s and early 1990s.

The government has made formal inquiries into the maternity services roughly every decade since the 1950s. In 1991 the House of Commons Health Committee again chose to examine maternity services; however, unlike earlier studies that were inquiries into perinatal death, this committee explicitly sought to examine the experience of normal birth and to focus on the scientific evidence available to address this question. The unexpected result was a recommendation from the Health Committee calling into question the argument for hospitalizing birth. The Health Committee, however, could not make policy but could only recommend changes. The Department of Health in turn chose to establish an "Expert Maternity Group" to explore the issues raised by the Health Committee and make *its* recommendations. The result was the report, *Changing Childbirth,* which noted that "most women were given little choice about the place of birth . . . . A [national study found that] 72% would have liked at least the option of a different system of care and delivery. [Of these], 22%

FIGURE 1–2.
Percent Home Births, United States and United Kingdom, 1989–1997.

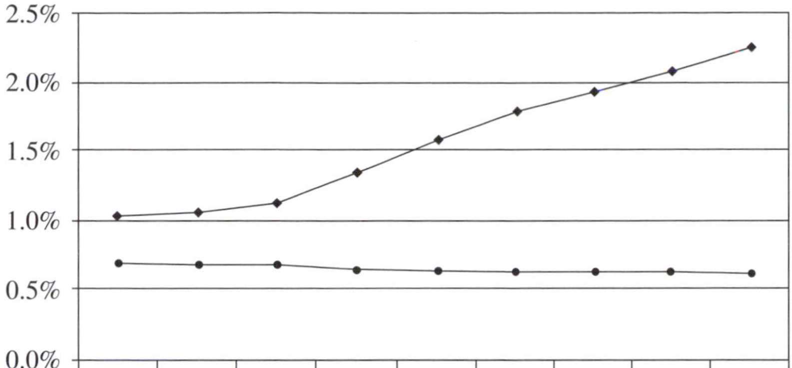

	1989	1990	1991	1992	1993	1994	1995	1996	1997
U.K.	1.01%	1.04%	1.11%	1.33%	1.56%	1.78%	1.92%	2.06%	2.23%
U.S.	0.69%	0.67%	0.67%	0.64%	0.63%	0.62%	0.62%	0.61%	0.60%

SOURCES: U.K. Data: 2000. *Birth Counts: Statistics of Pregnancy and Childbirth,* 2nd ed., vol. 2, tables by A. MacFarlane, M. Mugford, J. Henderson, A. Furtado, J. Stevens, and A. Dunn (London: The Stationary Office). U.S. Data: Annual Reports of Final Natality Statistics (Hyattsville, MD: NCHS).

[i.e., 14% of the total sample] said they would like the choice of a home birth" (p. 23). The Expert Maternity Group concluded: "Women should receive clear, unbiased advice and be able to choose where they would like their baby to be born. Their right to make that choice should be respected and every practical effort made to achieve the outcome that the woman believes is best for her baby and herself" (Department of Health Expert Maternity Group, 1993, p. 25).

There have been several developments stemming from the Changing Childbirth initiative. First has been a growth in research in the United Kingdom on home birth. In 1996 a single issue of the *British Medical Journal* devoted four articles and an editorial to home birth (Ackermann-Liebrich et al. 1996; Davies et al. 1996; NRPMSCG 1996; Springer & Van Weel 1996; Wiegers et al. 1996). Second, there have been efforts to examine different schemes (e.g., combinations of GP, midwife, and emergency support arrangements) by which home births can be supported. Third, different combinations of midwife groups have been developed with an eye toward regaining the skills for attending home births and providing more support for mothers who choose this option. As home birth becomes more common it will appear less unconventional and may appeal to a broader range of the population. The actual proportion of women giving birth at home may in fact be less important than having a real choice, wherein one will be attended by a provider skilled at home birth, backed up by a system of rapid transfer and support at a hospital upon arrival.

Norway: Normal Hospital Birth—To Centralize or Decentralize?

Norwegian debates on how health services should be organized often revolve around the particular geographical conditions of the country. When it comes to hospital birth, it is argued that a population scattered about in isolated communities presents a special challenge. As in the Netherlands, however, natural circumstances cannot completely explain the organization of maternity care. In fact, the issue of a scattered population has been used both to advocate decentralization of hospital birth *and* to defend its centralization. This case, based on a review of the recent literature on childbirth in Norway, highlights the complexity of the issue of hospital birth and calls attention to the important influence of the organization of the hospital system.

Until World War II, the majority of Norwegian women delivered at home. As in the other countries studied here, the situation was substantially altered in the period of 1940–1960. The number of maternity hospitals tripled between 1940 and 1949. (Blom 1988, p. 178). By the 1960s, nearly 98 percent of births were in hospitals (Blom 1988, p. 224); today, more than 99 percent of Norwegian women deliver in hospitals—the vast majority of them in large hospitals (Births in Norway 1999).

The postwar increase in hospital births resulted in a decline in the number of midwives. A second development to weaken the position of midwifery in Norway was that—unlike in other Nordic countries—GPs became the primary providers of prenatal care services that were organized in the 1940s (NOU 1998, Chapter 8). Before the hospitalization of birth, community midwives provided the bulk of domiciliary care in Norway. The system was organized through the Midwives Act of 1898 that divided the country into midwife districts, with midwives in some districts required to have special qualifications. The number of practicing midwives in Norway peaked at 1,590 just prior to World War II. By 1950, the number of midwives in practice declined to 1,397; over the next two decades, the figure fell rapidly. Only 744 midwives, primarily based in hospitals, were practicing by 1970 (Kjølsrød 1993, p. 18).

After the early 1970s, changes in maternity care policy resulted in a slight increase in the number of midwives. Legislation in 1984 and 1995 required communities to provide midwife services (NOU 1998, p. 13). Between 1987 and 1996 midwifery practice in communities (measured by midwifery work-years) more than doubled (*Statistisk sentralbyrå* 1997).

The return of midwives to community health care reflects the influence of consumer interest group activity on Norwegian maternity care policy. These interest groups have also questioned the organization of birth care in Norway. In the last thirty years, these groups have emphasized that birth is a normal event that is important for the whole family, and they have asked for more opportunities for the mother and father to influence childbirth and for the availability of birth at home. In many cases they cited the precedent of the Netherlands where strict risk selection criteria work well, resulting in perinatal outcome statistics comparable to the Nordic countries.

Opponents of their view emphasize the fact that the population in Norway is more scattered than that in the Netherlands. In the Netherlands, transportation to a hospital during delivery was reported in only 12 percent of primiparous and 4 percent of multiparous women with unexpected complications (Phaff 1986). These figures are used to raise questions about the applicability of the Dutch model in Norway. Thus far, the efforts of home birth advocates have not resulted in any significant increase in the number of planned home deliveries. In 1996 only 0.4 percent of births (269 out of 61,314) in Norway were at home (Births in Norway 1999), and many of these were not planned. An earlier study (1975–1976) found only 13.2 percent (20 of 152) of out-of-hospital births in Norway were planned (Bakketeig & Bergsjø 1977). A recent *Norges Offentlige Utredninger* (NOU) report regarding maternity wards and transportation in Norway does not recommend any strengthening of home deliveries in the public health service, although it *does* acknowledge the need for improved transportation facilities in connection with home deliveries, as the numbers appear to be slightly increasing (NOU 1998, p. 9).

Proponents of home birth have not been the only critics of the policy of centralizing normal birth at large hospitals in Norway. For the other pressure groups, the central goal has been to keep small maternity hospitals or maternity homes (*fødestuene*) a viable option for childbearing women. Criticism of the concentration of all births in large hospitals in Norway began in the early 1970s (Kjølsrød 1993). In 1974, Bakketeig and Bjerkedal published a report that called attention to increased risks associated with the transportation of laboring women to centralized hospitals. In the anti-institutional climate of the 1970s the discontent of childbearing women caught media attention. Women from peripheries *and* those from urban centers complained about the move of birth to large hospitals. Women from rural areas were forced to come to the city days beforehand to await birth or to accept the risk of delivery during transport in a car or boat. Women in urban areas did not like the crowded hospitals and shortage of personnel. According to media reports, hospitals could not even guarantee a bed for all women in childbirth.

The issue of whether normal birth should be decentralized or centralized continues to the present day. In 1997, a report from the Norwegian Board of Health (*Statens helsetilsyn*) recommended *three* levels of the maternity units in Norway: Level 1, with at least 1,500 deliveries a year with a midwife, obstetrician, anesthesia team, and pediatrician available twenty-four hours a day; Level 2, with at least 400–500 deliveries a year with a midwife available 24 hours and an obstetrician and anesthesia team on call; and Level 3, with at least 40–50 deliveries a year with only midwives on call.

Nonetheless, only a minority of Norwegian women are able to choose to give birth at a small maternity hospital. Nearly 90 percent of the deliveries in Norway occur in maternity institutions with more than 500 deliveries a year. Recent studies suggest that even when no risk factors for complication during delivery have been identified during the prenatal care, 5–10 percent of the primiparae and 1–2 percent of the multiparae will need operative assistance during delivery (*Statens helsetilsyn* 1997). Thus, a stricter selection of the women allowed to deliver at the maternity wards located far from the specialized units has been recommended.

The advantages of small-scale birth settings are constantly weighed against the potential risks associated with childbirth care that lacks access to technologies available in the centralized settings. For instance, a recent governmental review on women's health (NOU 1999) states that healthy multiparous women can give birth at small maternity hospitals, but that women with medical problems often need specialized medical services.

One important consequence of the continued attention on the issue of how childbirth services are organized is that the debates have forced changes in the practice policies of the large, centralized delivery units. The criticism kept alive by the groups promoting home birth and defending small maternity hospitals appears to have brought about a gradual change in attitudes within all maternity wards. The strict hygienic routines are being replaced with a cozier atmosphere that combines medical safety with a better tolerance for individual needs. In recent years, some hospitals have also built "Alternative Birth Care" units in which the large hospitals try to accommodate the wishes of their clients (see Chapter 13).

It remains to be seen whether, and to what extent, small maternity hospitals will manage to survive as a viable option in Norway, combining a homey setting with what health policymakers, the medical profession, and women consider safe.

Conclusion

What accounts for the powerful trend toward hospitalization of birth in industrialized countries? Several factors are found in all of the cases presented here. First, *birth hospitalization was a by-product of the rise of hospitalization of health care in general.* Those of us who study maternity care may want to emphasize the uniqueness of the factors that shape its setting and practice, but the hospital building boom in many countries in the 1940s and 1950s coincides strongly with the surge in the hospitalization of birth. The building of these hospitals was not solely or primarily for the purpose of bringing birth into centralized settings, but their presence had an undeniable influence on the location of birth. The building of hospitals provided an economic incentive for governments and (in the United States) the private sector to centralize maternity care there and satisfied a growing demand for hospitalization of birth.

Second, *political and financing mechanisms have indirectly shaped the movement of birth into the hospital.* While explicit government attempts such as that in the United Kingdom to influence the place of birth are noteworthy, it is the overall structuring of the system of regulation and financing that has most affected the place of birth. From the development of private insurance in the United States to the public systems in Finland, the Netherlands, Norway, and the United Kingdom, the way maternity services are paid for has a powerful influence on practice. Interestingly, most of the changes in financing that influenced birth practices were general changes that included maternity care rather than explicit attempts to alter the treatment of pregnancy and birth. The most notable exception is the *Primaat* in the Netherlands, which has proved to be a very important factor in slowing the hospitalization of birth there.

The impact of *primaat* is a reminder of the third factor: *Midwives and home birth are inextricably linked.* Midwives are central to maternity care in virtually all the countries in the world and provide supportive care to mothers in hospital settings as well as at home. It is not surprising that in the industrialized country where midwives have the greatest independence of practice (the Netherlands) home birth has persisted, while in the country where home birth disappeared first (the United States) the campaign against midwives was an essential part of the hospitalization of birth. Likewise, the mild resurgence of home birth in the United Kingdom has corresponded with an effort by midwives to elevate their status. The ability of midwives and mothers to shape practice is more limited in large hospitals than in homes and small hospitals, and a cultural setting that supports midwives is more likely to support home birth.

Finally, *the attitudes of women have been an essential part of both the past hospitalization of birth and the renewed interest in bringing birth home.* Women's wishes concerning maternity care are examined more thoroughly in Chapter 13, but a few comments related to the desires of women are relevant here. We have seen that the desire of women to avoid pain in childbirth has allowed hospitals to use the provision of anesthetics as an incentive for hospitalization. Similarly, many women have accepted the argument that birth in the hospital is inherently safer than home birth. Different contributors to this chapter have referred to a small but vocal core of women in various countries who have fought for either home birth or a return of birth to smaller hospitals. The success of these women is a testimony to the ability of a tiny but committed group to shape policy in democratic states. It must be remembered, however, that women's views are not uniform regarding the place, attendant, and role of technology in maternity care, and, when faced with divided opinion, the political systems of industrialized states are inclined to do little.

Two additional notes in closing. First, we have learned that safe and rewarding birth experiences are not the exclusive domain of either home or hospital births. Second, our work has taught us that the designation "hospital birth" can have very different meanings in different countries or in different locations within one country. "Hospital birth" may describe an assembly line procedure, complete with the use of all associated technology, or it may refer to a birth in a quiet birthing room with family members and caregivers respectfully standing by.

Examining the place of birth is helpful in developing an understanding of a society's approach toward maternity care. Beginning this book with a look at the setting of birth serves as a reminder of the importance of context in understanding comparative differences in maternity practices. Subsequent chapters broaden our understanding of the way context, culture, and setting combine to create different maternity care policies and practices.

References

Abraham-Van der Mark, E. (ed.) 1993. *Successful Home Birth and Midwifery: The Dutch Model.* Westport, CT: Bergin and Garvey.

Ackerman-Liebrich, U., Voegeli, T., Gunter-Witt, K., Kunz, I., Zullig, M., Schindler, C., Maurer, M., and Zurich Study Team. 1996. Home versus hospital deliveries: Follow up study of matched pairs for procedures and outcome. *British Medical Journal* 313: 1313–1318.

Alestalo, M., and H. Uusitalo. 1986. Offpring Finland. In *Growth to Limits. The Western European Welfare States Since World War II,* ed. R. Flora (European University Institute, Political and Science Series C). Berlin: Walter de Gruyter.

Arestad, F. H., and M. A. McGovern, 1950. Hospital service in the US. *JAMA* 143(1): 25–37.

Bakketeig, L. S., and P. Bergsjø. 1977. Transportfødsel i Norge. (Birth during transportation in Norway.) *Tidskrift for Den norske lægeforening* (Journal of the Norwegian Medical Association) 94: 2306–2310. (In Norwegian.)

Births in Norway. 1999. *Medical Birth Registry of Norway 1967–1996. Births in Norway Through 30 Years.* Bergen: University of Bergen.

Blom, I. 1988. *"Den haarde Dyst".* Fødsel og fødselshjelp gjennom 150 år. ("The Tough Fight." Births and Birth Assistance through 150 Years.) Oslo: Cappelen. (In Norwegian.)

Borst, Charlotte. 1995. *Catching Babies.* Cambridge, MA: Harvard University Press.
Borst-Eilers, E. 1997. Health policy in the Netherlands. In *Health and Health Care in the Netherlands,* ed. A. J. P. Schrijvers. Utrecht: De Tijdstroom, pp. 15–19.
Campbell, R., and A. MacFarlane. 1994. *Where to Be Born?* 2nd ed. Oxford: National Perinatal Epidemiology Unit.
Chydenius, J. J. 1931. Mihin suuntaan olisi synnytys- ja naistentautialan sairaalaoloja maassamme kehitettävä? (What direction should obstetric and gynaecologic hospital conditions be developed?) *Suomen lääkäriliiton aikakauslehti* (Journal of the Finnish Medical Association) 10: 1–11. (In Finnish.)
Davies, J., Hey, E., Reid, W., and G. Young, for the Home Birth Study Steering Committee. 1996. Prospective regional study of planned home births. *British Medical Journal* 313: 1302—1306.
Declercq, E. 1998. "Changing Childbirth" in the UK: Lessons for US health policy. *Journal of Health Politics, Policy and Law* 23(5): 833–860.
Department of Health Expert Maternity Group. 1993. *Changing Childbirth.* Part I. London: HMSO.
Devitt, N. 1979. Hospital birth vs. home birth: The scientific facts past and present. In *Compulsory Hospitalization or Freedom of Choice in Childbirth?,* vol. 2, eds. D. Stewart and L. Stewart. Marble Hill, MO: NAPSAC, pp. 477–504.
DeVries, R. 1996. *Making Midwives Legal.* Columbus: Ohio State University Press.
Hingstman, L. 1993. Primary care obstetrics and perinatal health in the Netherlands. *Journal of Nurse-Midwifery* 39(6): 379–386.
House of Commons Health Committee. 1992. *Second Report, Maternity Services* Vol .1. London: HMSO.
Kjølsrød, L. 1993. *Jordmor der mor bor? En sosiologisk studie av jordmoryrket etter 1945.* (Midwife Where the Mother Lives? A Sociological Study of the Midwifery Occupation after 1945.) Oslo: Universitetslaget. (In Norwegian.)
Leppo, E. 1943. Äitiyshuollosta ja sen kohottamisesta Suomessa. (About maternity care and its improvement in Finland.) *Suomen Lääkäriliiton Aikakauslehti* (Journal of Finnish Medical Association) 22: 217–260. (In Finnish.)
Litoff, J. 1978. *American Midwives: 1860 to the Present.* Westport, CT: Greenwood Press.
Marland, H. 1993. Guardians of normal birth: The debate on the standard and status of the midwife in the Netherlands around 1900. In *Successful Home Birth and Midwifery: The Dutch Model,* ed. E. Abraham-Van der Mark. Westport, CT: Bergin and Garvey, pp. 21–44.
NRPMSCG (Northern Region Perinatal Mortality Survey Coordinating Group). 1996. Collaborative survey of perinatal loss in planned and unplanned home births. *British Medical Journal* 313: 1306–1309.
NOU. 1998. Hvis det haster . . . Faglige krav til akuttmedisinsk beredskap. Norges offentlige utredninger NOU 1998:9. (If there is an emergency . . . Professional requirements for emergency treatment. Official Reports of Norway.) http://www.odin.dep.no/nou/1998-9, ISSN 0806-2633 (NOU Computerfile). Sosial- og helsedepartementet, Oslo, accessed December 22, 1999.
Phaff, J. M. L. 1986. The organisation and administration of perinatal services in the Netherlands. In *Perinatal Health Services in Europe: Searching for Better Childbirth,* ed. J. M. L. Phaff. London: Croon Helm, pp. 117–127.
Pitkänen, H. 1960. Äitiyshuoltotyön saavutuksista maassamme. (On the achievements of maternity care in our country.) *Kätilölehti* (Journal of Midwifery) 65: 244–267. (In Finnish.)
Pott-Buter, H. 1993. *Facts and Fairy Tales about Female Labor, Family and Fertility.* Amsterdam: University of Amsterdam Press.
Rybczynksi, W. 1986. *Home.* New York: Penguin.

Springer, N., and C. Van Weel. 1996. Home birth: Safe in selected women, and with adequate infrastructure and support. *British Medical Journal* 313: 1276–1277.

Starr, P. 1982. *The Social Transformation of American Medicine.* New York: Basic Books.

Statens helsetilsyn. 1997. *Faglige krav til fødeinstitusjoner 1, 1997.* (Professional Requirements in Maternity Wards.) Oslo: Statens helsetilsyn. (In Norwegian.)

Statistisk sentralbyrå. 1997. Lege, fysioterapi og førebyggjande tenester i kommunehelsetenesta, 1996. Førebels tal: Ein av seks kommunar utan jordmortilbod. (Medical, physiotherapy and preventive services in municipal health services 1996. Advance figures: One in six municipalities without midwife services.) *Ukens statistikk* (Weekly Statistics) 26. http://www.ssb.no/www-open/ukens_statistikk/utg/9726/l.html, accessed September 22, 1998. (In Norwegian.)

STM. 1977. *Synnytyskipujen lievittäminen. Lääkintöhallituksen työryhmän mietintö.* (The Relief of Pain in Labor. A Committee Report for the National Board of Health.) Helsinki: The Ministry of Health and Social Affairs. (In Finnish.)

Torres, A., and M. Reich. 1989. The shift from home to institutional childbirth: A comparative study of the United Kingdom and the Netherlands. *International Journal of Health Services* 19 (3): 405–414.

Vallgarda, S. 1996. Hospitalization of deliveries: The change of place of birth in Denmark and Sweden from the late nineteenth century to 1970. *Medical History* 40: 173–196.

Van Andel, F. G., and N. Brinkman. 1997. Government policy and cost containment of pharmaceuticals. In *Health and Health Care in the Netherlands,* ed. A. J. P. Schrijvers. Utrecht: De Tijdstroom, pp. 152–162.

Van Daalen, R. 1988. De groei van de ziekenhuisbevalling: Nederland en het buitenland. (The growth of hospital birth: The Netherlands and elsewhere.) *Amsterdams Sociologisch Tijdschrift* (Amsterdam Journal of Sociology) 15(2): 414–445. (In Dutch.)

Van Teijlingen, E. R. 1990. The profession of maternity home care assistant and its significance for the Dutch midwifery profession. *International Journal of Nursing Studies* 27: 355–366.

Ventura, S. J., Martin, J. A., Curtin, S. C., Mathews, T. J., and M. M. Park. 2000. *Births: Final Data for 1998* (National Vital Statistics Reports, Vol. 48, No. 3). Hyattsville, MD: National Center for Health Statistics.

Viisainen, K., Gissler, M., and E. Hemminki. 1994. Birth outcomes by level of obstetric care in Finland: A catchment area based analysis. *Journal of Epidemiology and Community Medicine* 48: 400–405.

Viisainen, K., Gissler, M., Hartikainen, A.-L., and E. Hemminki. 1999. Accidental out-of-hospital births in Finland: Incidence and geographical distribution 1963–1995. *Acta Obstetricia et Gynecologica Scandinavica* 78: 372–378.

Vuorjoki, K. 1958. Vuoden vaihtuessa. (At the change of the year.) *Kätilölehti* (Journal of Midwifery) 63: 6–8. (In Finnish.)

Wertz, R., and D. Wertz. 1977. *Lying In.* New York: Free Press.

Wiegers, T. 1997. Home or Hospital Birth: A Prospective Study of Midwifery Care in the Netherlands. Utrecht: NIVEL.

Wiegers, T., Kierse, M., van der Zee, J., and G. Berghs. 1996. Outcomes of planned home and planned hospital births in low risk pregnancies: Prospective study in midwifery practices in the Netherlands. *British Medical Journal* 313: 1309–1313.

Ziekenfondsraad. 1999, January. *Vademecum Verloskunde: Eindrapport van het Werkoverleg Verloskunde van de Ziekenfondsraad.* (Final Report of the Sickness Funds Council Work Group on Obstetrics) Amsterdam: *Ziekenfondsraad.* (In Dutch.)

CHAPTER 2

The State and Birth/ The State of Birth

MATERNAL HEALTH POLICY IN THREE COUNTRIES

Sirpa Wrede, Cecilia Benoit, and Jane Sandall

Introduction

When we think about the quality of care given to new and expectant mothers we tend to think small—looking at client characteristics, professional-client relationships, or clinical contexts. It is easy to forget that what happens in a maternity care clinic is a product of work done in legislative assemblies and ministries of health. State policies influence everything from the interactions between caregivers and clients to the clinical outcomes. In this chapter we take a close look at maternal health service policy in three countries—the United Kingdom, Finland, and Canada—giving special attention to the gendered implications of these policies. We believe that the post–World War II emergence and later transformation of "Western" welfare states has had the most important influence on maternal health service designs in high-income countries.

We define the welfare state as "a state commitment of some sort which modifies the play of market forces in an effort to realize greater social equality for its population" (Ruggie 1984, p. 11). In the words of Palme (1990, p. 8), "[Welfare state social policies] weaken the whip of the market and promote working-class political solidarity." Welfare states shoulder responsibility for the well-being of inhabitants; this obligation cannot be easily consigned to the individual, private business firm, or local community. All high-income countries have some form of welfare state, although the amount of state expenditure, the range of social programs available to citizens, and the degree of comprehensiveness of the public provisions provided vary extensively.

Of course, good intentions do not always lead to good results. Not all policies of the welfare state promote greater equality between different societal groups. Our comparative analyses of maternal health policies allow us to examine success of the welfare state in meeting the needs of women as mothers, caregivers, and health professionals.

All high-income countries have developed public policies to help inhabitants shoulder the economic consequences of childbearing as well as ill health and disability, but the type and degree of government involvement in health care systems are quite variable, ranging from minor interventions to control of the market. In the case of maternity care policy, some states do little more than offer licensure to maternity care providers. In other countries governments intervene in the marketplace enacting legislation that nearly eliminates private health insurers and private practitioners.

Limited state involvement in maternity health policy does not mean limited influence on the social organization of maternity care. Even the simple act of licensing has a tremendous impact on care delivery. When the health care division of labor is highly sex-segregated, state regulation can promote gendered power relations in the market. For example, until well into the twentieth century in both the United States and Canada, (mostly) female midwives were denied the opportunity to attain a secure license and mandate to practice. Such privileges, on the other hand, were generously awarded to their (mostly) male physician counterparts. By contrast, most European governments by the twentieth century had enacted legislation that secured legal status and a more or less secure mandate of practice for midwives as well as physicians, thereby promoting greater gender equality among maternity providers. Adopting a certain policy can also mean supporting a gendered division of labor, which may, in turn, marginalize some health professionals and disenfranchise health care recipients.

In this chapter, we focus, in particular, on one important aspect of maternity policy in three different states: access to care. Britain, Finland, and Canada are similar to the extent that each, at some point in the twentieth century, enacted policies that resulted in citizens/residents gaining the right of access to free maternity care services (Digby 1996; Maioni 1998; Malin & Hemminki 1992).

Despite this general similarity, maternal health policy in Britain, Finland, and Canada differs in significant ways. In Britain and Finland, for example, strong state intervention in the first half of the twentieth century shaped the organization of maternity care services (Hänninen 1965; Lewis 1980), but in the last two decades these two countries developed very different maternity policies. In Canada, the care of pregnant women, especially in urban areas, remained firmly in the hands of male physicians working in private practice until the 1960s. Until the emergence of national health insurance in the late 1960s, the role of the state was largely limited to provision of maternity education (Comacchio 1993). In the last decade, maternity care in Canada, as in Britain, has become politicized and provincial governments are seeking to change existing maternity care arrangements.

In our discussion of maternal health policy and the organization of maternity care in each country we consider two "critical moments" when a change of policy paradigms occurred. The first critical moment involves policy debates and policy changes that resulted in public provision for maternity care for all pregnant women. The second involves recent policy debates and policy changes unique to each country.[1]

The United Kingdom

The first critical juncture affecting maternal health services in the United Kingdom occurred in the 1940s when maternity care was made available at no charge to all women. A second turning point took place in the 1980s and 1990s when—for the first time—the government allowed women's maternity care preferences—not concerns with safety—to shape policy. Both of these historical moments had important implications for midwives as providers of maternal health services.

THE EMERGENCE OF THE NATIONAL HEALTH SERVICE

State involvement in the organization of maternity care in the United Kingdom gradually increased from the turn of the twentieth century on. In 1911, a National Insurance Bill was passed, enabling women in wage work to have a choice of midwife or doctor, but despite its title, the 1911 bill did not provide universal coverage. Wives of working men and unemployed women were not eligible for state-supported maternity care until 1948. In 1918, the Maternal and Child Welfare Act was passed. This act—precipitated by the war and by the campaigns of women's organizations that called attention to the connection between socioeconomic deprivation and mortality and morbidity in childbirth—increased the number of midwives in local government salaried service (Lewis 1990).

In the 1920s, as midwives in Britain were gaining public employment in the area of antenatal care, childbirth was being hospitalized and obstetricians were increasing their power within the health division of labor. Hospital childbirth increased throughout the 1920s (see Chapter 1). However, it is important to note that a 100 percent hospitalization rate was not a foregone conclusion before World War II. Both consultants and the government assumed that home confinements would continue, mainly because of the high cost of hospital birth. There was a broad agreement by all concerned with maternal mortality that the ideal structure of an effective maternal health service should be based on midwife-attended home birth deliveries for most women, with general practitioners serving as backup to the midwife. For women considered to be at risk for complications that would endanger safe birth at home, care in hospitals under the direction of obstetricians was advocated.

The 1936 Midwives Act established a salaried domiciliary National Maternity Service (Peretz 1990). Local authorities and the Central Midwives Board were responsible for the service and community midwives were at the center of care. The main strengths of the newly established National Maternity Service included access to specialist hospital services, flexibility, continuity of care, and subsidized care at a time when general practitioner (GP) services were not free and midwives had little job security. However, as Peretz points out, the scheme also had drawbacks. The services were only free for women poor enough to pass the means test. Provision was varied and relied heavily on charitable help. The local authorities, with the responsibility to provide antenatal services since 1918, did not make adequate resources available for regular clinics. Women's attendance was low, and those who attended had a small number of visits (Peretz 1990). Prior to the introduction of the National Health Service (NHS) in 1948, the hospital was an expensive option.

World War II brought lasting change, in both the planning of local and national services and the promotion of hospital birth; by the end of World War II, the institutional confinement rate had passed 50 percent (see Chapter 1). The experience of population mortality in both wars led to the recognition of the importance of an expansion of health services in general and of maternal and child health services in particular. Two elements in the creation of the postwar welfare state had specific gendered consequences: the Beveridge Report (1942) and the introduction of the NHS (1948). Beveridge's view that "housewives as mothers have vital work to do in ensuring the adequate continuance of the British race" (Beveridge 1942) reflected traditional gendered assumptions about the role of women. Anxieties were focused on rebuilding the family following the dislocation of the world war. State assistance was provided as long as it promoted family life, that is, full-time motherhood. Beveridge assumed that a married women, regardless of whether she had children, would not work; thus her benefits were payable through her husband's insurance. This model for married women's entitlements was not changed until the 1970s. The result was that interventions that relieved mothers of childcare responsibilities were resisted (Riley 1983).

Maternity care services were thoroughly restructured in the NHS. With the introduction of the NHS, consultant led services expanded at the expense of local authority services (Honigsbaum 1979). Under the provisions of the NHS Act of 1946 maternity care included hospital services, domiciliary services, and GP services. For the first time, maternal health services were free at point of access for all women.

With the NHS, women's access to health services became better secured, but the organization of the services for pregnant women remained underfunded and patchy because the provision of antenatal care was now laid in the hands of three different parties—hospitals, GPs and the local authority clinics. The percentage of GPs providing antenatal care rose rapidly to 75 percent in the 1950s. GPs gradually took over the provision of community antenatal care from midwife-run local authority clinics. Care became more fragmented as more and more GPs and obstetricians became involved in "normal" maternity care. The result was a profound change in the midwife–birthing client relationship. The GP rather than the midwife was now women's first point of contact with the public maternal health service (Oakley 1984). The NHS eliminated economic competition between midwives and GPs, but it also established the midwife's subordination in the new hierarchy. There was an irony here. The NHS destroyed the economic basis of independent midwifery, but it provided long-term occupational security and improved working conditions for female health professionals and created the possibility of increased female agency in the new welfare state.

CHANGING CHILDBIRTH FOR WOMEN AND MIDWIVES

During these postwar years public pressure for hospital maternity services had grown (Lewis 1990), and obstetric knowledge and methods had classified more pregnancies as high risk. By 1970, the Peel Committee (Department of Health and Social Security 1970) was advocating a 100 percent hospitalization rate.

In the 1980s, maternity care became increasingly specialized and fragmented. Midwives were less free to use their clinical judgment. As midwives' skills grew rusty from infrequent use, they became increasingly concerned about the erosion of their role in normal pregnancy and childbirth (Robinson et al. 1983). Women's interest groups were also concerned about the increased medicalization and dehumanization of childbirth (see also Chapter 3). Women complained about impersonal care, lack of continuity of care, long waiting times, and unnecessary use of interventions in labor (Cartwright 1979; Oakley 1980). Women's concerns were supported by an accumulating body of research evidence that highlighted the benefits and hazards of routine maternity interventions (Chalmers 1989) and the safety of planned home birth (Campbell & MacFarlane 1987; Tew 1977).

Coupled with these clinical issues were concerns about escalating costs and equitable resource allocation. From 1984 onward there were increasing calls for professional and managerial accountability within the NHS, accompanied by greater financial restraints. The implementation of the NHS reforms (Department of Health 1989) took these earlier initiatives further. Central to this managerial revolution was a new relationship between management and medicine. It became acceptable for the effectiveness and efficiency of medical care to be questioned by politicians, the public, and the media, and the government began to challenge unacceptable professional power (National Audit Office 1990).

Maternity care came to the attention of the government for several reasons: Consumer opinion about this service received higher than average media attention, litigation was common (Ennif 1991), and it seemed a waste of resources. Evidence suggested that it was possible to reduce the workload of junior obstetricians through the adoption of the extended role of the midwife (McKee et al. 1992).

Thus, following two financial investigations into maternity services (Committee of Public Accounts 1990; National Audit Office 1990), the Health Committee of the House of Commons set up an inquiry into maternity services to "determine the extent to which resources and professional expertise were used to achieve the most appropriate and cost effective care of pregnant women and delivery and care of newborn babies." Their subsequent report highlighted three major themes:

- Women's need for continuity of care
- Women's desire for choice of care and place of delivery
- Women's right to control their own bodies at all stages of pregnancy and birth (House of Commons 1992, p. xiii, para. 38).

The report concluded that there should be a move away from mortality as the major outcome measure and toward a woman-centered approach that better met the needs of women themselves. Women should be offered choice in the place of birth and type of maternity services used with seamless care that minimized the number of professionals involved. These recommendations, announced in 1992, were seen as a milestone in maternity policy by consumer groups and midwives alike. For the first time, an independent committee at national level had focused on whether women received the kind of service they wanted, and not just questions about safety.

The government response, *Changing Childbirth,* was published in 1993 and identified three key principles of maternity care: woman-centered participatory care, accessible and appropriate services, and effective and efficient care (Department of Health 1993, p. 8). Ten key indicators of success were identified. The indicators fell into four areas: shifting the role and responsibilities between midwives and doctors with the aim of giving midwives greater autonomy, cost-effectiveness and efficiency, improving continuity of care, and increased client participation in care. *Changing Childbirth* was implemented as national policy in England in 1994 (National Health Service Management Executive 1994).

With a focus on woman-centered care, choice, and the efficient use of human resources, the aspirations of the midwifery profession coalesced with the ideological and political concerns of government. The publication of these reports could be seen as "the integration of feminist interests, the grass roots feelings of women, the heart of midwifery philosophy, and practice made possible through government policies" (Annandale & Clark 1996, p. 424). However, midwives did not agree on how such policies should be implemented, particularly with regard to the demands that team midwifery and caseload practice make upon their lives (Stock & Wraight 1993). The implementation of *Changing Childbirth* policy required midwives to change their working pattern from shift-based to a more flexible working pattern that included spending more time on call. Like all flexible workers, it was hoped that the "new" midwife would be highly trained, consumer-focused, committed, autonomous, and flexible in time commitment (Walby et al. 1994). This model of care was based on a blueprint that came from independent self-employed midwives, but very few midwives have worked in this way since the inception of the NHS. For the midwifery profession, this way of working has been more important as a symbol of independent professional autonomy (Bowler 1994).

As such, the image evoked by the "new" midwife has been a "genderless" image, a professional without family responsibilities, devoted to women and available twenty-four hours a day to meet their needs. Although it was recognized that providing continuity of care would be problematic for some midwives (Department of Health 1993, p. 16), policy documents, government publications, and the profession have been silent on the question of how midwives could work more flexibly. The notion of an ungendered job assumes a particular organization of domestic life and social production (Acker 1990) and is modeled on full-time work. Part-time work is perceived to be a nuisance and a disadvantage. The issues facing midwives in Britain represent a unique example of the issues that face all women who are combining work and family commitments.

A national study of the effects of the implementation of *Changing Childbirth* on the work and lives of midwives was published in 1998. The study—done with a 5 percent representative sample of the midwifery workforce in England (Sandall 1998a)—found about 30 percent of midwives working in "new" patterns of care such as teams or group practices. Midwives working in new team schemes tended to have a wider scope of practice compared to their counterparts in traditional settings. However, as newer appointees, they were also more likely to be on lower occupational grades and earn less money. Furthermore, midwives working in hospital teams had higher levels of burnout (Sandall 1998b).

The changes in maternity care following *Changing Childbirth* have not been uniform. In some places they have been discontinued because of a lack of funding and commitment by health providers. Continuity of care has not always resulted from the establishment of midwife schemes because team midwifery is more popular among midwives than is caseload midwifery. Most midwifery schemes, however, achieve high levels of demedicalized care and maternal satisfaction (Green et al. 1998).

In the new system midwives were being expected to work more flexibly, but without employer acknowledgment of, or support for, family commitments. In some popular areas of work, such as in community-based practice, fewer midwives were employed part-time. There was some evidence of an informal exclusion policy in these settings, where midwives with childcare commitments—or those who wished to work part-time—were not offered work. New patterns of care contain an inherent assumption about the "genderless" job, which required flexibility and availability, and ignored the needs of almost half the current midwifery workforce with children at home. It appears that the midwifery profession missed the opportunity to develop new paradigms of professional practice that incorporate a partnership with users and acknowledge the needs of both providers and clients.

SUMMARY OF THE BRITISH CASE

During the first decades of the twentieth century maternity care emerged as separate, midwife-provided services delivered by the local authorities and self-employed midwives in private practice. The emergence of the NHS that followed the critical years of World War II implied a new paradigm for maternity care. Health services were made universally accessible and free of charge. The NHS endorsed GPs, midwives, and obstetricians as caregivers at birth and had great concern with safety. This resulted in a shift to hospital birth and the medicalization of pregnancy and childbirth. Women received fragmented, dehumanized care and midwives lost autonomy in a system that underused their training and skills and where they worked in a role as a maternity nurse.

Decades later, after years of public and academic debates on maternity care, women's demands were given room in the shaping of maternity policy. However, the changes occurred in a context where British health policymakers were working under neoliberalist assumptions that were expressed in calls for restructured health services and cost containment. The new models for how maternity services should be provided reflected post-Fordist models of flexibility, entrepreneurship, and economical effectiveness.

The new policies have affected women and midwives differently. Although we are cautious about seeing "midwives" or "women" as homogenous groups, our analysis leads us to ask, "Does the new way of organizing care empower midwives, women, or neither?"

The Finnish Case

The Finnish case examines two changes in Finnish health policy that had significant consequences for the organization of maternity care. The first occurred between the mid 1930s and the mid 1940s, when a pronatalist and preventive care-based paradigm came to dominate Finnish politics. The new paradigm came into being as a result of the war and focused on providing services to childbearing women.

A second critical change occurred with the implementation of the Public Health Act in 1972. By this time the strong paradigm of the postwar years had been replaced by a new policy paradigm with less emphasis on maternity care. The Public Health

Act emphasized the role of primary care in health services. The organizational model associated with this paradigm resulted in the gradual decentralization of maternity care. Maternity care services came to be defined as a part of family care and are provided in the community.

THE FINNISH MATERNITY SERVICE EMERGES: THE WINTER WAR AS A CRITICAL MOMENT

Before World War II Finland was a rural country where the majority of the population worked in agriculture. Traditional birth attendants had a strong foothold in maternity care, even after a state policy to subsidize midwifery in rural municipalities was enacted in the 1920s. Hospital births were already common in cities, but for the majority of the population, home birth was the norm (Hänninen 1965). However, Finland was rapidly changing. After the great depression and severe political instability in the early 1930s, Finland entered a more stable and prosperous period, during which social policies such as maternity care were taken to the state agenda.

Following foreign examples, the Finnish Social Insurance Committee (1936) lobbied medical authorities for a reform of municipal midwifery and prepared a proposal to legislate a maternity benefit. In 1937 a Midwives' Act and a Maternity Benefit Act were passed. The system of municipal midwifery was expanded to the entire country, and the municipal midwife was assigned the task of providing prenatal care. These state provisions were limited, however, and did not cover the entire population. The maternity benefit was intended to cover only part of the cost of birth assistance and some necessary supplies (Social Insurance Committee 1936, p. 11). The services of municipal midwives were available free of charge only to the poor. Furthermore, the maternity benefit included a means test and favored agrarian women over working-class women. The committee drafted the new policy without direct influence from women politicians, despite their activism in the Parliament (Sulkunen 1989).

The Social Insurance Committee saw the new Municipal Midwives' Act as just *one* step toward the improvement of maternity care (1936, p. 11). The committee believed a more comprehensive maternity care policy included the development of maternity centers and maternity hospitals. Their hopes for new policies were realized in 1937 when the reform-friendly "red-green" coalition entered government. This new government set up two important parliamentary committees, both of which included maternity care on their respective agendas. The first—the Rural Health Committee—was initiated by several voluntary organizations, district governors, and the association representing rural municipalities. Its task was to examine how public health conditions in the countryside could be improved (Rural Health Committee 1939, pp. 7–10). The second—the Population Committee—was initiated by the Ministry of Social Affairs and was asked to prepare proposals for policies intended to solve the "population question" (Pesonen 1980, p. 629).

The Rural Health Committee gave its report in 1939, only a few months before the outbreak of the Winter War—Finland's entry into World War II.[2] The report encouraged increased state involvement in the provision of preventive health services and stated that public health was intimately linked with social policy. The committee concluded that access to health services, provided in a timely fashion, could prevent social problems (Rural Health Committee 1939, pp. 95–96). Nevertheless, access to no-cost municipal primary care services for free was suggested only for the poor.

The report of the Rural Health Committee also included outlines for a reformed maternity service, with a new emphasis on preventive care. The committee proposed that in each municipality at least one maternity center—headed by the municipal health officer—should be established and that the state should sponsor municipalities in the provision of this service (Rural Health Committee 1939, p. 67). The report favored a move toward hospital birth by encouraging the building of large specialist-headed central departments in which maternity and gynecological wards would be combined. Small municipal maternity wards were recommended only in peripheral areas. Furthermore, the committee claimed that the price of hospital birth could be made low enough to allow less-advantaged women to use this option (Rural Health Committee 1939, p. 69). The maternity care program of the Rural Health Committee corresponds closely to the goals of gynecologists that were also supported by the larger medical profession (see Chapter 1). The only female member of the committee was a home economist and a teacher, not a medical expert or politician, like the men on the committee. Her role fit with the ideology of the times according to which women could speak to matters concerning social policy only in their capacity as experts on family life and homes (see, e.g., Ollila 1993).

As a result of the need to effectively manage the social crisis caused by the Winter War, Finnish social and health policymaking changed rapidly.[2] The report of the Rural Health Committee, although influential, was used only as the basis for the reform of municipal maternity care. The policies suggested were not considered to be far-reaching enough. A political will to accept a strong authority for the central state had emerged during the war. More interventive strategy for health and social policy was proposed. One expression of this new, more interventive state was the rise of *family policy.* Maternity care came to be considered one of the central policies on the new family political agenda (Pesonen 1980; Suonoja 1992).

The Population Committee was the most central arena for the making of the new family policy. The committee continued its work until 1945, producing a total of five reports on various topics, including loans for couples to set up families, family allowances, and social policies for maternity protection. The Population Committee and the other parliamentary committees that worked during the 1940s were called on to develop family policies that could help solve the pressing problems of postwar Finnish society brought on by the material and human losses associated with the war (Suonoja 1992, pp. 390–399).

Unlike the more modest Rural Health Committee, the Population Committee recommended a sweeping transformation of maternity care policy. The previous committee was primarily concerned with maternal and infant mortality (Rural Health Committee 1939, pp. 64–69); the Population Committee saw maternity care as a wider population-political issue. The health of the mother was defined in relation to her role as childbearer, as caregiver to her family, and as the gatekeeper of optimum health of the child (Population Committee 1942, p. 1). Several women were involved with the Population Committee as politicians and as professional experts. Although women's political organizations participated actively in the making of population/family policy in this and other arenas, the central positions were occupied by men. Women's roles corresponded to traditional ideas about women's proper place in society as representatives of the family.

In this period, maternity care policy subordinated women's personal interests to the interest of the state. New policies were intended to establish and protect the position of the family as a basic unit of society (Nätkin 1997). Hence it is no surprise that state policies did not promote "family planning": Contraception and abortion were not available to ordinary women. The duty of the state was to "support the women who are giving birth to a new generation for the nation" (Pitkänen 1950, p. 88). Following this line of reasoning, the maternity benefit was made universal in 1941, and in 1944 the state established universal access to free maternity care through *municipal maternity centers*. These centers provided all women with free services in the community, including regular check-ups and advice on health and childcare; birth assistance provided by the municipal midwives was now free of charge to all women. Parallel to this reform, however, the Rural Health Committee policy of promoting hospital birth was adopted by the hospital system, although hospital birth was not made free.

The professional role of the municipal midwife was substantially transformed by these changes in maternity care. The emphasis in her practice came to lie on preventive services, and tasks defined as "social care" were added to her duties. (Hänninen 1965). The new midwife and the public health nurse who practiced at the new municipal child health centers represented a new type of health service professional that was to become more common when the Finnish welfare state services were built. Publicly employed professional groups with mandates provided by social policies have been central for the implementation of Finnish welfare state policies.

Nevertheless, the Finnish "national maternity service" cannot be compared with the welfare state policies that later were adopted in Finland. The wartime government was far more interested in the "survival of the nation" than in extending greater rights to pregnant women and their families:

> From the point of view of population policy, it is necessary to focus on the reproduction of the nation, especially due to the frightening loss of men during the long defensive war. It is certain, that a well-organized [maternity] training will save many thousand lives for the country and for the defence. (Government proposal cited in Pesonen 1980, p. 635)

MATERNITY SERVICES DECENTERED

Postwar maternity and child health services foreshadowed the way social policy goals could direct the organization of health services. It was not until the mid-1960s, however, that the real breakthrough in welfare state thinking in Finnish health policy occurred. The move toward the welfare state in Finland, at first, increased access to government-sponsored health care and, in the early 1970s, a comprehensive public program of free primary care services. The structure of health service delivery became a political concern in the 1960s. Not only was primary care considered underdeveloped in comparison with public delivery of hospital services, but outpatient services in municipalities—based on the separate practice of municipal health officers, midwives, and public health nurses—were also perceived as old-fashioned (Kuusi 1964).

These structural problems were exacerbated by the fact that the medical profession dominated hospital policy. The hospital sector constituted the sole "power base" of the health care system, and hospital physicians were able to profit by the great demand for their services at a time when physicians were in a scarce supply. Hospital physicians and medical authorities—primarily those located at the Finnish Medical Board—had continuous conflicts over such issues as physicians' fees for providing hospital medical services. The medical profession and the state were also doing battle over proposed national health insurance plans and demands for increased training of physicians (Pesonen 1974; Suonoja 1992). State officials and other health policy actors believed that stronger public primary care service would make the health care system more balanced and cost-effective. In 1965, the Public Health Committee formulated a plan for a two-step reorganization of medical services with the intent of promoting a better balance between outpatient and inpatient care. Primary medical services and preventive care were to be delivered directly by the municipality through one "umbrella organization" called the health center (Public Health Committee 1965, p. 34).

In 1966, the "red-green" government found strong support in the electorate for welfare policies that increased state involvement in service delivery. The health policy outlined by the new government aimed at universally accessible services. This political change and a new definition of disease based in a social science understanding that emphasized the social context of the individual in need of health services led to the Public Health Act of 1972. The act represented a new paradigm for health policy: There was a substantial increase in public funding of health care by both the state and the municipalities, and comprehensive municipal health centers were to provide universal access to both preventive services and primary-level medical care. All services were made free at the point of delivery after a transition period (Suonoja 1992).

These changes had a negative effect on midwives. The all-male Public Health Committee believed that maternity care no longer needed a separate legislatively defined organization. In the new system all primary care was to be based on a preventive approach, and this preventive care was to be integrated with the general services provided at the health center (Public Health Committee 1965, pp. 31, 61). Noting the decline of home birth in Finland, the committee saw no role for midwives in the new maternal health service (Public Health Committee 1965, p. 61). The decision to decentralize maternity care was based on a belief that women's health in general, and maternal health in particular, no longer constituted a problem. Maternity centers together with improved social conditions were credited for better health status of women. Because women would have access to free services during pregnancy, the organizational changes were not seen as a threat to their health (Kuusi 1964; Public Health Committee 1965).

The reform of primary care took shape above the heads of maternity care professionals, and midwives suffered as a result. They were unable to resist the changes in midwifery training that, after 1968, no longer qualified midwives for practice in primary care (Valvanne 1986). The revocation of the Municipal Midwives' Act of 1944 together with the provisions of the Public Health Act gradually excluded midwives from prenatal care during regular pregnancies. Even though many midwives remained a long time in the positions they had acquired before the 1972 legislation, the occupation no longer held the privilege of being the first contact for pregnant women.

Gynecologists, who had supported midwives because of shared goals, now had their own interests to pursue. In the early 1970s, gynecologists at hospitals were setting up outpatient maternity clinics intended to provide obstetric care to at-risk mothers. To establish the position of these clinics, gynecologists wanted to diminish the autonomy of maternity centers (Pyörälä 1970), and they eventually succeeded in getting the National Medical Board to issue a standardized indication list for sending mothers to maternity outpatient clinics (Hultin 1980).

Despite changes in the health system, the implementers of the 1972 legislation favored the maternity and child health care centers. Finnish maternity services kept the program of frequent prenatal visits modeled on the British program outlined in 1929 (Hultin 1980; see also Tew 1995). Because the former municipal midwives were still employed by municipalities in great numbers, it was easy to continue maternity service delivery in the same paths as before, even though maternity centers were subsumed in the health center organization.

Even though the maternity centers offering prenatal care in somewhat different shape survived the immediate blow of the Public Health Act, later organizational changes have eroded their role. The outpatient clinics have, since the 1970s, taken a major role in Finnish maternity care, even for women considered to be at low risk (Hemminki et al. 1990). From the point of view of pregnant women this development was regrettable. Research indicates that women are significantly less satisfied with the care they receive at maternity clinics compared to the maternity services at health centers (Kojo-Austin et al. 1993).

More important still is the continuous restructuring in the organizational context of maternity services within the health center throughout the 1980s. In response to claimed inefficiencies, the National Medical Board, supported by the Finnish Medical Association, initiated efforts to reorganize the health centers. The models that emerged to mend the problems, promoted as family-centered ways to organize primary care, viewed the GP as linchpin (e.g., Helenius et al. 1987). The subsequent Population Responsibility for Primary Care (PRPC) established a new division of labor based on *health care teams* consisting of primary care physicians and public health nurses. The team was to provide all central primary care services for a certain regionally defined population, working collaboratively and without specialization into particular services. The PRPC model was marketed as family care intended for all groups "from baby to the granddad." Continuity of care for pregnant women was defined as care during pregnancy by the same team that provided services to the *baby* (see, e.g., Liukko et al. 1990). By way of contrast, in the United Kingdom, for instance, continuity of care has been discussed in terms of the process that pregnancy, childbirth, and the postnatal period constitute.

For maternity service organization, the population responsibility reform reinforced the paradigm of decentralized maternity services expressed earlier in the Public Health Act. In the 1990s, these renewed efforts to decentralize the delivery of maternity services within primary care were met with sharp criticism, primarily from midwives' professional organizations and gynecologists. In addition, voluntary organizations in the area of public health expressed discontent with the new reforms (Wrede 1997), and experts at the national research and development center, STAKES, began to cautiously question the organization of maternity care (Poikajärvi and Mäkelä 1998).

The PRPC policy caught on in health policy in the late 1980s, when it was considered important to be flexible and cost-effective. Furthermore, it fit well with other measures the state took to decentralize health policymaking. In the early 1990s, after a deep recession intensified efforts to cut costs in health services, the PRPC model became part of the health policy paradigm that allowed rapid and substantial cuts in state spending on health services (Lehto & Blomster 1999).

In general, women appear to be satisfied with public maternity care services, although discontent with maternity clinics, the new power base in maternity care, remains (Kojo-Austin et al. 1993).

SUMMARY OF THE FINNISH CASE

The "national maternity service" created in Finland in 1944 gave midwives an unusually broad mandate to provide social and health care services to women in the community, autonomously and at "pram distance," as health officials proudly stated (Hultin 1980). However, the parallel policy of support for hospital birth soon started to erode the position of the municipal midwives. Paradoxically, the development of a new concern for women's health lessened support for midwifery among policymakers.

The predominantly male architects of the health services of the Finnish welfare state saw no need to put a *particular* emphasis on care during pregnancy and, consequently, after 1972, prenatal care came to be seen as a part of the jurisdiction of primary care public health nurses. Midwifery continued to "fade away" from primary care, when the services of midwives were defined as gatekeeping for hospital-based services. Other tasks of the municipal midwife were taken over by the public health nurse, who—in terms of health education and social care–related tasks—had a relatively similar professional profile. As in the United Kingdom, where midwives lost opportunities for broadly defined practice as a result of the NHS, the Finnish Public Health Act, together with hospitalization of birth (described in Chapter 1) limited the practice of Finnish midwives.

The Public Health Act, like the NHS, also had a fragmenting effect on maternity services. After the creation of the NHS in the United Kingdom consultant-led services expanded at the cost of community-based services, and three agencies—hospitals, GPs, and local authority clinics—each took a share of maternity services. In Finland, the Public Health Act institutionalized the role of the health centers as gatekeepers, paving the way for increasing influence of hospital-based services in maternity care during pregnancy. Furthermore, the Public Health Act removed formal responsibility for municipalities to provide domiciliary birth assistance. As a result, most pregnant women are cared for by three separate agencies—health centers providing maternity care, outpatient clinics at hospitals, and maternity hospitals. With the shift toward medically managed pregnancy at specialist-headed outpatient clinics there is increased dissatisfaction with care. Recent health reforms, aimed at flexibility and cost-effectiveness, have promoted generalist-provided primary care, a paradigm that has not included midwifery.

The Canadian Case

The Canadian case focuses on two critical periods for the organization of maternal health services. The first period takes place in the late 1960s, when the Canadian government established state-funded physician and hospital maternal services for all pregnant women. For the first time Canadian women enjoyed free access to maternity services and yet, not surprisingly, the new Canadian health care system favored medical and male approaches to maternal health.

The second, more recent, period was marked by the restructuring of maternity care services across the country in response to two intertwined pressures on the welfare state: (1) a fiscal crisis caused by cutbacks in federal health funds to the provinces and (2) consumer demand for greater choice in the organization of maternity care. An important outcome of this second period has been the legalization of midwifery in many Canadian provinces and the inclusion of midwives in a number of provincial health plans. However, apart from these changes on the midwifery front, no federal or provincial-wide maternity care policies have been enacted, and—because of a reduction in transfer payments for health services from the federal to provincial ministries of health—there are indications of growing inequalities in the access of Canadian women to crucial maternity-related services.

THE CANADIAN MATERNAL HEALTH SERVICE: A LONG TIME COMING

Compared to both Britain and Finland, Canada was a laggard in regard to the public funding of maternal health services and state recognition of midwives as an important profession for the care of women. To better understand the universal health care system of Canada and its effect on maternity care, we must set the historical stage.

Canadian midwives had been excluded from licensure in most provinces by the early decades of the twentieth century (Comacchio 1993). Further, in contrast to the case in industrializing Europe, no formal training programs for midwives developed in Canada during the first half of the twentieth century. The only exception was the eastern province of Newfoundland, which did not join the rest of Canada until 1949 (Benoit 1991). Midwifery remained a traditional craft across most jurisdictions of the country, and in many provinces physicians led successful campaigns to eradicate the occupation, depriving women of the option to seek out a midwife to care for them during pregnancy and childbirth (Oppenheimer 1983). Traditional "granny midwives" continued to practice in many areas of Canada, and they were often well respected and trusted by their local communities. In the long run, however, in most areas of the country midwifery was undermined. By World War II childbirth attendance was the mandate of the medical profession (Comacchio 1993). At the same time, women had no option but to pay for physician services out of their own pockets.

An important step to remedy this situation was taken in 1957, when the federal government of Canada introduced the Hospital Insurance and Diagnostic Act. This act provided payment for a number of medical services associated with hospitalization and medical testing. The payment structure determined by the federal government was a cost-matching scheme whereby provincial governments were reimbursed 50 percent for a fixed portion of the expenditures. This act, however, did not cover the cost of physicians' services. This meant that pregnant women across Canada had to pay for most of their maternity care—by now almost exclusively provided by a male-dominated profession—with their own money or (for more privileged women) through private insurance schemes.

Universal health insurance arrived with the passage of the federal Medical Care Act of 1968 (implemented in 1972). The act teamed national principles with provincial administration through an innovative program, eventually known as Medicare. Under this second act, physicians' fees were insured. Pregnant women in Canada now had access to physician and hospital services at no cost. The "conditions," or five fundamental principles, of the new Canadian health insurance Medicare plan included:

- **Universality of Coverage** The act stipulated that 95 percent of all residents of Canada had to be covered within two years.
- **Portability** Provincial governments had to ensure that the benefits would be portable from one province to another.
- **Comprehensiveness** Provincial governments had to cover all "medically necessary" services inside or outside of hospitals, as well as dental surgery performed inside of hospitals.
- **Accessibility** Provincial governments had to ensure medical services were "reasonably" accessible, were provided on "universal terms and conditions," and were free of any barriers to access (such as extra billing by physicians).
- **Public Administration** Provincial governments were to administer their health care plans directly or through a nonprofit public agency fully accountable to the provincial government.

Physicians were initially resistant to the implementation of a "socialized" health care system for Canada (an infamous "doctors' strike" protested the government Medicare plan), but in the end, the medical profession in general—and obstetricians in particular—gained much by the new welfare state policy. First, services were reimbursed through the public purse, virtually guaranteeing practitioners' economic security. Second, Medicare solidified physicians' dominance over maternal health services, granting them a monopoly over the provision of care to pregnant women. Third, physicians retained their right to remain private entrepreneurs, establishing their practices wherever they deemed appropriate and making available a range of medical services to women that physicians themselves, not their clients, deemed necessary. Finally, hospitalization of childbirth had long been a goal of the Canadian medical profession. Medicare solidified the hospital as the linchpin to the maternity care system. One important reason for doctors to promote hospital birth rather than domiciliary care was a consequence of the need for the physicians to be able to use substitute health providers to assist them in the care of birthing women and their newborns (Benoit 1991). Canadian physicians thus gave their support to the training of obstetrical nurses (rather than autonomous midwives), a strategy that was enthusiastically supported by the nursing lobby. Physicians were interested in forming relationships with "nursing assistants," who were expected to take a complementary role and show "wifely obedience to the doctor, motherly self-devotion to the patient and a form of mistress/servant discipline to those below" (Buckley 1979, p. 134).

PHYSICIAN DOMINANCE CHALLENGED

In the decades following the implementation of Medicare, the Canadian welfare state was both praised and scorned for its policies regarding maternity care. On the one hand, by the early 1970s all pregnant women in Canada were receiving public coverage for physician and hospital care. But on the other hand, the maternity care system put in place was criticized for being overly medicalized, with physician attendants and large hospitals the only viable choices for maternity clients.

The Canadian welfare state had enshrined *medical dominance* over the country's maternal health services. What this means in practice is that provincial health ministries (the agencies that oversee health service provision and negotiate physicians' reimbursement) allow physicians to work as private entrepreneurs who, through their provincial medical associations, bill the government for medical services that physicians alone deem essential to adequate maternity care. Each province had a Medical Practitioners Act that, until the 1990s, restricted the performance of "midwifery services" exclusively to licensed members of the College of Physicians and Surgeons. An "exceptions" clause was put in place in rural and northern areas that allowed trained midwives to "catch babies" and not be held liable for doing so (Benoit 1994). Public funds for maternity care services have been available almost exclusively for specific activities performed by licensed physicians. Until recently, so-called "alternative" health services, such as midwifery, remained uninsured under the health care plans in all Canadian provinces. The result has been inaccessibility of midwifery services to women.

As a result of physicians' exclusionary strategies Canadian women have not had access to midwives as primary attendants, unless they had money to seek such services on the private market. Private practice midwives in Canada had to work outside of the official health care system and formal health care settings (see Chapter 4). Typically, a client seeking midwifery services received her prenatal and postnatal care at the midwife's home and gave birth—assisted by the midwife—in her own home. When a home birth was not practical, the midwife has worked as a "labor coach" in the hospital. For these varied services, the client would have paid the midwife from her own pocket. Fees varied greatly across midwifery practices, ranging from $800 to $2500, sometimes even higher for a reputable midwife in an urban setting. Given this situation, most Canadian women who used private practice midwives have come from a small pool of educated, middle-class women with some measure of discretionary income.

For midwives this situation was less than ideal. While some had adequate economic resources to allow them to do midwifery as a "sideline," many others were forced to support their "midwifery habit" with a second or even third part-time job. Private practice midwives, some of whom lived near or below the poverty line, also had to contend with an absence of employment benefits of any kind, the persistent threat of being charged with criminal negligence, and a lack of control over their work and personal schedules: "The midwife's personal and professional lives are more intertwined than most, with no time of day reserved for herself or her family. Clients' personal crises and unpredictable timed labors intrude on a 24-hour basis. Each midwife either cop[ed] with this or retir[ed] according to the limits of her stamina and her support systems" (Barrington 1985, p. 50).

The situation of midwives must be seen in the larger context of an ongoing critique of the Canadian health system. For some time health critics have been calling for a refocusing of the Canadian health care system "upstream," in the direction of health promotion and illness prevention for all citizens. These critics have pointed out that the health care system in Canada is inefficient and very costly—in 1996, total health expenditures were 9.5 percent of the gross domestic product (GDP), one of the most expensive systems among high-income countries (Macionis, Benoit, & Jansson 1999, p. 346). The restructuring of health care services has been seen by many advocates—not the least of whom are women health activists, midwives, and maternity clients—to be a step toward improved health outcomes and increased efficiency of service delivery.

The legalization of midwifery and regulation of midwives' practice is an example of such reform (Shroff 1997). Following the lead of Ontario in the early 1990s, legislation enabling the integration of midwives into the health care system is now in existence in a number of Canadian provinces (Bourgeault & Fynes 1997). British Columbia was the first province to follow along Ontario's path, and more recently midwives have been regulated in the provinces of Alberta, Saskatchewan, Quebec, and Manitoba. The remaining provinces are likely to follow suit in the near future. These recent developments have extended access to midwifery services to clients from less privileged backgrounds and have improved midwives' working conditions and overall social status (see Chapter 6).

Nevertheless, the small number of midwife-attended births in Canada hardly signifies a revolutionary change from earlier decades of medical dominance over maternity care. In 1998 midwives attended only 3 percent of Ontario births, and the figure was even smaller in British Columbia, where licensure was established more recently (Benoit 2000). The overall Canadian figure is still less than 2 percent, and the demand for midwifery services continues to outpace availability in many regions of both provinces. Further, it is unsettling that the likelihood of publicly funded midwifery services in at least two Canadian provinces remains uncertain. Alberta, for example, recently legalized and regulated midwifery, but provides no public provision for services (James 1997). Saskatchewan also followed this path, leaving midwives' services on the private market. Birthing women still have to pay for their midwife in these two provinces. In Alberta, the fees of midwives have increased to $2000–$3000 since legalization because of provincial government requirements forcing midwives to purchase malpractice insurance. Quebec and Manitoba provide more positive cases, where the provincial governments announced that the services of midwives would be funded, as in Ontario and British Columbia by the public purse.

Unfortunately, these positive developments regarding the public funding of midwifery services have been accompanied by a reduction in federal health care funding for maternity and other health care services. One result has been sharp discontent among the Canadian family physicians and obstetricians who still provide the bulk of maternity care in Canada, many of whom are now unwilling to take on new maternity clients. The resulting "physician shortage" has left rural pregnant women and their counterparts in the low income areas of large cities in a catch-22: There are too few physicians willing to attend them, while at the same time they cannot arrange care with one of the few publicly funded midwives (Benoit 2000).

Summary of the Canadian Case

Substantial resources have been spent in Canada to fund the professions of obstetrics and gynecology and to provide hospital care for birthing women. Despite important reductions in maternal and infant mortality and morbidity, significant problems remained, even after the country established its public health care system in the late 1960s. Maternity care services remained largely under the control of male physicians and hospital bureaucrats, who allowed women little say in important decisions about their births. At the same time, women healers, not the least of all midwives, were deprived of an active role in women's health maintenance.

One of the central aims of recent restructuring of the health care systems of different Canadian provinces has been to eliminate such weaknesses while enhancing system efficiency. Whether the aims of health care planners in Canada have been realized remains to be seen, however. While midwives have been awarded public legitimacy and urban middle-class women have gained greater choice in regard to both primary childbirth attendant and place of birth, these positive developments appear to have been accompanied by increasing inequality among Canadian women in regard to access to key maternity care services. The shortage of family physicians and obstetricians who are willing to provide maternity services in rural areas and the inner cities is especially noteworthy in this regard. Few provincial governments, let alone the federal government, have been able to remedy this situation in any organized fashion, which among other things might challenge physicians' control over maternal health services in Canada.

Discussion

The organization of maternity services in the three countries examined here is framed by three very different welfare state projects. Even though important differences are visible, the consequences of state involvement in the care of pregnant women are surprisingly similar across our three case examples.

In Britain, social and health programs for mothers were created early on, but a critical moment occurred in 1948 with the creation of the NHS, when all women were granted access to free services. The universal policy did not consider women's particular maternity care needs, however, resulting in the fragmentation of care. In Finland, a similar process took place in the early 1970s, when the building of a Nordic welfare state—intended to increase access to comprehensive health services for all—resulted in the fragmentation of care.

The welfare state health service models in both Britain and Finland placed increasing power in the hands of hospital specialist physicians, a development that had occurred earlier in Canadian health policy. However, in Britain and Canada the state responded to demands from groups representing women and midwives, enacting policies that compromised the power of specialist physicians in favor of midwives. In Finland, policymakers also responded to women's demands, although in a different manner. The traditional family-centeredness of the pronatalist policy paradigm was replaced by an *equality*-driven family-centeredness. Paradoxically, within maternity care this development highlighted the family at the cost of pregnant women themselves.

The Canadian and British cases, although positive examples of an increased responsiveness to women's interests in policy, point at rather weak state engagement in these goals. In both cases, the welfare state's interest in maternity care appears to be predominantly pragmatic. Maternal health is not a cause of dramatic concern as it was in earlier decades. Consequently, cost containment, flexibility of the workforce, and other organizational concerns tend to override consumer concerns.

Interestingly, the U.K. and Finnish cases indicate that despite other adverse consequences, early pronatalist policies benefited both consumers and providers of services in terms of how services were organized. In more recent years, when these welfare states "updated" their policies, the gendered position of women—as clients and providers of care—was often not considered. For example, we have seen that new policies enhanced the professional position and status of midwives (one of the so-called "women's professions") in a way that was gender-blind. Midwives welcomed these changes, but their new position also created contradictions, with their professional goals and their personal lives pulling them in different directions.

Notes

1. The data sources for this chapter are varied. U.K. data sources include primary and secondary sources. Primary sources comprise published and unpublished reports and monographs, including government documents and policy-related debates in consumer and professional journals, and also draw on a study of the impact of U.K. maternity policy on midwifery work and midwives' lives (Sandall 1995, 1996, 1998a). Secondary sources include academic debates on maternity care providers and services in the United Kingdom. Finnish sources were collected and analyzed for a study on Finnish maternity care policy and the role of midwives as an interest group in relation to the Finnish state (Wrede, forthcoming). Some preliminary results from the study have been published (Wrede 1997, 1998). The data used in this article come from both primary and secondary sources on public policymaking. The primary sources cited are central policy documents and related materials, such as reports from parliamentary committees from the two critical periods, official statements made by interest groups, and policy-related debates in professional journals. Secondary sources include academic writings on health care, history books on organizations and professional groups, and memoirs by central policy actors. The Canadian data analyzed for this chapter are also collected from both secondary and primary sources. The secondary sources comprise published and unpublished reports and monographs, including government documents and academic writings of a general sort in the area of health care and, more specifically, on maternity care providers and services in Canada collected over the last decade and a half. Primary sources include empirical materials collected through a series of projects dealing with women's mothering/family role, comparison of health organizations and professions, gender and the health division of labor, the role of midwives as women's primary care providers, and family/employment tensions of health professionals (Benoit 1989, 1991, 1992, 1994, 1998; Benoit & Heitlinger 1998).

2. World War II resulted in three wars for Finland: two wars against Russia (the Winter War of 1939–1940 and the Continuation War of 1941–1944) and a third war, the War in Lappland against Germany (1944) (see, e.g., Klinge 1997).

References

Acker, J. 1990. Hierarchies, jobs, bodies: A theory of gendered organizations. *Gender and Society* 4(2): 139–158.

Annandale, E. C., and J. Clark. 1996. What is gender? Feminist theory and the sociology of human reproduction. *Sociology of Health and Illness* 18(1): 17–44.

Barrington, E. 1985. *Midwifery Is Catching.* Toronto: NC Press Ltd.

Benoit, C. 1989. Traditional midwifery practice: The limits of occupational autonomy. *The Canadian Review of Sociology and Anthropology* 26(4): 633–649.

———. 1991. *Midwives in Passage: The Modernization of Maternity Care.* St. John's: Memorial University of Newfoundland, ISER Books.

———. 1992. Midwives in comparative perspective: Professionalism in small organizations. *Current Research on Occupations and Professions* 7: 203–220.

———. 1994. Paradigm conflict in the sociology of the professions. *Canadian Journal of Sociology* 19(3): 303–329.

———. 1998. Rediscovering appropriate care: Maternity traditions and contemporary issues in Canada. In: *Health and Canadian Society,* 3rd ed., eds. D. Coburn, C. D'Arcy, and G. Torrance. Toronto: University of Toronto Press, pp. 350–378.

———. 2000. *Women, Work and Social Rights: Canada in Historical and Comparative Perspective.* Ontario: Scarborough, Prentice Hall Canada.

Benoit, C., and A. Heitlinger. 1998. Women's health caring work in comparative perspective: Canada, Sweden and Czechoslovakia/Czech Republic as case examples. *Social Science and Medicine* 47(8): 1101–1111.

Beveridge, W. 1942. Report on Social Insurance and Allied Services, *CMD* 6404 (VI): 53.

Bourgeault, I., and M. Fynes. 1997. The integration of nurse- and lay midwives in the US and Canada. *Social Science and Medicine* 44(70): 1051–1063.

Bowler, I. 1994. Midwifery—independent practice in the 1990's? In *Qualitative Studies in Health and Medicine,* eds. M. Bloor and P. Taraborrelli. Avebury: Aldershot, pp. 60–75.

Buckley, S. 1979. Ladies or midwives? Efforts to reduce infant and maternal mortality. In *A Not Unreasonable Claim: Women and Reform in Canada 1880s–1920s,* ed. L. Kealey. Toronto: Women's Press, pp. 131–149.

Campbell, R., and A. MacFarlane. 1987. *Where to Be Born? The Debate and The Evidence.* Oxford: National Perinatal Epidemiology Unit.

Cartwright, A. 1979. *The Dignity of Labor? A Study of Childbearing and Induction.* Tavistock, London: Institute for Social Studies in Medical Care.

Chalmers, I. 1989. Implications of the current debate on obstetric practice. In *Effective Care in Pregnancy and Childbirth.* eds. I. Chalmers, M. Enkin, and M. J. N. C. Keirse. Oxford: Oxford University Press, pp. 3–38.

Comacchio, C. R. 1993. *Nations Are Built of Babies. Saving Ontario's Mothers and Children 1900–1940.* Montreal: McGill-Queen's University Press.

Committee of Public Accounts. 1990. *Thirty Fifth Report, Maternity Services* (House of Commons Sessions, 1989–90, HC 380). London: HMSO.

Department of Health. 1993. *Changing Childbirth, Part 1: Report of the Expert Maternity Group.* London: HMSO.

Department of Health and Social Security. 1970. *Report of the Subcommittee on Domiciliary and Maternity Bed Needs,* (Peel Committee). London: HMSO.

Digby, A. 1996. Poverty, health and the politics of gender. In *Gender, Health and Welfare,* eds. A. Digby and J. Stewart. London: Routledge, pp. 69–70.

Ennif, M. 1991. Change in obstetric practice in response to fears of litigation in the British Isles. *Lancet* 338(8767): 616–618.

Green, J. M., Curtis, P., Price, H., and M. Renfrew. 1998. *Continuing to Care, the Organisation of Midwifery Services in the UK: A Structured Review of the Evidence.* Cheshire: Books for Midwives Press.

Hänninen, S.-L. 1965. *Kätilötyön vaiheita.* (Phases in Midwifery.) Helsinki: Otava. (In Finnish.)

Helenius, M., Marjamäki, P., Pekurinen M., and I. Vohlonen. 1987. *Sosiaali- ja terveysministeriön omalääkärikokeilu.* (The Ministry of Health and Social Affairs Demonstration Project on Family Physicians. (Lääkintöhallituksen tutkimuksia [Research Reports of the Finnish Medical Board] 42). Helsinki: Lääkintöhallitus (The Finnish Medical Board). (In Finnish.)

Hemminki, E., Malin M., and H. Kojo-Austin. 1990. Prenatal care in Finland: From primary to tertiary health care. *International Journal of Health Services* 20: 221–232.

Honigsbaum, F. 1979. *The Division in British Medicine, A History of the Separation of General Practice from Hospital Care 1911–1968.* London: Kogan Page.

House of Commons. 1992. *The Health Committee Second Report: Maternity Services, Vol 1.* London: HMSO.

Hultin, H. 1980. Role of the midwife: The Finland experience. *Child Health* 3: 110–124.

James, S. 1997. Regulation: Changing the face of midwifery? In *The New Midwifery: Reflections on Renaissance and Regulation,* ed. F. Shroff. Toronto: The Women's Press, pp. 181–200.

Klinge, M. 1997. *A Brief History of Finland,* 2nd ed. Helsinki: Otava.

Kojo-Austin, H., Malin, M., and E. Hemminki. 1993. Women's satisfaction with maternity health care services in Finland. *Social Science and Medicine* 37(5): 633–638.

Kuusi, P. 1964. *Social Policy for the Sixties. A Plan for Finland.* Helsinki: Finnish Social Policy Association.

Lehto, J., and Blomster, P. 1999. 1990-luvun alun lama ja sosiaali- ja terveyspolitiikan suunta. [The recession of the early 1990s and the direction of health policy.] *Yhteiskuntapolitiikka* [Social Policy] 64(3): 207–221. (In Finnish.)

Lewis, J. 1980. *The Politics of Motherhood. Child and Maternal Welfare in England, 1900–1939.* London: Croom Helm.

———. 1990. Mothers and maternity policies in the 20th century. In *The Politics of Maternity Care: Services for Childbearing Women in 20th Century Britain,* eds. J. Garcia, R. Kilpatrick, and M. Richards. Oxford: Clarendon Press, pp. 15–29.

Liukko, M., Perttilä, K., Aro, S., Husman, K., Notkola, V., Pellinen, S., Peurala, M., and K. Räsänen. 1990. *VPK Väestövastuisen perusterveydenhuollon kokeilut.* (PRPC. The demonstration projects in population responsibility for primary care.) (Julkaisuja [Publications] 156). Helsinki: Lääkintöhallitus (Finnish Medical Board). (In Finnish.)

Macionis, J., Benoit, C., and M. Jansson. 1999. *Society, The Basics: Canadian Edition.* Scarborough, Ontario: Prentice Hall Canada.

Maioni, A. 1998. *Parting at the Crossroads: The Emergence of Health Insurance in the United States and Canada.* Princeton, NJ: Princeton University Press.

Malin, M., and E. Hemminki. 1992. Midwives as providers of prenatal care in Finland—past and present. *Women and Health* 18(4): 17–34.

McKee, M., Priest, P., and M. Ginzler. 1992. Can out of hours work by junior doctors in obstetrics be reduced? *British Journal of Obstetrics and Gynaecology* 99(3): 187–202.

National Audit Office. 1990. *The Maternity Services: Report by the Comptroller and Auditor General* (HC 297). London: HMSO.

National Health Service Management Executive. 1994. *Woman-Centred Maternity Services* (EL(94)9). Leeds: Department of Health.

Nätkin, R. 1997. *Kamppailu suomalaisesta äitiydestä. Maternalismi, väestöpolitiikka ja naisten kertomukset.* (The Struggle for Finnish Motherhood. Maternalism, Population Policy and Women's Narratives.) Helsinki: Gaudeamus. (In Finnish.)

Oakley, A. 1980. *Women Confined: Towards a Sociology of Childbirth.* Oxford: Martin Robertson.

———. 1984. *The Captured Womb: A History of the Medical Care of Pregnant Women.* Oxford: Basil Blackwell.

Ollila, A. 1993. Suomen kotien päivä valkenee . . . Marttajärjestö suomalaisessa yhteiskunnassa vuoteen 1939. (The days of Finnish homes get brighter . . . The Martha organization in Finnish society until 1939.) Helsinki: Suomen Historiallinen Seura (Finnish History Society). (In Finnish.)

Oppenheimer, J. 1983. Childbirth in Ontario: The transition from home to hospital in the early 20th century. *Ontario History* 65(1): 36–60.

Palme, J. 1990. *Pension Rights in Welfare Capitalism: The Development of Old-Age Pensions in 18 OECD Countries 1930 to 1985* (Dissertation Series, No. 14). Stockholm: Swedish Institute for Social Research.

Peretz, E. 1990. A maternity service for England and Wales: Local authority maternity care in the inter-war period in Oxfordshire and Tottenham. In *The Politics of Maternity Care: Services for Childbearing Women in 20th Century Britain,* eds. J. Garcia, R. Kilpatrick, and M. Richards. Oxford: Clarendon Press, pp. 30–46.

Pesonen, N. 1974. *Lääkärinä ja virkamiehenä. Lääkintöhallituksen pääjohtaja muistelee.* (As a Doctor and a Civil Servant. General Director of the National Medical Board Thinks Back.) Porvoo: WSOY. (In Finnish.)

———. 1980. *Terveyden puolesta—sairautta vastaan. Terveyden- ja sairaanhoito Suomessa 1800- ja 1900-luvuilla.* (Promoting Health—against Illness. Health- and Medical Care in Finland during the 19th and the 20th centuries.) Porvoo: WSOY. (In Finnish.)

Pitkänen, H. 1950. Äitiyshuollon viimeaikaisesta kehityksestä maassamme. (On the recent development of maternity care in our country.) *Suomen lääkärilehti* [Finnish Medical Journal] 5: 483–526.

Poikajärvi, K., and M. Mäkelä . 1998. *Seksuaaliterveyspalvelut puntarissa. Onko neuvola järjestelmää uudistettava?* (Sexual Health Services Consided. Should the Counseling Services be Reformed?) (Aiheita [Topics] 32). Helsinki: STAKES.

Population Committee. 1942. *Väestökomitean mietintö n:o 2 äitiys- ja lastenhuollon neuvoloista ja kunnallisesta kätilöntoimesta.* (Population Committee Report No. 2 on Maternity and Child Health Care Centers and Municipal Midwifery.) (Komiteamietintö [Committee Report] 1942, 18). Helsinki: Finnish Government. (In Finnish.)

Public Health Committee. 1965. *Kansanterveyskomitean mietintö.* (The Report of the Public Health Committee.) (Komiteamietintö [Committee Report] 1965, B72). Helsinki: Finnish Government. (In Finnish.)

Pyörälä, T. 1970. Äitiysneuvolan merkitys terveydenhuollossa. (The relevance of maternity centers for health services.) *Suomen Lääkärilehti* (Finnish Medical Journal) 25: 105–107.

Riley, D. 1983. *War in the Nursery: Theories of the Child and the Mother.* London: Virago.

Robinson, S., Golden, J., and S. Bradley. 1983. *A Study of the Role and Responsibilities of the Midwife* (NERU Report 1). London: Kings College, University of London.

Ruggie, M. 1984. *The State and Working Women.* Princeton, NJ: Princeton University Press.

Rural Health Committee. 1939. *Maaseudun terveydenhoito-olot ja niiden kehittäminen. Maaseudun terveydenhoitokomitean mietintö.* (Health Service Conditions in Rural Areas and Their Development. The Report of the Rural Health Committee.) (Komiteanmietintö [Committee Report] 1939, 9). Helsinki: Finnish Government. (In Finnish.)

Sandall, J. 1995. Choice, continuity and control: Changing midwifery, towards a sociological perspective. *Midwifery* 11: 201–209.

———. 1996. Continuity of midwifery care in Britain: A new professional project. *Gender, Work and Organisation* 3(4): 215–226.

———. 1998a. *Midwifery Work, Family Life and Well-Being: A Study of Occupational Change.* Unpublished doctoral thesis, Department of Sociology, University of Surrey.

———. 1998b. Occupational burnout in midwives: New ways of working and the relationship between organisational factors and psychological health and wellbeing. *Risk, Decision and Policy* 3(3): 213–232.

Shroff, F. (ed.) 1997. *The New Midwifery: Reflections on Renaissance and Regulation.* Toronto: The Women's Press.

Social Insurance Committee. 1936. *Sosialivakuutuskomitean ehdotus laiksi äitiysavustuksesta. (Mietintö n:o 2.)* (The Proposal of the Social Insurance Committee for Maternity Benifit Act. [Report No. 2.]) (Komiteanmietintö [Committee Report] 1936, 1). Helsinki: Finnish Government. (In Finnish.)

Stock, J., and A. Wraight. 1993. *Developing Continuity of Care in Maternity Services: The Implications for Midwives* (Report for Royal College of Midwives). Sussex: Institute of Manpower Studies.

Sulkunen, I. 1989. *Naisen kutsumus. Miina Sillanpää ja sukupuolten maailmojen erkaantuminen.* (The Calling of a Woman. Miina Sillanpää and the Separation of the Social Worlds of Men and Women.) Helsinki: Hanki ja jää. (In Finnish.)

Suonoja, K. 1992. Kansalaisten parhaaksi—yhteistuntoa ja politiikkaa. Sosiaali- ja terveysministeriö 1939–1992. (For the best of the citizens—solidarity and politics. Ministry of Health and Social Affairs 1939–1992.) In *Suuriruhtinaskunnasta hyvinvointivaltioon. Sosiaali- ja terveysministeriö 75 vuotta,* (From a grand duchy to a welfare state. Ministry of Health and Social Affairs 75 years). Helsinki: Sosiaali- ja terveysministeriö (Ministry of Health and Social Affairs), pp. 323–739.

Tew, M. 1977. Where to be born? *New Society* 1: 120–121.

———. 1995. *Safer Childbirth? A Critical History of Maternity Care,* 2nd ed. London: Chapman and Hall.

Valvanne, L. 1986. *Rakkautta pyytämättä. Valtakunnankätilö muistelee.* (Love without Asking. The Midwife of the Nation Thinks Back.) Helsinki: Tammi.

Walby, S., Greenwell, J., Mackay, L., and K. Soothill. 1994. *Medicine and Nursing, Professions in a Changing Health Service.* London: Sage.

Wrede, S. 1997. The notion of risk in Finnish prenatal care: Managing risk mothers and risk pregnancies. In *Images of Women's Health. The Social Construction of Gendered Health,* ed. E. Riska. Turku: Institute of Women's Studies at Åbo Akademi University, pp. 133–180.

———. 1998. Reorienting professional strategies in prenatal care: Professional groups and health care reform. In *Professions, Identity and Order in Comparative Perspective,* eds. V. Ogliati, L. Orzack, and M. Saks. Onati: IISL Onati, pp. 217–229.

———. (forthcoming) *Maternity Care Services Decentered. The Finnish Politics of Maternity Services and Midwives as an Interest Groups.* Doctoral thesis, Department of Sociology, Åbo Akademi University, Turku.

CHAPTER 3

Changing Birth

INTEREST GROUPS AND MATERNITY CARE POLICY

Ivy Lynn Bourgeault, Eugene Declercq, and Jane Sandall

Introduction

On a variety of occasions and in a variety of ways those who use maternity care services have made organized efforts to change the way care at birth is given. How have these consumer actions affected maternity care policies? We use case studies from three countries—Canada, Britain, and the United States—to explore the strategies and outcomes of consumer efforts to reshape maternity care. These three countries represent a continuum in the politics of maternity care. In Canada and the United States, the maternity care division of labor is characterized by medical dominance; midwives play a minimal, supportive role (Bourgeault & Fynes 1997). Britain, on the other hand, has a long tradition of independent midwifery practice, although maternity care policies created after World War II have favored physicians and hospital birth.

Each of our case studies focuses on policies developed in the 1980s and the 1990s, and in each case we examine three questions:

1. How do the users of maternity care services act as interest groups in the shaping of maternity care policy?
2. What relationship do consumer interest groups have with the providers of maternity care services?
3. What accounts for the varying influence of consumer interest groups on governmental committees and agencies, the policies they create, and the implementation of these policies?

Before we embark on a cross-country comparison of maternity care policy, it is critical to understand that every political system has a different policymaking process. To allow meaningful comparison between widely different systems we must articulate a shared conceptual framework. We begin with a common definition of maternity care policy: *enforceable government legislation, institutional policies, or everyday practices that occur within the system of care for childbearing women.* With regard to the policymaking process, we use Kingdon's (1995) four-stage model, which includes: (1) the setting of the policy agenda, (2) the specification of alternatives from which a choice is to be made, (3) an authoritative choice among those alternatives, and (4) the implementation of the decision. Because we are primarily interested in consumer action, we focus mainly on the first and arguably the most critical stage of the policymaking process—agenda setting. Here, Kingdon describes three separate streams in agenda setting—problems, policies, and politics—which must come together at a "window of opportunity" for issues to be taken seriously by policy decision-makers.

Central to the agenda-setting process are interest groups that call attention to a problem. Our shared definition of interest groups is: *organizations of individuals with shared interests in bringing about change in government or institutional policy* (Walt 1994). We distinguish two kinds of interest groups: *insider groups* and *outsider groups.* The former are accepted as respectable by government policymakers and often play a consultative role in policy creation; the latter are not perceived as legitimate and find it difficult to penetrate the policymaking process (Grant 1984).

Traditionally, the interest groups most involved in maternity care policy have been maternity care providers, including physicians, midwives, nurses, and, in some cases, labor assistants. With the rise of the women's health and home birth movements, maternity care clients have become involved in the policymaking process either overtly through political organizations or latently through demands for particular services. In several cases, consumers have joined with providers, midwives in particular, to create a kind of advocacy coalition (Sabbatier 1988) to push for changes in maternity care policy. In countries where the government is involved in public health and health insurance, the state is an important actor in the maternity care policy process (see Chapter 2).

A final player in the policymaking process is the *policy entrepreneur.* Policy entrepreneurs work within interest groups and the government; they are those who are willing "to invest their resources—time, energy, reputation, and sometimes money—in hope for a future return. That return might come in the form of policies of which they approve" (Kingdon 1995, pp. 122–123). Their involvement in early stages of the agenda process often involves a battle over shaping the definition of the problem in the public's mind in a way that furthers their cause (Rochefort & Cobb 1994).

Our first case study examines recent efforts to (re)integrate midwifery into the Canadian health care system.

The Campaign of Canadian Consumer Groups: Increasing Choices in Childbirth with the Integration of Midwifery

In the past twenty years there has been no more important maternity care policy initiative in Canada than the integration of midwifery into various provincial health care systems. Prior to the 1970s, there were few midwives in Canada, and their practice was neither legal nor officially recognized. In fact, Canada had the dubious distinction of being the only Western industrialized nation without any formal provisions for midwifery care. Yet by the end of 1993 midwifery in one Canadian province, Ontario, became fully licensed, integrated into, and funded by the provincial health care system. Legislation integrating midwives has followed in the provinces of Alberta and British Columbia; is soon to follow in Quebec, Manitoba, and Saskatchewan; and is quite likely in Nova Scotia and Newfoundland (Bourgeault 1998). It took a mere decade for midwifery in Canada to move from obscurity to an officially recognized maternity care option. How and why has this happened, and—more to the point—what role did consumers play?

The policy process in the province of Ontario represents an illustrative case in point for the Canadian situation. It should, however, be emphasized that midwifery legislation in other Canadian provinces has not been implemented in exactly the same way as it has in Ontario. Indeed, there are many differences between provinces, but it is clear that the developments in Ontario helped put the issue of midwifery on the policy agenda in the other provinces.

The data used in this case description come from a collection of over twenty years of primary and secondary source documents (from medical, nursing, and midwifery newsletters, journals, policy documents, and reports) and semistructured interviews with over fifty key informants knowledgeable and influential in the Ontario midwifery integration process (Bourgeault 1996; Bourgeault & Fynes 1996/7).

THE DEVELOPMENT OF CONSUMER INTEREST GROUPS TO INTEGRATE MIDWIFERY IN ONTARIO

In Ontario, interest groups intent on integrating midwifery into the Ontario health care system evolved from a social movement of people interested in alternatives in childbirth, particularly those interested in having and/or attending home births (see Chapter 4). It is important to note that, numerically, this group never represented a majority opinion. Planned home births were rare in Ontario, particularly in the late 1970s and early 1980s. Even more recently, the numbers have only approached 1 to 2 percent of all births in the province. For one of these groups, the initial impetus for its creation was a change in policy. A group of community nurses decided to discontinue providing nursing care at home births attended by a few physicians across the province. In response, groups of concerned home birth physicians, consumers, and supporters organized to lobby the government to reinstate the service. These groups were unsuccessful in their bid, leaving labor support at home births to be taken up by a newly emerging group of would-be midwives.

The "would-be" midwives that emerged from this group were not formally trained; they were women interested in promoting childbirth alternatives through helping at home births. Often their own home birth experience sparked their interest. Home birth consumers, supporters, and assistants subsequently formed several midwifery support and study groups across the province, often as an offshoot of the initial home birth lobby groups. These groups helped foster a model of midwifery care that came to include *informed choice, choice of birthplace,* and *continuity of care.* Such woman-centered principles of practice resulted in significant consumer support for midwifery care.

A WINDOW OF OPPORTUNITY: AN INQUEST INTO A BABY'S DEATH

Midwives practiced in relative obscurity in the province in the early 1980s. However, an inquest into a baby's death initially planned as a home birth brought their practice broader public attention. The possibility of serious legal repercussions spurred the home birth community to abandon its "low-profile" strategy and to take more decisive action. Capitalizing on the media coverage of the inquest, midwives and their supporters, which now came to include not only midwifery consumers but also women's health activists, organized a public demonstration to increase public awareness and support for midwifery and home birth.

The inquest also brought the issue of midwifery to the attention of the province's medical regulatory body, the College of Physicians and Surgeons of Ontario. Subsequent to the inquest, the college issued a directive strongly discouraging the few physicians who were willing to assist or provide backup for home births from continuing to do so. The directive did little to curb the demand for home birth attendance, however, which was now taken up by midwives practicing independently of physicians. At the same time, the directive did highlight the precarious legal environment within which midwives were practicing. Although not illegal, as it was in some other Canadian provinces, there were no formal provisions for midwives' practice in Ontario or for their protection as practitioners. Midwives' concern with this situation propelled them to push for the formal integration of midwifery into the provincial health care system. They set up a professional organization of midwives across the province including a group of like-minded foreign-trained nurse-midwives—the Association of Ontario Midwives (AOM)—and began to lobby for integration into the health care system.

Consumers and supporters of midwifery care set up a separate advocacy organization, the Midwifery Task Force of Ontario (MTFO), to help support midwives' integration process. In part because of the structure of midwifery care in the province (i.e., not being publicly funded and available only as an "underground" option), many midwifery consumers were well educated and/or well connected in important women's health networks; in general those who used midwife care came from middle- to upper-middle-class backgrounds (particularly the leaders of the consumer group). They were very effective in their tasks of public education, lobbying, and fund-raising to help support the attempts to achieve legislation.

PUBLIC POLICYMAKING ARENAS

The Health Professions Legislation Review

The creation of AOM and MTFO was timely, as shortly thereafter the provincial government appointed a committee to review the regulation of all health care professions in the province, the Health Professions Legislation Review (HPLR). Initially set up to settle several outstanding issues involving numerous health professions in the province, the review created a ready context for efforts to integrate midwifery. Consumer advocates supported midwives by entering a Midwifery Coalition, which prepared a joint submission to the HPLR that expressed a strong desire for midwifery to become integrated according to the International Definition of a Midwife. This included self-regulation for midwifery as a profession distinct from nursing and medicine, access to both hospital and home birth practice, public funding of midwifery services as a means to increase the accessibility beyond those clients who could pay for it directly, and multiple routes of entry to practice, nursing not being a prerequisite.

The window of opportunity that had opened for the efforts to integrate midwifery continued throughout the review. Due to competing concerns, other professional interest groups, including nursing and medical organizations, were poorly committed to the issue of midwifery. In comparison, the submission prepared by the Midwifery Coalition stood strong with its reliance on international research and policy precedents (see Chapter 6).

In making a recommendation to the Ministry of Health regarding the inclusion of midwifery in the broader legislative package, the review committee was also influenced by an ongoing media and public awareness campaign actively pursued by midwives and their consumer supporters around several focusing events, not the least of which was another coroner's inquest in 1985, which became a public inquiry into midwifery in the province. Here, consumer supporters—who organized letter-writing campaigns and massive public demonstrations—were instrumental in bringing the media to a pro-midwifery perspective (initially they were quite critical of the practice of home birth). Through their efforts, midwifery was quickly becoming a politically charged issue that the government wanted to "get off the front pages" of the daily papers. Following recommendations made by the review, the provincial government formally announced in January 1986 that it was indeed going to integrate midwives into the Ontario health care system, and it established the Task Force on the Implementation of Midwifery in Ontario to investigate how this would be accomplished.

The Task Force on the Implementation of Midwifery in Ontario

Appointed to the task force by the government were a feminist lawyer, the lawyer who headed the HPLR, a family physician, and a nurse who had some midwifery training, all of whom were generally supportive of midwifery. The task force began a two-year process that involved the solicitation of written submissions, oral presentations, public hearings, and meetings among provincial stakeholder groups, including midwives, consumers, nurses, physicians, and hospital representatives. Consumer presentations made a particularly strong impression on the task force members. Consumers continued to advocate strongly for midwifery as a self-regulating profession available at home and in the hospital and funded through the provincial health care system, lending strong support to the midwives' proposals. In contrast, nursing and medical organizations expressed preference for a model of midwifery as a specialty of nursing available only in hospital.

When the task force presented its over 400-page report to the government in November 1987, it recommended that midwifery be implemented largely in the manner consumers and their midwives advocated. This included self-regulation, multiple routes of entry to midwifery education (without a nursing prerequisite), that midwives practice as primary caregivers in both home and hospital, and that midwives be funded by the provincial health care system (Eberts et al. 1987). The task force provided strong support for midwifery and for the specific model of care for which consumers and practicing midwives lobbied. Midwifery was later integrated into the health care system in 1993 in almost the exact manner proposed by midwifery advocates in their first submission to the Health Professions Legislation Review ten years earlier (see Chapter 6).

Presently, there are over 150 midwives licensed to practice in Ontario, and, according to College of Physicians and Surgeons of Ontario statistics, the total number of midwife-attended births have exceeded 3,000 per year (approximately 40 percent of which take place at home). This represents between 2 and 3 percent of all births in the province (Wolgelerenter 1998). Given that midwives continue to turn away almost 40 percent of clients who seek midwifery care, the expansion of midwifery in this province, not to mention the country, is a likely scenario.

SUMMARY OF CANADIAN CASE

The midwifery integration process in Ontario offers an example of a maternity care policy initiative fueled by organized consumer support. At critical events such as the inquests and presentations at governmental reviews, midwifery consumers and supporters successfully garnered media and public support for their pursuits. For midwives, having an active and visible group of consumer supporters was especially important: It gave their professional aspirations credibility with both the media and government representatives.

The success of the consumer groups in shaping the health policy agenda of Ontario resulted from several factors. First of all, these outsider organizations soon received support from health policy insiders, among which some figures turned out to be prepared to become "policy entrepreneurs" for maternity care policy. That is, key actors within the government offered significant support for the integration of midwifery in the health care system. This was manifested by the establishment and funding of midwifery policy committees, the purposive appointment of pro-midwifery persons to these committees, and government's actions on these committees' recommendations. Government support for the midwifery initiative was forthcoming for two main reasons. First, the argument that midwifery was a cost-effective form of care suited the state's current efforts regarding the rationalization of the health care system. Second, the government could also be publicly viewed as being progressive in supporting women's issues and promoting women's rights. It is also not insignificant that the Ministers of Health throughout the midwifery integration process were women who were personally supportive of the midwifery initiative (Bourgeault & Fynes 1996/7). Added together, these conditions created a conducive environment for this maternity care policy initiative. As we shall see in the next case study in Britain, similar influential factors were also present when new issues were set on the British maternity care policy agenda in the early 1990s.

A Consumer Campaign to Enhance Continuity of Care in Britain: Reestablishing the Midwife's Role as Primary Caregiver

One of the most commonly expressed wishes of pregnant women in Britain is that they be attended during their pregnancy, labor, and postnatal period by a midwife with whom they have an established relationship. In Britain in the 1980s, very few women had access to such care due to fragmentation of maternity care associated with the National Health System (NHS) (see also Chapter 2). During the 1960s, a fundamental shift in maternity care occurred, with more general practitioners (GPs) and obstetricians becoming involved in "normal" maternity care. In turn, the work of both hospital and community midwives became increasingly specialized and fragmented. By the 1980s the sphere of practice of midwives had been constrained and continuity of care severely limited.

Interestingly enough, this desire of pregnant women for continuity of care became a key theme in three government reports on maternity care in Britain in the 1900s: the *Winterton Report* (House of Commons 1992), *Changing Childbirth* (Department of Health 1993), and *Midwifery: Delivering the Future* (SNMAC 1998). Each of these reports critically reassessed the roles of health professionals in maternity care and each used the views and experiences of women in making policy recommendations. In these reports the government recommended shifting routine maternity care from the hospital to the community and making the midwife the "lead professional" in maternity care.

The move to enhance continuity of care and reestablish the role of midwife as a primary caregiver gives us a second example of consumer concerns influencing maternity care policy. The data used in this case study come from policy documents and published commentary on changes to maternity care in Britain.

CONSUMER PRESSURE: BUILDING A WINDOW OF OPPORTUNITY

As pregnant women began to depend more on doctors and larger hospitals there was an increased emphasis on "humanized" care in the maternity services literature. As early as 1961, there was enough concern to issue a policy statement called *Human Relations in Obstetrics* (Ministry of Health 1961). This report by the Maternity Services Committee described a general complaint that many hospitals had little regard for the personal dignity and emotional condition of women during pregnancy. It is noteworthy that most of the evidence was given by women's organizations, much of it coming from mothers. Acknowledging this testimony, the report suggested that hospital confinement should, in these respects, achieve as nearly as possible the atmosphere of home confinement.

Throughout the 1970s and 1980s women's distress caused by fragmented care was a topic of discussion. Although doubts were expressed about obstetric practice in the academic literature, it was the consumer organizations, in particular the National Childbirth Trust (NCT), the Association for Improvement in Maternity Services (AIMS), and the Maternity Alliance, that played the key role in the debate around childbirth, generating both media and parliamentary interest. The NCT—created in the 1950s to promote the ideas of Grantly Dick Read—is a national organization providing information and support to childbearing women. In contrast, AIMS has an explicit campaigning role focused on reproductive technology and the medicalization of childbirth, choice, and place of birth. The Maternity Alliance focuses on wider policy issues such as parental rights, benefits and childcare, inequalities in maternity care, risks and benefits of reproductive interventions, and working conditions of NHS staff. Together these organizations became a mouthpiece for consumer complaints about the existing maternity care system.

As in Canada, consumer groups were adept at publicizing ongoing research by social scientists to support their case. Continuity of care by the midwife was seen as an "ideal" way to overcome problems of fragmented medicalized care. It was advocated on three grounds: first, that if women got to know a few of the care providers available for them well, they were more likely to feel confident about expressing concerns; second, midwives were more likely to detect abnormalities; and third, the social support literature suggested beneficial effects of continuity of care for pregnancy outcome (Elbourne et al. 1989). The Maternity Services Advisory Committee (1982, para. 1.10) had already recommended the use of midwives in a more independent capacity, being aware of the "numerous consumer complaints about the so-called impersonal nature of care in hospitals, where maternity services are now concentrated." Nevertheless, continuity of care was considered by government policymakers to be too difficult to achieve in practice (Social Services Committee on Perinatal and Neonatal Mortality, House of Commons 1980, para. 292).

The issue of continuity of care was not buried for good, however, and in the early 1990s the topic reemerged in policy debates, where it was again associated with the role of midwifery in maternity care. In the 1990s the government became concerned about the underuse of midwifery skills. Reports on maternity services from the National Audit Office (1990) and Committee of Public Accounts (1990) led the Health Committee of the House of Commons to set up a special inquiry into maternity care. The committee wished to determine the extent to which resources and professional expertise were used to achieve the most appropriate and cost-effective care of pregnant women and delivery and care of newborn babies. The report that resulted from the inquiry was the *Winterton Report.*

THE WINTERTON REPORT: STATE ARENA FOR AGENDA SETTING

In the past, inquiries about maternity services focused on mortality; this time, however, the Health Committee of the House of Commons stressed that central to the inquiry was the management of normal pregnancy and birth. The committee comprised a selection of political party representatives, although one of the driving forces was Audrey Wise, a labor party politician. An independent-minded chairman (Nicholas Winterton) enabled an inquiry that received 400 representations and took oral evidence from individual women and their representative groups, researchers, and health professionals. The report concluded that there should be a move away from a concentration on mortality rates as the major outcome measure for the maternity services and toward a woman-centered approach that better met the needs of women and offered them a choice of place and type of service, with seamless care that minimized the number of professionals involved.

To promote continuity of care the committee recommended a move away from the old system of shared care. In its place the committee recommended unified care throughout the antenatal, intrapartum, and postnatal periods; the extension of the professional role of the midwife to include full responsibility for a set caseload of women; the provision of routine maternity care by community-based teams of midwives; and an increase in midwife-managed delivery units adjacent to obstetric units (House of Commons 1992, para. 219 and 344).

These recommendations, announced in March 1992, were seen as a milestone in maternity policy by consumer groups and midwives alike. For the first time, an independent committee at the national level had focused on whether women had received the kind of service they wanted rather than focusing only on safety. Furthermore, the committee recommended measures to combat social influences on pregnancy outcome, such as poverty. In response to the Health Committee report, the government established a departmental task force to address wider issues in the organization of care (Department Health 1992a), including a national study of team midwifery (Wraight et al. 1993) and a study of midwifery and GP-led units (Department of Health 1993). The government response to the *Winterton Report*, entitled *Changing Childbirth* (Department of Health 1993), was published in 1993.

CHANGING CHILDBIRTH: STATE ARENA FOR POLICY FORMULATION

In 1992 the government created the Expert Maternity Group (EMG) under the chairmanship of Baroness Cumberlege. The EMG drew its membership from the women who use NHS services and the professionals who provide care. Members included an obstetrician, a pediatrician, the chair of the National Childbirth Trust, the coordinator of the Asian Family Counselling Association, a professor of midwifery, a journalist, an NHS manager, and a GP. The purpose of the EMG was to "review policy on NHS maternity care, particularly during childbirth, and to make recommendations" (Department of Health 1993, p. 1). The group gathered evidence from a wide range of organizations and individuals with an interest in maternity care. The expert group also visited a range of maternity units, organized a consensus conference, and commissioned a survey of women conducted in their first language.

The ENG endorsed most of the *Winterton Report.* It identified three key principles of maternity care: woman-centered participatory care, accessible and appropriate services, and effective and efficient care (Department of Health 1993, p. 8). Ten key indicators of success, which fell into four key areas, were identified: shifting the role and responsibilities between midwives and doctors (with the aim of giving midwives greater autonomy), cost-effectiveness and efficiency, improving continuity of care, and increased client participation in care. In January 1994, the NHS Management Executive (National Health Service Management Executive 1994) told all regions, districts, and trusts to review their maternity services and develop a strategy to implement the recommendations, defining ten key indicators of success to be met within five years.

The policy focus on midwifery implied a lessened role for doctors in the provision of maternity care. As might be expected, the initial response of the medical profession was a defensive one. The profession critiqued the research evidence as inadequate (Dunlop 1993), emphasized concerns with safety (RCOG 1993), and debated the respective roles and responsibilities of midwives and obstetricians (British Medical Association 1995, 1997; RCGP 1995). Not surprisingly, the *Changing Childbirth* report was welcomed by consumer groups (Edwards 1993; Hutton 1995), midwifery organizations (Warren et al. 1993), and Health Authorities (NAHAT 1993).

SUMMARY OF BRITISH CASE

The policy recommendations of the early 1990s were, in part, a response to the consumers' critique of maternity care—a critique supported by academic research—and were situated in a context where the cost-effectiveness of health care was being scrutinized. The governmental reports of the 1990s were radically different from earlier reports. The focus on woman-centered care and reference to "evidence-based practice" coalesced with the ideological and political concerns of a government interested in the efficient use of human resources. The publication of these reports can be seen as "the integration of feminist interests, the grass roots feelings of women, the heart of midwifery philosophy, and practice made possible through government policies" (Annandale & Clark 1996, p. 424).

As was the case in Canada, consumers and midwives were successful at lobbying behind the scenes. In this case a window of opportunity was opened by a powerful member of the House of Commons Health Committee, who was able to push maternity care onto the political agenda, and by the Health Minister, who had a long-standing interest in women's health and in extending the autonomy of nurses and midwives.

It is important to note that, despite thirty years of consumer activism in the area of maternity services, government reform of maternity care policy only began to take place in the 1990s when the interests of consumers coalesced with the state interest in cost containment. It might be said that government policymakers used the argument of women's interests to pursue particular economic aims around the organization of maternal health services. In his analysis of the situation, Mason (1995) makes the claim that the visionary statements of the *Winterton Report* were transmuted by the economic rationalism of the government response in *Changing Childbirth*. The *Winterton Report* embodied a variety of perspectives that coalesced around childbirth during the early 1990s. In contrast, *Changing Childbirth* emphasized individual choice, personal continuity, and control. This second report ignored the wider range of social and environmental effects on health in favor of a strategy that treated maternity care services provision as a vehicle for the expression of consumer values (Declercq 1998; Streetly 1994).

There is little consensus about the implementation of the new policies (Stock & Wraight 1993). The changes appear beneficial for clients, but for midwives as workers the consequences are more complex (see Chapter 6). From the point of view of consumers, the implementation of the government reports has turned out to be patchy, a problem not likely to be remedied in the near future. Key figures in maternity care interest groups and in the government have left. Important interest groups have moved on to other issues, such as poverty, disability, and the increasing use of interventions such as prenatal screening and cesarean section. As maternity care has dropped off the political agenda, the pilot projects funded by *Changing Childbirth* money have been dropped. In 1998 the NCT lobbied parliament with a ten-point plan to keep maternity care on the political agenda, but until new relationships can be built with the fresh faces in government, professional organizations, and interest groups, little is likely to occur. Despite these problems, the British case demonstrates the central role consumer organizations can play in a state-centered policy system. The U.S. case, to which we now turn, serves as an example of a very different kind of opportunity for consumer influence on policy.

Consumer Policy without Consumer Input: The Case of U.S. Policies on Early Postpartum Discharge from the Hospital

In the United States, there is no such thing as public policy regarding maternity care. The U.S. health system is based on private providers and institutions supported by mostly private funding. The government *does* influence the process, but it does so indirectly or, on occasion, in a spasm of politically motivated and media-driven legislative activity. This kind of system is inclined toward the maintenance of the status quo. Lobbying groups seeking to identify and ultimately influence the pressure points of the system are often frustrated. How can lobbying succeed if there *is* no system and hence no pressure points?

The case study presented here focuses on government legislation related to early postpartum discharge. The data used come from review of the statutes, hearings, and supporting documents regarding early discharge and interviews with legislators, staff, insurers, and lobbyists involved in the process. For a more complete discussion of sources, see two related studies from which this analysis is drawn (Declercq 1999; Declercq & Simmes 1997).

THE ISSUE OF EARLY POSTPARTUM DISCHARGE IN THE UNITED STATES

Prior to May 1995, there was no reference to minimum periods of hospitalization for new mothers and babies in state or national laws in the United States (Wright et al. 1995). By the end of 1996, twenty-eight states had passed what are termed "early discharge" laws. Comparable bills were also introduced in the U.S. House and Senate in June 1995, and on September 26, 1996, President Clinton signed a national law mandating insurers to cover longer postpartum hospital stays. What caused this flurry of legislative activity?

In the past quarter century, the average postpartum hospital stay in the United States has been cut in half and now ranks among the shortest of all the countries studied in this volume. In 1970, the average postpartum length of stay for vaginal births in the United States was 3.9 days; by 1994 the rate dropped to 2.0 days. Likewise, the average postpartum stay for cesarean births was 7.9 days in 1970 and 3.9 days in 1994 (Curtin & Kozak 1998). These national averages mask considerable regional variation within the United States, with one study finding postpartum stays of one day or less in 1994 to be 2.5 times as common in the West (87.6%) than the Northeast (33.8%) (Gazmararian & Koplan 1996). Decreasing lengths of postpartum stays also occurred within a context of general reductions in hospital stays in all countries for all diagnoses (OECD 1999).

Underlying the debate over early discharge in the United States is the assumption that widespread hospitalization for birth and the postpartum period is desirable. This is a broadly held but not universally accepted belief (Campbell & MacFarlane 1994). Home care in general, and specifically postpartum home visiting, is much less common in the United States than in the other countries studied here. Comparatively, the United States has the least generous postpartum leave policies in the developed world. Many European countries have paid (at rates of 50–100 percent of salary) family leaves of at least twelve weeks (Ierodiaconou 1986), while in the United

States legislators struggle to pass a law to protect parents from losing their jobs for taking any *unpaid* family leave.

As insurers began to reduce the permitted length of postpartum stays, concerns about the health of mothers and babies—sent home to fend for themselves—arose. Some argued that it was dangerous to send mothers home without sufficient instruction and surveillance; others insisted moms and babies would do better in their own homes. There was little empirical evidence to support either side of the argument (Braveman et al. 1995). Most studies of early discharge suffer from serious methodological flaws, and both insurers, who reduced stays, and policymakers, who sought to lengthen them, could find individual studies to support their case. Ultimately, the policy process that led to early discharge laws centered on the question of who (mothers? doctors? funders?) controlled the decision on how long the hospital stay should be.

AGENDA SETTING BY THE MEDIA AND BY KEY PROVIDER GROUPS

The issue of early discharge came to the attention of the public in an era of dissatisfaction with managed care in the United States. The media framed the issue as a contest between mothers, babies, and doctors on one side and faceless insurance bureaucrats on the other and drew their evidence from personal anecdotes. In the face of powerful anecdotes evidence of low neonatal hospital readmission rates did little to sway public opinion.

The public was only mildly interested in this issue. Without the activity of the American Association of Pediatricians (AAP), the American College of Obstetrics and Gynecologists (ACOG), and the American Medical Association (AMA), early discharge would not have advanced to the policy agenda of state and national legislative bodies. There was nothing like a nationally coordinated campaign, and organized consumer involvement was minimal. The Center for Patient Advocacy joined the debate over a national law, but their primary concern was with reforming *managed care*, not *maternity* care (Center for Patient Advocacy 1996).

Because no major consumer organization made an effort to push for any particular solution, provider groups and politicians had room to maneuver and to make the compromises needed to pass legislation. The position of provider groups on proposed legislation was related to the nature of their service. Kingdon (1995) suggests that policy advocates often look for problems that they can solve with their existing practices. For those (physicians and nurses) trained in hospital-based care, an extra day of hospitalization was a perfectly sensible policy, while those involved in home care saw additional hospitalization as a waste of limited resources. As is often the case in health policy issues, self-interest and concern with patients' well-being became entangled.

POLICY FORMULATION AT THE STATE ARENAS

Maryland was the first state to pass an early discharge law. The original impetus for enacting early discharge legislation came from the medical community: Representatives from ACOG and AAP approached the bill's sponsor with concerns about their patients being discharged "too soon." Indeed, a lobbyist from AAP wrote most of the text of the bill, and the sponsor's constituents did not voice their support until after the bill had been announced. The positive publicity associated with passage soon led other states to consider similar policies, and by the end of 1995 four states had new laws. By the end of 1996, a national election year, twenty-eight of the fifty states had passed legislation mandating insurance coverage for postpartum hospital stays, one other (New Mexico) adopted comparable insurance regulations, and three more (Arizona, Colorado, and Michigan) had voluntary agreements with insurers. The remaining states would ultimately be covered by the national law, which allowed states with stronger provisions to have their law supersede the national requirements in their states.

The success of the legislation at the state level involved a more subtle dynamic than simple group pressure. Those legislators who proposed the laws (two-thirds of whom were women) truly believed in the need for the legislation, with many citing their own or friends' negative experiences with managed care companies (many of which had nothing to do with early discharge) as an impetus. For legislators at large it represented an easy vote. It cost the state little—most states excluded publicly funded births from the provisions—and gave the legislators a chance to symbolically appeal to upper-middle-class women, a key constituency. The legislation also fit the general political mood. The American public is concerned with the performance of the health system but is opposed to a general restructuring of health care delivery.

POLICY FORMULATION AT THE FEDERAL ARENA

In 1996, the U.S. Congress passed its version of an early discharge law. A national law was necessary to address an existing federal provision that severely limited the scope of the state early discharge laws. In the United States, companies who insure their own employees (i.e., do not buy insurance from another company) are exempted from state laws governing health insurance. In some states as many as half of all women are insured by their employers and thus not covered by state law on early discharge. A new national law would rectify that problem and also extend coverage to women in states without their own law. In cases where the state provisions were stronger (e.g., mandating a home visit) than the national provisions, the states' law would be applied.

The same professional organizations that sought state laws (ACOG, AAP) advocated for the national law, although interviews with legislative staff involved in the issue suggest that the issue was moving through the system largely on internal momentum, given some key Senate supporters and its symbolic political appeal. President Clinton also weighed in with his strong support for the bill, citing the issue in both of his campaign debates with Senator Robert Dole.

For the most part, opposition to the new laws stayed in the background. Insurers did not want to take too strong a public position in opposition to this popular issue. A coalition of groups opposed to the legislation was formed with the typically benign name Coalition for Optimal Maternity Care. Its members ranged from insurers (Health Insurance Association of America, Blue Cross Blue Shield) to business groups (U.S. Chamber of Commerce, National Association of Manufacturers) to the

American College of Nurse-Midwives (ACNM) and the National Association of Childbearing Centers. The ACNM opposition was based on a desire to more carefully examine the nature of postpartum care in both the hospital and at home, aptly summarized in their legislative testimony:

> Since nurse-midwives were among the first supporters of early discharge for selected patients with adequate and appropriate mechanisms for follow-up, we know that the problem is not timing of discharge. The problem is—what is the patient's condition at discharge and what services are available once a mother arrives home with a newborn baby. It is our position that the current debate and the proposed solution do not address the real problem. (Committee on Labor and Human Resources, 1995, p. 72).

While the ACNM position was similar to that of some national legislators who opposed the bill, opponents were not the biggest challenge the legislation faced. The major obstacle to an early discharge law in Congress was the fact that the new Republican leadership of the House of Representatives did not consider it a priority. After a series of tortured internal legislative maneuvers (the final bill was never directly voted on in the U.S. House), the U.S. Congress passed the law in the late summer of 1996, in time for all parties to claim credit during the upcoming fall election campaign.

SUMMARY OF THE U.S. CASE

Maternity care consumers remain outsiders to the U.S. policy process, and their exclusion is reinforced by their lack of collective organization in a system that rewards organization. The glacial pace of the U.S. legislative process and a reluctance of legislators to dictate medical practice means that significant, consumer-based change is very difficult to accomplish. The tendency to defer to physicians when it comes to medical practice issues further limits the potential for consumers or midwives to influence the policy process. Interestingly, an early version of the national law included a "mother's veto," which would give new mothers the right to decide when they went home. The provision was dropped for a more politically acceptable clause that gave the provider the right to decide the time of discharge in consultation with the mother.

Why, then, did the legislation on early discharge get enacted so quickly, if no consumer pressure fueled issue formulation? Declining postpartum length of stay can be seen in different ways. It could be seen as testimony to the medical system's sensitivity to mothers' wishes to be home sooner or as a reflection of the ability of medical technology to shorten unnecessary hospital stays. This case study has shown that in the United States in the early 1990s, the media and organizations representing key providers defined early discharge as an economic decision imposed on mothers and doctors by greedy insurers. Consequently, the passing of the early discharge legislation was a politically symbolic process, capturing the frustration of consumers and physicians with managed care. The laws also represent one of the few victories physicians have had in their recent dealings with managed care organizations. The kind of personal anecdotes that dominated this debate also serve media and advocates' need for emotional stories. The widely shared view of early discharge as a consequence of insurers' wish to cut costs opened a window of opportunity for the early discharge laws and helped this legislation pass with unprecedented speed.

We have also shown that the issue of a guaranteed minimum length of postpartum stay gained political support quickly because it did so little. It narrowly focused on postpartum discharge and avoided more difficult choices about funding maternity care for the poor or the efficacy of hospitalized birth in general. It was portrayed as a nontechnical matter of common sense and had an apparently simple, clearly defined solution—an extra day in the hospital. Another alternative, increased home care, is not so easily defined (when and how often would visits occur? what training would home visitors have?) as a solution and may conflict with the U.S. cultural predisposition toward individualism and privacy.

What does the U.S. experience with early discharge legislation tell us about the main focus of this chapter, the role of maternity care consumer interest groups in maternity care policy? Simply put, it reminds us of their general insignificance in terms of shaping maternity care practice in the United States. The impetus for this bill came from provider groups who were hospital-based and who (not surprisingly) proposed more hospitalization. What it did not consider was the nature of that care or, to any large extent, the perspectives of consumers. Consumers supported the legislation in a general sense but were largely unaware of the campaign for the new law.

Conclusion

Having described our three cases in some detail we can return to the three questions posed in the introduction, highlighting differences between countries.

1. INSIDERS AND OUTSIDERS, MATERNITY POLICY PROCESS, AND THE POSITION OF CONSUMER INTEREST GROUPS

We have seen that the effectiveness of consumer interest groups in shaping maternity care policy is determined by the health policy process. In Canada and Britain the state plays an important role in health policymaking. Because liberal democratic states need to maintain legitimacy vis-à-vis its electorate, the government offers consumer groups a ready and relatively responsive audience. In the United States, where the state is minimally involved in health care, there is no ready policy arena where consumer group activities can be played out. The interests of U.S. maternity care consumers *have* been represented by midwifery movements and home birth activists, but these social movements are only occasionally involved in policy.

In Canada and Britain consumer groups succeeded in becoming and remaining insider groups in maternity care policymaking. Their voices were heard in government task forces and committees, and consumer efforts were central in keeping particular user-centered interests on the policy agenda. It seems consumer organizations in all locations need sympathetic politicians to be in the right place at the right time. It is safe to say that the success of consumer groups is tied to a receptive policy arena and to securing and maintaining an insider position. Policy windows can make insiders out of outsiders, as we have seen in the Canadian case.

2. RISING WOMEN'S INTEREST COALITIONS? RELATIONS BETWEEN CONSUMERS AND MATERNITY CARE PROVIDER GROUPS

Consumer groups wishing to influence maternity care policy face a fundamental problem. Traditionally, interest groups succeed by long-term, concerted efforts to change policy. Effective interest groups have sufficient resources, talent, and persistence. Consumer interest groups concerned with birth have a constantly changing constituency. The interest of parents in maternity care policies peaks around the time of birth but then quickly turns to matters of parenthood. Successful maternity care interest groups include providers—specifically midwives and doctors—who have a greater, longer-lasting stake in the issues involved.

In Canada and Britain consumer groups formed advocacy coalitions with midwives. In Canada, consumer groups and midwives united in a "midwifery coalition" to advocate the shared goal of the integration of midwifery into the provincial health systems. In Britain, consumer groups set the agenda for the new policies, but their efforts to promote midwife-led care were constantly supported by midwives.

In the policy process, the coalition representing the different groups of advocates for woman-centered maternity care has often, both in Canada and Britain, acted as representatives for women's interests in health care more widely. Gender has had an important influence on the relationship between consumer and provider interest groups. Maternity care consumers are women and their families, while maternity care providers include both male- and female-dominated groups. Feminist critiques of medicine and health care have helped to locate maternity care policy in the broader framework of women's interests in health care. In the case of midwifery in Canada, the "packaging" of midwives' integration efforts as a fundamental feminist issue of women controlling their reproduction resulted in sustained support by midwives, consumers, *and* women's health and feminist activists. Midwifery became a feminist issue, keeping it on the policy agenda and garnering wider consumer support. Maternity care policy campaigns in Britain were also fueled by feminist critiques of medicine and health care.

In the United States, early discharge was sometimes framed as a woman-centered policy, but the impetus of the policy resulted from a discontent with managed care among both providers and consumers. In general, however, consumers remained organized and unrepresented in the policy process. Anecdotes were used to represent consumer opinion; the media and other self-appointed advocates became de facto spokespersons for consumers. In the case examined here, physician perspectives dominated initial media coverage of early discharge. Such policy entrepreneurship fits the decentralized U.S. policy scene, where, at present, no "women's interest coalitions" can be discerned in maternity care.

3. FACTORS INTERNAL TO THE STATE: EXPLAINING THE VARYING INFLUENCE OF CONSUMER INTEREST GROUPS

All three cases highlight the state's overriding concern with cost containment. A central explanation for the quick passing of the early discharge policy in the United States was that it did not involve significant government expenditures. In Canada there was a strong sense that by integrating midwifery, the government would be "killing two birds with one stone": By implementing midwifery as a low-tech childbirth alternative it was possible to reduce health care costs *and* to respond to the feminist lobby, which was beginning to have significant power in swaying the "women's vote." The British government's recommendations were primarily concerned with continuity of care, but it is no coincidence that the policies outlined in *Changing Childbirth* also promise to save money.

Advocates for woman-centered maternity care have had some success in effecting policy changes in Canada and Britain, but it is clear that "woman-centeredness" was not a dominant interest in policymaking. Consumer interest groups must be continuously active if they intend to keep woman-centeredness on the policy agenda.

A FINAL WORD

Even though consumer groups must fight for their influence, they do have the potential to make the voices of service users heard in policymaking. This leaves us with an important question: Do consumer groups represent the desires of *all* maternity care consumers? Organized consumer groups often claim to represent all women, but it is clear that they overstate their case. Consumer groups may be interpreted as an *avant-garde* (see Chapter 4), or they may be seen as a fringe movement. If midwifery flourishes in Canada and Britain we can conclude that these groups were harbingers of change. On the other hand, if the status quo survives it suggests one of two things: Either these groups represented a minority viewpoint, or professional groups found a way to overwhelm state-sponsored change.

References

Annandale, E. C., and J. Clark. 1996. What is gender? Feminist theory and the sociology of human reproduction. *Sociology of Health and Illness* 18(1):17–44.

Bourgeault, I. 1996. *Delivering Midwifery: An Examination of the Process and Outcome of the Incorporation of Midwifery in Ontario.* Ph.D. Thesis, University of Toronto.

———. 1998, Autumn. Delivering midwifery in Canada: Obstructed labor? *Woman News-magazine,* p. 38.

Bourgeault, I., and M. Fynes. 1996/7. Delivering midwifery in Ontario: How and why midwifery was integrated into the provincial health care system. *Health and Canadian Society* 4(2): 227–262.

———. 1997. The integration of nurse- and lay midwives in the US and Canada. *Social Science and Medicine* 44(7): 1051–1063.

Braveman, P., Egerter, S., Pearl, M., Marchi, K., and C. Miller. 1995. Early discharge of newborns and mothers: A critical review of the literature. *Pediatrics* 96: 716–726.

British Medical Association. 1995. *Maternity Medical Services, Legal Advice, Guidance for GPs.* London: GMSC, RCGP.

———. 1997. *General Practitioners and Intrapartum Care: Interim Guidance.* London: GMSC, RCGP.

Campbell, R., and A. MacFarlane. 1994. *Where to Be Born: The Debate and the Evidence,* 2nd ed. Oxford: National Perinatal Epidemiology Unit.

Center for Patient Advocacy. 1996. Center lands historic victory with Newborns' and Mothers' Health Protection Act. *The Patient Advocate* (undated newsletter).

Committee on Labor and Human Resources, US Senate. 1995. *Hearings on Newborns' and Mothers' Health Protection Act of 1995.* Washington, DC: U.S. Government Printing Office.

Curtin, S., and L. Kozak. 1998. Decline in US cesarean delivery rate appears to stall. *Birth* 25: 259–262.

Declercq, E. 1998. Changing childbirth in the United Kingdom: Lessons for US health policy. *Journal of Health Politics, Policy and Law* 23(5): 833–859.

———. 1999. Making US maternal and child health policy: From "early discharge" to "drive through deliveries," to a national law. MCH *Journal* 3(1): 5–17.

Declercq, E., and D. Simmes. 1997. The politics of drive-through deliveries: Putting early postpartum discharge on the legislative agenda. *Milbank Quarterly* 75(2): 175–202.

Department of Health. 1992. *Maternity Services, Government Response to the Second Report from the Health Committee* (Session 1991-2, Cm 2018). London: HMSO.

———. 1993. *Changing Childbirth, Part 1: Report of the Expert Maternity Group.* London: HMSO.

Dunlop, W. 1993. *Changing Childbirth,* Commentary 2. *British Journal of Obstetrics and Gynaecology* 100: 1072.

Eberts, M., Schwartz, A., Edney, R., and K. Kaufman. 1987. *Report of the Task Force on the Implementation of Midwifery in Ontario.* Toronto: Queen's Park Printers.

Edwards, N. 1993. Cumberlege Report. *Aims Journal* 5(3): 1–5.

Elbourne, D., Oakley, A., and I. Chalmers. 1989. Social and psychological support during pregnancy. In *Effective Care in Pregnancy and Childbirth,* eds. I. Chalmers, M. Enkin, and M. J. N. C. Keirse. Oxford: Oxford University Press, pp. 221–236.

Gazmararian, J., and J. Koplan. 1996. Length-of-stay after delivery: Managed care versus fee for service. *Health Affairs* 15: 74–80.

Grant, W. 1984. The role of pressure groups. In *British Politics in Perspective,* eds. R. Borthwick and J. Spence. Leicester: Leicester University Press.

House of Commons. 1980. *Second Report from the Social Services Committee on Perinatal and Neonatal Mortality* (Paper 663-1). London: HMSO.

———. 1992. *The Health Committee Second Report: Maternity Services,* Vol. 1. London: HMSO.

Hutton, E. 1995. *Midwife Caseloads.* London: National Childbirth Trust.

Ierodiaconou, E. 1986. Maternity protection in 22 European countries. In *Perinatal Health Services in Europe,* ed. J. M. L. Phaff. London: Croom Helm.

Kingdon, J. 1995. *Agendas, Alternatives and Public Policies,* 2nd ed. New York: Harper Collins.

Mason, J. 1995. Governing childbirth: The wider view. *Journal of Advanced Nursing* 22(8): 835–840.

Ministry of Health. 1961. *Central Health Services Council, Standing Midwifery and Maternity Advisory Committee.* London: HMSO.

National Association of Health Authorities and Trusts. 1993. *NAHAT's Response to Changing Childbirth, the Report of the Expert Maternity Group.* London: NAHAT.

National Health Service Management Executive. 1994. *Woman-Centred Maternity Services* (EL(94)9). Leeds: Department of Health.

Rochefort, D., and R. Cobb. (eds.) 1994. *The Politics of Problem Definition: Shaping the Policy Agenda.* Lawrence: University of Kansas Press.

Royal College of General Practitioners and Royal College of Midwives. 1995. *Responsibilities in Intrapartum Care. Working Together.* London: Royal College of General Practitioners and Royal College of Midwives.

Royal College of Obstericians and Gynacologists. 1993. *Press release.*

SNMAC. 1998. *Midwifery: Delivering Our Future* (Report by the Standing Nursing and Midwifery Advisory Committee). London: Department Health.

Streetly, A. 1994. Maternity care in the 1990's. *Health For All 2000 News* 26: 14–15.

Stock, J., and A. Wraight. 1993. *Developing Continuity of Care in Maternity Services: The Implications for Midwives* (Report for Royal College of Midwives). Sussex: Institute of Manpower Studies.

Warren, C., Hughes, D., Bowman, L., and I. Kargar. 1993. A.R.M.'s response to *Changing Childbirth. Midwifery Matters* 59: 3–6.

Wolgelerenter, D. 1998, June 29. Controversy still lingers over the role of midwife. *Toronto Star,* pp. E1, E3.

Wraight, A., Ball, J., Seccombe, I., and J. Stock. 1993. *Mapping Team Midwifery. A Report to the Department of Health* (IMS Report Series 242). Sussex: Institute Manpower Studies.

CHAPTER 4

Reforming Birth and (Re)making Midwifery in North America

Betty-Anne Daviss

Social movements[1] demanding peace, protection of the environment, and equal rights for women and ethnic minorities swept Northern Europe and North America in the 1960s and 1970s. These movements evoked passion, caused unrest, and promoted social change. The alternative birth movement (ABM) was one of the many social movements of this time period. Drawing on movements promoting the rights of women and minorities, the ABM arose to help women reclaim their agency in childbirth. The movement was most visible in North America, although it was also evident in some European countries, notably the United Kingdom (see Chapter 13). The greater strength of the ABM in North America is due, in part, to the connection between the movement and efforts to restore and preserve midwifery. In the United States and Canada, unlike in Western Europe, midwifery was essentially eliminated by the middle of the twentieth century. Thus the ABM in North America had two tasks: reform of "medicalized" birth and the establishment of professional midwifery.

This study of the ABM is based on a detailed survey of Ontario midwives I carried out between 1996 and 1998, in-depth qualitative interviews I conducted with Canadian midwives about their history and their engagement with the ABM (Daviss 1999), and my own involvement with the ABM in both the United States and Canada throughout twenty-five years of midwifery activism and practice. I begin my analysis with a discussion of the circumstances that set the stage for the rise of the ABM and go on to show how it came into its own as a social movement, if in somewhat different fashions, in the United States and Canada. I then explore the characteristics of the ABM as a social movement and continue with examination of the concept of "radical" elements in social movements, investigating the role of what might be termed the "radical flank" of the ABM. Based on my analysis I argue that "success" for the ABM entails more than achieving legalization and regulation for midwives; success involves promoting larger changes in society. I conclude with a discussion of the future of the ABM.

The Rise of the Alternative Birth Movement

Classical "strain" theory holds that social movements arise in response to some breakdown in society (Lang & Lang 1961; Smelser 1962). That seems to be the case here: The ABM in the United States and Canada had its beginnings in the 1950s, when growing numbers of women began to feel alienated from the prevailing obstetrical techniques. Many women wrote letters to the women's magazines *Redbook* and the *Ladies' Home Journal* about the abusive nature of their childbirth experiences (Edwards 1984). Their letters documented the social isolation of laboring women and the dehumanizing effects of obstetrical care. Women reported being tied to their beds by their hands and feet and left alone and in pain for hours or even days, on the premise that scopolamine would wipe out their memories of the experience (Wertz & Wertz 1989). During the 1960s and 1970s, the ABM continued to grow as more and more women spoke out about their dissatisfaction with hospital birth and made alternative choices like giving birth at home.

The criticism of birth practices was not an isolated phenomenon. Rather, the ABM was part of large-scale structural and cultural changes that were occurring in the 1970s and 1980s, including antiwar protests, civil rights and minority activism, the rise of the counterculture, environmentalism, and the first stirrings of feminism (see Melucci 1989; Touraine 1978). A number of childbirth activists confirm that this generalized "amorphous movement" formed the context within which the ABM grew. For example, Joanne Myers-Ciecko, current director and one of the founders of the Seattle Midwifery School (the oldest direct-entry program for midwives who practice out of hospital in the United States), points to the combination of "the anti-war movement and the civil rights movement [and] self-help movements" as creating "a new feminist movement among women frustrated with male power and political models" (1988, p.71). This new feminist movement, she notes, was the catalyst for the creation of feminist self-help clinics around the United States as well as the creation of various midwifery programs, including the Seattle Midwifery School.[2] Sociologist Raymond De Vries, himself a long-time childbirth activist, writes:

> Collectively, we were referred to as "the alternative birth movement," giving us a home among the many movements that populated the American social landscape in the sixties and seventies. The better-known movements of that era—the civil rights movement, the women's liberation movement, the antiwar movement—were in fact our inspiration. Compared with the task of overturning centuries-old discriminatory laws or taking on the military-industrial complex, our mission seemed easy. We were confident we could

"de-medicalize" pregnancy and childbirth, making a place for birth at home and for mid-wife-assisted birth (1996, p. xi).

However, in both Canada and the United States, many childbirth reformers did not realize at first that they were a part of a specific "alternative birth movement." Ina May Gaskin, who became one of the movement's early leaders, said, "Women interested in childbirth began serving as attendants in different parts of the country, unaware of one another, an illustration of how much this new kind of midwifery was an expression of the *Zeitgeist*. For all some of us knew, we were the only kind of midwives in the country (1998, p. 54)." Similarly, a former midwife living in Ontario, Canada, remembered that even as late as the early 1980s, she was not yet connected to any network:

> I wasn't aware of movements. I wasn't aware of some title for it, so I couldn't have been a part of it at first because I didn't know it had a name. I was part of getting back to the land, mothering, and spirituality, but when I became a parent, I didn't have contact with other people doing these things and didn't have a support group or even know that one existed. I remember feeling so ecstatic when I found out that there was a woman in my town (Cornwall) who wanted a home birth and to know that there was someone I could relate to. It wasn't until I started attending meetings in Ottawa that I realized that we were a part of a larger movement (Terri Forrester, personal communication, 1998, in Daviss 1999).

The ABM was given focus and impetus in North America during the 1970s by the publication of a number of influential books.[3] Those with the greatest impact on midwifery include Raven Lang's *The Birth Book* (1972), which was the first to describe the home births being attended by the pioneers of the lay midwifery renaissance; Suzanne Arms's *Immaculate Deception* (1975), which called public attention to the abuses of women in the obstetrical management of birth; and Ina May Gaskin's *Spiritual Midwifery* (1975), which articulated a cohesive and successful alternative approach worked out by the "hippie" midwives of the Farm in Summertown, Tennessee. The movement was given organizational structure by the founding of the first childbirth education organizations in the 1960s, including the International Childbirth Education Association and the American Society for Psychoprophylaxis in Obstetrics (now known as Lamaze International). These organizations were created to resist the obstetrical domination of birth by educating women about their bodies, their rights, and their options, including midwifery care. The same literature and organizations affected Canada.

U.S. versus Canadian Developments of the ABM

At first, consumers and birth practitioners in both North American countries formed joint organizations, one of the most influential being the National Association of Parents and Professionals for Safe Alternatives in Childbirth (NAPSAC). In Canada and many of the states, the distinction between mothers and midwives was neither encouraged nor apparent because the midwives in the movement were often mothers who were learning how to accompany other mothers at birth. In Ontario the midwives and the consumers had the same newsletter until 1983. However, by the early to mid-1980s, in the United States and most Canadian provinces consumers and mid-wives had separated into different groups. The influence of NAPSAC and other such parent-professional coalitions was gradually replaced by the growth of multiple asso-ciations of childbirth professionals that successfully sought to create a wider aware-ness of midwifery as an alternative form of birth assistance.

Although members of the American College of Nurse-Midwives (ACNM, founded in 1955) had worked for decades to develop midwifery as a profession in order to provide better health care to women and babies, midwifery did not garner widespread cultural attention until the home birth midwives who formed the Mid-wives' Alliance of North America (MANA) in 1982 entered the scene. Perhaps the most symbolic act of rebellion perpetrated by midwives and mothers was bringing birth out of the hospital and back into women's lives and homes. This "coming out" was accomplished in part through the publication of books about home birth that dis-played photographs of nude women birthing their babies in full view of partners, families, friends, and, shamelessly, the photographer. Such behavior represented obvious resistance to dominant social norms, which insisted that birth should be hid-den from the public view.

Following as they did on a repressive era in which many women were embarrassed to be seen in public when they were pregnant, such ostentatious acts attracted the attention of society's institutions. California midwives have suggested that the graphic photos in Raven Lang's *Birth Book* (1972) may have been what motivated the district attorney to send a pregnant couple disguised as two hippies to catch Raven Lang and her partner, Kate Bowland, in the act of practicing midwifery. Shortly after their initial consult with this couple-in-disguise, the district attorney sent eight police cars to raid Lang and Bowland's birth center in Santa Cruz (Kate Bowland, personal communication, 1998). Handcuffing the midwives and confiscat-ing diapers, toy stethoscopes, and birth baskets (luckily all their client charts were at Stanford University) was the state's way of taking control of this out-of-control situ-ation. In the ensuing twenty-five years this scenario has been repeated numerous times in various states, the most recent being a raid that took place in July 1999 on the birth center of an unlicensed direct-entry midwife in upstate New York. Ironi-cally, such persecutions often provide added stimulus to the movement by rallying public support.

In Canada, relations between home birth midwives and government authorities have been rather more tame. The Canadian ABM generated no provocative publica-tions, with the possible exception, in 1985, of Eleanor Barrington's *Midwifery Is Catching*. Its more discreet black-and-white photos did not appear to overstress pub-lic sensibilities: Royal Canadian Mounted Police have not impersonated potential midwifery clients nor raided midwives' birth centers or homes. To date no Canadian midwives have been dragged off in handcuffs. Gloria LeMay, the only birth attendant who has been tried (and acquitted) for criminal negligence, reports that the police were very polite. Canadians are shocked when they hear that police in California arrested Faith Gibson, a Mennonite midwife; the Mennonite midwives in Canada, long before legalization, had been allowed to practice under an umbrella of immunity because of their religious beliefs. It seems clear that the polarization was greater between authorities and social activists in the United States than between similar players in Canada.

A shared feature for the ABM in both the United States and Canada is that the white middle-class groups in the ABM made the loudest noise and were an important ingredient for social movement success. Government "crackdowns" on traditional birth in the 1970s and 1980s, such as the removal of the licenses of the black "granny midwives" in the American south (Susie 1988) and the forced evacuations of Inuit women from northern Canada to hospitals in southern Canada (Daviss 1997) increased the need for these cultural groups to seek political help, validation, and solidarity from their white sisters. In some places, the rise of the ABM and the needs of traditional midwives converged just in time. For example, ABM home birth midwives settled in the Inuit community of Povungnituk and began training Inuit women to be professional midwives and attend births in their community, so that women could receive safe care and avoid forced evacuation to the South (Daviss 1997). And when state officials tried to take away the license of Gladys Milton—the last practicing black granny midwife in Florida—home birth midwives who were members of MANA, an organization that has always identified itself with the ABM, supported her. They rallied around her and helped her gain licensure under their new law. By way of contrast, ACNM—a group that prides itself on being a professional organization—has been more reluctant to support midwives who are not nurses.

The difference in the way the ABM has developed among Canadians and Americans sheds light on the struggles between the different factions that emerged in both countries. In the following pages I describe both the increased momentum and increased discordance of philosophy and tactics within the ABM.

The ABM as a Social Movement

Social movements share particular features that distinguish them from other forms of collective behavior. For example, social movements often represent the interest of the "have-nots," while political movements represent the interest of the "haves" (Baer & Bostitis 1993); social movements consist of informal networks of multiple autonomous groups, while political movements often have one individual or organization designated as leader (Diani 1992; Lawn-Day 1994). When we look at the North American ABM in terms of these primary characteristics of social movements we get a clearer picture of its frailties and its strengths. In the following pages I discuss and, to some extent, compare the ABM in the United States and Canada in terms of six characteristics commonly associated with social movements: shared ideology and common goals, collective action, informal networks, fragmentation, non-institutionalized type of action, and significant size.

A SHARED IDEOLOGY AND SOLIDARITY AROUND A COMMON GOAL
(BRANDWEIN 1985; DIANI 1992).

The ABM has been described as a reaction by women against a predominantly Western and male medical establishment that controls obstetrical care (Mathews & Zadak 1991) and disseminates that control to all parts of the world (Davis-Floyd & Sargent 1997; Jordan 1993). Thus we would expect to find more active proponents of the ABM where birth is most medicalized. The aim of the ABM has been and is to change childbirth by minimizing medical intervention and maximizing women's choice. The shared ideology heralds birth as a normal physiologic event. Members profess a belief that women should have a major role to play in decision-making and should be given enough information to make an informed choice (including the choice about where to give birth). Furthermore, members of the ABM suggest that midwives are the practitioners best qualified to empower women and facilitate their ability to give birth normally. Like all social movement ideologies, the goal of the ABM creates a group consciousness in participants "so strong that it overcomes competing differences such as class, religion, age, etc." (Lawn-Day 1994, p. 29). The mandate of the ABM has proven powerfully motivating, mobilizing practitioners and consumers alike: Midwives exhausted from attending births find time to attend inordinately long meetings, while mothers and fathers—busy with careers and newborns—create space for hours of volunteer work, all "for the cause."

COLLECTIVE ACTION ON CONTROVERSIAL ISSUES (DIANI 1992)

During the 1970s and 1980s, members of the ABM worked both individually and collectively across the United States and Canada to introduce childbirth reform, winning success on a number of fronts. Cumulatively they were able to:

- Make it possible for partners to be in labor and delivery rooms
- End the abuses of the scopolamine era by insisting that women had the right to be "awake and aware" during childbirth
- Introduce rooming-in and the use of a single room for labor, delivery, and recovery in many hospitals
- Create alternative birthing centers in hospitals
- Win women the right (in some hospitals) to drink liquids and eat light foods during labor
- Allow a woman's other children to be present at the birth of their new sibling
- Make childbirth education—and thus, more informed choice—universally available to pregnant women

These successes were accompanied by dramatic rises in electronic fetal monitoring, cesarean section, and the use of pain-relieving drugs, especially the epidural. In other words, women's expanded choices within the hospital were accompanied by intensified medical interventions in birth (Davis-Floyd 1992). Thus the preservation of independent midwifery and out-of-hospital birth became even more important to the members of the ABM, many of whom felt that their efforts to transform hospital birth had been co-opted by the dominant system (Rothman 1981).

PARTICIPATION BY INFORMAL NETWORKS OF MULTIPLE AUTONOMOUS GROUPS, WITH NO SINGLE LEADERS OR ORGANIZATIONS AND LARGELY DEALING WITH A PREVIOUSLY UNMOBLIZED GROUP (DIANI 1992; LAWN-DAY 1994; TARROW 1983)

The most obvious previously unmobilized group that could become engaged in the ABM was a large contingent of quietly dissatisfied birthing women. Suzanne Arms (1975) discovered that women who were made to feel that they should be grateful for their interventions became increasingly unhappy with their experience as time passed. Around the United States and Canada, the informal interactions of activists, mothers, and childbirth practitioners coalesced into functional networks and then into the creation of multiple professional organizations. Nurses, childbirth educators, midwives, doulas, and some physicians worked together formally and informally to try to transform childbirth locally, nationally, and internationally. A number of these organizations crossed the border into Canada, including NAPSAC, International Childbirth Education Association (ICEA), American Society for Psychoprophylaxis in Obstetrics (ASPO) (now Lamaze International), and MANA. Over time these networks, especially those generated by *Midwifery Today* and the International Confederation of Midwives, have come to feel like a global sisterhood to many of their members.

The strategy chosen by the emerging midwives' associations has turned out to be crucial for the relationship between midwives and the ABM. There are some important differences between the national midwifery organizations in Canada and the United States in this respect. MANA—originally started as a Canadian/American organization, but now dominated by American membership—has been a leading organization devoted to keeping the spirit and ethics of the midwifery ABM alive. It has steadfastly refused to become an exclusive professional organization, choosing instead to keep its membership open to all midwives so that it can continue to be a forum for the social movement rather than the professionalizing enterprise. Trying to accommodate multiple realities, MANA created the North American Registry of Midwives (NARM) to provide professional certification, while MANA, as a separate nonprofessional organization, could go on performing iconoclastic tasks.

Canadian midwives have not had an organization that represents the social movement or provides a forum where revolutionary ideas are celebrated and nurtured in the same way that they are in MANA. Some provincial associations have allowed the open and diversified activity needed to maintain the movement, but the midwife associations of British Columbia and Ontario have focused the professional project, and midwives are discredited should they stray (Daviss 1999). The Canadian Confederation of Midwives (CCM) is a small organization that only allows membership by province. The meetings are closed to most midwives and consumers, and the organizational aim, like the aforementioned provincial organizations and the ACNM, is on promoting the profession. For these reasons, some Canadians continue to maintain their memberships in MANA.

Fragmentation (Melucci 1989)

While shared beliefs and solidarity create a collective identity and sense of belonging, such cohesiveness "does not imply homogeneity of ideas and orientations within social movement networks" (Diani 1992, p. 9). Each of the organizations that forms part of the ABM has its own particular ideology and agenda, ranging from increasing public awareness about prenatal psychology to lowering the cesarean rate and increasing the rate of vaginal births after cesareans (VBACs). Sometimes these conflict, pitting members of the overarching movement against each other in various ways. Such conflicts have been particularly evident in the struggles over appropriate standards for midwifery education and professionalization (see Chapter 7).

Accompanying the fragmentation of the ABM is its lack of a single leader, another defining characteristic of social movements. In most major centers in Canada and the United States there were a few midwives, consumers, and the odd physician who worked hard to bring alternatives to their local area and/or to contribute to a particular national or international organization. Some of these became internationally known figures who have served to focus public attention on the ABM and its agenda of childbirth reform, including physicians such as Robert Bradley and Marsden Wagner; childbirth educators and activists who wrote popular and influential books, such as Lester Hazell, Marjorie Karmel, Elisabeth Bing, Doris Haire, Suzanne Arms, and Nancy Wainer Cohen; home birth midwives, such as Raven Lang, Ina May Gaskin, and Elizabeth Davis; nurse-midwives, such as Penny Armstrong; and social scientists, such as Brigitte Jordan, Barbara Katz Rothman, Emily Martin, and Robbie Davis-Floyd. While all these people are internationally known and all have made significant contributions, none of them can be said to be the leader or even the most important figure in the ABM. In Canada, the ABM also has several leaders, but it is a well-known Canadian sensibility that we do not create heroes and heroines—"stars"—as do our American counterparts. In fact, a person who becomes well known in Canada is often frowned upon as an attention-seeker, a perspective that extends to foreign authors, who are usually listened to diplomatically but regarded with some suspicion. In Canada, conferences that bring in well-known personalities in the childbirth field are not favored as much as meetings using local experts and resources.

ACTION THAT TAKES PLACE LARGELY OUTSIDE THE INSTITUTIONAL SPHERE AND DAILY ROUTINES OF SOCIAL LIFE (DIANI 1992)

Some authors have suggested that noninstitutionalized forms of protest like demonstrations, marches, and sit-ins are intrinsic characteristics of social movements (Marx & McAdam 1994). Other scholars concur, claiming that the fundamental distinction between movements and other social political actions is to be found in the contrast between conventional styles of political participation and public protest (Diani 1992). Public dramatics in the United States and Canada have included marches such as that carried out by *Naissance Renaissance*—the consumer group in Quebec threatened with the elimination of home birth in that province; the occupation of the provincial legislature in Ontario by all of the MANA delegates who were gathered in Toronto for the annual conference in 1984 when the first Ontario midwifery bill was being voted on; and a number of political rallies in the various U.S. states to support midwives who were on trial (see De Vries, 1996). In both countries, however, activists are giving up on demonstrations in favor of increasing efforts to lobby government legislatures; write books, journal articles, and letters to the editors of newspapers; and educate women about their rights. Despite this recent shift in strategy, the ABM in both the United States and Canada has clearly been extrainstitutional, developing outside of hospitals, outside of education programs, and regardless of the type of health care system in place. Activists in both countries have worked from the outside to effect change.

Any comparison between home birth midwives in Canada and the United States will note that American midwives seem to be less compromising, more radical, and more fiercely committed to breaking down structures than are their Canadian sisters. This difference is attributable to the more marginal position of American home birth midwives, who have been subject to a variety of legal actions by the FBI, various district attorneys, and the American College of Obstetricians and Gynecologists (ACOG). The Canadian midwives' ultimate willingness, like American nurse-midwives, to compromise and accept university-based education reflects the fact that they have not been persecuted to the same extent and so felt freer to adopt what would be acceptable to the authorities. Many MANA midwives, in contrast, have felt that, just as they have tried to help childbearing women avoid institutionalization in hospitals at the time of birth, they have wanted to avoid the institutionalization of midwives in the "ivory towers" of the university setting.

SIGNIFICANT SIZE AND AGGREGATES OF COLLECTIVE ACTION (LAWN-DAY 1994; MARWELL & OLIVER 1991)

During the 1970s, Suzanne Arms's *Immaculate Deception* (1975), the book that did the most to spur the creation of the ABM, sold over 250,000 copies. Over time, Ina May Gaskin's *Spiritual Midwifery* (1975) sold over 400,000 copies worldwide. In 1994, Lawn-Day identified forty national organizations involved in the ABM in the United States, almost all of which have chapters at the local or state levels. The best estimate of how many individuals and organizations are involved in the ABM in the United States today comes from the Coalition for Improving Maternity Services (CIMS), a meta-organization in which most of the groups in the ABM have participated to create the "Mother-Friendly Childbirth Initiative: 10 Steps to Mother-Friendly Hospitals, Birth Centers, and Home Birth Services." Twenty-seven organizations whose membership totals over 90,000 have endorsed the CIMS initiative in the U.S.[4]

Looking at these six features of the ABM has given us a more complete picture of the history and influence of this social movement and of the differences and similarities between the two countries. There is, however, a further characteristic of social movements that requires our attention: I am speaking of the tendency of social movements to include a radical or fringe group that takes the movement's agenda to extremes that other—more conservative—participants may not be comfortable supporting. This feature of social movements has special bearing on our analysis of the ABM in Canada and the United States. Unlike the ABM in the United States, there are no organizations of midwives in Canada that have the protection of the movement as their main focus, and there are no Canadian counterparts to the umbrella organization CIMS. Some Canadians fear that while Canadian midwives are largely ahead of the Americans in midwifery legislation (see Chapter 6) and have been busy gaining credibility with the ministries of health and medical associations, there are few forums that encourage social protest or the healthy disruption of institutions. In the following section I discuss the social history of the radical flank of the ABM in Canada and the United States.

Home birth and the Radical Flank of the ABM

Many nurses who were midwives in both Canada and the United States were horrified when the lay midwives appeared on the cultural scene in the form of a social movement. These same women were shocked when lay midwives were successful despite their countercultural style. These midwives and others considered home birth to be a radical aspect of the ABM. Ironically, many of the British-trained midwives hired as nurses in Canadian hospitals had attended home births in their own country, and American nurse-midwives had attended births almost exclusively at home until the mid-1950s (Rooks 1997). By the early 1970s, the American nurse-midwives had completely shifted to hospital-based practice, and in 1973 the American College of Nurse Midwives (ACNM) adopted a "Statement on Home birth" that described the hospital as "the preferred site for childbirth because of the distinct advantage to the physical welfare of the mother and infant" (Rooks 1997, pp. 66). This statement was reviewed and retained in 1976. Most of the nurse-midwives of the 1970s (many of whom were also certified childbirth educators) aligned themselves with the literature and agenda of the emerging ABM, but some believed the renaissance of lay midwifery and the growth of the home birth movement to be a radical fringe that threatened the credibility of the midwifery profession or the movement as a whole. This attitude aligned this group more closely with physicians, who were outraged at the trend toward home births. In the early 1970s, the ACOG went on the offensive against lay midwives by issuing a press release that asked all physicians to report deaths associated with intentional home deliveries to ACOG, as well as a statement that referred to home births as "child abuse" and "maternal trauma" (Pearse 1977).

As different factions emerge in social movements, participants must negotiate among themselves to realign intentions (Melucci 1989; Snow et al. 1986). Haines (1984) suggests that two things can occur in the presence of radical flanks. The first is a negative effect in which moderates are hurt by the presence of the radical wing that is not perceived to be credible or fundable. The second is a positive effect where radicals provide a foil for moderates or effect a redefinition of their demands. Lawn-Day identifies the radical flank of the ABM in the U.S. as the Home Birth Movement (HBM), and she asserts that it had a positive rather than a negative effect:

> As the prominence and number of participants in the HBM increased, hospitals and doctors were forced to change standard procedures or be affected financially. The development and use of LDRs (Labor-and-Delivery-Rooms) and hospital based birthing centers with home-like settings and perks such as champagne dinners and limo rides (Miller 1988; Jordan 1993) were the direct result of the economic pressure imposed by the HBM (1994, p. 5).

Lawn-Day also points out the differing agendas of various ABM participants regarding home birth: Some wanted to promote it as an important goal in itself, while others considered home birth too radical and were interested only in using its existence as leverage to improve birth inside the hospital.

Lawn-Day's (1994) description of the home birth movement as a "radical element" of the ABM is useful, but it can cause us to miss an important contribution made by these activists. The reintroduction of home birth as a viable option is, in fact, a key part of the movement because it constitutes an important ingredient in providing ultimate control and choice for women, a central theme of the ABM ideology. This is true in both countries, but most dramatically so in Canada, where 100 percent of the midwives in the Ontario survey (Daviss 1999) said that the home birth movement was crucial to the overall ABM, even if they did not originally attend home births themselves. It was midwives who learned their profession by attending births at home who drove the legalization of midwives in Canada.

My research shows that those considered to be radicals in Ontario were not home birth proponents—the radicals were the ones who proposed informed choice to clients on more "fanatical" issues such as waterbirth and VBACs at home. Unlike simple home birth, these practices were less acceptable to local physicians. As a consensus in Canada developed around laws that would legalize and regulate midwives and require a university-based education, it became radical to support other approaches to midwifery regulation and education, such as the decriminalization of midwifery, an option that would give midwives more freedom from regulation at the expense of exclusion from the Canadian health care system, or the preservation of apprenticeship and the development of regional vocational schools.

In many respects, the issues that have come to be more contentious than home birth in Canada have also replaced home birth as the gauge of how radical members of the U.S. ABM are. Although home birth is still considered radical, consensus among the American members of the ABM that home birth should be preserved as a viable option actually developed as early as 1980, when the ACNM rescinded its earlier position and came out with a statement supporting women's right to planned, midwife-attended home birth. Disagreements over the validity of apprenticeship and vocational training, on the other hand, continue. Those midwives who wish to preserve these forms of midwifery education are now considered radical by some members of the ABM; more radical still are the midwives who reject any form of licensure or regulation[5] (see Chapter 7).

What Constitutes Success for the Alternative Birth Movement?

Some have come to define success for the ABM as preservation of choice of birth place and protection of informed choice through the legalization and regulation of midwifery as an autonomous profession. In this light, the movement can be said to have succeeded in almost all provinces of Canada (British Columbia, Alberta, Saskatchewan, Manitoba, Ontario, and Quebec), while these battles are still being fought in most of the United States. Various explanations for this difference offer themselves. First, Canadian activists were less ostentatious (read, more socially acceptable) than their American counterparts, and the Canadian authorities have been less heavy-handed in putting down the movement. Second, except in a few places (such as Quebec until 1972, Newfoundland, and the North), midwives were not recognized at all in the health care system before the 1970s–1980s movement began. This meant that no preexisting schools or programs tied midwives to the mainstream health care system, which meant in turn that there was no strong contingent of midwives to fight the practicing community midwives attending home births, as the members of the ACNM have often done in the United States.[6]

A third reason for the difference in the pattern of the ABM in Canada compared to the United States can be found in the differences between the Canadian and American feminist movements. Canadian feminists Vickers, Rankin, and Appelle (1993, pp. 45–46) point out that whereas American feminists tended in the 1970s and 1980s to reject the ordinary political process and replace politics with individual consciousness-raising, English Canadian feminists of the same time period tended to be pro-state and politically proactive. In other words, American feminism has had more of a focus on individual transformation, while Canadian feminism has focused more on mobilizing resources and political structures. In such a context, Canadian midwives and institutions have been more amenable to legalizing and professionalizing midwives. My 1996–1998 survey of Ontario midwives (Daviss 1999) demonstrated their high degree of involvement in the feminist movement, while the movement toward "spiritual enlightenment" was a considerably lower priority. In contrast, American home birth midwives have tended more often to embrace the kind of spiritual focus described in Gaskin's *Spiritual Midwifery* and Davis' *Heart and Hands* (1997). Even those connected to the Boston Women's Health Collective, considered more feminist, were still strongly attached to a modus operandi of individual transformation. Canadian midwives, who from the early 1980s on sought to mainstream their services, learned not to associate with the more spiritual and less culturally acceptable "radical fringe." For example, a would-be Canadian translator of *Spiritual Midwifery* into French reported being discouraged by the "hippie" image of the book.

Given that the goals of the ABM are rather different than the professional strategies of established professional groups, it seems important to look beyond the ability of the Canadian midwives to mobilize resources and claim success. The success that social movements seek is often not purely political: The spirit of the movement is an important consideration. American midwives seem to be able to preserve organizations and styles that continually distrust and disrupt institutions.

The fact that there was less fragmentation in the Canadian than in the American alternative birth movement does not mean it was not there. The desire of Ontario midwives to protect the image and credibility of the midwifery profession has caused them to become more conservative in practice and to keep a constant eye on their image for the purposes of demonstrating to the government, other health care professionals, and the public that they can self-govern. Some of the strategies used to silence dissenters suggest that the ethics of the original social movement have been left behind (Daviss 1999). There has been query in British Columbia and Ontario, for instance, over whether midwives are being eliminated, not because their clinical skills are wanting but because their social activist behavior has become an embarrassment to the professional project (Daviss 1999). Sixty-five percent of respondents to my Ontario survey felt that expectations of them had changed in the two to five years that they have been practicing legally: Conformity and technological knowledge are perceived to be more rewarded now than before. Several mentioned that in times past, spirituality was a focus, whereas some implied what one midwife said: "Now midwives are dismissed as real midwives if [spirituality] is one of their main focuses."

The respondents to my Ontario survey did not agree on the issue of whether or not they got the revolution they wanted by obtaining professional status. Sixty-four percent do not feel that the movement is completed now that midwives are legal and regulated. Many are concerned that the "hidden" skills of the midwives who formed the movement—touching, nurturing, intuition, praying, and other cultural unmentionables—are in danger of being erased, ridiculed, and marginalized because they are not in keeping with the supposed image of the professional. Some may think that the early rituals (the use of candles, blessing ways) are fringy and childish and that singing and waterbirth are marginal. But trying to hide the fact that midwives have such leanings, or to ridicule and ostracize those who promote them, threatens the continued success of the movement. I suggest that such tactics subtly undermine the diversity of the movement in the guise of legitimizing and professionalizing it. What good did the movement do, we might ask, if midwives become too much like the obstetricians they have sought to replace?

There are also concerns that as midwives become more successful, consumer involvement wanes. An interesting turn of events in the ABM in both countries occurred when the legitimization of midwives became the major focus. The term "consumers" was adopted to refer to parents who used midwives' services. This term transforms parents into a group in need of a commodity and the midwife into a provider of that commodity, which she can sell in the capitalist system. Whereas in Quebec, the consumer group *Naissance Renaissance* took on a role of advocating for all consumer demands, some consumer groups in the other Canadian provinces, called "Midwifery Task Forces" (MTFs), took on a single-purpose agenda: to get midwives legalized. Some advocates were concerned about this singular focus and the seeming hierarchy that accompanied it, asking, "Who owns this movement anyway?" (Mason 1988, 1990). In Ontario, the main consumer organization, the MTF, disbanded when midwives became legal and consumer interest and involvement in the ABM fell away. A new consumer group trying to revive the passion that occurred prior to legislation is asking, "Where have all the women gone?" (address of the president of the Ontario Midwifery Consumer Network at the meeting of the Association of Ontario Midwives 1999). Similar occurrences have been reported in the United States in states where legalization has been achieved (see De Vries 1996). Susan Hodges, a leader in the national consumer organization, *Citizens for Midwifery*, says:

> There is no question that consumers are much more likely and willing to come forward when there is a crisis. . . . If they have been organized mainly for constituent pressure to get a bill passed, it is understandable that they will disband when the bill is passed. If the organization is working for larger issues (promoting the Midwifery Model of Care overall, health freedom in general, etc.) then they are more likely in for the long haul and will keep going even when legislation is passed (personal communication, 1999).

If we define true success for the midwifery ABM as achieving its policy goals while retaining the movement's spirit and impetus toward cultural change, then certain states in the United States where both aims have been accomplished may turn out to have a more successful ABM than the Canadian jurisdictions where the policy goals have been reached but the "citizen surge" (Lofland & Johnson 1991) is on the wane. In Washington state, for example, ABM activists have succeeded in mobilizing their resources, legalizing midwifery, raising the percentage of home births, and obtaining insurance reimbursement while retaining a spirit of "appropriate" insurgency and continuing to work for cultural reform.

Conclusion

This chapter has suggested that one of the critical victories of the ABM in the United States and Canada was its legalization of midwifery; at the same time, it is important not to confuse legalizing midwifery with the larger ABM, which has multiple goals and participants. Keeping the spirit and ethics of a movement alive cannot be achieved simply by legalizing practitioners and providing informed choice. If one looks at the ABM as distinct and separate from the professional/legislation project, then one can be freed of the temptation to judge the health of the movement in any jurisdiction solely by whether the midwives secure more legal power, more power over the medical profession, or more status from higher education. Connection with the movement can be crippled when midwives are too well established and they and their clients cease to work for political change.

In the new millennium, the flowers and placards of the early ABM period may be passé, but the sense of belongingness and collective identity that a social movement creates is still needed. The wane in consumer interest in the ABM following midwifery legislation may just be a lull in the "citizen surge" of interest in natural childbirth, or it may mark the effective end of the movement. As midwives begin to focus on evidence-based practice and friendly relations with the medical establishment, it would be a real loss if they forget their history and their historical, political, and spiritual sisterhood with their clients. Some Ontario midwives report experiencing a longing for the old laid-back hippie client and the former relationship in which clients in the movement took care of the midwife as much as the other way around. The consumer age is upon us, with informed choice for everything and service on demand. Said one midwife: "Clients . . . think they've bought a midwife and they can call you about their hemorrhoids at 2 a.m. and they think you care. . . . [With] my former clients, midwives were very respected" (anonymous midwife, personal communication, quoted in Daviss 1999).

In both the United States and Canada, serious questions still remain about how to transform the governance apparatus of midwifery so that fundamental change can be consistent with the radical potential of the movement. And in the provinces that have secured legal midwifery (British Columbia, Alberta, Saskatchewan, Manitoba, Ontario, and Quebec) midwives are coping with perhaps their biggest challenge to date: finding a way to maintain their ideals and their holistic, nonmedicalized style of practice as they attend more and more hospital births.

In the United States, nurse-midwives have long been legal and regulated in all fifty states, and direct-entry midwives have a new national certification that is helping to legitimate them in the public eye. But despite incontrovertible evidence that midwives provide better care and have better outcomes, cumulatively all (U.S.) midwives attend a mere 7 percent of births, and intervention rates in the vast majority of hospitals remain unnecessarily high (Rooks 1997). Perhaps in both countries, midwives and their supporters need to reframe involvement with the ABM as a redeeming player in reform whose participants are not on the fringe, but rather, on the frontier. I base this conclusion on a strong belief in social movements: From labor reform to feminism, the historical effectiveness of social movements gives us cause to trust their strategies of critiquing society, reevaluating power relations, disrupting institutions and processes, and creating positive change. Birth activists can rest assured that the ABM, like any other social movement, can be fragmented without being ineffective and that the roles played by the "radical flank" can be beneficial to the movement as a whole.

Acknowledgments

The author would like to thank Robbie Davis-Floyd for her kind advice and useful suggestions on this chapter.

Notes

1. A social movement is a distinct form of collective action, distinguished by the involvement of previously unmobilized populations and by the theatrical tactics used in the effort to secure change (Scott 1990). Politeness and social conformity are characteristic of special interest and lobby groups; social movement protesters tend to be more irreverent and dramatic, carrying placards, organizing demonstrations, and otherwise engaging in unruly (and hopefully newsworthy) behavior (Lofland & Johnson 1991).
2. For a discussion on social movements, feminism, counterculture and childbirth, see Umansky 1996.
3. Wertz and Wertz 1989, pp. 304–314, have compiled a bibliographical essay that covers well the central literature associated with the ABM in the United States.
4. The U.S. organizations that have endorsed the CIMS initiative include, among others, the American College of Nurse-Midwives (ACNM), the Association of Women's Health, Obstetrical and Neo-Natal Nurses (AWHONN) Physicians for Midwives, Midwives Alliance of North America (MANA), Lamaze International, the International Childbirth Education Association (ICEA), the Bradley Method, the Association of Labor Assistants & Childbirth Educators (ALACE), Doulas of North America (DONA), La Leche League, and the International Lactation Consultants Association (ILCA), and many others. For more information, see www.motherfriendly.org.
5. Many direct-entry midwives who insist on preserving apprenticeship are increasingly perceived as moderate because they have developed and actively support NARM certification for home birth midwives and the Midwifery Education Accreditation Council (MEAC) accreditation of direct-entry programs. Today the most radical members of the ABM are midwives (usually with a religious orientation) who resist all forms of regulation and the tiny minority of women who plan unassisted home births (Shanley 1994).
6. Most foreign-trained midwives in Canada, concerned about their immigration status and their jobs, refrained from working as midwives until they could do so legally. (For a discussion on the reasons why midwives licensed outside Canada did not become part of the ABM when they came to Canada, see Daviss 1999; Schroff 1997.)

References

Arms, S. 1975. *Immaculate Deception.* Boston, MA: Houghton-Mifflin.

Baer, D. L., and D. A. Bostitis. 1993. *Politics and Linkage in a Democratic Society.* Eaglewood Cliffs, NJ: Prentice Hall.

Barrington, E. 1985. *Midwifery Is Catching.* Toronto, Ontario: Vintage Books.

Brandwein, R. A. 1985. Feminist thought-structure: An alternative paradigm of social change for social justice. In *A Conference in Search of Strategies for Social Change: March 23–25, 1984,* eds. D. Gil and E. A. Gil. Cambridge, MA: Schenkman Publishing.

Davis, E. 1997. *Heart and Hands: A Midwife's Guide to Pregnancy and Childbirth.* Berkeley: Celestial Arts.

Davis-Floyd, R. 1992. *Birth as an American Right of Passage.* Berkeley: University of California Press.

Davis-Floyd, R., and C. Sargent. 1997. *Childbirth and Authoritative Knowledge; Cross-Cultural Perspectives.* Berkeley: University of California Press.

Daviss, B. A. 1997. Heeding warnings from The Canary and The Whale: An analytical framework for authoritative knowledge. In *Childbirth and Authoritative Knowledge; Cross-Cultural Perspectives,* eds. R. Davis-Floyd and C. Sargent. Berkeley: University of California Press, pp. 441–456.

———. 1999. *From Social Movement to Professional Midwifery Project: Are We Throwing Out the Baby with the Bath Water?* Master's thesis in Canadian Studies, Carleton University, Ottawa, Ontario.

De Vries, R. 1996. *Making Midwives Legal.* Columbus: Ohio State University Press.

Diani, M. 1992. The concept of social movement. *The Sociological Review* 40(1): 1–25.

Edwards, M. 1984. *Reclaiming Birth: History and Heroines of American Childbirth Reform.* Trumansburg, NY: The Crossing Press.

Gaskin, I. M. 1975. *Spiritual Midwifery.* Summertown, TN: The Book Publishing Co.

———. 1988. Midwifery reinvented. In *The Midwife Challenge,* ed. S. Kitzinger. London: Pandora Press, pp. 42–60.

Haines, H. H. 1984. Black radicalization and the funding of civil rights: 1957–1970. *Social Problems* 32(1): 31–43.

Jordan, B. 1993. *Birth in Four Cultures: A Cross-Cultural Investigation in Yucatan, Holland, Sweden and the United States,* 4th ed. Prospect Heights, IL: Waveland Press.

Lang, K., and G. Lang. 1961. *Collective Dynamics.* New York: Thomas Crowell.

Lang, R. 1972. *The Birth Book.* Ben Lomond, CA: Genesis.

Lawn-Day, G. 1994. *Using Institutionalized Social Movements to Explain Policy Implementation Failure: The Case of Midwifery.* Doctoral thesis, University of Oklahoma.

Lofland, J., and V. Johnson. 1991. A domain in movement studies and a perspective on peace activism in the 1980's. *Research in Social Movements, Conflicts and Change* 13: 1–29.

Marx, G., and D. McAdam. 1994. *Collective Behaviors and Social Movements. Process and Structure.* NJ: Prentice Hall.

Mason, J. 1988. Midwifery in Canada. In *The Midwife Challenge,* ed. S. Kitzinger. London: Pandora Press, pp. 99–133.

——— 1990. *The Trouble with Licensing Midwives.* Ottawa, Ontario: CRIAW/ICREF.

Matthews, J., and K. Zadak. 1991. The alternative birth movement in the United States: History and current status. *Women & Health* 17: 39–56.

McAdam, D. 1982. *Political Process and Development of Black Insurgency 1930–1970.* Chicago: University of Chicago Press.

Melucci, A. 1989. The symbolic challenge of contemporary movements. *Social Research* 52(4): 789–816.

Miller, A. 1988. Butlers, Limos and Labor Pains. *Newsweek* 111: 49.

Myers-Ciecko, J. A. 1988. Direct-entry midwifery in the USA. In *The Midwife Challenge,* ed. S. Kitzinger. London: Pandora Press, pp. 42–60.

Pearse, W. H. 1977, July. The home birth crisis. *Bulletin of the ACOG.*

Rooks, J. 1997 *Midwifery and Childbirth in America.* Philadelphia: Temple University Press.

Rothman, B. K. 1981. Awake and aware, or false consciousness? The co-option of childbirth reform in America. In *Childbirth: Alternatives to Medical Control,* ed. S. Romales. Austin: University of Texas Press, pp. 150–180.

Schroff, F. 1997. *The New Midwifery: Reflections on Renaissance and Regulation.* Toronto, Ontario: Women's Press.

Scott, A. 1990. *Ideology and the New Social Movements* (Controversies in Sociology). London: Unwin Hyman.

Shanley, L. K. 1994. *Unassisted Childbirth.* Westport, CT: Bergin and Garvey.

Smelser, N. J. 1962. *Theory of Collective Behavior.* New York: The Free Press.

Snow, D. A., et al. 1986. Frame alignment processes, micromobilization, and movement participation. *American Sociological Review* 51: 464–481.

Susie, D. A. 1988. *In the Way of Our Grandmothers: A Cultural View of Twentieth-Century Midwifery in Florida.* Athens: University of Georgia Press.

Tarrow, S. 1983. *Struggling to Reform: Social Movements and Policy Change during Cycles of Protest.* (Western Societies Program Paper No. 15). Ithaca, NY: Center for International Studies, Cornell University.

Touraine, A. 1978. *The Production of Society.* Chicago: University of Chicago Press.

Umansky, L. 1996. *Motherhood Reconceived. Feminism and the Legacies of the Sixties.* New York: New York University Press.

Vickers, J., et al. 1993. *Politics as If Women Mattered.* Toronto, Ontario: University of Toronto Press.

Wertz, D., and R. Wertz. 1989. *Lying-In. A History of Childbirth in America,* expanded ed. New Haven, CT: Yale University Press.

CHAPTER 5

Looking Within

RACE, CLASS, AND BIRTH

Margaret K. Nelson and Rebecca Popenoe

Introduction

Much can be learned by examining the many ways maternity is organized and by looking at the different outcomes associated with various systems of care, but we must not forget that comparisons *between* countries can conceal important variations that exist *within* countries. Consider, for example, rates of infant mortality. These rates are widely used to assess the quality of a nation's maternity care system, a measure of how well different nations are caring for their youngest citizens and their mothers. However, when looking at mortality rates it is also important to know the extent of variation in those rates across different regions and population groups within a single country. Looking at the two countries examined in this chapter—Sweden and the United States—we find a telling difference in intracountry variation. The infant mortality rate in Sweden accurately reflects the risk for *most* Swedish women, but the U.S. rate represents an average computed from *wide* variations by social class, race/ethnicity, and immigration status. For some U.S. women the infant mortality risk is akin to that in low-income countries, while for others it resembles the low rates of Sweden and other Western European social democracies.

The analysis we offer in this chapter reminds us international comparisons of maternity care experiences and outcomes must take into account the impact of class, race/ethnicity, and immigration. To highlight the range in *intracountry* variation we compare maternity care in the United States and Sweden. We chose these two countries because they represent a dramatic contrast in the degree to which class, race/ethnicity, and immigration shape childbirth and the organization of maternity care. These differences derive from the sharp distinctions between the two countries, both in the nature of health care delivery and in the degree to which cultural uniformity is an accepted—perhaps even expected—norm. The United States has a largely privatized health care system, and it values (in word if not in deed) individual choice and inno-vation while downplaying the necessity of equality and any "right" to health care. Sweden, by contrast, considers health care a right to which all should have equal access and has guaranteed universal health care, including maternity care (like most other high-income countries).

As one might expect, the American focus on individual choice means that more has been written about women's desires concerning, and responses to, childbirth in the United States than in Sweden, whereas Sweden's emphasis on "equality of outcome" means that much of the research has focused on uncovering differences in measurable birth outcomes. In light of these different foci of research, we discuss each country's system separately, highlighting the issues that have been on each nation's research agenda while still, we hope, making plain the relevant points of comparison.

Sweden

THE MATERNITY CARE SYSTEM

Several studies have demonstrated that maternity care in Sweden is egalitarian, not only in principle, but also in fact (Elmèn 1995, p. 62; Håkansson 1994; *Socio-ekonomiska förhållanden* . . . 1996; Sundström-Feigenberg 1988, p. 43). The general equality of birth outcomes and childbirth experiences extends across both class and ethnic differences. Of course there is some variation in birth outcomes, but, as we will show in what follows, it seems largely attributable to behavioral and background issues—especially higher rates of smoking among less privileged women—rather than uneven maternity care. Unlike the United States, then, one description of the maternity system suffices to explain the experience of virtually all women in Swe-den, cutting across both social class and ethnic lines.

The initial cornerstone of Sweden's current maternity care system of maternal health centers and family-friendly policies was laid in the 1930s (Sundström-Feigen-berg 1988, p. 35). All female citizens as well as permanent residents are entitled to regular prenatal check-ups, childbirth in a hospital, and postnatal care, including home visits. Working women have a right to paid sick leave before a child is born if the pregnancy is difficult and up to one year's parental leave after childbirth at 80 per-cent of their salary.[1]

A reporter for the *Swedish Medical Journal* recently described the Swedish approach to childbirth: "Nature should prevail, but with the hospital safety net always at the ready" (Wilhelmson 1995; p. 2600). This combination of a relatively "natural" approach to childbirth yet with the constant nearby presence of a high tech-nology medical system is reflected in a number of aspects of Swedish maternity care:

1. Almost all women give birth in hospitals, and are routinely attended by nurse-midwives, but an anesthesiologist, an obstetrician, and a pediatrician are available for about 95 percent of all births.
2. Sweden's C-section rate has fluctuated between 11 and 13.4 percent since 1980, an average that is just over half the U.S. rate (between 17 and 24 percent).

The C-section rate was actually quite stable in Sweden between 1980 and 1990, when many other countries had rising rates (Notzon 1990), but between 1995 and 1998 the Swedish rate rose by 15 percent, from 11.6 percent to 13.4 percent. Researchers have attributed this rise to the requests of women themselves who are fearful of vaginal births for various reasons (Pineus 1999).

3. The vast majority of Swedish women receive pain medication when in labor,[2] although clinics increasingly offer alternatives such as massage, hot water baths, and acupuncture (administered by specially trained midwives).

4. Swedish women have long been encouraged to give birth in a position they find comfortable and they only rarely lie on their backs to give birth.

Most prenatal and maternity care is provided by nurse-midwives who have one and a half years midwifery training after a three- or four-year nursing program. Pregnant women normally make their first visit to a nurse-midwife at a maternity clinic at twelve weeks and have monthly visits through week twenty, when the number of visits increases first to biweekly and then to weekly. For women with normal pregnancies, two visits to a physician are also scheduled (but only one visit for a second child), one early in the pregnancy to do an ultrasound and determine the time of delivery, and one nearer the time of delivery. If a woman's pregnancy shows signs of complications, or if she simply requests it, more visits to a physician are scheduled. Women with pregnancy complications and women over the age of thirty-five are informed of the options to have amniocentesis and other tests. The majority of maternity clinics are government-run, but there are additional privately run clinics that are also covered by national health insurance. Private clinics meet a perceived need for more personal care, a softer or more holistic approach, and more convenient opening hours, but, apart from this and possibly interior decorating details, they do not differ significantly from government clinics.

As we noted earlier, all but a minute number of births in Sweden take place in hospital maternity clinics. A small but growing interest in home births in the 1980s (Ahlenius et al. 1997, p. 1275) had waned by the 1990s. A nurse-midwife almost always attends the few women who do choose home birth. In addition, one Alternative Birth Care center opened connected to a Stockholm hospital in 1989, offering a more "home-like" atmosphere in which to give birth (Waldenström 1992), but so far this phenomenon has not spread widely.

In Sweden the practitioner who sees the pregnant woman prenatally is not the same as the one who sees her through delivery.[3] This is partly because the prenatal clinics and the hospital birthing clinics are spatially and administratively separate from one another in Sweden, but it may also be influenced by the fact that Swedish labor laws are strong so that expecting midwives to be available at any time of day or night to help a woman in labor is thought unreasonable. The midwives who see women prenatally do, however, have contact with the midwives who work in hospital delivery wards.

Although midwives routinely handle all normal deliveries, physicians frequently play some role. A study at one academic hospital (Lund) found that physicians were involved in some way in half of all deliveries (Wilhelmson 1995, p. 2599). Again one sees the tendency of the Swedish system to treat birth as a natural and relatively unproblematic occurrence in the first instance, but not to hesitate to ensure safety and a healthy outcome with a high level of technology when at all necessary. This is in line with the tendency in Swedish society as a whole to appreciate safety and security.

In her cross-cultural study of birth, done in the 1970s, Jordan (1993, p. 63) noted that in Sweden the woman giving birth is treated by the midwife as "a competent person for whom she provides certain kinds of services." According to Jordan, giving birth is seen as a personal achievement for a woman in Sweden, and the atmosphere in birthing clinics is one of "quiet, intense concentration," rather than the "vocal panic and despair" she observed in the physician-run, highly medicalized U.S. birthing wards. Here is where culture meets the health care system; as Jordan points out, each birthing system is in some way attuned and adapted to the culture in which it exists, and it is therefore logical that the same characteristics that shape Swedish life in general—respect for personal autonomy, expectations of personal responsibility, and acceptance of nature but with a high need for safety measures and assurance—inform the Swedish system of birth.

Keeping in mind the relative uniformity of birthing practices in Sweden, we now turn to examine the variations in birthing experiences that do exist in Sweden.

SOCIOECONOMIC STATUS

The steady and largely successful assault of sixty years of social democracy on class inequalities in Sweden has had the somewhat paradoxical effect of keeping class awareness at the forefront of the social imagination. This is especially apparent in public policy, including health care, where since 1984 a conscious, consistent goal has been to reduce if not eliminate any lingering class differences in care, and indeed in health outcome (Elmèn 1995, p. 75). We discuss class variation first, looking at studies of birth outcomes, and then consider the smaller body of literature on variations in care. Since differences in birth outcome that correlate with social class can be the result of many factors—mother's and father's educational level, household income, mother's and father's occupation, mother's marital status, smoking, and others—we will also look at the studies that have tried to disentangle just what aspect of socioeconomic status seems responsible for class variations in birth outcomes.

Comparative studies have shown that socioeconomic differences correlate with health differences in Sweden as in other countries, but that they do so to a relatively small extent (see Koupilova et al. 1998). Because of limited socioeconomic differences among social classes in Sweden and because the perinatal mortality rate is already so low, many studies that have looked for socioeconomic differences in birth outcomes have compared the *most* privileged to the *least* privileged groups in order to find signs of a gap, rather than looking at the population as a whole (*Socioekonomiska förhållanden . . .* 1996). Differences of mean birthweights emerged in four studies that took this approach (Elmèn 1995; Ericson 1993; Koupilova et al. 1998; Nordström and Cnattingius 1996). A study that examined feto-infant mortality in Sweden in 1986 found that the rate of fetal or infant death during the first year of life was 1.4 times as high for underprivileged mothers as for educated mothers of privilege, but infant mortality statistics include a range of factors that affect children in the first year of life that do not have to do with childbirth per se. By contrast, a study of perinatal mortality (up until seven days after birth) found that when maternal age and parity were taken into account, a difference between the most and least privileged groups that emerged in the 1980s had disappeared by 1991 (*Socioekonomiska för-hållanden* . . . 1996). Recall that the differences uncovered in the studies emerged when comparing the richest 10 percent of the population to the poorest 10 percent. In other words, on the whole, socioeconomic differences in childbirth outcomes are admirably low.

One form of social inequality that has been on the rise in recent years is related to growing segregation in larger cities, often related to immigrant settlement, and correlates of this segregation are reflected in health and maternity statistics. A study in Göteborg, Sweden's "second city," found that there was a steady correlation between birthweight and neighborhood, where neighborhood was a proxy for socioeconomic status. The difference in mean birthweights between the most and least privileged neighborhoods was 191 grams, 146 grams when birthweights were adjusted for gestational age and sex (Elmèn 1995). Another study examining perinatal complications in Sweden's third largest city, Malmö, found that such problems arose more frequently for women from lower-income areas (Gudmundsson et al. 1997).

These differences in birth outcome according to neighborhood, as well as the ones related purely to socioeconomic status, raise the inevitable question, "What accounts for these differences: biology? behavior? quality of care?" A number of Swedish studies have tried to answer this question. Few studies seem to find or even consider that the care provided to those of lower socioeconomic status is actually worse than that provided to those of higher socioeconomic groups. The data that do exist, while scant, do not demonstrate significant variations in care. Even Håkan Elmèn, who embarked on his study of segregation and health in Göteborg after being struck by the lower-than-average health status of the population in the lower-income neighborhood where he worked as a physician, does not criticize the quality of care there, although he notes that the health care administration was not particularly sensitive to the needs of these neighborhoods and that they were low-status places to work for health care professionals.

Several factors that tend to accompany lower socioeconomic status emerge as significant for birth outcomes in different studies, in particular smoking, educational level of the mother, and whether or not the mother lives with the father. Most research has found that higher rates of smoking among women of lower socioeconomic classes explains part of the differences in birth outcomes (e.g., Elmèn 1995, p. 70). One small-scale study found that taking smoking rates into account explained away nearly all of the differences in birthweight according to socioeconomic status (Nordström & Cnattingius 1996).

In two studies (Haglund 1993—cited in Elmèn 1995, p. 71—and Nordström et al. 1993), maternal education was correlated with birth outcomes, and in one of these it was significantly more predictive than socioeconomic status as a whole. Single mothers have also been shown to have worse birth outcomes, but this correlation disappears if the single mother has a high educational level (Elmèn 1995, p. 71; Ericson et al. 1993), again suggesting that education is a highly important factor for predicting birth outcomes, even in egalitarian Sweden.

Statistics show that a much higher number of children are born "out of wedlock" in Sweden than in the United States, but it must be understood that "out-of-wedlock" has very different meanings in the two different countries. In Sweden cohabitation has been a legally and culturally recognized norm for several decades, and thus the majority of the 53 percent of children born "out-of-wedlock" are born to cohabiting rather than single (living alone) parents. Only women who are neither married nor cohabiting run a higher risk of lower birthweight infants and more preterm births than average (Ericson & Smedby 1989; Koupilova et al. 1998; Vågerö et al. 1999).

Turning our attention to the health care system, we now ask if there is any variation in the care that women receive. At least one carefully done study at three prenatal clinics in southern Sweden with women representative of the Swedish population as a whole found that "both manual (blue collar) and non-manual (white collar) working women appear to enjoy equal antenatal health and receive equal antenatal care" (Håkansson 1994). Few researchers seem to blame inequality of care at prenatal clinics or hospitals for different birth outcomes among women of different socioeconomic levels. Instead, they suggest that more research be done to discover the nature of the risks to which women of lower socioeconomic classes are exposed (Cnattingius & Haglund 1992; *Socioekonomiska förhållanden och fölossningsutfall i Sverige* 1996), so that prevention measures can be taken against these behavioral factors themselves (e.g., smoking prevention programs; see 1996). Other lines of approach would be to look at what distinguishes the behavior and/or the general health of women of high socioeconomic class; one study, for example, found that women who choose alternative birth centers tend to be older, better educated, and healthier (Waldenström 1992).

IMMIGRANTS

Approximately one in ten Swedes today are of immigrant background, having themselves been born, or having at least one parent born, outside of the country. While most of these are from other European countries, a walk down the main street of most Swedish towns and cities quickly alerts one to the fact that the blond, blue-eyed stereotype is everywhere punctuated by people of African, Asian, Mediterranean, and Latin American origin.

Yet issues of race, ethnicity, and immigrant status have a different meaning in Sweden than in, for example, the United States. First of all, since the Swedish population has historically been very homogeneous (with the vast majority of newcomers historically arriving from other northern European countries), the term "immigrant" in common Swedish parlance today usually implies a newcomer from southern Europe, the Middle East, or a low-income country (see Pineus 1999). Second, since Sweden has until recently been ethnically homogenous, with the exception of the Lapps in the north (about 17,000) and Finns, both of which groups are white and of Nordic background, ethnicity, race, and immigrant status can largely be lumped together, as their use in Sweden tends to refer to the same group of more recent arrivals from lands to the south.

Earlier studies of immigrants' birth outcomes compared to native-born Swedes did not uncover significant differences (Aurelius & Ryde-Blomqvist 1978; Ericson & Smedby 1979; Ericson et al. 1989), but a recent analysis of all births between 1978 and 1993 uncovers moderately worse birth outcomes for women from Africa south of the Sahara, Asia, and Denmark (*Förlossningsresultat bland invandrarkvinnor i Sverige* 1998). Danish women's smoking habits partly explain their higher risk of low birthweight infants, and Asian women's smaller stature seems to largely explain their increased frequency of C-sections and of what are classified as low birthweight infants. Only women from sub-Saharan Africa had significantly higher perinatal mortality than native-born Swedes. Regardless of land of origin, refugees also have significantly worse birth outcomes than native-born Swedes and than other immigrants on average.

As the authors of this study of immigration conclude, "Whether or not [the worse birth outcomes among immigrants] depend on social factors in Sweden, communication problems in Swedish maternity care, genetic factors, or conditions in the women's lands of birth, Swedish maternity care and birthing care need to devote special attention to these groups" (*Förlossningsresultat bland invandrarkvinnor i Sverige* 1998, p. 38). Although communication factors are undoubtedly a problem for many immigrants, all immigrants are entitled to interpreters when they use any health facilities. For many of these women as well, the quality of the health care they receive is superior to what they receive in their homelands, even if the social conditions may be uncomfortable for them. Here, too, however, Sweden has tried to adapt; it is perfectly acceptable, for example, for a number of family members to accompany an immigrant woman giving birth. In fact, although few studies have actually looked for differences in care of immigrants and nonimmigrants in Sweden, there is no evidence that immigrants receive a different quality of care than Swedish-born women within the maternity care system.

One quantitative study of actual care of pregnant women found no difference in the degree to which women of Swedish and immigrant origin were given pain medication during childbirth during the years 1973–1995 (Ahlenius et al. 1997, p. 1272). Unlike in the United States (as we will show later), there is also little evidence that birth outcomes for immigrants change significantly depending on how long they have been in the country (Aurelius & Ryde-Blomqvist 1978; *Förlossningsresultat bland invandrarkvinnor i Sverige* 1998; p. 23).

The apparent lack of differences in care of immigrants and Swedes, while seemingly impressive, may, however, be read in less positive terms. In her review of the use of pain medication during childbirth, one physician notes that between 1973 and 1995 women of non-Swedish background received pain medication to the same extent that women of Swedish origin did. These data suggest that perhaps birthing clinic traditions in Sweden are deciding how a woman gives birth, rather than the distinct wishes of the pregnant women themselves (Ahlenius 1997; p. 1275). In short, the emphasis on uniformity of care in Sweden may in fact prevent women of different cultural backgrounds from having the type of childbirth they would prefer.

A qualitative study of prenatal and child health care among immigrants in Sweden came to similar conclusions (Olin Lauritzen 1990). The researcher sat in on numerous encounters between health care personnel and immigrant clients and found that systematic Swedish health care routines were on the whole uniformly and kindly applied to immigrants, but that the cultural miscommunication that did occur resulted from the structure of health care itself, rather than practitioners. Western patterns of diagnosis may not be in line with how people from non-Western cultures understand illness. Or, as the author puts it, the health care provider may not be aware of "what type of ground she is planting her advice in" (p. 136) when she conveys health advice to an immigrant woman, and therefore her advice may go misunderstood or simply missed.

In general, this research suggests that while immigrants may be technically treated equally within the Swedish maternity care system, this uniformity may not be suited to immigrants' circumstances. More studies need to be done not so much on the quality of care offered, which is consistently high by Western standards, but on the experience of women from different cultural backgrounds undergoing this care, as well as on different types of care that immigrants may prefer, given the option.

While the Swedish maternity system does not seem to be adapting itself to the special needs of immigrants yet, some other modest changes are afoot. Studies such as one that exposed high regional variation in the use of anesthesia during delivery (Ahlenius et al. 1997) are encouraging ever greater uniformity and equality of care, but there are also growing worries that budget pressures and staff shortages are decreasing the quality of care in birthing clinics (Wilhelmson 1995). After some publicized incidents of maternal and neonatal deaths and misdiagnoses in the early 1990s, it has also been suggested that something of an "American" way of thinking has come to birthing practice in Sweden—said one doctor, practitioners have begun to think: "better one C-section too many than that I miss something" (Wilhelmson 1995, p. 2599). At the same time, one obstetrician points out, parents have become more demanding of health practitioners, expecting constant personal engagement from the midwife (p. 2600), which contrasts with the relatively detached style of midwife attendance that Brigitte Jordan describes for Sweden in the 1970s.

All in all, however, while socioeconomic and ethnic differences in birth outcomes persist in Sweden on a small scale, little of this variation seems attributable to the health care system.[4] Indeed, as this brief portrait has tried to show, compared to other nations Sweden cares well for its pregnant women, regardless of their socioeconomic status, ethnicity, or immigration status: Maternity care is guaranteed for all women; there is very low morbidity and mortality; the birthing environment is generally relatively free; birth is treated generally as a natural occurrence, even if technology is available; and parental leave policies enable mothers and fathers to spend time with their newborns. However, as noted earlier—and as we will review in the conclusion of this chapter—there are some down sides to the uniformity of an otherwise admirably fair and high-quality system.

The United States

THE MATERNITY CARE SYSTEM

Women in the United States, like those in Sweden, can be said to have a typical birth experience: The vast majority of women receive prenatal care, give birth in a hospital, and have a physician in attendance during labor and delivery. However, unlike Sweden there is little uniformity in either the events leading up to—or the outcomes of—this typical birth. Indeed, the United States has wide intracountry variations in almost every aspect of childbirth. This wide variation can be attributed to two sets of factors. First, the United States is unique among high-income countries in not guaranteeing universal health care, including maternity care. Second, the United States is the most economically stratified of high-income countries (Bradsher 1995) and is also highly diverse in terms of race and ethnicity. As we show in this section, socioeconomic status, race, ethnicity, and immigration status are all relevant to producing comparatively enormous intracountry variations in maternity care in the United States.

In addition, in word, if not in deed, the United States values individual choice to an extent perhaps not found in any other high-income country. The well-formulated critique of medicalized childbirth that emerged in the 1960s is tied to this value insofar as it regards with mistrust the degree to which medical professionals, by controlling the birth process, deny agency to individual women. This critique also contains a bias against intervention in what is regarded as an essentially natural process in which the woman can trust her body and her (preferably female) supporters (see Fox & Worts 1999). Hence some of the U.S. scholarship on childbirth appears to place a premium on the availability of options (and is suspicious of medical management). Here too there is a sharp difference from Sweden, where the public provision of health care is assumed to carry general societal consensus (and where medical intervention appears to be more readily accepted). Ironically, however, women in the United States may be less able to exercise individual agency in issues surrounding childbirth than are women in Sweden.

SOCIOECONOMIC STATUS

Teasing out the manner in which socioeconomic status affects childbirth is difficult. The United States keeps no detailed information about either the income or social class status of mothers (Krieger et al. 1993), and the available data reflect biases. On the one hand, social accounting, combined with a special concern about reproduction among the poor, results in numerous (predominantly quantitative) studies designed to assess the impact of public policies on behavior. On the other hand, qualitative studies of attitudes toward, and experiences of, childbirth generally find recruits in childbirth education classes and thus end up with unrepresentative samples weighted toward the middle and upper classes.[5] Moreover, because of the robust relationships among class, race/ethnicity, and immigration status, it is often difficult to tell which of these factors is operating in a given situation.

Even so, the evidence (much of which uses education as a proxy for social class) suggests that in the United States three sets of factors related to socioeconomic status are relevant. There are distinct social class differences in the context in which women give birth (e.g., timing of first birth and the marital status of mothers), in access to (and the quality of) health care, and in the choices concerning (and evaluations of) the childbirth experience.

The Context of Birth

In the United States, age at first birth is increasingly tied to social class. Whereas during the post–World War II years, both rich and poor women had their children early, starting in the 1980s more affluent women began postponing their first birth, leaving poorer women as the only ones engaging in early childbearing (Luker 1996). Although teen birth rates have been declining in recent years (as have *all* birth rates), there remains a bifurcation in the population with respect to age at first birth. Poor women have births at young ages and often drop out of high school because of these pregnancies; more affluent women wait until they have completed their education, and increasingly, until their thirties and forties (Ventura et al. 1999). There is also a bifurcation in the population with respect to the variable of total lifetime fertility. Women with less education tend to expect they will have more children than women with a college degree ("Women's Health" 1997), and one year of college or more predicts significantly lower fertility rates over the course of a lifetime (Mathews & Ventura 1997).

The bifurcation in the timing of a first birth is accompanied by differences in marital status. In Sweden there are many mothers who are technically "single" but who are living in legally recognized common-law relationships. In the United States the picture is quite different. Not only are common-law relationships less frequent (and without legal status), but "single" mothers often give birth outside of an ongoing significant relationship with the father. In 1997 over three-quarters (78 percent) of all U.S. teenagers who gave birth were unmarried (and may well have been unconnected to the baby's father). By way of contrast, a quarter (26 percent) of those over twenty were unmarried when they gave birth (Ventura et al. 1999).

Not surprisingly, the group of women who are younger, unmarried, and poor are likely to face different risks associated with fertility and childbirth than are those who are older, in stable relationships, and better-off financially. As is true in Sweden, those who are less well-off by virtue of income and education, and those women who are younger, are more likely to engage in substance abuse and in poor eating habits, which can produce birth defects (NIDA 1999). This group is also more likely to live in areas of environmental pollution and to hold down jobs that pose occupational hazards to the health of the mother and the fetus. In addition, in the United States intention status—with more unintended pregnancies among those who are younger, unmarried, lower-income (Henshaw 1998), and less educated (Kost & Forrest 1995)—has been linked to the full range of behaviors surrounding childbirth, from seeking early prenatal care through to breastfeeding and well-child check-ups (Kost et al. 1998a, b). Young mothers are also more likely to experience abuse and battering from male partners during pregnancy (U.S. Department of Health and Human Services 1994) and postpartum depression following birth (Deal & Holt 1998). However, because teenage mothers are not a random sample of the population, but carry with them a host of social and economic disadvantages, it is difficult to disentangle cause and effect. Some of the problems found among teenage mothers are also found among similarly situated mothers who are considerably older. Indeed, some research suggests that, far from being the cause of subsequent difficulties, not only is teenage parenthood a response to a disadvantaged status, but even that early childbearing might be optimal in some disadvantaged subpopulations (Hoffman 1998).

Moreover, it is not the poor (or young) alone who face risks associated with behaviors that are correlated with age and socioeconomic status. Because of the decline in fertility associated with aging, those who delay having children until they are older increasingly turn to high-technology forms of assisted reproduction; they also face other special risks associated with first-time mothers over forty, such as having babies that are premature, short-lived, and of very low birthweight or of having multiple births (Luker 1996, p. 171; Ventura et al. 1999). Those who are older are also more likely to be in the labor force and thus have to negotiate with workplace policies concerning job discrimination and parental leaves. Whereas Sweden, like most European countries, ensures paid parental leave, in the United States those who are in the labor force are *ensured* only unpaid leave (and only if they work for companies with over fifty employees). Women who return to work shortly after giving birth risk high rates of postpartum depression (McGovern et al. 1997).

Variations by Payment

Perhaps even more important than variations by the context in which birth occurs are those correlated with, and even imposed by, the means through which maternity care expenses are covered. In the absence of a universal health care system, the availability and quality of health care depends on income (and employment status), and an analysis of class differences cannot be separated from the mechanism through which health care services are made available.

The poorest Americans have their health care costs covered through Medicaid, a means-tested, government-sponsored insurance program.[6] As a result of expansions of this program in the 1980s (combined with higher birthrates among the poor), by 1994, 39 percent of all births were covered by Medicaid (Swartz 1997). The vast majority of the population *not* covered by Medicaid rely on private health insurance, usually made available through employment. Still, 17.6 percent of the U.S. population under sixty-five remains with neither health insurance nor Medicaid coverage (Steinhauer 1999). While pregnant women are more likely to be eligible for special assistance for the cost of medical care (e.g., through state extensions of Medicaid) than are other women (and men) at similar income levels, learning about, and thus gaining access to, these programs remain significant issues for poor women. Those who are entirely without insurance—likely to come from the population known as the working poor—pay for childbirth-related services out of pocket.

In the United States, the fact that health care for the poor alone is provided through public moneys leads to public concern about whether these policies are pronatalist and will have the effect of increasing the birth rate among an "underclass" (Clarke & Oleson 1999). Hence, the specific content of these programs (e.g., whether they pay for fertility treatment and birth control), the range of income groups covered, and, indeed, the very existence of these programs themselves, are subject to public debate (Joyce et al. 1998). Some groups (e.g., legal immigrants in California and illegal immigrants elsewhere) were recently cut off from public insurance altogether, while other women were crowded out of private insurance and thus were subject only to Medicaid coverage or no insurance at all (see Currie & Gruber 1997, p. 7). These shifts have enormous consequences for the options available to individuals affected by them.

Medicaid does not cover either abortion or the full cost of infertility services (Roberts 1999). This does not mean that the fertility of the poor is ignored entirely. Poor women (and their advocates) in the U.S. have had to resist sterilization in the past and, more recently, the mandatory use of long-lasting contraceptives like Norplant. But, control over fertility is not assured for those who are in a position to purchase private health insurance either. Although between 1985 and 1991 ten states passed laws requiring insurance coverage of infertility services, the trend toward mandatory inclusion seems to have come to a halt (Roberts 1999, p. 253). Ironically, cutbacks in private insurance mean that infertile couples pursue the most aggressive strategy in an effort to get pregnant quickly (Vobejda 1998). Hence they are likely to experience a high level of multiple births and all the associated medical problems.

Despite the fact that access to prenatal care has become almost universal in the United States, class differences in quality remain. Because private obstetricians may be unwilling to accept Medicaid patients—Gifford (1997) found that only 36.7 percent of obstetricians accepted new Medicaid patients—those relying on Medicaid might have to rely on public clinics, which offer few of the amenities available to those whose care takes place in a private physician's office (Lazarus 1997, p. 141). In addition, there is evidence that the care offered to low-income women in some kinds of public clinics is not as effective in reducing risks as is that offered by private physicians (Johnson 1997).

However, there are some unexpected ironies in the prenatal care data. Most of those who study prenatal care assume that only benefits result (see, e.g., Fiscella 1995). Yet prenatal care carries hazards both for those who are poor and for those who are relatively well off. For those often seen as most in need of prenatal care—teenagers, racial and ethnic minorities—not only does prenatal care bring one under the supervision of providers whose values and outlooks are culturally disparate (and who might well hold prejudices about one's membership group)—but it can also lead to the identification as an individual who is behaving in ways that are punishable, particularly when these behaviors are seen to pose threats to the fetus (Balsamo 1999; Roberts 1999). Moreover, because it is *only* the poor in the United States who receive *public* funds for prenatal care, they might be subject to special scrutiny (Rapp 1993, p. 63).

At the same time, the intensive prenatal care given to more privileged women—and especially those who have delayed childbirth—might have its own dangers: Amniocentesis carries the risk of possible miscarriage (Grady 1998), some argue that repeat ultrasound creates health problems (Saul 1994), and the knowledge obtained from prenatal diagnosis can create enormous psychological burdens and ethical or moral dilemmas (see Chapter 9).

The expansion of Medicaid has not only increased access to prenatal care for poor women, but it may also have had the effect of reducing variation in the way women in the United States give birth. Because Medicaid only reimburses for charges in hospital births, and not for home births, it has virtually completed the movement of childbirth from home to the hospital among the very poor in the United States (Germano 1997). Medicaid expansion may also have had the effect of increasing the use of four procedures—C-section, fetal monitoring, induction of labor, and ultrasound—among women likely to have moved from the status of no insurance to Medicaid (Currie & Gruber 1997) because it brings women from a situation where physicians and hospitals may be reluctant to offer services for which they cannot be assured of payment to one where medical care providers know they will receive at least a moderate reimbursement. Meanwhile, because those crowded out of the private insurance market by Medicaid expansions were likely to have shifted to a less intensive regime (since physicians receive less from Medicaid than they do from private insurance programs), overall Medicaid expansions might have had the effect of equalizing (at least some kinds of) treatment of more advantaged and less advantaged groups of mothers (but see also Lenaway et al. 1998).

This greater equalization, however, does not ensure that all groups get equally good care or even that they get good care at all. The high maternal mortality rate in United States (which is sixteenth in the world) has been attributed to two factors related to the form of payment for care. One affects large numbers of women without private health insurance who are likely to receive publicly funded care and thus go to overcrowded hospitals staffed by overworked and inadequately trained physicians. The other factor affects those who do have private insurance: U.S. doctors want their patients to be in the hospital but the physicians themselves are office based and there-fore not necessarily available. As the earlier discussion has shown, this pattern is in contrast with Sweden—and indeed with every industrialized country in Europe—where obstetricians are primarily hospital-based specialists and where midwives are crucial to health care delivery (United States: Maternal Mortality . . . 1998).

As is the case for prenatal visits, there are sharp differences between giving birth in a hospital under the auspices of a private insurance plan and giving birth in a public hospital without this protection. A recent *New York Times* article describes how one woman experienced this difference (Steinhauer 1999, p. A1):

> Seven years ago, [Peggy Paraga] had a baby in [a hospital], which accepted her managed care plan, offered good prenatal care, and even served her and her husband a celebratory champagne dinner. In 1996, pregnant again but uninsured, she could afford only a clinic . . . and endured a chaotic and unpleasant delivery by a doctor she had never met before.

The implied critique of delivery by an unknown doctor highlights the difference between expectations in the United States (personalized service from prenatal care through delivery) and Sweden (where women as a rule are assisted at birth by a person they have not previously met). Indeed, the champagne dinner described in this piece may indicate a growing difference between those who are better off and those who are poor—and between the "best" offered in the United States and the norm in Sweden—as managed care programs and hospital maternity services, faced with declining num-bers of women in the peak years for childbearing and declining birth rates, begin to court pregnant women with prenatal and postnatal frills (Braus 1996).

As a cost-saving technique, *both* public and private insurance have shortened hos-pital stays following delivery to a brief period dubbed "drive-through deliveries." Prior to legislation designed to ensure that mother and child could remain in the hos-pital for at least forty-eight hours following delivery, managed care organizations developed guidelines to restrict post-delivery hospitalization to twenty-four hours or less (for an interesting analysis, see Germano 1997; see also Chapter 2). While the reduction in length of hospital stays has affected almost all women and while the evi-dence is mixed with no clear evidence about outcomes for shorter or longer stays (Braveman 1996), some argue that significant numbers of mothers discharged from the hospital early manifested health and social risk factors associated with poor out-comes for both mother and child (Blood-Siegfried et al. 1998; Margolis et al. 1997). Indeed, unlike Sweden, where early discharge is the norm, lack of private insurance or receipt of Medicaid for delivery is associated with early discharge. Moreover, unlike Sweden and other European countries where there is a rich experience with universal postpartum nurse home visiting, not all states in the United States ensure this practice and thus jeopardize continuity of care during the early postpartum period (Braveman 1996).

In short, these data suggest that in the United States some class differences in childbirth are disappearing as Medicaid expansions increase the range of services for the poor at the same time as managed care reduces the range of services for the middle class. Even so, significant differences remain among those who have private insurance, those who rely on Medicaid, and those who have no insurance at all.

Childbirth Choices

As was true of much associated with the second wave of feminism, the alternative birth movement appealed largely to middle-class women who saw in that movement a possibility for enacting a set of ideals that included reclaiming control from male health care providers and from technology itself. Some of the ideas gradually spread to other social classes, especially through childbirth education (Mathews & Zadak 1991).

Regardless of their desires, there is evidence that middle-class women who wish to avoid a technological birth find it difficult to sustain those choices. In a study of a group of thirty-one women recruited from childbirth education classes (all residents of a large West Coast city who tended to be middle to upper middle class), Monto (1997) found that despite commitments to nonconventional childbirth, medical definitions intruded during the prenatal period, and as they did, the women found their previous choices challenged.

While these challenges may well have resulted from a combination of what was deemed medically necessary intervention *as well as* the manner in which a hegemonic birth was imposed regardless of choice or necessity, many researchers suggest that because resistance to technology is ambivalent at best, women themselves play a role in altering their choices as they approach the birth itself (Lazarus 1997; Monto 1997). Recently, in fact, there are signs that the middle-class resistance to technology is breaking down altogether. Doctors have reported a rise in "elective" cesareans (Gilbert 1998); Lazarus (1997, p. 147) reported as well that she had interviewed well-educated and professional women who had requested cesarean sections because they believed that technological control would ensure a safe birth and a healthy baby (see also Grady 1999, p. A1).

Information about the childbirth choices of those who are less privileged is scantier. Browner and Press (1997, p. 115) found "no significant differences by ethnicity or social class . . . in . . . women's attitudes toward prenatal care or their pregnancy practices" and Lazarus (1997, p. 141) reported that the poor women she studied, when asked to participate in birth-related decisions, "often did not have enough information to make such decisions." Other data suggest that, regardless of choices, less privileged women—like those who are better off—have relatively little control over what happens to them during labor and delivery (Stewart 1998; Nelson 1983.)

RACE AND ETHNICITY

In the United States race and ethnicity are clearly associated with almost every aspect of childbirth, from fertility rates, marital status, and timing of first birth to infant and maternal mortality rates. Because race and ethnicity are so closely associated with social class and immigration status, it is difficult to identify the causes in these different patterns.

In the discussion that follows we first identify "raw" differences in racial/ethnic childbirth experiences in the United States.[7] We then argue that at least some of these racial/ethnic differences—and in particular those between African American and white women—in the United States can be attributed to a complex legacy of racism and inequality in general (see Krieger 1993; Krieger et al. 1993). Finally, we consider the issue of racial/ethnic differences in choices surrounding childbirth.

Birth rates of all racial and ethnic groups generally declined during the 1990s. Still, sharp differences remain between different groups. At 102.8 (births per 1,000 women of childbearing ages), the fertility rate of Hispanic women overall continues to be higher than that of the other racial/ethnic groups. While the fertility rate of 72.4 births per 1,000 women among African American births represents a historic low, it is still higher than that among whites, which stands at 57 (Ventura et al. 1999; see Table 5–1).

These differences in fertility rates conceal further differences both *within* specific racial/ethnic groups and *among* them. One example of the first set of differences is the range in fertility rates among the Hispanic population from 116.6 among Mexican women to 57.4 for Cuban women (a difference that probably represents class as much as it does ethnicity). With respect to differences among ethnic groups, in 1997 when 32.4 percent of all births occurred among unmarried women, nonmarital births were far more common among African American women (representing 69.2 percent of births in this group) than among white (21.5 percent) or Hispanic (40.9 percent) women (Ventura et al. 1999). Teen birth rates varied by race and ethnicity as well: The 1997 rate of 90.8 births per 1,000 women among African American teens represents a fall of 24 percent since 1991; Hispanic young women have replaced blacks as the teenagers with the highest birthrate (97.4 per 1,000); white teenagers continue to have a considerably lower rate (36 per 1,000) than their African American and Hispanic peers (Ventura et al. 1999).

As noted earlier, the vast majority of pregnant women in the United States now have access to prenatal care. Nevertheless, racial/ethnic differences remain in timing of initiation and utilization of prenatal care. In 1997 84.7 percent of white mothers began prenatal care in the first trimester, in comparison with 73.7 percent of Hispanic and 72.3 percent of black mothers (Ventura et al. 1999), and while only 3.2 percent of white mothers received no prenatal care or prenatal care only starting with the third trimester, this was the case for more than twice as many black women (7.3 percent) and women of Hispanic origin (6.2 percent) (Pyle 1999).

Racial/ethnic differences are also found in procedures related to pregnancy, labor and delivery, and birth outcomes. Among North Carolina Medicaid recipients hospitalization during pregnancy was higher among black women than among white women (Bennett et al. 1998). Although in 1997 the rate of cesarean deliveries rose slightly after a seven-year decline (after having risen dramatically in the 1980s), the C-section rate remains twice as high as that in Sweden, and it varies by race and ethnicity. African Americans have a higher rate (21.8 percent) than either whites (20.7 percent) or Hispanics (20.2 percent) (Ventura et al. 1999). Even with more intensive intervention for blacks, a recent study by the Centers for Disease Control and Prevention in

Atlanta reported that black women in the United States had maternal mortality rates nearly four times as high as did white women.[8] More specifically, between 1987 and 1996 1 black woman died for every 5,102 who gave birth, whereas among white women the figure was 1 in 18,868. The disparity (which has remained about the same for the last four decades despite sharp improvements in all maternal mortality rates) holds true even for women who are middle class and have health insurance (State-Specific Maternal Mortality among Black and White Women—United States, 1987–1996, 1999; Stolberg 1999). Of special interest is the fact that black and white women generally suffer the same types of complications, but *mortality* is about four to five times higher among blacks, whereas morbidity or complications are only 1.5 times higher (see Stolberg 1999).

With respect to birth outcomes for the infant, the proportion of very low birth-weight black infants (3.0 percent) is about triple that for white (1.1 percent) and His-panic (1.1 percent) babies; the infant mortality rate among black infants (14.2 per 1,000) remains more than double the rate for white and Hispanic infants (6.0 and 5.8 per 1,000, respectively) (Ventura et al. 1999).[9]

Obviously, many of the differences just noted can be attributed to two factors—social class differences and accompanying differences in the circumstances under which women give birth: African American women and Hispanic women are more likely to be poor and are more likely to be having children as unmarried teens. But some disparities among ethnic and racial groups remain even after controlling for mothers' education, income, and age; they thus elude easy explanation. For example, higher infant mortality rates are found among college-educated black women than among their similarly situated white peers (Williams & Collins 1995). Indeed, the evidence among some studies suggests that differences in black-white infant mortal-ity rates are narrowest among women who have not completed high school and high-est among women with a college education (Williams & Collins 1995).

TABLE 5–1

Comparison of White, Black, and Hispanic Childbirth Outcomes in the United States

	White	Black	Hispanic
Fertility rates (births per 1,000 women of childbearing ages)	57.0	72.4	102.8
Percentage of births to unmarried women	21.5%	69.2%	40.9%
Teen birth rates (per 1,000 teenagers)	36	90.8	97.4
Percentage of mothers who begin prenatal care in first trimester	84.7%	72.3%	73.7%
Percentage of mothers with no or late prenatal care	3.2%	7.3%	6.2%
C-section rate	20.7%	21.8%	20.2%
Percent very low birthweight infants	1.1%	3.0%	1.1%
Infant mortality rates (per 1,000)	6.0	14.2	5.8

SOURCE: Ventura et al. 1999.

To some extent, Williams and Collins (1995) argue the reason for the persistence of racial differences despite adjustment for socioeconomic status (SES) is that the commonly used SES indicators do not fully capture the economic status differentials between households of different races. But, there is also distinct evidence that racial/ethnic discrimination and its legacies affect these outcomes (Williams & Collins 1995). Several examples suffice to demonstrate this point.

First, there is evidence that even when financial barriers in access to prenatal care have been reduced, race-related barriers to obtaining *adequate* prenatal care remain in place among middle-class blacks (Warner 1997). In addition, while among whites education beyond high school reduces the risk of infant mortality by 20 percent, it has little effect among African Americans (Din-Dzietham & Hertz-Picciotto 1998).

Second, the manner in which individuals are perceived—and therefore treated—can depend entirely on race. Telfair and Nash (1996, p. 5), for example, note that "health care providers tend not to make class distinctions among African Americans, the result being erroneous assumptions about clients' backgrounds and health care experiences that perpetuate stereotypes, miscommunication, and conflicts between practitioner and client."

Finally, a legacy of discrimination has caused mistrust of a white-dominated health care system and thus affects the choices individuals make. While those who have always benefitted from the health care system can opt to forego some of its privileges (as is the case for middle-class women who eschew technology), those who have never had those privileges might see their absence as further evidence of racism. It is thus not surprising that Stewart (1998, p. 234) found that education affects the probability of the choice of a midwife for pregnancy and delivery differently among whites and non-whites: Whereas among whites higher educational attainment increases the probability of midwife use, among blacks the reverse is true, suggesting that "the use of midwives may not be part of an ideology of childbirth for educated, middle-class nonwhites."

We are reluctant to ascribe most of the differences between the African American and white population in the United States to "cultural" and "behavioral" factors—explanations can just as easily be found in class differences and in patterns related to the history of racism within mainstream institutions—but clearly culture and behavior make a difference in some places and among some groups.

The evidence about cultural influences on childbirth activities is mixed, however. Browner and Press (1997, p. 115), in their small study of 158 pregnant women who were enrolled in prenatal care at a branch of a health maintenance organization, found no significant differences by ethnicity either in women's attitudes toward prenatal care or in their actual pregnancy practices. Similarly, in a study of low-income Puerto Rican (N = 27) and European-American (N = 26) obstetrical patients at a U.S. inner-city hospital, Lazarus (1988, p. 36) reported that, "Puerto Rican and white women held similar beliefs about pregnancy and birth, managed these events in a similar fashion, and behaved similarly in their clinic interactions."

On the other hand, some research on specific groups does report *desired* variations from the hegemonic birth experience—regardless of whether or not these are medically advised. The research of Campanella et al. (1993, p. 333) on the very distinctive group of the Amish, for example, shows although they do not automatically reject medical technology, they select only "those aspects that are congruent with, and that will support and maintain their way of life." Similarly, the Hmong in

Wisconsin choose avoidance of prenatal care as a mechanism for resisting certain aspects of childbirth (e.g., pelvic examinations—particularly by a male physician—during pregnancy). However, unlike the Amish, who are able to isolate themselves to sustain their cultural practices, the Hmong have not necessarily been able to avoid other procedures (e.g., episiotomies, newborn blood tests) that violate their own strongly held cultural beliefs (Jambunathan 1995).

IMMIGRANTS

Immigration to the United States can affect childbirth experiences in a variety of ways. Not only are new immigrant groups likely to experience the kind of culture clash with the dominant medical paradigm described for the Hmong and Amish, but their health outcomes might also be adversely affected by the breakdown of traditional practices even if they have emigrated to a country in which the overall quality of health care services is better than in their homeland. And while some immigrants find themselves in relatively advantaged economic and social positions within the U.S. class structure or find upward mobility possible, other groups, even if they experience improved living conditions in comparison to those in their country of birth, face discrimination and relative poverty. Moreover, because of the general problems associated with the U.S. health care system, even immigrant groups that hold a relatively advantaged position when they relocate to the United States might experience a decline in health outcomes. Research that focuses explicitly on immigration to the United States suggests a complex interplay among this broad range of factors.

Taken as a whole, these studies suggest that immigration to the United States is bad for one's health and that this is true both for those who come to the United States from impoverished areas and fare poorly in the United States (e.g., Mexican Americans) *and* for those who come to the United States from countries with good health care systems and whose U.S. experience is one of relative affluence (e.g., the Japanese).

Several studies show that although Mexican immigrants have surprisingly positive birth outcomes given their low levels of educational attainment, income, and access to health care, problems increase in succeeding generations: Mexican women who are born in the United States have higher rates of low birthweight babies and infant mortality than do women in the immigrant generation (Sherraden & Barrera 1997). Sherraden and Barrera's (1995, p. 465) qualitative interviews help interpret these findings by noting the influence of culture breakdown and, more particularly, the role played by the presence (or absence) of support by a childbearing woman's mother.

A similar finding regarding the negative influence of immigration is reported by Alexander et al. (1996). These researchers found that even among the Japanese who have "exemplary" pregnancy indicators both in the United States and in Japan, foreign-born Japanese American immigrants have modestly better low birthweight percentages and lower infant mortality rates than U.S.-born Japanese Americans. And although, as is the case for the Mexican Americans, Japanese American immigrants might experience cultural breakdown and thus the loss of supportive mechanisms protecting women during their childbearing years, the Japanese experience differs from the Mexican experience because they move from a situation of good health care to one that is less good.

The awareness of cultural differences in choices surrounding childbirth—whether among new immigrants or among established subgroups—has led to calls for care that is more sensitive to the culture of patient, families, and friends. Clarke and Olesen (1999, p. 18) warn, however, that we be cautious about this kind of "culturally competent care." They note that although such care can be offered in a manner that is respectful of individuals, "it can also become commoditized in Health Maintenance Organization competitions for racial/ethnic market segments"; they also note that an array of other problems might result: "Cultural *formulas* do not work well in clinical practices. Cultures are neither uniform nor static—nor are people. Some versions of culturally competent care (or some people attempting to provide it) are reinscribing traditions, including gendered patriarchal traditions."

Conclusion

As we stated in our introduction, one of this chapter's main aims was to show that simple country-to-country comparisons can obscure considerable intracountry variation in class, race, and immigrant experiences of childbirth. The example of the United States illustrates just how vast these variations can be, while the example of Sweden illustrates that, at least in a small, relatively homogenous country, it is possible to provide highly uniform quality care to women.

The usefulness of this comparison is partly to be judged on what each country can learn from the other. We believe that the United States has more to learn from Sweden than vice versa. It must be recognized, however, that Sweden's excellent maternity system is part and parcel not only of a general public health system of high quality but also of a society that has aimed at and largely achieved equality among its population not only in maternity care but in all respects. The system is funded by taxes that are levied at among the highest levels in the world, and it functions within a national population that, until recently, at least, has been unusually homogeneous, as well as small (at just under nine million, approximately the size of the U.S. state of New Jersey). A country's maternity system exists against a background of political, social, economic, and cultural features that strongly predispose its form. When immigrants enter a country, they get absorbed by the system in place. In Sweden this involves receiving care at the standard of all Swedes, and in the United States, it means falling into one or another position in the steep class and race structures with all that implies for variations in care.

Although we are enthusiastic about the equality found in the Swedish system, it is only fair to note some of its limitations, in particular its relatively hegemonic nature. That is, while maternity care of good quality is guaranteed to all women in Sweden, women have relatively little choice about the type of care they receive (and they receive less "personalized" care at every stage than is the case for the most elite consumers in the U.S. system). Even so, it is interesting to note that the Swedish system does seem able to absorb some demands for change relatively easily. For example, there have been calls to increase home births and to allow alternative forms of therapy into the birthing process. These quiet demands are met for the most part within the system: A very small number of state midwives have begun attending home-births, some midwives are trained in acupuncture, women can give birth in the position they find most comfortable, and hospital birthing clinics have begun experimenting with more home-like decors. By way of contrast, even middle-class women in the United States have found it difficult to fight their way through to nontechnological births or the use of "alternative" medical practices, and, for the most part, women who desire home births must leave the system altogether and rely on traditional midwives (see De Vries 1996).

As Brigitte Jordan (1993, p. 45) points out, "as long as [birthing] systems are stable, they are generally experienced as appropriate from within" and are not critically assessed by participants. In conflict-averse, relatively egalitarian Sweden, there is no *large-scale* movement afoot to alter prenatal and birthing practices in any way.[10]

In the United States, on the other hand, it is in part the diversity of people, traditions, and birth options available that makes some women relatively opinionated about the type of childbirth experience they want to have. Ironically, however, these opinions often clash with a system that, in many ways, is equally (if not more) hegemonic as that of Sweden. Indeed, as we have suggested throughout, variation in the United States comes less from individual choice (whether shaped by class or racial/ethnic group membership) than it does from the nation's failure to provide a universal, just system of maternity care.

Notes

1. For more detailed information see http://www.si.se/sverige/svfr1e.html.
2. In 1995, between 85 percent and 97 percent of all women giving birth in Sweden received some form of pain medication, varying according to region of the country. Between 1990 and 1995 the most common type of pain medication was nitrous oxide, followed by petidin/morphine derivatives, followed by epidurals. Women giving birth for the first time were also much more likely to receive medication than multiparous women (Ahlenius et al. 1997).
3. An exception to this is the Alternative Birthing Centers that were started in Sweden just in the last decade which have located prenatal care and delivery wards in the same location, giving women the possibility of seeing the same midwife before, during, and after delivery (Hörnfeldt 1998, pp. 21–22).
4. Where differences in care have persisted is across regions: One large-scale study of anaesthesia use during delivery all over Sweden found that there were strong regional differences in what medications were used and how often (Ahlenius et al. 1997), and another recent study on the rise of C-sections in Sweden between 1995 and 1998 found that counties varied in the percentage of C-section deliveries they performed from 8.1 to 17.1 percent (Pineus 1999). A common maternity science and even a uniform maternity care system, it seems, do not necessarily lead to uniform application of maternity procedures. Whether or not these differences are significant for birth outcomes is another question (the differences are certainly significant from a financial standpoint, however). There is also evidence that perinatal mortality (up to day 7 after birth) differed regionally up through the mid-1970s in Sweden, with some rural areas having over twice the rate of some urban areas (15/1,000 vs. 6/1,000). By the 1980s, however, this difference had been erased, suggesting that the system had successfully eliminated what regional inequalities in care existed and that most of the remaining deaths are due to biological factors (Sundström-Feigenberg 1988, p. 43).

5. For a representative sample of women's experiences and behaviors before, during, and shortly after pregnancy with respect to a limited number of issues, see Centers for Disease Control and Prevention 1999.

6. Prior to the early 1980s Medicaid was restricted to very-low-income single mothers and children who received cash welfare payments under the Aid for Families with Dependent Children program. Beginning in the early 1980s and particularly after 1987 eligibility for Medicaid coverage of the expenses of pregnancy and childbirth was greatly expanded. By 1992 all states were required to cover the expenses of pregnancy and childbirth for women in households with incomes up to 133 percent of the poverty line and were permitted to extend eligibility up to 185 percent of the poverty line (Singh et al. 1994).

7. Similar data are not available for other countries, which are more reluctant to identify race on birth certificates (Williams & Collins 1995, p. 359). See also Williams and Collins 1995, p. 370) for an interesting discussion of problems with measurements of race and ethnicity in the United States.

8. Maternal deaths were defined as "deaths that occurred during pregnancy or within 42 days after pregnancy termination, regardless of pregnancy duration and site, from any cause related to or aggravated by the pregnancy, but not from accidental or incidental causes" (State Specific Maternal Mortality among Black and White Women—United States, 1987–1996, 1999, p. 492).

9. Evidence that the high infant mortality rates among the U.S. African American population is not the result of genetic predispositions derives from studies showing that birthweight is lower among infants of U.S. born than African born black women (David & Collins 1997), thereby suggesting that the answer is more likely to be found in barriers to good health care and other factors associated with minority status in the United States (including maternal behavior). For a study of black and white infant birthweights that controls for maternal demographic factors and medical complications of pregnancy, see Hulsey et al. 1991.

10. Indeed, the homogeneity of the Swedish population (until recently at least) means that diversity of options are less sought out by women themselves. In one perhaps telling study, pregnant women in Lund who were actively involved in making "birth plans" in which they partook in the preplanning of their deliveries (an idea that came from England) were not more satisfied with their care than were pregnant women not involved in this trial (Dykes 1998). (Both sets of women were, in fact, quite satisfied.)

References

Ahlenius, I., Ericson, A., Odlind, V., and P. Otterblad-Olausson. 1997. Ojämn Fördelning av Obstetrisk Analgesi. (Uneven distribution of obstetric analgesia.) *Läkartidningen* (The Journal of the Swedish Medical Association) 94: 1269–1275.

Alexander, G. R., Mor, J. M., Kogan, M. D., Leland, N. L., and E. Kieffer. 1996. Pregnancy outcomes of US-born and foreign-born Japanese Americans. *American Journal of Public Health* 86: 820–824.

Aurelius, G., and E. Ryde-Blomqvist. 1978. Pregnancy and delivery among immigrants. *Scandinavian Journal of Social Medicine* 6: 43–48.

Balsamo, A. 1999. Public pregnancies and cultural narratives of surveillance. In *Revisioning Women, Health and Healing,* eds. A. E. Clarke and V. L. Olesen. New York: Routledge, pp. 231–253.

Bennett, T. A., Kotelchuk, M., Cox, C. E., Tucker, M. J., and D. A. Natedau. 1998. Pregnancy-associated hospitalizations in the United States in 1991 and 1992: A comprehensive view of maternal morbidity. *American Journal of Obstetrics and Gynecology* 178: 346–354.

Blood-Siegfried, J., Hoey, C., and E. Matheson. 1998. The challenges of early discharge: Common newborn problems in the first few weeks of life. *ADVANCE for Nurse Practitioners,* 35–40.

Bradsher, K. 1995. Income disparity grows. *New York Times,* April 17, 1995: 2A.

Braus, P. 1996. The mother market. *American Demographics* 18: 36–41.

Braveman, P. A. 1996. Short hospital stays for mothers and newborns. *Journal of Family Practice* 42: 523.

Browner, C. H., and N. Press. 1997. The production of authoritative knowledge in American prenatal care. In *Childbirth and Authoritative Knowledge: Cross-Cultural Perspectives,* eds. R. E. Davis-Floyd and C. Sargent. Berkeley: University of California Press, pp. 113–131.

Campanella, K., Korbin, J. E., and L. Acheson. 1993. Pregnancy and childbirth among the Amish. *Social Science and Medicine* 36: 333–342.

Centers for Disease Control and Prevention. 1999. *PRAMS 1996 Surveillance Report.* Atlanta, GA: Division of Reproductive Health, National Center for Chronic Disease Prevention and Health Promotion.

Clarke, A. E., and V. L. Olesen. 1999. Revising, diffracting, acting. In *Revisioning Women, Health and Healing,* eds. A. E. Clarke and V. L. Olesen. New York: Routledge, pp. 3–48.

Cnattingius, S., and B. Haglund. 1992. Socio-economic factors and feto-infant mortality. *Scandinavian Journal of Social Medicine* 20: 11–13.

Currie, J., and J. Gruber. 1997. The technology of birth: Health insurance, medical interventions, and infant health. In *NBER Working Paper Series.* Stanford, CA: National Bureau of Economic Research.

David, R.J., and J. W. Collins. 1997. Differing birth weight among infants of US-born blacks, African-born blacks, and US-born whites. *New England Journal of Medicine* 33: 1209–1214.

Deal, L., and V. Holt. 1998. Young maternal age and depressive symptoms: Results from the 1988 National Maternal and Infant Health Survey. *American Journal of Public Health* 8: 66–270.

De Vries, R. 1996. *Making Midwives Legal.* Columbus: Ohio State University Press.

Din-Dzietham, R., and I. Hertz-Picciotto. 1998. Infant mortality differences between whites and African Americans: The effect of maternal education. *American Journal of Public Health* 88: 651–656.

Dykes, A. 1998. Gravida Kvinnors Möjlighet till Information, Autonomi, och Delaktighet i Vårdens Planering. (Pregnant women's possibilities for information, autonomy, and participation in the planning of their care.) *Vård: Utbildning, Utveckling, Forskning* (Healthcare: Education, Development, Research) 3: 80–84.

Elmèn, H. 1995. *Child Health in a Swedish City: Mortality and Birth Weight as Indicators of Health and Social Inequality* (NHV Report 1995:2). Göteborg: The Nordic School of Public Health.

Ericson, A., and B. Smedby. 1979. Perinatal dödlighet bland barn till invandrarkvinnor. (Perinatal mortality among children of immigrant women) *Läkartidningen* (The Journal of the Swedish Medical Association) 76: 2889–2892.

Ericson, A., Eriksson, M., Källén, B., and R. Zetterström. 1989. Socio-economic variables and pregnancy outcome: Birthweight in singletons. *Acta Paediatrica Scandinavia, Supplement* 360: 48–55.

———. 1993. Secular trends in the effect of socio-economic factors on birth weight and infant survival in Sweden. *Scandinavian Journal of Social Medicine* 21: 12–16.

Fiscella, K. 1995. Does prenatal care improve birth outcomes? A critical review. *Obstetrics and Gynecology* 85: 469–479.

Förlossningsresultat bland invandrarkvinnor i Sverige. (Birth Outcomes among Immigrant Women in Sweden.) 1998. Epidemiologiska Centrum (EpC) Rapport 1998: 1.

Fox, B., and D. Worts. 1999. Revisiting the critique of medicalized childbirth: A contribution to the sociology of birth. *Gender and Society* 13: 326–346.

Germano, J. 1997. Home birth and short-stay delivery: Lesson in health care financing for providers of health care for women. *Journal of Nurse-Midwifery* 42: 489–498.

Gifford, B. 1997. Obstetricians' receptiveness to teen prenatal patients who are Medicaid recipients. *Health Services Research* 32: 265–282.

Gilbert, S. 1998. Doctors report rise in elective caesareans. *New York Times,* September 22: F7.

Grady, D. 1998. Research finds risk in early test of fetus. *New York Times,* January 27: B15.

———. 1999. What's missing in childbirth these days? Often, the pain. *New York Times,* October 13: A1, A16.

Gudmundsson, S., Bjorgvinsdottir, L., Molin, J., Gunnarsson, G., and K. Marsal. 1997. Socioeconomic status and perinatal outcome according to residence area in the city of Malmö. *Acta Obstetrica Gynecologica Scandinavia* 76: 318–323.

Håkansson, A. 1994. Equality in health and health care during pregnancy: A prospective population-based study from southern Sweden. *Acta Obstetrica et Gynecologica Scandinavica.* October 73(9): 674-9.

Henshaw. 1998. Unintended pregnancies in the US. *Family Planning Perspectives* 30: 24–29.

Hoffman, S.D. 1998. Teenage childbearing is not so bad after all . . . or is it? A review of the new literature. *Family Planning Perspectives* 30: 236–240.

Hörnfeldt, H. 1998. *Det naturliga födandets politik.* (The politics of natural childbirth.) In T. I. Fjell et al., eds., *Naturlighetens Positioner: Nordiska Kulturforskare om Födsel och Föräldraskap.* (Natural Positions: Scandinavian Culture Researchers on Birth and Parenthood.) Åbo: Nordiskt Nätverk för Folkloristik.

Hulsey, T.C., Levkoff, A.H., Alexander, G.R., and M. Tompkins. 1991. Differences in black and white infant birth weights: The role of maternal demographic factors and medical complications of pregnancy. *Southern Medical Journal* 84: 443–446.

Jambunathan, J. 1995. Hmong women in Wisconsin: What are their concerns in pregnancy and childbirth? *Birth* 22: 204–210.

Johnson, K. A. 1997. What assures good outcomes in Medicaid-financed prenatal care? *Public Health Reports* 112: 133(2).

Joyce, T., Kaestner, R., and F. Kwan. 1998. Is Medicaid pronatalist? The effect of eligibility expansions on abortions and births. *Family Planning Perspectives* 30: 108–127.

Jordan, B. 1993. *Birth in Four Cultures: A Cross-Cultural Investigation of Childbirth in Yucatan, Sweden and the United States,* rev. and expanded ed. Prospect Heights; IL: Waveland Press.

Koupilova, I., Vågerö, D., Leon, D.A., Pikhart, H., Prikazsky, V., Holcik, J., and M. Bobak. 1998. Social variation in size at birth and preterm delivery in the Czech Republic and Sweden 1989–1991. *Paediatric Perinatology and Epidemiology* 12: 7–24.

Kost, K., and D. Forrest. 1995, January/February. Intention status of US births in 1988: Differences by mothers' socioeconomic and demographic characteristics. *Family Planning Perspectives* 27: 11–17.

Kost, K., Landry, D. J., and J. E. Darroch. 1998a. The effects of pregnancy planning status on birth outcomes and infant care. *Family Planning Perspectives* 30: 223–230.

———. 1998b. Predicting maternal behaviors during pregnancy: Does intention status matter? *Family Planning Perspectives* 30: 79–88.

Krieger, N. 1993. Analyzing socioeconomic and racial/ethnic patterns in health/health care. *American Journal of Public Health* 83: 86–87.

Krieger, N., Rowley, D. L., Herman, A. A., Avery, B., and M. T. Phillips. 1993. Racism, sexism, and social class: Implications for studies of health, disease, and well-being. *American Journal of Preventive Medicine* 9(6 suppl.):82-122.

Lazarus, E. S. 1988. Theoretical considerations for the study of the doctor-patient relationship: Implications of a perinatal study. *Medical Anthropology Quarterly* 2: 34–59.

————. 1997. What do women want: Issues of choice, control, and class in American pregnancy and childbirth. In *Childbirth and Authoritative Knowledge: Cross-Cultural Perspectives,* eds. R. E. Davis-Floyd and C. Sargent. Berkeley, CA: University of California Press, pp. 132–158.

Lenaway, D., Koepsell, T. D., Vaughan, T., van Belle, G., Shy, K., and F. Cruz-Uribe. 1998. Evaluation of a public-private certified nurse-midwife maternity program for indigent women. *American Journal of Public Health* 88: 675–679.

Luker, K. 1996. *Dubious Conceptions: The Politics of Teenage Pregnancy.* Cambridge, MA: Harvard University Press.

Margolis, L. H., Kotelchuk, M., and H. Chang. 1997. Factors associated with early maternal postpartum discharge from the hospital. *Archives of Pediatric and Adolescent Medicine* 151: 466–472.

Mathews, J. J., and K. Zadak. 1991. The alternative birth movement in the United States: History and current status. *Women and Health,* 17: 39–56.

Mathews, T. J., and S. J. Ventura. 1997. Birth and fertility rates by educational attainment: United States, 1994. *Monthly Vital Statistics Report* 45: 1–80.

McGovern, P., Dowd, B., Gjerdingen, D., Mosovice, I., Kochervar, L., and W. Lohman. 1997. Time off work and the postpartum health of employed women. *Medical Care* 35: 507–521.

Monto, M. A. 1997. The lingering presence of medical definitions among women committed to natural childbirth. *Journal of Contemporary Ethnography* 26: 292–715.

Nelson, M.K. 1983. Working-class women, middle-class women, and models of childbirth. *Social Problems* 30: 284–296.

NIDA (National Institute on Drugs and Alcohol). 1999. Pregnancy and drug use trends. http:// www.nida.nih.gov/Infofax/pregnancytrends.html.

Nordström, M., and S. Cnattingius. 1996. Effects on birthweight of maternal education, socio-economic status, and work-related characteristics. *Scandinavian Journal of Social Medicine* 24: 55–61.

Nordström, M-L., Cnattingius, S., and B. Haglund. 1993. Social differences in Swedish infant mortality by cause of death, 1983–1986. *American Journal of Public Health* 83(1): 26–30.

Notzon, F. 1990. International differences in the use of obstetric interventions. *JAMA* 263(24): 3286–3292.

Olin Lauritzen, S. 1990. *Hälsovård som rutin eller relation: svensk mödra- och barnhälsovård möter invandrarfamiljer.* (Health Care as a Routine or a Relationship: Swedish Prenatal and Child Health Care Meet Immigrant Families.) Doctoral dissertation, Stockholm University, Department of Education.

Pineus, I. 1999. Andelen kejsarsnitt har ökat kraftigt. (The percentage of cesarean sections has risen sharply.) *Dagens medicin* (Medicine Today).

Pyle, A. 1999. Many Latinas lack health insurance, study finds. *Los Angeles Times,* January 28: B1.

Rapp, R. 1993. Accounting for amniocentesis. In *The Anthropology of Medicine and Everyday Life,* eds. S. Lindenbaum and M. Lock. Berkeley: University of California Press, pp. 55–78.

Roberts, D. 1999. *Killing the Black Body.* New York: Vintage.

Saul, H. 1994. Screening without meaning? *New Scientist,* March 19: 14–15.

Sherraden, M. S., and R. Barrera. 1995. Qualitative research with an understudied population: In-depth interview with women of Mexican descent. *Hispanic Journal of Behavioral Sciences* 17: 452–470.

————. 1997. Family support and birth outcomes among second-generation Mexican immigrants. *Social Service Review* 71: 607–633.

Singh, S., Benson, Gold R., and J. Frost. 1994. Impact of the Medicaid eligibility expansions on coverage of deliveries. *Family Planning Perspectives* 26: 31–33.

Socioekonomiska forhållanden och förlossningsutfall i Sverige. (Socioeconomic Circumstances and Birth Outcome in Sweden.) 1996. (Epidemiologiskt Centrum Rapport 1996:2). Stockholm: Socialstyrelsen.

State-specific maternal mortality among black and white women—United States, 1987–1996 1999. *Morbidity and Mortality Weekly Report* 48: 492–496.

Steinhauer, J. 1999. For the medically uninsured, tough, and creative choices. *New York Times,* March 2: A1, A21.

Stewart, S. D. 1998. Economic and personal factors affecting women's use of nurse-midwives in Michigan. *Family Planning Perspectives* 30: 231–235.

Stolberg, S. G. 1999. Black mothers' mortality rate under scrutiny. *New York Times,* August 8: A1, A17.

Sundström-Feigenberg, K. 1988. Reproductive health and reproductive freedom: Maternal health care and family planning in the Swedish health system. In *Government Policy and Women's Health Care: The Swedish Alternative,* eds. G. Westlander and J. M. Stellman. New York: The Haworth Press, pp. 35–45.

Swartz, K. 1997. Babies are coming: Don't cap Medicaid (editorial), *JAMA* 277: 42.

Telfair, J., and K. B. Nash. 1996. African Americans. In *Cultural and Ethnic Diversity: A Guide for Genetics Professionals,* ed. N. Fisher. Baltimore: Johns Hopkins University Press, pp. 36–59.

United States: Maternal mortality inexcusably high and increasing. 1998. *WIN News* 24: 24–25.

U.S. Department of Health and Human Services. 1994. Physical violence during the 12 months preceding childbirth–Alaska, Maine, Oklahoma, and West Virginia, 1990–1991. *Morbidity and Mortality Weekly Report* 43: 132.

Vågerö, D., Koupilova, I., Leon, D.A., and U.-B. Lithell. 1999. Social determinants of birthweight, ponderal index, and gestational age in Sweden in the 1920s and the 1980s. *Acta Paediatrica* 88: 445–453.

Ventura, S. J., et al. 1999. Births: Final data for 1997. *National Vital Statistics Reports* 47: XX.

Vobejda, B. 1998. Multiple births keep growing in number. *Washington Post,* July 1: A8.

Waldenström, U. 1992. ABC—En Ny Vårdform vid Barnafödande. (A new form of care for childbirth.) *Vård* (Healthcare) 9(2): 21–26.

Warner, G. 1997. Racial differences in the hurdling of prenatal care barriers. *Review of Black Political Economy* 25: 95–120.

Wilhelmson, B. 1995. Ökad Centralisering Ger Bättre Säkerhet. *Läkartidningen* (The Journal of the Swedish Medical Association) 92(25): 2594–2597.

Williams, D. R., and C. Collins. 1995. US socioeconomic and racial difference in health: Patterns and explanations. *Annual Review of Sociology* 21: 349–386.

Women's health. 1997. *Washington Post,* June 10: 5.

PART II
Providing Care

Introduction to Part II

Edwin R. van Teijlingen

The organization of professions plays a significant role in the way care at birth is delivered. Because midwifery is "where the action is" in terms of professional "jurisdiction"—arguments about the most appropriate caregiver at birth—all four chapters in Part II put midwives at the center of their analysis: Midwifery is used as a way of illustrating the professional activity in maternity care systems.

Sandall and her colleagues open Part II with an examination of interprofessional rivalries among maternal health professions in the latter half of the twentieth century. Using case studies from Germany, the United Kingdom, Canada, and the Netherlands, Chapter 6 examines how the process of professionalization changes the nature of midwifery work, relationships with clients and colleagues, and the standing of midwives in society. These four countries were selected because they represent three different processes of professionalization. Midwifery in the United Kingdom exemplifies an occupation that appears to be strong but is struggling to find independence. Midwifery in the United Kingdom is state-funded; midwives are university-educated, and they attend the majority of all births. But as salaried employees of the National Health Service, most midwives work in a very hierarchical system and complain about long hours and poor pay. Midwifery in Germany has a long tradition, but today most midwives work under the supervision of an obstetrician. In the Netherlands midwives practice as private entrepreneurs at home and in the hospital. Dutch midwives benefit from legislation that limits competition from both family doctors and obstetricians, but their status is uncertain and their pay modest. Midwifery in Canada had largely vanished by the 1980s, but is now reappearing with the support of the state.

Chapter 7 analyzes midwifery education. Education is central to all professions, offering the training and socializing necessary to transform lay people into professionals. In "Designing Midwives," Benoit et al. look at education in the widest sense of the word—ranging from informal unofficial hands-on training by apprenticeship to formal and official education that leads to a government-endorsed license. The authors discern three educational models and illustrate and analyze them with case studies from different countries.

Chapter 8 uses midwifery case studies to breathe real life into the sociology of the professions. Van der Hulst has developed a case study model as a tool to link midwifery theory and practice. In this chapter, British, Canadian, and Dutch midwives tell us stories from their practices, and Van der Hulst uses these stories to shed new light on the profession of midwifery and its relation to other occupational groups.

In Chapter 9, Rothman offers a case study of the ways Dutch midwives have used (and not used) the technologies of prenatal diagnosis and screening. Using data from focus groups. the author allows us to listen to Dutch midwives' concerns about these new technologies. We hear a deep uncertainty about a technology that can, and often does, "spoil the pregnancy."

Part II moves us from the macro perspective represented by several of the chapters in the first section to a meso perspective that looks at the role of professional groups in organizing and delivering maternal health care.

Chapter 6

Deciding Who Cares

WINNERS AND LOSERS IN THE
LATE TWENTIETH CENTURY

Jane Sandall, Ivy Lynn Bourgeault, Wouter J. Meijer,
and Beate A. Schücking

Studies of midwifery (or any profession, for that matter) often begin with a simplistic notion of professional success. State sanction and a measure of status are seen as signs that midwifery has arrived, securing its place in the "system" of professions. However, as DeVries (1993) points out, professional success for midwives must be measured in *three* dimensions: the interests of midwives *as persons,* the interests of midwifery *as an occupation,* and the interests of midwifery *as a service* that promotes the health and well-being of women and babies. When we recognize that professional success is a multidimensional concept, we begin to see that the interests of midwifery as an occupation can be at odds with those of midwives and their clients. For example, in the Netherlands self-employed Dutch midwives have a great degree of autonomy, but the hours are long and family life is difficult (Bakker et al. 1996; McKay 1993, p. 120;). Benoit's (1999) research on the "new" midwifery in Canada and Sandall's (1995, 1997) on the reemergence of autonomous midwifery in Britain also confirm the incompatibility of midwives' concerns as workers and the needs of clientele.

A broader view of professional success allows us to see how changes in midwifery affect women as both *providers* of care and *receivers* of care, and it helps us understand the many ways the occupational role and status of midwives are situated in the social structure of health care. This chapter addresses recent changes in midwifery in Canada, the Netherlands, Britain, and Germany, paying special attention to how the delivery of care by midwives is shaped by: occupational structures; the links between health care systems and other political, educational, legal, and economic organizations; and the culture of the people served by the midwife.

Professional Projects in Midwifery

To understand the development of midwifery as an occupation we must examine the role of specialized knowledge in securing and maintaining professional privileges. In general, professional power and status are achieved through a process of *professionalization,* either by securing an occupational monopoly (Larson 1977) or by a having a privileged position in the class structure (Johnson 1972). Larkin (1983) argues that aspiring professions have to negotiate boundaries with other professions. He describes *occupational imperialism*: "'poaching' skills from others or delegating them to secure income, status, and control." The outcome of occupational imperialism, he argues, is largely shaped by the differential access of each group to external sources of power. Abbott (1988) calls this *conflicts over jurisdiction.* He explains how the division of expert labor is negotiated in a modern society and suggests that there are four areas where jurisdictional claims are made: (1) the legal system, (2) public opinion, (3) the state, and (4) the workplace. The success of a profession is strongly related to the situation of its competition; because professional jurisdictions are always in dispute, new professions can develop and old ones disappear. For a profession to be successful in the marketplace it must control a particular body of knowledge and its application (Abbott 1988, p. 19).

Our case studies look at the way the state and interest groups—representing professionals and clients—participated in the definition of midwifery as an occupation. In each country we consider two interlinking themes:

1. How the process of professionalization influences the nature of midwifery work and relations with clients and colleagues.
2. How the social structure of health care influences the occupational role and status of midwives.

We begin by examining recent developments in Canada.

The Integration of Midwifery in Canada

Ontario was the first Canadian province to regulate midwifery. In the second half of the twentieth century there were several attempts to introduce midwifery in Canada. In the face of opposition from the medical and nursing professions and the inability of midwives to organize, these efforts failed initially (Buckley 1979; Connor 1994; Rushing 1991). Pockets of midwifery practice remained in tightly knit ethnic communities and/or in northern outposts where British-trained nurse-midwives practiced unofficially (Benoit 1991). By the late 1960s changes in health policy resulted in a general decline in most of these and a general convergence toward physician-attended birth in hospitals (Benoit 1991; Mason 1988). In the early 1970s there was some interest in nurse-midwifery, but the idea had little political support (Bourgeault

& Fynes 1997). Until 1993, Canada was the only industrialized nation not to have any provision for midwifery care.

In the late 1970s, as a result of the influx of ideas from the United States, lay midwifery experienced a "rebirth" in Canada. These "lay" midwives were often empirically trained, coming to the practice as a result of an experience with home birth. Many began practicing as assistants to physicians who attended home births; they were present to coach the woman through labor and to offer advice, reassurance, and comfort. This form of midwifery care focused on serving both the physical and emotional needs of the woman, providing her with information and following her lead in how she wanted to give birth. Originally midwifery practice was limited to childbirth attendance, but eventually lay midwives began to provide prenatal and postnatal care. Midwives organized prenatal clinics independently of the physicians they assisted (Barrington 1985), and they assisted women and their babies for up to six weeks after the birth. Continuity of care thus became an integral component of their care.

For the most part, midwives' assistance at childbirth was restricted to home births. On occasion women who were not comfortable with a home birth but who wanted midwife care asked for their assistance at a hospital birth, but lack of official status severely limited midwives in the hospital. At home, midwives sometimes "caught" the baby even if the physician was present, but this was not allowed in the hospital setting.

In 1983, a formal directive from the College of Physicians and Surgeons made it impossible for physicians to attend home births. As a result, midwives became primarily caregivers at home births. This change did nothing to improve their status in hospitals, however; midwives remained unable to provide continuity of care for a woman choosing to birth in a hospital. Given these conditions, the model of midwifery practice that evolved in the late 1970s and early 1980s focused on continuity of care, informed choice, and, to a limited extent, choice of birth place. When the government-appointed Health Professions Legislation Review (HPLR) contacted midwives in 1983, this is the model of care they proposed.

A JOINT MIDWIFERY PROJECT

Created by the Ontario government to assess the organization of the health professions, the HPLR cast a wide net in its study of midwifery. The panel contacted the lay midwives' group and the relatively inactive nurse-midwives' group. These two organizations explored the possibility of joining forces to pursue integration. Nurse-midwifery representatives were impressed by the commitment and political will of lay midwives, who were willing to challenge the system by practicing in a less than ideal legal environment. Furthermore, by merging with practicing midwives nurse-midwives could achieve a more autonomous form of midwifery than they had originally envisioned. Finally, nurse-midwives would also benefit from the consumer support lay midwives had garnered, which proved to be a key factor in pushing midwifery onto the political agenda (see Chapter 4). For their part, lay midwives realized that a nurse-midwifery model presented a more acceptable form of practice to the nursing and medical professions. Although lay midwives resisted changing the model of practice they had developed, they realized that nurse-midwives would be a good political ally. With nurse-midwives on their side lay midwives had a better chance to challenge the viability of the midwifery models proposed to the review by medical and nursing organizations. In unifying, the groups created a larger and more forceful midwifery lobby, and, in the end, lay midwives convinced nurse-midwives to support their independent model of midwifery care.

In 1993, midwifery was introduced in Ontario in almost exactly the same form as nurse and lay midwives had requested. Midwives were regulated by a board separate from nursing and medicine, nursing was not a prerequisite for practice, continuity of care was assured by allowing both home and hospital practice, and access to midwifery services was assured through public funding.

IMPLICATIONS FOR OCCUPATIONAL BOUNDARIES

The integration of midwifery into the health care system in Ontario occurred despite medical opposition. The Ontario Medical Association expressed the view that midwifery services were not *needed.* Similarly, the College of Physicians and Surgeons of Ontario claimed to have no reservations, since "the inclusion of midwifery services has been demonstrated to be successful and well received in other countries"; nevertheless it warned against duplication of services and significant increase in costs if midwifery was introduced. Generally speaking, responses of the nursing and medical professions to the proposals were very brief. Unlike the material submitted by midwives, most of the arguments from these groups were *not* substantiated with reference to the international literature. This may have been partly because they themselves were also undergoing review by the HPLR, but it may have also been owing in part to a sense of arrogance that midwifery was really a "nonissue." For example, consider this comment from a representative of the medical association:

- HPLR was dominated by major issues for us. Midwifery would have been absolutely out on the periphery (OMA Policy Advisor, 1993)

And a representative of Ontario's nurses said:

- The majority of the effort was not spent on dealing with the midwifery issue. It was really spent on dealing with the issues that were more directly related to nursing (RNAO executive, 1993).

The general lack of interest in the "midwifery issue" on the part of the medical profession may have also been the result of an exodus of physicians from obstetrics because of (1) its demand on lifestyle and (2) prohibitively expensive malpractice insurance fees. Only a minority was deeply interested in the possible integration of midwifery, as the majority was preoccupied with other more salient issues.

In Abbott's (1988) terms, a vacant occupational space was created by the withdrawal of family physicians from the provision of community-based, low-risk maternity care, space that came to be "occupied" by practicing midwives. It might also be argued that the filling of a vacant occupational space is a strategy especially suited to the "professional projects" of female occupations. Occupational groups dominated by women, disadvantaged in direct competition for jurisdiction, find it easier to assume empty spaces in the professional system.

In the provinces of Quebec and British Columbia the medical profession has been much more vehemently opposed to the integration of midwifery (Kornelson & Carty forthcoming, Vadeboncoeur forthcoming). There physicians were *not* undergoing a concurrent review at the time midwifery was introduced, and in British Columbia physicians are not leaving the practice of obstetrics in any great numbers. The fact that midwives succeeded in gaining practice in Quebec and British Columbia despite resistance from a medical profession is evidence of the state's overriding interest in midwifery.

IMPLICATIONS FOR MIDWIFERY WORK

The professional project of midwives in Ontario has significant implications for midwifery work. One of the key elements of midwives' professional project is the provision of continuity of care. This worthy goal can make working as a midwife somewhat unbearable. The provision of continuity of care is something of a dilemma for midwives, putting their interests as workers in direct conflict with the interests of the users of their services. The legislation in Ontario attempted to minimize this "caring dilemma" for midwives. The law provides childbearing women with assurance of continuity of care and caregiver (midwives are available twenty-four hours on call), long prenatal and postnatal visits, choice of birth place (all midwives practice both at home and in hospital), shared decision-making expressed in a model of informed choice, and public funding to help ensure access. The law also supports midwives by calling for moderate caseloads, remunerating work in pairs (or group practices), and allowing for part-time work and time off-call.

The integration of midwifery changed the structural relationship between midwives and their clients. In the "golden age" of unregulation a midwife would contract with her client directly for an agreed set of services regardless of risk factors; the midwife-client relationship was personal and unique (see De Vries 1996a). Midwives now have numerous layers of bureaucratic accountability between them and their clients. The provincial Ministry of Health controls funding, the hospital determines admitting privileges, and the regulatory board sets standards for midwives' practice. Though most of these layers of bureaucracy are in the stated interests of midwifery clients, they do increase the potential for contradictions in midwives' accountability to individual clients (Bourgeault 2000).

The true measure of the "caring dilemma" for midwives is found in the everyday work of the profession. Here we find a flood of new work not directly related to caring for women, including committee work to maintain hospital admitting privileges, preceptor work to mentor new midwives, and paperwork for the Provincial Ministry of Health. Several midwives describe the personal and familial role conflicts that arise from being on-call twenty-four hours a day. In Ontario, the "caring dilemma" seems to create most conflict in the midwives' roles as spouse and mother (Bourgeault 1996).

The Reemergence of Autonomous Midwifery in Britain

The 1970s and 1980s marked a low point for professional midwives in Britain. Maternity care was fragmented, with both general practitioners (GPs) and obstetricians caring for "low-risk" women. Women were now going to GPs, not midwives, to confirm pregnancy. The incidence of obstetric interventions was rising sharply, partly because of the dominant notion that childbirth was only "normal in retrospect." Some midwives were providing continuity of care through "domino schemes" (where the community midwife provided both antenatal and postnatal care *and* attended the birth in hospital), but this way of working was not common. Midwives were not free to use their clinical judgment, and they were increasingly concerned about the erosion of their role (Robinson et al. 1983).

In 1979, the Nurses, Midwives and Health Visitors Act abolished the Central Midwives Board and replaced it with the United Kingdom Central Council for Nurses, Midwives and Health Visitors. New education proposals (UKCC 1986) defined midwifery as a nursing specialty, and midwifery schools were incorporated into higher education, resulting in fears among midwives about losing control over the educational process. By the mid-1980s the sphere of practice of midwives had been constrained in three key areas: clinical practice, licensing, and education. The care women received was fragmented, midwives' skills were underused, obstetric interventions were rising, and midwifery was on the verge of becoming a nursing specialty.

Not all midwives accepted these changes passively. Midwives who were unhappy with their increasingly subordinate role formed an alliance with women who wanted more control over birth. The efforts of these midwives to (re)gain independence and autonomy involved campaigns around licensing, education and practice. In 1986, the Association of Radical Midwives (ARM 1986) published *The Vision,* which outlined radical change in the division of labor, such as:

- Midwife-led care–midwives would be responsible for about 80 percent of normal births.
- Community-based care–70 percent of midwives would work in a community base.
- Independent caseload/group practice model contracting services into the NHS.
- Continuity of care throughout childbearing for both "high"-risk and "low"-risk women.
- Women's choice in childbirth.

The ARM was able to push their proposals for continuity of care onto the professional and political agenda as members became active in mainstream professional organizations and moved into teaching, research, and managerial posts. *The Vision* appealed to the state to initiate changes that would enhance the autonomy of midwives (Sandall 1995). The ARM plan challenged existing arrangements of power in several ways.

- By proposing that midwives set up in their own practices and contract their labor to the health authorities, they challenged managerial and medical domination within the NHS.
- By establishing direct client access to midwives and providing continuity of care throughout the process of reproduction, from preconception to the postnatal period, midwives would be established as the lead professional in maternity care, challenging the traditional hierarchical division of medical and midwifery labor.
- By providing continuity of care to all women in a geographically defined area regardless of risk categorization, they challenged traditional boundaries of

the medical profession, including their right to define and control risk and the right to decide on referral.

The ARM's strategy focused on autonomy for midwives because it believed that strong, autonomous midwives would be better able to deliver woman-centered care. This strategy was eventually taken up by more conservative elements as part of a struggle for survival of the midwifery profession in the 1970s and 1980s (RCM 1987).

The concerns of government regarding the inefficient use of midwifery skills remained an issue well into the 1990s. Following several official reports on the maternity services, the Health Committee of the House of Commons set up an inquiry into maternity services to determine the extent to which resources and professional expertise were being used to achieve the most appropriate and cost effective care of "normal" pregnant women and their babies. In 1992, the Health Committee (1992, p. xiii) published the *Winterton Report* highlighting three major themes, namely,

- Women's need for continuity of care.
- Women's desire for choice of care and place of delivery.
- Women's right to control their own bodies at all stages of pregnancy and birth.

The report concluded that it was time to move away from a concentration on safety and mortality rates as the major outcome measure for the maternity services. This represented a move from a medically dominated paradigm—that childbirth was a risky affair—toward a woman-centered approach that offered choice in place and type of service and seamless care that minimized the number of professionals involved. The report also recommended an extension of the role of the midwife to include full responsibility for a caseload of women, routine maternity care provided by community-based teams of midwives, and an increase in midwife-managed delivery units (Health Committee 1992, Para. 219 and 344). These recommendations were seen as a milestone in maternity policy, since this was the first time an official committee focused on whether women had received the kind of service they wanted rather than on safety.

The government response was published the following year. *Changing Childbirth* (Department of Health 1993), the report of the "Expert Maternity Group," endorsed most of the *Winterton Report* and identified three key principles of maternity care: woman-centered participatory care, accessible and appropriate services, and effective and efficient care (Department of Health 1993, p. 8). The report also identified ten key indicators of successful change in maternity care. The indicators fell into four key areas: (1) shifting the role and responsibilities between midwives and doctors with the aim of giving midwives greater autonomy, (2) cost-effectiveness and efficiency, (3) improving continuity of care, and (4) increased client participation in care. Finally, the government emphasized individual choice and personal control, reflecting a strategy that took maternity care as a vehicle for enhancing choice while promoting efficiency (Declercq 1998). The midwives' professional project in the late 1980s was successfully merged with state and consumer interests in maternity care (Sandall 1995).

IMPACT OF *CHANGING CHILDBIRTH* ON MIDWIFERY

While the changes initiated by *Changing Childbirth* have given midwives a wider scope of practice—they can now suture, start infusions, and do neonatal examinations—they have not given midwives control over organizational aspects of their work (Sandall 1998). Developing new technical skills and task substitution for doctors may not result in the increase in status midwives hoped for.

A postal survey in 1995 provides an overview of the organization of midwifery work in both new and traditional care settings in the post–*Changing Childbirth* era (Sandall 1998). One-third of the midwives were working in community or hospital-based teams, but only 3 percent were in group practices or carried their own caseloads. The implementation of the "new midwifery" has involved a renegotiation of occupational boundaries, but it remains to be seen whether the proposed division of labor has occurred in practice and whether the important boundary of "risk" has changed. Early evidence suggests that risk assessment guidelines have *restricted* women's choice about place of birth (Campbell 1999). Thus, a policy designed to increase women's autonomy has been substantially diluted in practice.

It is possible that "new" U.K. midwives are operating in a bounded occupational space and that the existing power relations will remain unchanged. It remains to be seen if the changes made in the 1990s are part of a traditional professionalization strategy by midwives, reasserting their autonomy and control over the process of birth, or the beginning of a powerful new alliance between midwives and women that will usher in a new paradigm of professional partnership and practice.

The Revival of Independent Midwifery and Home Birth in Germany

In Germany, maternity services are one of many health care sectors affected by post-unification economic reform. German midwives (*Hebammen*) were well established as birth attendants as a result of a 1938 law that made them the primary caregivers at every birth, *Hinzuziehungspflicht* (Zindars & Sauer 1955). In the economic and social turmoil of postwar West Germany, however, the number of midwives declined, particularly as many of them aged and there were few recruits to take their place. The postwar decline of German midwifery was paralleled by an increase in American influence on German society in general, and with it, a preference for medicalized birth. As a result, more and more women delivered in hospitals; by 1953, 48.9 percent of births in West Germany were in hospital, and 66.3 percent in 1960 (Trombik 1985). In East Germany, a socialist system of maternity care was adopted after the war. Prenatal care and birth had to take place in hospitals under an almost inflexible regime of hygiene and control as compared to the West; intervention rates remained at a low level, comparable to, for example, Czechoslovakia. Midwives worked only in hospitals under the control of doctors, and women's childbirth options were few.

This trend in both the East and the West was exacerbated by prenatal and postpartum maternity care guidelines developed by Western obstetricians in 1968, with the support of politicians and insurance companies, *Mutterschaftsrichtlinien*. Every pregnant woman was to have her prenatal and postpartum activities documented by an obstetrician and entered in a small blue book resembling a passport, the *Mutterpass*. In practice, the guidelines imposed by the *Mutterpass* served as controls, assuring the medicalization of birth as well as the obstetricians' role in normal pregnancies. The guidelines also mandated sick fund coverage of the costs of care at all births. Therefore, it is not surprising that mothers and midwives moved to the hospitals. By 1971, 96.2 percent of all births took place in hospitals. In less than twenty years, the number of midwives in West Germany dropped precipitously (Bartholomeycik 1978), from 11,601 in 1953 (mostly independent) to 8,107 in 1960 to 5,713 by 1975 (3,288 employed in hospitals). Paralleling this decline was a shift from independent home birth to hospital-based practice. In 1953 most midwives worked independently, but by 1975, 58 percent worked in hospitals. By 1985, 4,115 of the 5,934 midwives in West Germany were employed by hospitals. Regular working hours and steady pay made hospital employment more desirable than the on-call hours and irregular income of independent midwifery.

In the 1990s midwives and consumers began to lobby for a more independent role for midwives and a revival of home birth. Their campaign was successful, resulting in policy changes that increased the professional status of independent midwives (MDK-Info, 1997). How did this change come about?[1]

REVIVING THE PRINCIPLE OF A MIDWIFE AT EVERY BIRTH

The first wave of postwar midwifery reform in West Germany began in the early 1980s as a new generation of women entered midwifery. These young midwives longed for the professional autonomy of years past, and, enlisting the few remaining practicing home birth midwives as teachers, they attempted to revive the traditional home birth model of midwifery. When the young midwives realized they could not live on what they earned as independent midwives, they began to fight for better wages and legal reform. Although the lobbying efforts of West German midwives were focused on achieving better wages for independent practice, it was also their intention to create a shift from medicalized hospital-based birth attended by obstetricians to less medicalized birth in the community attended by independent midwives.

When these midwives began actively pursuing midwifery reform in the early 1980s, they had two major obstacles to overcome. First, their numbers were quite small in comparison to the numbers of obstetricians who had nothing to gain from legal legitimization of independent midwifery. Second, although the existing law mandated that midwives be primary caregivers for every birth, the law dated back to the Nazi regime and carried with it the present-day animosity toward that period.

The first step in promoting independent midwifery practice was to renew the principle of *den Hebammen vorbehaltene Tätigkeit* (tasks reserved for midwives). Here, consumer groups joined together with midwives and the German Society of Childbirth Education (GfG) to promote the old principles of the midwives' law. The movement was started by women who were discovering that programmed birth did not respect their individual rights and needs. Many went into childbirth education and broadened this profession's task from prenatal gymnastics to a more holistic approach that included accompanying pregnant women and empowering them to an active birth. At the same time, the European Community had agreed to a common standard of midwifery education that would apply to West Germany. Because the nursing and medical professions never sought to abolish midwifery (they preferred to keep it as a weak profession), politicians had no incentive to withdraw midwives' rights. In fact, midwives were supported by the liberal-democratic party under the flag of empowering independent professions.

By 1985, the female coalition of midwives (and their consumer supporters) succeeded in getting a new law passed that retained the old principle (HebG, 1985). Every woman was given the right to see a midwife during her pregnancy and the government insurance system would pay for it. Still, most German women choose to have their prenatal care in a gynecologist's practice, and many did not even know about midwives' competence in this field. But the midwife gave all birthing women some kind of intrapartum care, either in hospital, a birth center, or at home. Postnatal care was the exclusive domain of midwives, but many women did not know about their rights and did not find a midwife.

The new law also affirmed that a doctor, legally speaking, need not be present at every birth. In hospitals, however, doctors continued to be present at nearly every birth. The new law also had the important proviso that when both a doctor and a midwife were present, the midwife must serve as the doctor's assistant. In practice, then, few midwives worked independently. Those midwives who did choose to work independently could now legally provide prenatal and postpartum care and education beyond the hospital walls, but they had to do so without a fixed salary and living wage. Even with health insurance reimbursements midwives could not survive solely on earnings from independent practice. Most were forced to retain hospital employment as well.

REVIVING HOME BIRTH AND INDEPENDENT PRACTICE THROUGH WAGE INCREASES

The second wave of midwifery reform in the late1980s picked up where the 1985 law left off. Young midwives interested in professionalizing independent midwifery formed their own association, *Bund freiberuflicher Hebammen* (Association of Independent Midwives) (BfHD), separate from the general German Association of Midwives (BDH). They joined forces with the GfG and the women's movement. Birthing women dissatisfied with medicalized birth also joined the ranks of what became known as the "Home Birth Movement." Together, they formed a strong coalition promoting home birth and outpatient postpartum care.

The Home Birth Movement used television discussions, publications, and yearly celebrations of international midwives' day to bring public and government attention to the issue. The medical profession was opposed to the idea of out-of-hospital birth, declaring it dangerous and irresponsible. But the doctors' influence on health politics was not as strong as it used to be, and politicians knew that increased medical involvement would be expensive. Furthermore, developments in other countries helped promote the efforts of German midwives and feminist activists. For example, although both the British *Winterton Report* (Health Committee 1992) and *Changing Childbirth* report (Department of Health 1993) were ignored by German health politicians and doctors, politically active midwives had read these papers and disseminated the recommendations among their colleagues. They also translated the *Guide to Effective Care and Pregnancy and Childbirth* (Enkin et al. 1995), which was published in German in 1999.

Around 1990, health promotion in all fields reached a peak in publicity, and consumer organizations and midwives were able to win public support. Politicians needed to be convinced that even under growing economic pressure (reunification was showing its first consequences) investing in midwives would strengthen women's health. In 1993, after much politicking, a change in midwifery law resulted in a 20 percent rise in insurance reimbursements for independent midwifery services. However, reimbursement for home birth assistance was excluded and wages were still too low to support independent practice, causing midwives to go public with their demands for reform.

Even though their actions garnered them a formal invitation to meet with the Minister of Health, midwives remained dissatisfied and opted to strike. The midwifery strike, which lasted several days, resulted in the Conservative Minister of Health (a father himself) establishing a commission to recategorize midwifery services and revise the payment schedule for those services. As a result a list of activities was produced that was not only the basis for payment but also the first official acknowledgment of the broad spectrum of midwives' duties from pregnancy counseling to postnatal care. The commission's recommendations were passed by parliament in 1997.

For the first time in the history of German midwifery, midwives are now paid for prenatal care given before the sixth month and breastfeeding consultations for up to six months after birth. With the passage of the 1997 legislation, midwifery wages were increased by 30 percent, and included equitable reimbursement for attending home births ($380, up from $175) and prenatal care. German midwives are now in a position to choose between two financially viable options, hospital or independent work. Nevertheless, the majority of midwives continue to work in hospitals, and many of those who are leaving make an effort to keep a part-time arrangement because hospital employment has become a guarantee of financial security. It is also true that midwives' training concentrates on hospital birth; there is a need for better training in prenatal and postnatal care. Hospital-based midwives have also begun to lobby for better working conditions, and the creation of midwife-led units will make hospitals more attractive places to work.

IMPACT ON MIDWIFERY

The German case study shows a renaissance of independent midwifery amidst economic debates and changes in the health care system. It also suggests an important change in health care politics: Public and government support for midwifery care can be interpreted as an effort to reduce the medicalization of healthy people. As in the United Kingdom and Canada, midwives succeeded in reestablishing policy support for their status as primary caregivers at childbirth. After succeeding with this, midwives pursued more changes to establish independent midwifery as a viable career option.

These recent legislative changes cannot be attributed to pressure from a single group, but rather to a convergence of political, economic, and social forces. Although the midwifery associations took the lead, politicians who were ideologically committed to professional autonomy in the freemarket system also supported midwives. In several cases, personal experience with midwifery care and fatherhood prompted politicians and journalists to speak out in favor independent midwives. These political factors converged with the belt-tightening economic pressures of German reunification and a groundswell of public support to bring about legislative changes.

It is not easy to distinguish the role played by consumers. In 1980 consumers were challenging midwives, but during the next twenty years, many of them trained in midwifery, birth education, or health sciences, and their influence from these various positions cannot be underestimated. However, less than 5 percent of births are either at home or in a freestanding birth center.

The Obstetricians' Association strongly opposed midwifery reform (*Berufsverband* 1997), particularly with regard to payment for home birth, but it did not have enough political support to change the recent reforms. Real opposition may not be seen for a few years and could possibly be contingent on whether or not the total number of midwives increases and whether or not midwives resume an active role not only as birth room attendants and childbirth educators but as primary caregivers as well.

During this period, hospital birth has also changed. Fathers are now welcomed into delivery rooms, parents are encouraged to "bond" with their newborn soon after birth, and obstetrical wards have been remodeled to appear more "homey." Early discharge is also becoming the general rule, now that insurance companies pay German hospitals a fixed sum for each birth. Postpartum hospital stay declined from ten days in 1980 to six days in 1990 to three to five days in 1998 (NPExtra 1998, 2000). These cost-saving changes in hospital politics were made possible with an additional investment in outpatient care, most of which is given by midwives. Although doctors have warned that early discharge would lead to higher morbidity both in women and infants, their views were not taken into account. Midwives and consumer groups have welcomed early discharge, building up networks of postnatal care, including not only midwifery care but also household helpers, breastfeeding support, postnatal gymnastics, and baby groups. However, the number of independent midwives is still too small to completely meet the countrywide need for postpartum care. Of the approximately 14,000 German midwives, one-third are working independently, one-third work both in hospital and free practice, and one-third work only in a hospital (BDH 1997).

IMPACT ON INTERPROFESSIONAL BOUNDARIES

As in Canada and the Netherlands, the structure of the health care payment system supports midwives. Midwives are now paid by the sick funds for birth education, displacing the former lay activists who developed birth education and breastfeeding support. Thus, midwives have gained jurisdiction over childbirth, taking over work previously done by lay groups and doctors.

Midwives are well organized. Of the 14,000 practicing midwives, 12,000 are members in the German Midwives Association (BDH), and they welcome the increased range of opportunities to change from hospital to independent work, or do both part-time, depending on personal circumstances. There is little public critique of high intervention rates; cesarean section rates, for example, are about 19 percent (NPExtra 1998, 2000). Germans see "natural birth" as less important than "birth as an event," and many choose to go to a hospital that offers high-tech care in "homey" surroundings.

Maintaining a Lead Role in Maternity Care: Midwifery Care in the Netherlands

Midwifery practice in the Netherlands is often seen as a model for midwives in other countries (Van Teijlingen 2000). In our examination of the Dutch maternity care system we pay particular attention to the role of the state and of health insurance organizations in supporting a primary role for midwives and in attenuating the impact of occupational boundaries.

The Dutch system of maternity care is regarded as unique because of the high percentage of home births. In 1993, 31 percent of all babies in the Netherlands were born at home (CBS 1999). The union of a high number of home births and good outcomes is made possible by unique features of the Dutch system, including: its division into primary care—provided by autonomous midwives and (to a lesser extent) GPs—and secondary care—provided by obstetricians; the Dutch philosophy of maternity care; the existence of maternity home care assistants; the funding scheme administered by the Sick Funds; and political support for midwifery and home birth (De Vries 1996b; Van Daalen 1988).

PRIMARY AND SECONDARY OBSTETRIC CARE

The sharp and consistent division between primary and secondary obstetric care in the Netherlands is based on the principle that pregnancy and childbirth are essentially natural events that do not need to be medicalized. Different from other Western countries, primary obstetric care is provided not only by GPs but also on a large scale by independent midwives. Dutch midwives are qualified to provide obstetric care autonomously, and, like GPs, they are entitled to refer patients directly to obstetricians. Midwives are trained in recognizing early signs and symptoms of pathology, and they are competent to do minor obstetric interventions such as episiotomies. In their philosophy, the guidance of physiological pregnancy and birth requires a noninterventionist attitude that stimulates the confidence of the women in their own potential to give birth.

Secondary obstetric care is provided by, or under the responsibility of, an obstetrician. The Sick Funds, the insurance companies, remunerate obstetricians only when there is a medical indication for secondary obstetric care (Van Teijlingen & McCaffery 1987, p. 179). Consequently, primary care (midwife-led or GP-led) and secondary care (obstetrician-led) are distinguished by the type of the responsible caregiver, *not* by the place where the care is provided. Indeed, in most general hospitals it is possible for midwives and general practitioners to assume responsibility for deliveries.

A midwife will guide an expectant mother during her pregnancy, delivery, and postnatal period. In cases where a GP is obstetrically active (mostly in rural area), a woman may be attended by her own GP. Only when a medical indication for secondary obstetric care is present will she be referred to an obstetrician. In terms of risk selection, a woman at low risk may choose a "short-stay hospital" delivery or a home birth. For women at "intermediate" risk, a short-stay hospital birth is preferred.

Adequate obstetric risk selection is an essential condition for the effective operation and the division of labor between obstetricians and primary caregivers (midwives or GPs) in the Netherlands (Treffers 1993). Obstetric risk selection implies an interaction between a midwife (or GP) and an obstetrician. In the case of a straightforward transfer to an obstetrician, this interaction may be no more than providing medical information to the obstetrician. In less simple cases, the midwife or GP may wish to receive advice from an obstetrician on the necessity of primary versus secondary care. For such advice, the woman is sent to the obstetrician for a consultation. Alternatively, the obstetrician may be asked for advice without sending the woman in (referred to as a "deliberation"). In both situations (consultation and deliberation) there is an interaction between the primary caregiver (midwife or GP) and the obstetrician; ideally, their communication results in a shared decision on who will be responsible for further guidance of the woman.

STRATEGIES TO COUNTERACT THE TREND TOWARD SECONDARY OBSTETRIC CARE

For decades, it had been the government's policy to promote primary health care in general and, in the case of obstetric care, primary obstetric care and home births (Van Teijlingen 1990, pp. 360–361). As recent as December 1999 the Dutch Minister of Health, Welfare and Sport stated in parliament, "My policy is aimed at maintaining and, where possible, strengthening the home delivery." However, as noted in chapter 1, there has been a continuous decline in the percentage of home births: 53 percent in 1972, 44 percent in 1975, stabilizing at around 36 percent between 1978 and 1983, and decreasing to 31 percent in 1993 (Central Bureau of Statistics [CBS] 1999). Also, the percentage of women under specialist care has increased greatly, from 26 percent in 1971 to 46 percent in 1979. The presence of considerable regional variations (from 40 percent to 80 percent) suggests that many women are under specialist care without a proper obstetric indication (Working Group Revision Kloostermanlijst 1987). To counteract this trend, the Health Care Insurance Board issued referral guidelines in 1983, which aimed to regulate the referrals to obstetricians (Working Group Revision *Kloostermanlijst* 1987). The aim of the guidelines was to discourage medicalization of obstetric care and to promote home birth. The board included the national health insurance organizations through which more than 70 percent of Dutch citizens were insured. A committee was commissioned to revise the then current list of medical indications for secondary obstetric care, the Kloosterman List. This list classified conditions into two categories: low risk (primary care, that is, midwife-led or GP-led care) and high risk (secondary care, that is, obstetrician-led care) (Kloosterman 1985).

The committee presented a new list of indications, the so-called New Obstetric Indications List, which distinguished four areas of decision-making:

- What is the nature and the seriousness of the complication(s) with regard to the increased risks?
- What are the possibilities of preventing the occurrence of the complication(s)?

- What is the likelihood that any complication(s) that may occur will be promptly recognized?
- What are the possibilities of adequate intervention in the event of complication(s)?

With the help of these practical questions, referral policies were drawn up based on 124 detailed indications. Like the Kloosterman List, this list distinguished low and high risk, but the new list also introduced an intermediate category of risk. The introduction of this category was aimed at reducing the number of women transferred to obstetricians. An "intermediate risk" implied that the midwife (or GP) should consult an obstetrician who gives advice so that the midwife or GP could decide classification into low or high risk. In other cases, however, intermediate risk would remain intermediate. This was called a "medium-risk situation." In such a medium-risk situation the woman would be at slightly elevated risk of complications and would require a delivery in the hospital under the responsibility of a midwife or GP. It was necessary that an obstetrician had seen the woman beforehand and that (s)he had agreed that the delivery would take place in the hospital and that (s)he would be able to come in time if needed. The most frequent "medium risk" condition was maternal age (thirty-six years for first-time mothers and forty for others).

The New Obstetric Indications List was agreed upon by the Health Care Insurance Board and was issued to the insurance companies in 1987. The Dutch Organization of Midwives and the Association of Dutch Care Insurers (*Vereniging van Nederlandse Zorgverzekeraars,* VNZ) accepted the list as the basis of contracts between insurers and midwives. However, the majority of obstetricians rejected these guidelines, making appeals to safety (Riteco & Hingstman 1991) and women's choice. The Dutch Society of Obstetrics and Gynecology (1987) rejected the list on several grounds. Compared to the Kloosterman List, the new list gave more responsibility to the midwife and GP in caring for women with possible complications. The Dutch Society of Obstetrics and Gynecology rejected the competence of the midwife and the GP to decide on risk status and suggested that the most competent professional (the obstetrician) should be responsible for risk selection. The society also argued that a woman should have the freedom to choose the professional in whom she had the most confidence and that it was unacceptable to make the choice of primary care or secondary provider solely on the basis of risk factors. On medical-epidemiological grounds, it was also argued that the list underestimated the degree of risk for many single risk factors, and the society opposed the construction of the so-called "medium-risk situation" because the responsibilities of the midwife and the obstetrician would overlap. It argued that the responsibilities should be clearly divided. For example, a woman with a previous third-degree perineal tear—now allowed to stay with her midwife in consultation with the obstetrician—would, under the society's proposals, be attended by an obstetrician and, by definition, have a hospital delivery (Van Teijlingen & Bryar 1996, p. 26).

Finally, obstetricians argued that by aiming to strengthen primary care through enforcing regulations, the quality and safety of care would be affected. The society argued that over the period 1970–1984, the Netherlands had lost its excellent position in the ranking of perinatal mortality figures and that the trend of the Dutch perinatal mortality rates compared unfavorably with other countries. One of the suggested causes was the system of Dutch obstetric care with home birth and greater obstetric autonomy of Dutch midwives and GPs.

As a consequence of obstetricians' concerns about the perinatal mortality figures and the government's concerns that the obstetric risk selection could be negatively influenced by poor cooperation between midwives and obstetricians, an Advisory Committee on Obstetric Care was established by the State Secretary of Welfare, Health and Culture (*Adviescommissie Verloskunde* 1987). In its response to the recommendations of the advisory committee, the government summarized its long-term policy on maternity care:

- A midwife or a GP should care for a pregnant woman, unless there was a medical indication for obstetrician-led care.
- Home birth was regarded as the natural and preferable way of birth. For this system risk selection was considered to be essential, and for adequate risk selection the caregivers (midwife, GP, and obstetrician) should cooperate.
- Such cooperation had two aspects: cooperation in the care for an individual woman and an institutionalized form of cooperation.

The government response relativized concerns about the Dutch national perinatal mortality rates, arguing that the differences with other countries could be explained by differences in registration and prenatal screening policy. It regarded mortality as an increasingly inadequate measure of the outcome of obstetric care and considered morbidity to be a more suitable indicator. This view conflicted with the position of the Dutch Society of Obstetrics and Gynecology, a difference of opinion that has been a source of persisting disagreement and an obstacle to reaching consensus on policy measures.

The effect of the new list of indications was evaluated in one region (Van der Lugt et al. 1991). Compared to national data, there was less secondary care when using the list in the antenatal period, but this was counteracted by a higher rate of transfers during and after delivery. In view of the lack of consensus, the Health Care Insurance Board commissioned a new committee in 1994 to further develop referral guidelines for obstetric care (Health Care Insurance Board 1999). The committee (including representatives from GPs, midwives, and obstetricians) had hoped to develop evidence-based guidelines, but finding very little epidemiological research on populations of low-risk pregnant women, the guidelines were based on consensus and expert opinion. The new guidelines were finally accepted by all professional organizations and were issued in 1999 (Health Care Insurance Board 1999).

The guidelines continue to respect the professional responsibilities of midwives and GPs for normal pregnancy, delivery, and postnatal care. Midwives and GPs remain responsible for selecting women with certain risk indications. The new list eliminated the overlap of responsibilities between primary and secondary care, giving responsibility for the short-stay hospital delivery to the midwife or GP.

Agreement on an indications list is only the first step in improving relations among maternity care providers. The *Adviescommissie Verloskunde* (1987) also proposed local obstetric cooperation groups (OCGs) as a way to improve working relationships and to promote a shift from obstetrician-led care to midwife-led or GP-led care, resulting in more home and short-stay hospital births. An OCG is a local interprofessional group of maternity caregivers who work jointly to improve the quality of their care, and it may include midwives, GPs, obstetricians, pediatricians, hospital obstetric nurses, and maternity home care assistants (or their representatives). An evaluation of the OCGs showed that they did not eliminate competition between maternity care occupations. Indeed, midwives also reported feelings of competition among themselves. However, the evaluation established that conditions favorable to cooperation included mutual respect, trust, openness, regular meetings, and well-functioning channels of communication (De Veer & Meijer 1996).

IMPLICATIONS FOR OCCUPATIONAL BOUNDARIES

Obstetric risk selection defines the division of labor for maternity care in the Netherlands. As we have seen, effective obstetric guidelines must have the support of midwives, GPs, and obstetricians and their professional organizations. The Dutch experience shows that agreement on major issues can be reached only if the professional organizations of midwives, GPs, and obstetricians are on equal footing. It is interesting that in both the Netherlands and the United Kingdom obstetricians felt that they had not been sufficiently represented in the government's chief advisory committee. The Dutch obstetricians complained of being underrepresented in the working group for the revision of the Kloosterman List, and British obstetricians were upset that they were not (formally) represented in the expert maternity group (Walker 1995).

The role of the midwife in the Dutch maternity care system has been actively protected by the state. The state organization of the Sick Funds and its regulation of the practice of GPs and obstetricians carved out a niche for midwives. This state support has not gone unchallenged by obstetricians and GPs. Obstetricians believe midwifery is less safe than physician care, and GPs insist that midwives do not offer continuity of care. Nevertheless, midwives in the Netherlands feel secure in their professional status. Unlike midwives in Canada, the United Kingdom, and Germany, Dutch midwives have made no efforts to create a political alliance with consumer organizations. Of course this security is won at a price. Midwives in the Netherlands have very high caseloads and often feel undervalued for the work they do (Bakker et al. 1996).

Conclusion

In our comparison of the contemporary roles of maternal health professions in four countries we discovered four themes. First, the state plays a key role in legitimating and protecting jurisdictional claims of midwives. Second, in all four countries, supportive political players arose during important "windows of opportunity" in policymaking and implementation. Third, in the three countries where midwives were attempting to gain (or regain) independent practice, alliances with consumer groups were a critical factor. Fourth, in the struggle to maintain control over their practice, midwives emphasized community-based care and home birth.

IMPLICATIONS FOR MIDWIFERY WORK

In all four countries midwives use a model of practice that emphasizes independent caseload practice and continuity of care as benchmarks of their autonomy. This model of practice emphasizes the role of the midwife as the lead provider of maternity care and is a useful strategy for obtaining the status of an independent profession.

Midwifery organizations and pressure groups welcomed the policy changes in Canada, the United Kingdom, and Germany, all of which allowed midwives more occupational freedom. Midwives and clients alike assumed that occupational autonomy would translate into more "woman-centered care." However, we have seen that the ideas of "women-centered care" and "continuity of care" can result in the exploitation of midwives by their clients (Annandale & Clark 1996) and by the state (Mason 1995). These models of practice create the so-called "caring dilemma." Providing continuity of care is difficult for any occupation. It is even more difficult for a female-dominated occupation like midwifery because conflicts of interest arise between professional and domestic roles. In Canada and Germany, the rights of midwives as women workers have been addressed to a certain extent in order to provide a sustainable model of practice. In the United Kingdom, workers' rights have been a low priority, with the result that the rhetoric of continuity of care is not substantiated by the reality. Not surprisingly, U.K. midwives report disillusionment with new organizational changes and burnout (Sandall 1999). In the Netherlands a high workload and burnout exists among community midwives. Midwives claim that their reimbursement per case is too low, which forces them to have a too high workload, something which the government is only beginning to address.

Task substitution for medical work and taking on new skills may not result in the increase in status that midwives have hoped for. Skill is a gendered concept (Atkinson & Delamont 1990), and there is always the possibility that tasks performed by a female-dominated occupation will lose their status. Even though the occupational boundaries have been redrawn, the essential map is left unchallenged.

The professional projects of midwives in Germany, Britain, and Canada developed in response to the exclusion of midwives from the official health care system. Midwifery leaders hoped that with inclusion their services would be more accessible to a wider clientele and that they would secure protection from legal harassment. It is ironic, then, that in attempting to become integrated into the health care system, midwifery leaders often employed exclusionary strategies of their own. In Ontario, for example, it was decided that the success of the "integration project" required the exclusion of those who did not fit the midwives' model of care (i.e., those who did not have home birth experience or who did not want to attend home births). Such exclusionary measures, whether intentional or not, resulted in a large amount of work to be accomplished by a small number of practitioners. When midwifery was officially integrated in Ontario at the end of 1993, approximately sixty midwives had to staff a midwifery education program, set up a self-regulatory body *and* an association, secure hospital admitting privileges, create new practices, and negotiate funding contracts with the provincial ministry of health. Although there are now over 150 midwives practicing in the province, this is a very small group to manage a profession.

Current attempts to develop professional status are dependent on state mandate, funding, and political expediency (Declercq 1994, 1998). There is a danger that the independent caseload model—an ideology arising from a profession aiming to increase its autonomy and sphere of practice—may lead midwifery down a path of unsustainable practice. In creating new models for their profession, midwives must continually ask three questions: Does the new way of organizing care empower my profession? Does it allow me to live a fulfilling professional and personal life? Does it provide the best service to my clients?

Note

1. The data used here are drawn from participant observation conducted for more than four years by Schüecking, who served as a medical consultant to the German Midwives Association. Data are also drawn from documents on German midwifery written and collected by the Midwifery Research Group at the University of Osnabrück as well as from research comparing European systems of maternity care (Schüecking 1997).

References

Abbott. A. 1988. *The System of Professions: An Essay on the Division of Expert Labour.* Chicago: University of Chicago Press.

Adviescommissie Verloskunde. 1987. *Verloskundige organisatie in Nederland: uniek, bewonderd en verguisd.* (Obstetric Organization in the Netherlands: Unique, Admired and Abused). Rijswijk, the Netherlands: Ministry of Welfare, Health and Culture. (In Dutch.)

Annandale, E. C., and J. Clark. 1996. What is gender? Feminist theory and the sociology of human reproduction. *Sociology of Health and Illness* 18: 17–44.

Association of Radical Midwives. 1986. *The Vision—Proposals for the Future of the Maternity Services.* Ormskirk, Lancs: ARM.

Atkinson, P., and S. Delamont. 1990. Professions and powerlessness: Female marginality in the learned professions. *Sociological Review* 38: 90.

Bakker, H. C., Groenewegen, P. P., Jabaaij, L., Meijer, W. J., Sixma, H., and A. de Veer. 1996. "Burnout" among Dutch midwives. *Midwifery* 12: 174–181

Barrington, E. 1985. *Midwifery Is Catching.* Toronto: NC Press Limited.

Bartholomeycik, E. S. 1978. Die Entwicklung des Berufsstandes der Hebamme (Volkszählung 1970). (The development of the occupation of midwife [Census 1970]) *Bundesgesundheitsblatt* 21 (12 May): 145 ff. (In German.)

BDH. 1997. *Erhebung.* (Data.) Karlsruhe, Germany: BDH.

Benoit, C. 1991. *Midwives in Passage: A Case Study of Occupational Change.* St. John's, Newfoundland: ISER Press.

———. 1999. Midwifery and health policy: equity, workers rights and consumer choice in Canada and Sweden. In *Professional identities in transition, cross-cultural dimensions,* eds. I. Hellberg, M. Saks, and C. Benoit. Sodertalje, Sweden: Almquist and Wiksell International.

Berufsverband der Frauenärzte e. V., Deutsche Gesellschaft für Gynäkologie und Geburtshilfe e. V. 1997. Gemeinsames Statement. (Joint statement). *Der Frauenarzt* 38: 1401–1405. (In German.)

Bourgeault, I. L. 1996. *Delivering Midwifery: The Process and Outcome of the Incorporation of Midwifery in Ontario.* Unpublished Ph.D. thesis, Department of Community Health, University of Toronto, Toronto.

————. 2000. Delivering the "new" Canadian midwifery: The impact on midwifery of integration into the Ontario health care system. *Sociology of Health and Illness* 22: 172–196.

Bourgeault, I. L., and M. Fynes. 1997. Integrating lay and nurse-midwifery into the U.S. and Canadian health care systems. *Social Science and Medicine* 44: 1051–1063.

Buckley, S. 1979. Ladies or midwives: Efforts to reduce infant and maternal mortality. In *A Not Unreasonable Claim: Women and Reform in Canada, 1880s–1920s* ed. L. Kealey. Toronto: The Women's Press, pp. 131–149.

Campbell, R. 1999. Review and assessment of selection criteria used when booking pregnant women at different places of birth. British Journal of Obstetrics and Gynaecology 106: 550–556.

CBS. 1999. *Tijdreeksen Mens en maatschappij, Gezondheidszorg, zorg rond de geboorte* (People and society: Health care, care at birth). CBS StatWeb, web pages, http://argon2.cbs.nl/statweb/indexned.stm.

Connor, J. T. H. 1994. "Larger fish to catch here than midwives": Midwifery and the medical profession in nineteenth-century Ontario. In *Caring and Curing: Historical Perspectives on Women and Healing in Canada,* eds. D. Dodd and D. Gorham. Ottawa: University of Ottawa Press, pp. 103–134.

Daalen, R. van. 1988. Dutch obstetric care: Home or hospital, midwife or gynaecologist? *Health Promotion* 2: 247–255.

Declercq, E. R. 1994. A cross-national analysis of midwifery politics: Six lessons for midwives. *Midwifery* 10: 232–237.

————. 1998. *Changing Childbirth* in the United Kingdom: Lessons for U.S. health policy. *Journal of Health Politics, Policy and Law* 23: 833–859.

Department of Health. 1993. *Changing Childbirth, Part 1: Report of the Expert Maternity Group.* London: HMSO.

DeVries, R. 1993. A cross national view of the status of midwives In: *Gender, Work and Medicine: Women and the Medical Division of Labour,* eds. E. Riska and K. Wegar. London: Sage, pp. 131–146.

————. 1996a. *Making Midwives Legal, Childbirth, Medicine and the Law,* 2nd ed. Columbus: Ohio State University Press.

————. 1996b. The social and cultural context of birth: Lessons for health care reform from Dutch maternity care. *The Journal of Perinatal Education* 5: 25–30.

Dutch Society of Obstetrics and Gynaecology. 1997. *Commentaar op het eindrapport van de werkgroep bijstelling Kloostermanlijst.* (Commentary on the Final Report of the Committee Changing the Kloosterman List.) Utrecht: Dutch Society of Obstetrics and Gynaecology. (In Dutch.)

Enkin, M., Keirse, M. J. N. C., Renfew, M., and J. Neilson. 1995. *A Guide to Effective Care in Pregnancy and Childbirth.* Oxford: Oxford University Press.

Health Care Insurance Board. 1999. *Lijst van Verloskundige Indicaties.* (List of Obstetric Indications.) Amstelveen: College voor Zorgverzekeringen. (In Dutch.)

Health Committee. 1992. *Maternity Services Second Report,* Vol. 1 *Winterton Report* London: HMSO.

Johnson, T. J. 1972. *Professions and Power.* London: Macmillan.

Kloosterman, G. J. (ed.) 1985. *Medische indicaties voor specialistische behandeling.* (Medical Indications for Specialist Care. *De voortplanting van de mens.* (Human reproduction.) Weesp, the Netherlands: Center. (In Dutch.)

Kornelson, J., and E. Carty. Forthcoming. Interprofessional relations in midwifery in British Columbia. In *Reconceiving Midwifery: The New Canadian Model of Care,* eds. I. L. Bourgeault, C. Benoit, and R. Davis-Floyd. Ann Arbor: University of Michigan Press.

Larkin, G. 1983. *Occupational Monopoly and Modern Medicine.* London: Tavistock.

Larson, M. S. 1977. *The Rise of Professionalisation.* Berkeley: University of California Press.

Lugt, B. J. A. M. van der, Remmink, A. J., Canten, J., Elferink, W., and M. Kempers. 1991. Enkele verloskundige resultaten bij selectie volgens de nieuwe medische indicatielijst. (Some obstetric results of selection by applying the new medical list of indications.) *Nederlands Tijdschrift voor Obstetrie en Gynaecologie* 104: 54–58. (In Dutch.)

Mason, J. 1988. Midwifery in Canada. In *The Midwife Challenge,* London: Pandora, pp. 99–133.

———. 1995. Governing childbirth: The wider view. *Journal of Advanced Nursing* 22: 835–840.

McKay, S. 1993. Models of midwifery care: Denmark, Sweden and the Netherlands. *Journal of Nurse-Midwifery* 38: 114–120.

MDK-Info. 1997. *Eckpunkte aus der Sicht der Medizinischen Dienste.* (Key Points from the Point of View of Medical Services.) Essen: AOK Bundersverband (German Health Insurance Organizations). (In German.)

HebG. 1985. *Gesetz über den Beruf der Hebamme und des Entbindungspflegers (Hebammengesetz-HebG).* (Act regarding the occupation of midwifery and maternity nurses.) *BGBL* 1: 902. (In German.)

NPExtra. 1998. *Niedersächsische und Bremer Perinatal- und Neonatalerhebung.* (Lower-Saxon and Bremer perinatal and neonatal data.) Hanover: Ärztekammer Niedersachen (Regional Doctors' Association in Lower Saxony). (In German.)

NPExtra. 2000. *Niedersächsische und Bremer Perinatal- und Neonatalerhebung.* (Lower-Saxon and Bremer perinatal and neonatal data.) Hanover: Ärztekammer Niedersachen (Regional Doctors' Association in Lower Saxony). (In German.)

RCM (Royal College Midwives.) 1987. *Report of the Royal College of Midwives on the Role and Education of the Future Midwife in the United Kingdom.* London: RCM.

Riteco, J. A. and L. Hingstman. 1991. *Evaluatie invoering 'verloskundige indicatielijst'.* (Evaluation of the Implementation of the Obstetric List of Indications) Utrecht: Netherlands institute of primary health care (NIVEL). (In Dutch.)

Robinson, S., Golden, J., and S. Bradley. 1983. *A Study of the Role and Responsibilities of the Midwife* (NERU Report 1). London: University of London, Kings College.

Rushing, B. 1991. Market explanations for occupational power: The decline of midwifery in Canada. *American Review of Canadian Studies* (Spring): 7–27.

Sandall, J. 1995. Choice, continuity and control: Changing midwifery, towards a sociological perspective. *Midwifery* 11: 201–209.

———. 1997. Midwives' burnout and continuity of care. *British Journal of Midwifery* 5: 106–111.

———. 1998. Midwifery work, family life and wellbeing: A study of occupational change. Unpublished Ph.D. thesis, Department of Sociology, University of Surrey, Guildford.

———. 1999. Team midwifery and burnout in midwives in the UK: Practical lessons from a national study *MIDIRS Midwifery Digest* 9: 147–151.

Schüecking, B. 1997. Ein Schluessel zur Frauengesundheit: Hebammenbetreuung in acht europäischen Ländern. (A key to women's health: Midwifery care in eight European countries.) In *Frauen und Gesundheit: Ethnomedizinische Perspektiven* (Women and Health: Ethnomedical Perspectives), eds. C. Gottschalk-Batschkus and J. Schuler. Berlin: VWB-Verlag, pp. 193–198. (In German.)

Teijlingen, E. R. van. 1990. The profession of maternity home care assistant and its significance for the Dutch midwifery profession. *International Journal of Nursing Studies* 27: 355–366.

———. 2000. Maternity home care assistants in the Netherlands. In *Midwifery and the Medicalization of Childbirth: Comparative Perspectives,* eds. E. van Teijlingen, G. Lowis, P. McCaffery, and M. Porter. New York: Nova Science, pp. 163–171.

Teijlingen, E. van, and R. Bryar. 1996. Selection guidelines for place of birth. *Modern Midwife* 6: 24–27.

Teijlingen, E. van, and P. McCaffery P. 1987. The profession of midwife in the Netherlands. *Midwifery* 3: 178–86

Treffers, P. E. 1993. Selection as the basis of obstetric care in the Netherlands. In *Successful Home Birth and Midwifery. The Dutch Model,* ed. E. Abraham van de Mark. Westport, CT: Bergin and Garvey, pp. 97–114.

Trombik, E. 1985. Die Hebammen 1885–1985 (Midwives 1885–1985) *DHZ* 37: 174 ff.

UKCC. 1986. *Project 2000: A New Preparation for Practice.* London: UKCC.

Vadeboncoeur, H. (forthcoming). The legalization of midwifery in Quebec: A detour through experimentation. In *Reconceiving Midwifery: The New Canadian Model of Care,* eds. I. Bourgeault, C. Benoit, and R. Davis-Floyd. Ann Arbor: University of Michigan Press.

Veer, A. J. E. de, and W. J. Meijer. 1996. Obstetric care: Competition or co-operation. *Midwifery* 12: 14–20.

Walker, P. 1995. Should obstetricians see women with normal pregnancies? Obstetricians should be included in integrated team care. *British Medical Journal* 310: 36–37.

Working Group Revision of Obstetric Indications List (Werkgroep Bijstelling Kloostermanlijst). 1987. *Verloskundige Indicatielijst* (List of Obstetric Indications.) Amstelveen, the Netherlands: Ziekenfondsraad. (In Dutch.)

Zindars, K., and K. Sauer. 1955. *Hebammengesetz vom 21. 12. 1938 mit Erläuterungen und Anhang.* (Midwifery Act of 21-12-1938 with Comments and Appendix, 3rd ed.) Hannover: Staude-Verlag.

CHAPTER 7

Designing Midwives

A COMPARISON OF EDUCATIONAL MODELS

Cecilia Benoit, Robbie Davis-Floyd, Edwin R. van Teijlingen, Jane Sandall, and Janneli F. Miller

Introduction: Education and Socialization

How should aspiring midwives be prepared for their role as caregivers? What do midwives need to know? Who should teach them? Where should the education of midwives take place? There are no easy answers to these questions. All educational models have strengths and weaknesses. In the following pages we offer a cross-cultural comparison of the preparation of midwives that shows how educational programs are created and how different programs shape the way midwives practice.[1]

Becoming a midwife requires both *education* and *socialization*: In our analysis we examine both processes. We use the term "education" to refer to the formal requirements and organization of the midwife training program. We use the term "socialization" to signify the informal process—or "hidden curriculum" (Illich 1973)—by which a midwife acquires the "shared culture" of midwifery—its values, beliefs, attitudes, behavior patterns, and social identity. Our comparative study uncovers the many ways the wider sociocultural context shapes both educational programs and socialization processes: By looking at midwifery education in several different settings we see how the preparation of midwives is influenced by medical and technological advances, new pedagogical ideas, gender relations, state policies, and economic and cultural change.

We begin our analysis by distinguishing two transnational trends and describing the three basic models of midwifery education that serve as our analytical frame. To illustrate how these trends and models of care are influencing the education of midwives, we examine the state of the art in midwife preparation in four countries: the United States, the Netherlands, Canada, and the United Kingdom.

Transnational Trends and Types

When we look at midwifery education in the high-income countries of Western Europe and North America, we find two important trends: a move toward university education and the development of direct entry programs.

A TREND TOWARD HIGHER EDUCATION

In Western technocratic societies professional status and success requires ever-higher levels of education. This trend is influencing midwifery education. In the United Kingdom, for example, midwifery training was purely vocational until the late 1980s. Midwives were educated at small schools in National Health Service (NHS), hospitals with clinical teaching carried out in hospitals and the community. U.K. midwives now train in universities. In the United States, nurse-midwives succeeded in moving midwifery education to the postgraduate level by requiring an undergraduate degree as a prerequisite for entry into their educational programs.[2] There are a few exceptions to this trend. Midwives in the Netherlands resisted the trend toward university education, deliberately choosing to retain their vocational style of training, and in the United States, non-nurse midwives are preserving stand-alone apprenticeship as a viable educational path. Canadian midwives, struggling with the tension between their heritage of independent apprenticeship and strong cultural pressure to require a university degree, accepted university education at the undergraduate level but stopped short of following their American nurse-midwife colleagues into the postgraduate realm.

A TREND TOWARD "DIRECT-ENTRY" MIDWIFERY EDUCATION

Increasing numbers of midwives—from Canada to Australia—are questioning the need to be trained as a nurse in order to practice as a midwife. They believe that nursing education supports a structural subordination to physicians and leads to a lack of decision-making power. In many of the countries where midwifery is closely linked to nursing we find movements that seek to dissociate midwifery from nursing and to increase the autonomy of midwives. In the United Kingdom, for example, decades of emphasis on nurse-midwifery have given way to a revival of interest in direct-entry education and enrollment into direct-entry programs is on the rise. In the United States, nurse-midwives, solidly grounded in nursing for the past seventy years, have created a new direct-entry educational track. The newly established form of midwifery in Ontario, Canada, resulted from an early alliance between nurse-midwives and direct-entry midwives that included agreement that nursing would not be a requirement. Midwives in the Netherlands and the home birth midwives in the United States are proud that their educational models have never mixed nursing and midwifery. It is no accident that high degrees of autonomy characterize Dutch and Canadian midwives and American home birth midwives, all of whom are direct-entry, while British midwives (most of whom are also nurses) and American nurse-midwives often chafe against NHS and nursing hierarchies that subordinate them to physicians.[3]

It is important to understand that the term "direct-entry" is used in different ways in different countries. In the United Kingdom, Canada, and the Netherlands, as in most European countries, "direct-entry midwifery" means that one graduates from a formal, government-accredited training program that educates students as midwives without requiring them to gain a nursing qualification. In the United States the situation is more complex. As independent (i.e., non-nurse) midwives in the United States began to refine their knowledge and skills they developed state and national certification programs. In the early 1990s they began to call themselves "direct-entry" midwives, a term they adapted to mean that one enters directly into *any type* of midwifery education—including apprenticeship, vocational, and university-based programs—without first passing through nursing. When the American College of Nurse-Midwives (ACNM) developed its non-nursing certification, its members also began to use the term "direct-entry." In ACNM parlance the term means preparation through an *ACNM-accredited* program that does not require nursing as a prerequisite. The common feature that unites these varied definitions is agreement that nursing instruction is not a requirement for entry into midwifery education; it is in that broad sense that we use the term "direct-entry" in this chapter.

EDUCATIONAL MODELS

There is great variety in the educational programs for midwives in the countries of Western Europe and North America. To analyze that variety we have created a continuum that describes the possibilities for midwife education: This continuum ranges from hands-on apprenticeship through vocational training to university-based education. As with all typologies, these categories—apprenticeship, vocational, and academic—represent ideal types; programs in the countries we examine combine elements of all three models in ways that are unique to the existing social and cultural situation. This variation, coupled with a fascinating mix of reactions to the trends toward direct-entry and university education, offer rich ground for comparison and analysis.

In the sections that follow we explore these three educational models. Each section opens with a fictional story that provides a window into the experience of a midwife trained according to the tenets of that model. We then describe the model's characteristics, consider its advantages and disadvantages, and offer a detailed case study of its use in one country. We conclude each section with a short summary of the variations of the educational model found in other countries.

Apprenticeship

Imagine being in the shoes—or the wooden clogs—of Annika, a peasant girl growing up in a rural farming community in continental Europe three centuries ago. Annika is fifteen years old. She cannot read or write, but this is not uncommon; only a few of the adults in the village have the ability to decipher more than the odd word or two of written text. Although at the time there are a few schools in urban areas of the continent, these are completely removed from Annika's experience. She knows no one well who has attended school, save the local clergyman. Yet already for the past eight or nine years, Annika has been "at work," spending a part of her time accompanying the local midwife while she attends to the concerns of pregnant women in the community. Recently, Annika had the opportunity to actually take over for the midwife, who looked on as Annika assisted a local woman through her labor and delivery. Annika hopes to eventually become a full-fledged midwife after her teacher retires.

Annika has never left the area in which she was born, and in fact has spent most of her life within her village and its surrounding fields, only occasionally, during times of religious celebrations or weddings or funerals, traveling to other local villages and nearby craft towns. Annika will eventually marry a local peasant boy and, like the other women in her community, bear the children who will help plant and till the fields that are the main breadbasket for the villagers. Her younger brothers and sisters will do likewise, and thus continue with the cycle of peasant agriculture like their ancestors before them. And like the ancestors that preceded her in midwifery, Annika will serve the women of her community, supporting them through the pains of labor and guiding them as they give birth.

HISTORY AND CHARACTERISTICS OF APPRENTICESHIP

Although Annika is "uneducated," she is far from ignorant. At the age of fifteen, Annika has already developed a sensitive and deep understanding of family and kinship arrangements in her village, she is aware of the health status of most of the women, and she has observed a number of births in women's homes. Annika has a mastery of local customs and traditions, which will serve her well as she prepares for her role as village midwife.

Annika is an imaginary figure, a composite and somewhat romanticized picture of a typical peasant girl growing into adulthood in premodern Europe. Formal education of midwives is a relatively recent development, beginning with the development of written language and the city-states of ancient civilizations. Historically, there was but one type of knowledge transmitted to neophyte midwives—"lay" knowledge or "lifeworld" knowledge that was gained by watching an experienced midwife at work, and eventually by the trainee doing more and more of the work herself (Benoit 1989).

Apprenticeship learning is full-bodied and experiential, involving the senses (Davis-Floyd 1998a, b). In apprenticeship systems, even watching is participatory; the apprentice never simply observes. Rather, she is almost always involved in some way, carrying water, providing clean cloths, preparing food, or massaging the mother. This method of learning fits well with the demands of the job: The apprentice learns in the sorts of environments in which she will practice. Traditionally, midwives were also expected to acquire a body of cultural-religious knowledge, which included how to deal with such things as death in childbirth and how to dispose of the afterbirth. In acquiring this cultural-religious knowledge and the practical techniques needed to be a midwife, a young woman came to learn the shared values, codes of behavior, and common mores of those in her "lifeworld" (Böhme 1984).

Although superseded by more didactic vocational and university-based models in high-income countries, apprenticeship is still part of the curriculum. Like medical training, institutionally based education for midwives retains aspects of apprenticeship in the form of clinical training under preceptors. Hands-on, one-on-one interactions with preceptors reminiscent of apprenticeship characterize midwives' training in all high-income countries. Of course there are important differences between pure apprenticeship and clinical preceptorship. The most significant of these is the particularly close and intense quality of the student-mentor relationship in a pure apprenticeship model.

CASE STUDY: APPRENTICESHIP TRAINING IN THE UNITED STATES

History and Current Status

The United States is unique among developed countries in that all types of midwifery education exist there. The continued use of apprenticeship can be traced to the rise of American lay midwifery during the 1970s and 1980s. The pioneers of this social movement—including internationally known midwives Raven Lang, Ina May Gaskin, and Elizabeth Davis—learned about birth by attending the births of friends, reading books, and apprenticing with other midwives, nurses, or, on occasion, physicians. In time they developed a unique body of knowledge that reflected their lived experience of home birth. They created a sophisticated system of apprenticeship to preserve the knowledge they had gained and to avoid being incorporated into universities or subsumed into nurse-midwifery. The earliest midwives were self-taught, but as their knowledge base grew, they began to train others.

As these lay midwives gained licensure and regulation in various states, they developed a number of formal programs, including vocational schools. Eventually they dropped the appellation "lay" in favor of the more professional "direct-entry." But even as they professionalized, apprenticeship remained central to their sense of identity as autonomous and independent out-of-hospital practitioners. In 1982 they founded the Midwives' Alliance of North America (MANA), an organization that primarily represents direct-entry midwives who practice outside of hospitals. Throughout the 1980s MANA members developed standards for practice and core competencies to guide midwife training. In the early 1990s the North American Registry of Midwives (NARM)—an affiliate of MANA—developed a new national certification, the certified professional midwife (CPM); to date over 600 direct-entry midwives have obtained CPM certification.[4] The CPM is a competency-based credential—it is based on educational evaluation and testing of applicants to make sure they have the knowledge, skills, and experience deemed necessary by NARM for safe entry-level practice—and does not require a university degree. A primary motivator for the development of this credential was a desire among MANA members to legitimize apprenticeship through creating a mechanism for evaluating the knowledge, skills, and experience of the apprentice-trained midwife.

The apprenticeship training that produces many of today's independent direct-entry midwives takes various creative and original forms; fundamentally, it involves attending births with one or more practicing midwives, assisting them in myriad ways, and observing the way they interact with and care for pregnant, laboring, and postpartum women. Apprentices also watch and help with emergencies, discussing every detail of care. The experienced midwife and apprentice develop an intimate relationship that facilitates rapid learning within a context of trust. Countless hours are spent together as they perform prenatal and postpartum exams, attend home births, and manage the routine maintenance of equipment and clinic space. This often involves both mundane and essential tasks such as cooking, cleaning, childcare, public relations, pelvic exams, labor support, chart review, and attending workshops and conferences together. Through this contact the midwife and apprentice come to develop a deeply bonded relationship that many see as essential to successful midwifery education. All published descriptions of midwifery apprenticeship stress the importance of this relationship; two even contain sections on what to do when the relationship is not "working" as it should (Davis 1997; Steiger 1989). The average duration of such apprenticeships is around three years.

Strengths and Limitations of American Apprenticeship Training

The deep commitment of American direct-entry midwives to apprenticeship comes from two basic beliefs: (1) A fear of birth generates complications, and (2) midwives who trust birth profoundly can help women give birth more effectively. The argument used in favor of apprenticeship training is that "to trust a woman to give birth is to help her trust herself." Most of the time birth goes well and requires no intervention; thus, apprentice-trained midwives are, for the most part, exposed to women working hard and successfully giving birth. Although they have opportunities to experience pathology and emergency management over the course of their apprenticeship training, these form the periodic punctuation, not the defining ethos, of their clinical experience (Davis-Floyd 1998a). Apprentice-trained midwives develop a strong faith in themselves, in the inherent trustworthiness of the birth process, and in a woman's ability to give birth on her own. Their training gives them experience with the wide range of "normal" birth outside of hospitals. Apprentice midwives often include a stint in a high-volume midwifery service as part of their training. Here they encounter many complications, but this exposure takes place against an already-established background of trust in the power of women and in the normal process of birth.

There are additional benefits of apprenticeship training. Apprentice learning is financially and geographically accessible, allowing women to become competent practitioners even if they do not have the money or the mobility to attend a private school or university. Apprenticeship learning is connection-based. When an apprentice is at a birth where the woman hemorrhages, she will spend the next day studying every book she can find on postpartum hemorrhage and will quiz her mentor about its management. She knows, in an immediate and visceral sense, why this knowledge matters.

According to MANA midwives, "pure apprenticeship" is a long-term (usually three-year) learning process involving one teacher and one student with a focus on out-of-hospital birth. This is sometimes difficult to manage. Indeed, one of the limitations of pure apprenticeship is the relatively small number of experienced midwives available to serve as mentors.[5] More than other educational models, successful apprenticeship is tied to the motivation of the learner, the abilities of the teacher, and the quality of their relationship. If mentor and apprentice do not communicate well, if the student is unmotivated, or if the mentor is deficient in knowledge, clinical judgment, skills, or the ability to interact with clients, the student suffers. Other limitations of pure apprenticeship include the absence of in-hospital training and infrequent exposure to birth complications, which can be rare for midwives who learn purely through low-volume home birth practice.

Because of its special combination of intimacy and efficacy there is a growing trend in adult education toward revaluing apprenticeship as a viable educational style for the twenty-first century, although in a technocracy apprenticeship training alone is not recognized as a valid educational route to professional practice.[6]

The Convergence of Didactic and Experiential Models

In the United States, apprenticeship training in its pure form is increasingly rare. Today many apprentices work with more than one mentor to ensure that they have exposure to more than one style of practice. After two to three years of one-on-one apprenticeship, many students complete their training by working in high-volume clinics in the United States or in a low-income country where they can be exposed to the complications of birth and can learn to deal with them effectively.[7] Many direct-entry educators are combining apprenticeships with more didactic models, and mentors are creating semistructured curricula to make sure their students meet the standards set by NARM. These curricula include independent reading, weekly classes taught by midwives in their communities, and, in some cases, college courses in the basic sciences. This syncretistic trend reflects a growing convergence between apprenticeship models and more formal didactic models.[8]

Apprenticeship as an Educational Component in the Netherlands and Canada

Apprenticeship continues to play an essential role in midwifery education in many countries. The vocational training of Dutch midwives contains a large apprenticeship component—approximately half of the total learning experience in the curriculum. Most of this time is spent with practicing community midwives who have received training in being a midwifery mentor. Apprenticeships foster the education of Dutch midwives in three ways: (1) They make it possible for students to practice the technical aspects of obstetric/midwifery procedures, (2) they give them a means to put their acquired theoretical information into practice, and (3) they build students' insight and help them gain practical experience.

In Canada, many of the newly registered midwives were educated in one-on-one apprenticeships; in some cases they supplemented their training with formal lectures and/or preceptorships outside the country. In Ontario an altered form of preceptorship forms a part of the university education program, and in remote parts of Canada apprenticeship plays a role in midwife training (see Daviss 1997; Morewood-Northrop 1997; O'Neil and Kaufert 1990).

Vocational Training

Lou-Anne was born in a small outport community on the southwest coast of Newfoundland (Canada). Although now retired from midwifery practice, Lou-Anne still has vivid memories of her vocational training and subsequent practice in the local cottage hospital serving the people of her own and neighboring communities. In the 1980s, the provincial highway connected Lou-Anne's community to the larger urban areas, and the new regional hospitals located there led to the demise of the cottage hospital system, and eventually the vocational style of training midwives as well.

However, prior to these developments of modernization, Lou-Anne and her co-workers literally "ran the show" on the cottage hospital maternity ward and were held in high esteem by the local birthing women and their families.

Lou-Anne stresses that she is a trained midwife; in her view acquisition of skills via practical experience and specialized formal knowledge achieved through a vocational program are both essential for qualified midwifery practice. Lou-Anne also stresses that her formal qualifications and practical experience have given her a government license and access to public employment, granting her a kind of occupational status and economic security not enjoyed by her predecessors. Lou-Anne states, "The more I found out about maternity work, the more I wanted to become educated in it." Her vocational midwifery training included formal lectures, technical training on the use of obstetrical instruments, and extensive clinical experience both on the hospital's maternity ward and in women's homes. As Lou-Anne explains, "What I didn't learn from the midwifery training, I could learn on the cottage hospital ward because we had to do these things, emergency things as well as the practical delivery of babies." Today Lou-Anne's workplace, the cottage hospital, is confined to the northern areas of the province, and the vocational style of training midwives for practice in Canada has completely disappeared.[9]

HISTORY AND CHARACTERISTICS OF VOCATIONAL TRAINING

As high-income countries began to industrialize, a new form of "vocational" midwifery education emerged. This new approach required students to read about obstetrics and attend lectures given by obstetricians and senior midwives. The lectures took place in formal settings—cottage hospitals, birthing centers, and, later, larger hospitals where student midwives could observe women during labor and delivery. At first, these formal midwifery training programs ran for only a number of weeks, but they were gradually extended as the twentieth century unfolded (Benoit 1991; Carter & Duriez 1986). Didactic learning in the classroom was complemented with hospital observation and practical experience with birthing mothers, many of whom were poor women without adequate living conditions for home birth. Apprenticeship was not absent from the vocational model. Midwives in vocational training continued to learn much of their art and science by actually doing midwifery, observing and assisting the senior midwives in a variety of locations.

STRENGTHS AND LIMITATIONS OF VOCATIONAL TRAINING

Vocational programs focus exclusively on the occupation they are designed to teach, offering a balance of practical skills and theoretical knowledge oriented toward real-world application. Vocational training mixes experiential and didactic educational methods and concentrates on preparing students for the practical requirements of their jobs. Vocational curricula are formalized; to ensure the production of midwives of a measurable and uniform minimum standard, these curricula are evaluated for content and quality by an outside body. This system assures employers and clients that a midwife has knowledge of physiology, biology, psychology, and specified midwifery skills. Unlike apprenticeship, the quality of the learning is not based solely on the abilities of one or a limited number of mentors.

Generally speaking, vocational training in high-income countries carries less social status than does university education.[10] In countries where midwifery education is moving (or has moved) to universities, vocationally trained midwives often suffer from the stereotype of the "second-class citizen." Some have criticized vocational training in the United Kingdom for paying more attention to the organizational need for cheap labor than to the educational and developmental needs of the student midwives. These criticisms and the desire of midwives for more autonomy have been a driving force for moving midwifery education into higher education in the United Kingdom.

CASE STUDY: VOCATIONAL TRAINING IN THE NETHERLANDS

History and Current Status

In the Netherlands midwifery education is highly centralized. The annual intake of student midwives at the three Colleges of Midwifery is deliberately limited to guarantee every trained midwife a job (van Teijlingen 1994, p. 146). In the late 1990s approximately 1,000 applicants applied for the combined 120 openings for first-year students (Rooks 1997, p. 14). Five years of secondary schooling are required for entry to midwifery school. A university degree is not required, nor is nursing training (McKay 1993). In fact, having a nursing background on one's application form is seen as a disadvantage for entry into midwifery. Until recently, the training program took three years. In 1994, a fourth year was added. Dutch midwives are trained to provide antenatal and postnatal care, to attend normal low-risk deliveries in home and hospital settings, and to identify high-risk women during all stages of pregnancy and childbirth.

Obstetricians served as directors of the three midwifery schools until the early 1990s; today the directors of all three schools are midwives. The midwifery schools were established in the late nineteenth and early twentieth century and are regulated and accredited by Acts of Parliament. There is a Midwifery Schools Act and a separate Act Governing Midwifery Examinations (Committee for the Revision of the Curriculum of Midwifery Schools in the Netherlands 1991, p. 1). All three schools are state-funded through the Ministry of Welfare, Health and Sport. A supervisory agency of the Ministry of Welfare, Health and Sport oversees the educational institutions and ensures that they comply with the regulations. In this capacity, the Supervisory Agency maintains the quality of education and can issue warnings if necessary (Committee for the Revision of the Curriculum of Midwifery Schools in the Netherlands 1991, p. 16). Midwifery students spend about half of their education as an apprentice with a qualified midwife. The rest of their education consists of classroom, bedside, and theater teaching.

The first-year curriculum focuses on the normal physiological course of pregnancy, delivery, and postpartum period. In the second year, the focus shifts to obstetric pathology and related fields. In the third and fourth year students work on integrating the theoretical and practical knowledge acquired in the previous two years. In addition, student midwives learn how to conduct scientific research (including a course in statistics), how to run a midwifery practice, and how to determine primary obstetric management. The curriculum stresses the importance of skills training, in the form of (1) diagnostic skills, (2) therapeutic skills, (3) skills needed to manage pregnancies, (4) laboratory skills, and (5) social skills.

Midwifery students are socialized into the norms and values of Dutch professionals in general and those of midwives in particular. The latter consist of principles and tenets such as "labor and birth are normal physiologic processes"; "home is a safe place to have a baby"; "midwifery is a psycho-social as well as medical service"; "selection of high-risk mothers and babies is usually possible during pregnancy, labor and in the post-partum period"; and "midwives are bound to know more about normal pregnancy and delivery than doctors because the latter spend so much time learning about pathology."

Recent Developments in Dutch Vocational Training

The transnational trend toward higher education is being felt in the Netherlands, where some have called for moving midwifery education into the university. But there are no signs of this happening in the near future, in large part because both the state and Dutch midwives have very consciously resisted this trend. Midwives feel strongly that their vocational model works to preserve midwifery as separate, woman-centered, and unique. They do not want their profession "polluted" or "compromised" by being moved to the university and mixed with other health professions or sciences. They have, however, worked to create streamlined mechanisms through which midwives who want college degrees can easily obtain them.

Some see the recent European Union (EU) directives—the EU has mandated that midwife training in all member nations must be comparable, facilitating mobility of midwives between countries—as a threat to the Dutch midwifery profession. However, there is no evidence that midwives trained in other EU countries will establish practice in the Netherlands. One of the main obstacles for those who wish to practice midwifery in the Netherlands is the requirement that midwives speak Dutch to be able to communicate with pregnant women. The Dutch language is not widely spoken, and there are few places where it is taught.

Vocational Training in the United Kingdom, the United States, and Canada

Vocational training remained an important part of British midwifery education until the early 1990s. The London Obstetrical Society introduced the first formal training course and diploma for midwives in 1872. The Midwives' Institute campaigned throughout the latter period of the nineteenth century for state registration and formal education (Sandall 1996). The result was the 1902 Midwives' Act. All "bona fide" practicing midwives were permitted to receive state registration, and all new midwives were required to undertake formal vocational training. Interestingly, the length of the course did not seem to have been based on educational principles, but rather on financial requirements. A "three month course, it was thought, was all that many women would be able to afford" (Carter & Duriez 1986, p. 48).

Twentieth-century midwifery education in the United Kingdom continued to be driven by pragmatism. Until 1916, there was a single pathway into midwifery for nurses and non-nurses. Gradually midwifery training increased in length. By 1938 it took two years to become a midwife, and it was not until the passage of the Midwives' Act of 1936 that "unqualified" women were forbidden from attending women in childbirth, and only then once a qualified midwife was locally posted.

With the introduction of the National Health Service (NHS) in 1948 there was a shift away from direct-entry and toward nursing-entry. The midwifery curriculum was changed to reflect the changing nature of practice: The self-employed midwife working in the community was giving way to the salaried midwife working in both the hospital and the community. Many nurses studied midwifery solely to achieve promotion to a higher salary level within nursing and never actually practiced as midwives. Indeed, promotion prospects for midwives were always poorer for those without a nursing qualification. By the early 1960s, only 5 percent of student midwives passed through the direct-entry route, and many direct-entry programs were phased out. By 1985, only one direct-entry program remained active (Radford & Thompson 1988).[11]

Vocational midwifery training for registered general nurses was twelve months until 1981. In that year the training period was increased to eighteen months (three years for non-nurses) in response to European Community midwifery directives (Robinson 1991, p. 304). The extra six months were to be "used to develop clinical skills and to give opportunities for the midwife to become confident" (Stewart 1981). In these vocational programs, students spent 50 percent of their time in clinical practice (half community and half hospital) and 50 percent in school.

In recent years, midwives and those hoping to expand the autonomy of midwifery have criticized vocational midwifery training in NHS schools (Sandall 1996). They saw the educational needs of student midwives being sacrificed to the need of the NHS for cheap student labor, and they complained that educational programs were too nursing-oriented and socialized student midwives to accept subordination to the medical model and to the requirements of a medically dominated, hierarchical NHS. Both midwifery educators and students were dissatisfied with current educational preparation. They felt they were not preparing midwives for the kind of independent autonomous practice being advocated in U.K. maternity policy initiatives (House of Commons 1992). British vocational training was also criticized for discouraging critical enquiry in favor of an emphasis on following standing orders, for a lack of awareness of the increasing evidence on midwifery practice, and for its disdain for the contribution of other disciplines to midwifery education (Flint 1990; RCM 1987).

In the United States, vocational midwifery training, like apprenticeship, is being developed and preserved only by direct-entry midwives. Some nurse-midwifery educators, stressing the value of university-affiliated programs, dismiss vocational programs as "trade schools" that represent an outdated educational model. Nevertheless, for American direct-entry midwives vocational programs are proving to be viable means of expanding educational opportunities beyond the numerical limitations of one-on-one apprenticeship while still preserving their unique body of knowledge about out-of-hospital pregnancy and birth. Because such schools are usually private and not university-affiliated, their owners and teachers can codify and teach this body of midwifery knowledge free of the "hegemonic influence of technomedicine." They can offer highly tailored, focused, and formalized combinations of apprenticeship and didactic training that meet established standards without sacrificing their philosophy. Unlike vocational programs in the United Kingdom, these U.S. vocational schools put great emphasis on the development of a sense of autonomy and of critical thinking and decision-making skills. They usually offer clinical training and courses in women's studies, midwifery philosophy, and the practical side of how to run a midwifery business. Some vocational midwifery schools offer extensive additional training in herbs, homeopathy, and/or other forms of alternative medicine. Most educators in such schools seek to imbue their students with both technical knowledge and an ideology that stresses the importance of honoring and respecting the sacredness of women's bodies and the spiritual dimensions of pregnancy and birth. And, unlike in one-on-one apprenticeships, students in these schools can interact with and learn from each other and have exposure to several primary faculty members who are in teaching positions because of their demonstrated expertise.

The Midwifery Education and Accreditation Council (MEAC), founded in 1991, evaluates these formal direct-entry vocational programs and has accredited eight of them to date, including the Seattle Midwifery School in Washington state; Maternidad La Luz in El Paso, Texas; the Utah College of Midwifery; and Birthingway Midwifery School in Oregon. A few of these MEAC-accredited vocational schools have developed distance-learning programs. Most are three-year programs; some require a year of basic science prerequisites. Their tuition fees range from $8000 to $22,000.[12]

In Canada, a short-lived vocational School of Midwifery located in Vancouver, B.C., took in two classes of midwives in 1984 and 1985. The school was loosely affiliated with Seattle Midwifery School and was accredited by Washington state. Upon completing the Washington state's licensing examination and applying for a license, the successful midwife candidate gained the title Licensed Midwife (Rice 1997). The former British colony of Newfoundland initiated a vocational training program for midwives in the early 1920s in the capital city of St. John's. Graduate midwives found work in outlying clinics, in one of the eighteen small (thirty- to fifty-bed) cottage hospitals strategically located around the island of Newfoundland, or in one of the few parallel institutions located in the even more isolated northern region of Labrador. Formal union with mainland Canada in 1949, where midwifery had all but become defunct, led to a demise of vocational education for midwives in the renamed eastern provinces of Newfoundland and Labrador (Benoit 1989b, 1991).

On the European continent, vocational education still exists in Belgium, where vocational colleges offer midwifery training. Students study for three years, and in each year the proportion of apprenticeship increases, from six out of thirty weeks in the first year to eighteen out of thirty weeks in the third year. In addition, Belgian students can opt to do nursing training first (at the same vocational colleges) and subsequently complete their midwifery training in two years.

University Education

U.S.-born Joanne Bostick had always known that when she grew up she wanted to be involved in the health care professions, but as a college graduate at the age of twenty-two, she still had not been able to figure out which one. Sitting in a medical library in 1991, she leafed through a booklet listing all the professions in the healing arts until she came across the title "nurse-midwife." Chills ran down her spine as the realization swept over her that this was what she was to become. She had always been fascinated by babies and by birth, but she had never wanted to be a doctor, and until now she had not even known that midwifery was a professional option. Further investigation taught her that her potential educational pathways were many. Nursing was a prerequisite, but there were various ways to fulfill the nursing requirement. Not wanting to spend years of her life learning nursing, she chose the program at the University of California San Francisco that would put her through nursing training in one year and move her straight into two years of midwifery education, from which she would graduate with a master's degree. She did not enjoy that one year of nursing training, but she knew she was gaining valuable skills, so she held on. When she finally moved into the midwifery part of the program, she felt that she had come home. She loved everything about being a midwife, even the late-night work. The prerequisite basic science courses she had taken to augment her liberal arts education had not proved to be too much of a stretch, and now she was thrilled to be engaged in hands-on application of many aspects of the sciences she had studied, from taking throat cultures to doing Pap smears as part of her training in well-woman primary health care. She enjoyed her academic classes, during which she could engage in stimulating discussions of the various case studies she and her classmates were always reading. But she was happiest when she was learning hands-on midwifery skills, whether she was practicing pelvic exams and diaphragm-fitting on her fellow students or learning speculum insertion on the plastic dummies that lined shelves of their laboratory.

Once she began attending laboring women, she sometimes found herself torn between wanting to stay at the mother's side, gazing into her eyes and giving her emotional and verbal support, and wishing to be at the other end, watching every detail of how her preceptor was handling the birth. Soon she felt quite comfortable catching the baby, handing it to the mother, and supporting them to establish breastfeeding, as long as her supervisor was near. But the more she studied birth pathologies, learning academically about everything that can go wrong, the more nervous and tentative she found herself becoming. Her tension came to a head five months into her midwifery program during one awful week when she was faced in rapid succession with a mother who hemorrhaged massively and nearly died and the sudden deaths of two babies during what seemed like normal births. Terrified by these experiences, she went through a period of wanting to apply technological interventions at every birth because they made her feel safe. Understanding her fear, her supervisor consistently encouraged her to regain her trust in birth, reminding her that most births turn out fine without intervention and urging her to empower women with back rubs, hugs, and hands-on support instead of being so quick to intervene. Over time the encouragement worked, and Joanne developed special expertise in helping women give birth without perineal tears; she was proud when she managed to graduate without ever having cut an episiotomy. She was also proud of her mastery of sophisticated technologies like electronic fetal monitoring and vacuum extraction, although she vowed to use them as rarely as possible and to treat all her low-risk clients according to the noninterventive principles of the midwifery model of care she had been taught. During her first years of practice in a tertiary care center, she was met with resistance from both physicians and the older nurses and often was forced to use more interventions than she wanted to keep her job. But over time, as she gained her colleagues' respect and trust, she was increasingly able to make her practice match her ideals.

HISTORY AND CHARACTERISTICS OF UNIVERSITY TRAINING

Mid- to late-twentieth-century Europe and North America are marked by a new style of midwifery knowledge—academic—and a new site for imparting it—the university. Optimists such as Bell (1973) viewed the emerging "postindustrial" society of the second half of the twentieth century as nothing short of revolutionary because of its magical mix of technical efficiency and capital accumulation. According to Bell, the prime movers of postindustrial society are no longer capitalists but rather "knowledge workers" trained in academic institutions distinguished by their latest technological developments and scientific advances in knowledge production. Midwives, along with an assortment of other health providers, eventually found themselves drawn to the postindustrial academy for the training and socialization of new recruits to their profession.

Canada also took this route, although comparatively late in its development. In many high-income countries where midwifery survives, the neophyte's educational preparation follows this route: secondary school graduation, application to a university-level direct-entry or nurse-midwifery program of three to five years' duration, and, in some countries, advanced education at the master's level.

STRENGTHS AND LIMITATIONS OF UNIVERSITY EDUCATION

University-based training fits well with the values, beliefs, and status consciousness of mainstream society; it is often thought of as the minimum training required for service occupations. As a socially valued educational pathway, it affords social recognition and prestige, easy access to government loans, and straightforward routes to advanced degrees. Advanced professional degrees empower their recipients to teach, to start new programs, to effect changes in legislation, and to carry out research on client needs and various aspects of midwifery care. In short, academic credentials give midwives (and other professionals) "cultural capital" helping them to negotiate attractive work options and to compete on an equal standing with other similarly credentialed health professionals (Benoit 1991).

Presence on a university campus offers the distinct advantage of well-equipped facilities and a variety of educational and research opportunities. Moreover, academic institutions and university hospitals are often the sites of development for innovative knowledge and technologies about childbearing that midwives can use. As sites for creative developments in education, universities have developed sophisticated distance learning technologies and have advanced educational theories and methods. Distance learning offers some of the advantages of apprenticeship, allowing a student to remain grounded in her community and to gain clinical experience with a preceptor in her local hospital.

Students trained in the large teaching hospitals associated with universities develop expertise in dealing with individuals of diverse sociocultural and economic backgrounds, a wide range of birth complications and unusual health conditions, and the "latest and newest" in medical technologies (Benoit 1991). Educators work with students to help them develop good risk assessment skills, competence in giving culturally sensitive care, a critical sense of the value of technology, and good research skills that can enable them to sift the data for themselves.

In the United States, university education is paid for by the individual and can be prohibitively expensive, costing up to $100,000. Many U.S. students obtain scholarships or government loans to help with this financial burden. In Canada, the average university student pays tuition for only 20–25 percent of her education. In the United Kingdom midwifery is paid for by the state. Sources of funding are just one point of variation in university education. Programs also vary in the degree of medicalization of the curriculum, the distance placed between students and the lifeworlds of the women they serve, and the view of midwifery advocated.

University programs are particularly susceptible to the risk of divorcing the education of health practitioners from hands-on practice. Hunt (1996, p. 31) found that practicing midwives feel the danger of becoming more academically than clinically focused. Can those with more elaborate theoretical education translate this theoretical knowledge into practice? Some commentators are convinced that university education has great potential to improve clinical care (Alexander 1994, p. 25), while others question this assumption (Jackson 1993, p. 275).

In all the countries we study here the university training of midwives is carried out in institutions that are highly medicalized, patriarchal, and technocratic. Midwives in these institutions are often required to intervene in birth in ways contrary to both scientific evidence and the noninterventive principles of midwifery care in order to successfully graduate.

CASE STUDY: UNIVERSITY TRAINING IN SELECT CANADIAN PROVINCES

History and Characteristics

Until the late 1980s, three university nursing schools—located in Alberta, Nova Scotia, and Newfoundland—offered nurses additional courses in midwifery training under the rubric of an "Outpost Nursing" program. These academic programs were focused on placing nursing in northern and remote communities of the respective provinces (Benoit 1991).

In autumn 1993, a full-fledged direct-entry university program for training midwives began operation in three university sites in Ontario—McMaster, Ryerson Polytechnic, and Laurentain Universities. In September 1998, the Ontario government renewed the five-year initial pilot funding. Initially the program required the student to complete three years, with each academic year covering eleven months, after which time the successful candidate was awarded a Bachelor of Health Sciences degree. The program is now shifting to a four-year degree requirement, with eight-month academic years (in line with other university programs). At Ryerson, most midwifery students study part-time, allowing them to work part-time to support their midwifery studies. At the bilingual (French and English) Laurentain program and the McMaster program full-time study is the norm (Shroff 1996/97). Tuitions range from 3500 to 5000 Canadian dollars for each academic year; these fees may increase substantially because of recent deregulation of university student tuition fees in Ontario. As in the Netherlands, demand for student places in the three Ontario midwifery programs seriously exceeds supply.

In all three Ontario university programs, a "problem-based learning" model is employed, small group discussions are commonplace, and many of the classes are taught to students at a distance with the aid of special distance learning technologies. Preceptorship is an important part of all three programs. From their first day of study students are required to follow birthing clients throughout their reproductive cycles. In fact, it is fair to say that the Ontario midwifery educational model combines apprenticeship with university education. The defining principle of this model of educating midwives is, "The midwife follows the woman." This means that the midwife is trained to practice her profession in the woman's chosen setting—home, clinic, or hospital—and will accompany the woman wherever she may need to go. While attending women in their own homes, the midwife recruit observes the wide variety of home conditions, family structures, and cultural practices of birthing women. This hands-on knowledge helps the student midwife acquire in-depth knowledge of her birthing client as someone with an intricate history who is embedded in a complex web of social relations.

Despite its use of a combination of educational models, the university training program in Canada has its drawbacks. Students are often in their late teens or early twenties, savvy in intellectual ways of knowing, but with little in the way of life experience. The Ontario midwifery programs do select students on the basis of their expressed "calling" to be a midwife, but the ultimate criterion for admission is the ability to survive in a highly stressful academic setting (Sharpe 1997). The Ontario educational model also tends to privilege students along race, class, and ethnic lines. Midwifery students have to pay hefty tuition fees and need access to a vehicle to get to births, a pager, and—if mothers themselves—money for a babysitter. Compounding these structural forms of exclusion, it took some time for Ontario academic midwifery programs to develop alternative routes to licensure for midwives trained in other countries (Nestel 1996/97).

Recent Developments in Midwifery Training in Canada

In 1995, in response to the need for a way to incorporate foreign-trained midwives into the Canadian system, the College of Midwives of Ontario piloted a Prior Learning Assessment process for midwives trained outside the province. This program, now called Prior Learning and Experience Assessment (PLEA), assesses midwives' theoretical and clinical skills and offers resources, opportunities to be in contact with midwifery practices, an orientation to midwifery in Ontario, and clinical skills workshops. Midwife graduates from the PLEA Program now account for 23 percent of all registered midwives in Ontario. Potential applicants learn about this program from advertisements in Canadian newspapers. The Ontario government's Ministry of Citizenship funded start-up of the program and now works with the college to present information about it to other professions in Canada. As of 1999, Ontario midwifery has a greater proportion of registered professionals who were trained in other countries than any other regulated health profession in Canada. This group of registered midwives is critical to the development of midwifery services and the new profession of midwifery in Ontario. Many are experienced practitioners with valuable skills and leadership capability, and they contribute to developing a more diverse population of midwives who better reflect the population of the province. More than 80 percent have immigrated from other countries, about 40 percent are women of color, and about 80 percent speak languages other than English (Holliday Tyson, personal communication, January 13, 2000).

In summer 1999 the provincial government of Quebec approved the establishment of an academic training program for midwives in that province. The program started up in fall 1999 with sixteen students. Offered at the Health Sciences Faculty of the University du Quebec à Trois-Rivières (UQTR), it is designed as a four-year baccalaureate program (personal communication, Helene Vadeboncoeur, December 12, 1999).

There is always the danger that midwifery training will be co-opted by university education; this has not happened in Ontario because the educational model used there balances students' training in both home and hospital settings, allowing them to see both a low-tech noninvasive form of midwifery practice and its more high-tech counterpart.

The Development of University and Direct-Entry Education in the United States and United Kingdom

The United Kingdom

In the 1990s, midwifery education in the United Kingdom was dominated by three trends: (1) movement into higher education, (2) the creation of an internal market in the purchasing of nursing and midwifery education; and (3) a resurrection of direct-entry midwifery programs. The move of midwifery education was accompanied by the opening of a large number of new direct-entry programs that may eventually result in more psychological and actual autonomy for British midwives.

During the 1980s, new education proposals in the United Kingdom moved nursing training into higher education and redefined midwifery as a nursing specialty. The midwifery profession reacted by defending its distinct identity (UKCC 1986). The Association of Radical Midwives (ARM 1986) and the Royal College of Midwives (RCM 1987) produced separate reports emphasizing the importance of an autonomous role for midwives trained by a direct-entry route. This resurgence of interest in direct-entry training resulted from three major concerns: (1) the desire by midwives to establish midwifery as an autonomous profession separate from nursing, (2) government concerns that a population decrease in eighteen-year-olds would likely result in a decrease in entrants to midwifery, and (3) midwifery concerns that the majority of nurses who trained to be midwives did not practice midwifery.

Following a change in educational policy in the United Kingdom, schools began to compete for NHS training contracts (Department of Health 1989). By the mid 1990s, midwifery education in Britain had moved into the university sector and had begun to develop/regain its own educational identity separate from nursing. In addition to the standard midwifery diploma or degree, some universities began to offer postgraduate programs in midwifery. Merging with institutions of higher education presented opportunities for extending the knowledge base of midwifery and for increasing academic rigor (Roch 1993). Creating postgraduate courses, establishing an academic research base, and creating chairs in midwifery helped raise the status of midwifery as an academic discipline within the university setting, but did little to change the working conditions of midwives vis-à-vis physicians.

"Internal markets" were introduced to the NHS by a conservative government. This management innovation was intended to control costs by encouraging competition between different service-providers within the NHS. The competitive market has had some questionable consequences for midwifery education. Because contracts to train midwifery students must be renewed every five years, universities have no incentive to make long-term investments in infrastructure. The consortiums that oversee these five-year educational contracts are dominated by NHS managers whose main concern is to have a midwifery workforce trained in as short a time as possible at as low a cost as possible. It is likely that without the EU midwifery training regulations, midwifery would be suffering the downgrading that nursing education is currently going through in the United Kingdom, with a revision of educational aims from the education of a reflexive critical practitioner (UKCC 1986) to a worker fit for a specific purpose (UKCC 1999).

Around 1,600 students enter midwifery training each year in England; the overwhelming majority (99 percent) of midwifery students are female (ENB 1999). In 1999, 46 percent were on a direct-entry route, and the remainder were already qualified nurses. This is a dramatic increase in direct entry places since the 1980s. All students are either registered for a diploma or degree program. Forty-five percent of students were registered in a degree (i.e., baccalaureate) program, with the remainder registered for a diploma (nonbaccalaureate). Funding inequities remained between students registered in diploma and degree programs. Students registered for a degree are treated like other undergraduates in the United Kingdom. Their fees are paid, but they have to take out interest-free loans to pay for their living expenses. Students registered for a diploma are funded through the NHS and have their fees paid and receive a bursary of around £6,000 a year. Not surprisingly, some students are forced to drop out of degree programs because of financial difficulties, a problem that disproportionately affects direct-entry students who are older and often have childcare commitments.

Each university and the National Board for each country accredit all programs in the United Kingdom. The Royal College of Midwives plays no part in educational accreditation, its role being that of a professional organization and trade union. All programs fulfill EU requirements, and students spend 50 percent of their time in clinical practice in the NHS. Although all programs include hospital and community placements (community and hospital care is usually integrated in the United Kingdom), the quality of the placement depends on the provision of care provided by the "linked" maternity provider. One student may experience "caseload midwifery" in a group practice with plenty of home birth experience; another may find herself working in a regional high-tech unit. Further, some students rotate between several maternity providers during their training and others do not. The UKCC commission recognizes this variability in education and has suggested that NHS providers take on more responsibility for clinical training (UKCC 1999).

Thus, we find both continuity and change. In some places lecturers in vocational courses simply moved into the university system and the organization of clinical placements changed very little. Other universities introduced shared multidisciplinary learning, a problem-based learning curriculum and teaching from "pure subject" specialists, rather than generic midwifery lecturers. In addition, many qualified midwives are "topping up" their academic qualifications to first degree and master's level through part-time education programs. Student midwives enter training with high expectations, and their lecturers (who still work clinically) often encourage their students to think critically about maternity care. But during their training and subsequent employment in the NHS, midwifery students continue to encounter a medically dominated hierarchy, cost constraints, staff shortages, policies that are not family-friendly, and unequal opportunities. After graduation UK midwives have little choice about where they will work, since almost all maternity care is provided by the NHS and private health insurance does not cover normal pregnancy and birth. In the mid-1990s the Royal College of Midwives further limited midwives' options by withdrawing malpractice insurance coverage from midwives who are self-employed; in the late 1990s only a handful of independent midwives remained in practice.

On the whole the move into higher education has improved the lot of midwives: The number of direct-entry programs continues to grow, and there is government commitment to a 100 percent midwifery education at the degree level. Midwifery education is now free from nursing and medical dominance, and it has found a space for students and staff to develop midwifery theory and practice and to carry out postgraduate work and midwifery-driven research. At the same time, the clinical experience of students often incorporates the same overmedicalized elements found in vocational training. In some cases, the geographical separation of the university and the clinical sites has widened the gap between midwife and medical approaches to birth; in these situations university educators have no power to influence the quality of clinical experience and mentorship a student receives.

The United States

For American midwives, university training is by far the most common educational pathway (Roberts 1995; Rooks 1997). There are forty-eight nurse-midwifery educational programs; all are either university-based or are distance learning programs that are university-affiliated. All but one require prior nursing education and licensure,[13] and all are accredited by the American College of Nurse-Midwives' Division of Accreditation (DOA). This latter fact is especially significant, as in few other countries does the professional midwifery association hold sole accrediting power; it can thereby assure the uniform quality and content of every program.

American nurse-midwives have been an important force in the transnational trend toward university-based midwifery education. As of 1999, all forty-eight nurse-midwifery programs required the bachelor's degree for entry (see note 1). The master's degree is not required for practice; nevertheless, over 70 percent of nurse-midwives have master's degrees. It is important to keep in mind that nurse-midwives in the United States attend only 7 percent of all births; one of their strategies for establishing nurse-midwifery as a respected profession has long been to obtain higher degrees both for the credibility they bring and for the ability they bestow to carry out much-needed research on the effects of nurse-midwifery care and to assure that midwifery practice remains evidence-based.

All nurse-midwifery educational programs are designed to teach ACNM's core competencies, which have been expanded to include not only care for women during pregnancy, birth, and the postpartum period, but also well-woman gynecological care across the female life cycle. All equip their students to work in health care institutions (hospitals, birth centers, and managed care organizations) and sometimes to manage private practices. The majority of faculty in these programs must be nurse-midwives; experts in a given area, including doctors and nurse practitioners, can also hold teaching positions. Every program includes specific criteria for entrance, structured learning objectives, formalized didactic instruction, clinical experience with more than one clinical instructor, and involvement of several faculty members in judgment about the student's ability to provide beginning-level midwifery care. Clinical supervision is always the responsibility of midwives. In-hospital training is the norm. The availability and depth of both didactic teaching about and clinical experience in out-of-hospital birth can vary considerably from program to program. Unlike the Ontario system, out-of-hospital clinical experience is not required for U.S. certification or for program accreditation and is unavailable in most nurse-midwifery programs. Many student nurse-midwives are disturbed by their complete lack of out-of-hospital experience (Davis-Floyd 1998a, b), as they are aware that the location of birth has a major influence on both caregivers and the kind of care they provide (see Chapter 1).

Tuition in U.S. university-based programs ranges widely. Some programs have tuitions of under $20,000 for the entire program, and some cost over $100,000. Most common are tuitions in the $70,000 range. Some students finance their education with government loans; others avoid incurring debt by participating in work-study programs or working part-time, often as nurses, and applying for the many available scholarships and grants. Some government loans require repayment not with money but with time practicing in underserved communities.

The transnational trend toward direct-entry midwifery education is also having its effect in the United States: The American College of Nurse-Midwives now offers direct-entry certification and has accredited one direct-entry program (see note 13). ACNM's move into direct-entry has been motivated by multiple factors, among them a desire for increased autonomy for midwives and the wish to shorten the length of time required for midwifery education.[14] A lengthy passage through nursing can derail students' lives and career goals. During her interviews with forty-five nurse-midwifery students, carried out between 1997 and 1999, Davis-Floyd learned that there is a strong ethic in American nursing that all midwifery candidates should practice as labor and delivery nurses before entering midwifery programs. Such practice generally ensures a dual socialization into a nursing identity and a medicalized approach to birth. Many potential midwifery students thus feel pressured to undergo two years or more of nursing training and several years of clinical practice. Much less of this sort of pressure is experienced by students who enter the fast-track programs at Yale, Columbia, and UCSF, which are designed to make their students nurses solely so that they can become midwives; in such programs a briefer (one-year) passage through nursing is the norm. The type of socialization a student undergoes during nursing training is another powerful motivator to avoid it; most of the forty-five nurse-midwifery students Davis-Floyd interviewed strongly resented being socialized as nurses into an attitude of subordination to physicians that they must overcome once they begin clinical study as midwives.

A major trend in the United States is toward the creation of innovative distance learning educational options designed to make midwifery education more accessible to a wider spectrum of women. This transnational trend mirrors a similar trend in education in general, stimulated by the new availability of distance learning computer technologies, including the Internet. Nurse-midwives in the United States have taken full advantage of these technologies: Their largest educational program, the

Community-based Nurse-Midwifery Educational Program (CNEP), allows students to remain at home studying didactics online and learning clinical skills from preceptors in their communities.[15] And several formal direct-entry programs in the United States are moving toward a distance-learning format.[16]

A criticism sometimes leveled at university education for midwives is that its standardization stifles individual creativity. Davis-Floyd has not found this criticism to apply to the nurse-midwifery students she has interviewed, who are strongly encouraged by their teachers to think "out of the box." Nurse-midwifery educators have long been leaders in educational innovation, and they continue to develop and refine creative and interactive learning and teaching methodologies (Johnson & Fullerton 1998).

Tensions within American nurse-midwifery education—certain to be more intense than those in countries with lower intervention rates—center around the large gap between the evidence-based focus of midwifery educators and the tradition-based approach of most obstetricians. Student nurse-midwives, steeped in the evidence, frequently experience distress over the unnecessary interventions they are regularly expected to perform. And they often must spend more time learning to deal with hospital procedures and protocols than with birthing women.

The level of medicalization of nurse-midwifery education varies from program to program. Some university-based programs are highly humanistic and woman-centered in their approach; others are far more oriented toward technomedicine. This technomedical orientation in some programs applies not just to education but to socialization as well: A few nurse-midwifery students describe intense hazing and criticism, of the kind that obstetrical residents undergo, throughout their educational process. These students report extreme difficulty in reconciling the ways in which they were trained with they ways in which they are expected to practice, suggesting that how a midwife is trained will have a major effect on what kind of practitioner she becomes. According to Davis-Floyd's nurse-midwifery student interviewees, some of the most holistic nurse-midwifery programs, both in education and socialization, are the distance learning programs, which allow their students to study didactics on computer while preceptoring/apprenticing with one or more nurse-midwives in their communities. These programs are not located on a university campus, but do have university affiliations.[17]

Conclusion

We began this chapter with a simple question: How should aspiring midwives be prepared for their role as caregivers? Our survey of the existing models of education provides no definitive answers. Midwifery students have been prepared in many ways, and there is no single best way to "design midwives." Our survey has shown that the knowledge base and socialization of midwives are arbitrary; each is shaped by the larger culture and structure of society. We have also seen the degree of professional autonomy midwives achieve is strongly related to the way they are educated. The recent trend toward higher education has raised the status of midwives, granting them more authority vis-à-vis medicine and nursing. Academic education can enhance midwives' autonomy, but it can also socialize them into accepting hegemonic models and practices.

Despite their marginalized status, apprenticeship and vocationally trained mid-wives in the United States are far more autonomous than university-trained midwives are. This is a result of their education and the fact that they practice outside of hospitals and thus are not subject to institutional hierarchies and restraints. Vocationally trained midwives in the Netherlands also emerge from our comparison as relatively autonomous; their vocational training gives them a distinct identity and place in the division of labor.

In the final analysis, it is how midwives practice that matters most. Even when midwives are educated to adopt a woman-centered philosophy of care, they often find themselves unable to implement such a model inside the work world of tech-nomedicine. Midwives whose education did not include experience with out-of-hospital birth find it especially difficult to think of and to treat pregnancy and birth as normal. It is no accident that American nurse-midwives, who are trained to practice almost exclusively in hospitals, employ routine interventions as frequently as physicians (Curtin 1999, p. 349). We believe that systems that provide training environments where midwives can function fluidly in both home and hospital—like those of the Netherlands and Canada—are more beneficial to women than hospital-dominated systems like those found in the United Kingdom and the United States.[18]

Our survey indicates a move away from nursing as a required part of the education of midwives. In the Netherlands, midwifery education has always been direct-entry. In the United Kingdom, it is moving in that direction. In Canada, it was set up that way from the start. And in the United States, nurse-midwives themselves have opened their college to direct-entry members, have created one university-based direct-entry program, and are working on more. Why is it so important to these midwives to maintain their identity as such? Many women experience a spiritual calling to midwifery, viewing it as not just a profession but a sacred trust. Increasingly, midwives tend to agree on the unique nature of midwifery and its strong humanistic significance for today's women. This commitment to the preservation of midwifery as a crucial alternative to obstetrics makes midwives unwilling to dilute their identity by coding midwifery as an advanced form of nursing.

In this new millennium, we expect to find midwives around the world working to develop philosophies of care that are evidence-based and woman-centered and that encourage midwives' independence of mind, educational programs that effectively blend theory and practice in the full spectrum of settings, and work settings that encompass that full spectrum. Such developments will assist midwives to become fully respected as practitioners within their country's health care system and to more effectively do what they exist to do: give childbearing women the best possible care.

Acknowledgments

Robbie Davis-Floyd acknowledges with thanks the editorial comments provided by midwives Mary Ann Baul, Judith Rooks, and Mary Ann Shah, and midwifery educator Joanne Myers-Ciecko.

Notes

1. This chapter focuses on midwives in high-income countries only. In no way are we suggesting that similar circumstances exist for midwives in low-income countries, where, for a variety of reasons that we are not able to take up here, midwives' education and socialization are organized differently.

2. The American College of Nurse-Midwives' Division of Accreditation has set standards that allow for prebaccalaureate programs, but none have been proposed, so effectively the baccalaureate is a requirement for entry.

3. The correspondence we point to here between nursing training as a prerequisite to midwifery training and midwives' lack of autonomy does not hold for all countries. Swedish nurse-midwives, for example, enjoy extensive autonomy. Important factors influencing midwives' autonomy or lack thereof include the organization of medicine in a given country and its form of health care funding. Out-of-hospital practice also contributes: The fact that Dutch and Canadian midwives practice not only in hospitals but also in homes facilitates their independence—but then again, part of why they have been able to preserve home birth is because they have also preserved their autonomy. It is important to note that nurses too are struggling for increased autonomy and for working partnerships and collaboration with physicians. But they are having far more difficulty achieving these than midwives are, as in most cases they have neither prescriptive privileges nor decision-making authority. As one nurse put it in an interview with Davis-Floyd, "We are taught to think of ourselves as autonomous practitioners working on an equal basis with the docs. The problem is that nobody teaches that to *them.*"

4. The full list of requirements for CPM certification is available at www.mana.org.

5. Many non-nurse midwives in the United States are not licensed, registered, or certified and thus cannot be counted, so exact numbers cannot be provided here. The Midwives' Alliance of North America, which is the organization that represents American home birth midwives, has over 1,000 members (one-third of whom are nurse-midwives). It is estimated that there are approximately 3,000 practicing direct-entry midwives in the United States; cumulatively, they attend around 1 percent of American births.

6. An example comes from the high-tech computer industry, in which many young people without college degrees are receiving on-the-job training from mentors within a given company in specialized computer skills not taught in universities. It is worth noting that neither Bill Gates, founder of Microsoft, nor Steve Jobs, cofounder of Apple Computers, graduated from college.

7. An example of the eclectic form many contemporary apprenticeships take is provided by well-known childbirth educator Nancy Wainer Cohen, author of *Silent Knife* (1983), who underwent two years of apprenticeship training with a midwife in Boston where she lives, interspersed with periodic trips to Michigan for weeks at a time to apprentice with midwife Valerie El Halta. Toward the end of this process, she spent eight weeks in El Paso, Texas, at Casa de Nacimiento and two weeks at Victoria Jubilee Hospital in Jamaica under the tutelage of Shari Daniels; in both places, she attended many births in short order and learned to deal with a wide range of complications.

8. This new convergence between apprenticeship and more formalized educational models is intensifying. Two private vocational programs, the Utah School of Midwifery and the Midwifery Institute of California, have both developed distance learning apprenticeship programs in modules that can be adapted for use by mentors and apprentices anywhere in the country. The modular form ensures that learning objectives can be formally set, and that what the apprentice learns can be tracked and evaluated, so these two have become the first apprenticeship programs to receive formal accreditation from MANA's associate, the

Midwifery Education and Accreditation Council (MEAC). MEAC has applied for formal recognition by the U.S. Department of Education. If its application is successful, then all graduates of MEAC-accredited programs, including the two MEAC-accredited apprenticeship programs, will meet the international definition of a midwife ("one who graduates from a program duly recognized in the country") and will be eligible to apply for government loans to complete their educations.

9. Adapted from Benoit 1992, pp. 1–2.

10. On the other hand, vocational education, at least for women in low-income countries but also for less advantaged women in high-income countries, is likely to be much less expensive than university-based educational programs for educating midwives, thus allowing more women greater access to midwifery training. However, in countries where the state finances education (as in the United Kingdom and the Netherlands, for example), these financial differences are likely to be less acute.

11. Derby was the only place in Britain that had continued to offer direct-entry midwifery training throughout the 1970s and 1980s.

12. Unique among such programs is the Miami-Dade Community College in Miami, Florida, which offers a three-year curriculum (opened in 1996) leading to an Associate of Science degree in midwifery. In addition to didactic training in the basic sciences and humanities, the program includes a strong apprenticeship component. Additionally, students have access to high-tech equipment and a variety of clinical experiences in hospitals, public health facilities, birth centers, and home birth practices in Florida and at a high-volume hospital in Jamaica. This community college model combines the advantages of a college education with a deeply held commitment to independent midwifery and seems especially appropriate for replication elsewhere. Two of the private schools that are MEAC-accredited offer advanced degrees recognized by the states in which they operate: the Utah School of Midwifery in Springville, Utah, which offers bachelor's and master's degrees; and the National College of Midwifery in Taos, New Mexico, which offers degrees all the way up to the Ph.D. Both of these programs have strong apprenticeship components and are extremely affordable. Government funding for students attending MEAC-accredited vocational schools will become available if MEAC is successful in gaining Department of Education recognition (see note 8). For more information about American vocational programs, see Rooks 1997; Davis-Floyd 1998a, b. For up-to-date information about MEAC-accredited programs, contact MEAC, 220 W. Birch, Flagstaff, AZ 86001; meac@altavista.net, or www.mana.org/meac.

13. The only currently operating nurse-midwifery program that does not require nursing training is located at the State University of New York (SUNY)–Health Science Center at Brooklyn, in New York City. At this date of writing, only fourteen direct-entry midwives have been certified by the ACNM; legislation is pending in many states to create legal status for them as their numbers grow. An update on the status and number of nurse-midwifery programs is published every year in the *Journal of Nurse-Midwifery.* For up-to-the-minute information, contact the ACNM national office in Washington, D. C., (info@acnm.org; 202-728-9860) and ask to speak to a member of the Education Department.

14. See Davis-Floyd (1998a, b) for a detailed discussion of what motivated ACNM's move into direct-entry certification.

15. For a detailed description of the CNEP program, see Rooks 1997, pp. 167–170.

16. Some Canadian university programs employ technologies that allow students to participate at a distance, and one educational proposal being discussed involves a distance learning program accessible to midwives in perhaps the three most Western provinces (personal communication, Susan Issacs, BC Ministry of Health, 1998).

17. In addition to the CNEP program, a number of other DOA-accredited programs also offer distance tracks for nurse-midwifery students, and a distance program for the direct-entry

students at SUNY-Brooklyn is under development. (For up-to-date information, see www. acnm.org.)

18. There are over 8,000 nurse-midwives in the United States; fewer than 200 of them attend home births. Many more would like to do so, but are required by law to have physician backup and malpractice insurance for home birth. Since these are often impossible to obtain, CNMs are effectively prevented from attending home births. Likewise, many direct-entry midwives would like to be able to practice in hospitals, but almost no hospitals will allow them to do so.

References

Alexander, J. 1994. Degree of difference. *Modern Midwife* 4(8): 24–26.

Association of Radical Midwives. 1986. *The Vision-Proposals for the Future of the Maternity Services.* Ormskirk, Lancs: ARM.

Bell, D. 1973. *The Coming of Post-Industrial Society.* New York: Basic Books.

Benoit, C. 1989a. Traditional midwifery practice: The limits of occupational autonomy. *The Canadian Review of Sociology and Anthropology* 267 (4): 663–649.

———. 1989b. The professional socialization of midwives: Balancing art and science. *Sociology of Health and Illness* 11(2): 160–180.

———. 1991. *Midwives in Passage: The Modernization of Maternity Care.* Memorial University of Newfoundland: ISER Press.

———. 1992. Midwives in comparative perspective: Professionalism in small organizations. *Current Research on Occupations and Professions* 7: 203–220.

Böhme, G. 1984. Midwifery as science: An essay on the relationship between scientific and everyday knowledge. In *Society and Knowledge,* eds. N. Stehr and V. Meja. New Brunswick, NJ: Transaction Books, pp. 365–385.

Carter, J., and T. Duriez. 1986. *With Child: Birth through the Ages.* Edinburgh: Mainstream Publishing.

Cohen, N., and L. Estner. *Silent Knife: Caesarian Prevention and Vaginal Birth After Caesarian (VBAC).* South Hadley, MA: Bergin and Garvey Publishers.

Committee for the Revision of the Curriculum of Midwifery Schools in the Netherlands. 1991. *Revision of the Curriculum of Midwifery Schools.* Rijswijk: Department of Welfare, Health & Cultural Affairs. (English Translation Commissioned by The American Foundation for Maternal and Child Health, New York).

Curtin, Sally 1999. Recent changes in birth attendant, place of birth, and the use of obstetric interventions, United States, 1989–1997. *Journal of Nurse-Midwifery* 44(4): 349–369.

Davis, E. 1997 (originally published 1983). *Heart and Hands: A Midwife's Guide to Pregnancy and Birth,* 3rd ed. Berkeley, CA: Celestial Arts.

Davis-Floyd, R. 1998a. The ups, downs, and interlinkages of nurse- and direct-entry midwifery. In *Getting an Education: Paths to Becoming a Midwife,* eds. J. Tritten, and J. Southern. Eugene, OR: Midwifery Today, pp. 67–118.

———. 1998b. Types of midwifery training: An anthropological overview. In *Getting an Education: Paths to Becoming a Midwife,* eds. J. Tritten and J. Southern. Eugene, OR: Midwifery Today, pp. 119–133.

Department of Health. 1989. *Education and Training* (Working Paper 10, Cmnd 555). London: HMSO.

———. 1998. *Midwifery: delivering our future: Report by the Standing Nursing and Midwifery Advisory Committee.* London: DH.

English National Board. 1999. *Students Statistics Report 1993/4–1997/8*. London: English National Board.

Flint, C. 1990, March. The demise of the midwifery profession. *Midwives, Health Visitor and Community Nursing,* pp. 66–67.

House of Commons Health Committee. 1992. *Second Report, Maternity Services* Vol. 1. London: HMSO.

Hunt, S. C. 1996. Marketing midwifery education: Findings from a survey. *Midwifery* 12(1): 31–36.

Illich, I. 1973. *Deschooling Society.* Harmondsworth: Penguin.

Jackson, K. 1993. Midwifery degree programmes: Who benefits? *British Journal of Midwifery* 1(6): 274–275.

Johnson, Peter G., and J. T. Fullerton. 1998. Midwifery education models: A contemporary review. *Journal of Nurse-Midwifery* 43(4): 351–357.

McKay, S. 1993. Models of care: Denmark, Sweden, and the Netherlands. *Journal of Nurse-Midwifery* 38(2): 114–120.

Morewood-Northrop, M. 1997. Community birthing project: Northwest territories. In *The New Midwifery: Reflections on Renaissance and Regulation,* ed. F. Shroff. Toronto: Women's Press, pp. 343–356.

Nestel, S. 1996/1997. A new profession to the white population in Canada: Ontario midwifery and the politics of race. *Health and Canadian Society/Sante et Societe Canadienne* 4(2): 315–341.

O'Neil, J., and P. A. Kaufert. 1990. The politics of obstetric care: The Inuit experience. *In Births and Power: Social Change and the Politics of Reproduction,* ed. W. P. Handwerker. Boulder: Westview Press, pp. 53–68.

Radford, N., and A. Thompson. 1988. *Direct Entry, a Preparation for Midwifery Practice* (Report to the English National Board). Surrey: University of Surrey.

Rice, J. A. 1997. Becoming regulated: The re-emergence of midwifery in British Columbia. In *The New Midwifery: Reflections on Renaissance and Regulation,* Toronto: Women's Press, pp. 149–180.

Roberts, Joyce 1995. The role of graduate education in midwifery in the USA. In *Issues in Midwifery,* ed. Tricia Murphy-Black. Edinburgh: Churchill Livingstone, pp. 119–161.

Robinson, S. 1991. Preparation for practice: The educational experiences and career intentions of newly qualified midwives. In *Midwives, Research & Childbirth,* Vol. 2. eds. S. Robinson and A. M. Thomson. London: Chapman & Hall, pp. 302–345.

Roch, S. 1993. Excellence in midwifery education. *Modern Midwife* 3: 36–38.

Rooks, Judith P. 1997. *Midwifery and Childbirth in America.* Philadelphia: Temple University Press.

Royal College of Midwives. 1987. *Report of the Royal College of Midwives on the Role and Education of the Future Midwife in the United Kingdom.* London: Royal College of Midwives.

Sandall, J. 1996. Continuity of midwifery care in Britain: A new professional project. *Gender, Work and Organization* 3(4): 215–226.

Schroff, F. 1996/1997. Walking the diversity talk: Curriculum within first year midwifery education. *Health and Canadian Society/Sante et Societe Canadienne* 4(2): 389–444.

Sharpe, M. 1997. Ontario midwifery in transition: An exploration of midwives' perceptions of the impact of midwifery legislation in its first year. In *The New Midwifery,* ed. F. Schroff. Toronto: Women's Press, pp. 201–244.

Stewart, A. 1981. The present state of midwifery training. *Midwifery, Health Visitor and Community Nurse* 17(7): 270–272.

Teijlingen, E. R. van. 1994. *A Social or Medical Model of Childbirth? Comparing the Arguments in Grampian (Scotland) and the Netherlands.* Ph.D. thesis, University of Aberdeen, Aberdeen.
UKCC. 1986. *Project 2000: A New Preparation for Practice.* London: UKCC.
———. 1999. *Fitness for Practice: The UKCC Commission for Nursing and Midwifery Education.* London: UKCC.

U.K. WEB SITES

Association Radical Midwives, http://www.radmid.demon.co.uk/index.htm
English National Board, http://www.enb.org.uk/
Scottish National Board, http://www.nbs.org.uk/
Welsh National Board, http://www.wnb.org.uk/
UKCC, http://www.ukcc.org.uk/

U.S. WEB SITES

American College of Nurse-Midwives, http://www.acnm.org
Midwives' Alliance of North America, http://www.mana.org

CHAPTER 8

Telling Stories of Midwives

Leonie van der Hulst and Edwin R. van Teijlingen
WITH CONTRIBUTIONS FROM
Betty-Anne Daviss, Myriam Haagmans-Cortenraad,
Annie Heuts-Verstraten, Jillian Ireland,
and Marike Roos-Ploeger

Introduction: Putting Stories on Paper

Put midwives together and they will start talking about their work, about the unusual or difficult situations they have faced, how they reacted, and what the outcomes were. These narratives provide insight into the actual work of midwives and put some flesh on the bones of social scientific analysis of the professions and professionalization.

Why do professionals tell stories to each other? Midwives (and other professionals) have a high degree of responsibility in areas touching on life and death; talking to their peers relieves some of the tension that is produced by this responsibility. Story telling allows professionals to

- Come to terms with, and get feedback on, significant events
- Get recognition and acknowledgment from colleagues for the way a case was handled and solved (as well as "permanent education" or "life-long learning")
- Shape, support, and strengthen professional identity

There is a growing awareness among midwives worldwide of the need to develop one's own identity (see Chapters 4, 6, and 7). The stories midwives tell—case studies, if you will—present a picture of the range and scope of the daily work of the profession. These recollections from practice both *describe* the content of professional work and *shape* its future. When put into writing, stories from experience surpass oral history: They provide sociological insight, strengthen the professionalization process, and shape professional identity. Analyzing these stories helps formulate midwifery theories that can be used to improve the quality of care.

The methodology we use here was designed by Van der Hulst (1999b) using stories from Dutch midwifery. This work provides the frame of reference for our analysis; in what follows we describe the important features of Van der Hulst's method for using case studies from midwives. To expand her original work to midwives in other settings, we asked midwives from the United Kingdom and Canada to write about cases that dealt with at least one of the theoretical subthemes derived from Van der Hulst's work.

The Nature of Midwifery Care

The starting point in a theoretical analysis of case studies is a good definition of "the work done by midwives." Van der Hulst (1999a, b) suggests that four aspects shape the daily work of midwives in the Netherlands (see Table 8–1).

Obstetric-technical care embodies all midwifery procedures done for the woman, such as performing internal/external examinations, episiotomies, and providing medication.

Risk selection is care based on the selection between low-risk and high-risk pregnant women, women in labor and the postpartum, and neonates. It involves screening for risk factors *and* making the appropriate medical referral. (Van Teijlingen & Bryar 1996, p. 24).

Social environment of the client refers to the fact that midwives harmonize their care with the personal situation of women, noting their social position, perceptions, expectations of pregnancy and birth, needs, and values. This aspect of midwifery care deals with intrapersonal psychosocial factors embedded in the client herself. Midwives are convinced that these factors stimulate (or obstruct) the physiological course of pregnancy, delivery, and lying-in.

Relational care revolves around efforts to establish a connection based on trust between care-provider and care-receiver. Equality, self-activation, empowerment, and open communication are important elements of a relationship that facilitates the natural birth process. This aspect of care is focused on the communicative and interactional aspects between midwife and client and requires the care provider to reveal her personal character.

This four-part model of midwifery care enables us to analyze the case studies, or stories of midwives. We readily acknowledge that theoretical analysis is, by its

TABLE 8–1
Theoretical Care Themes of Midwifery

Obstetric-technical
Risk selection
Social environment of the client
Relational care

FIGURE 8–1.
Overview of midwifery care and its four theoretical subthemes.

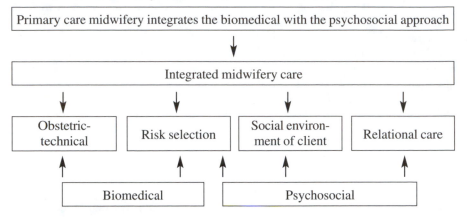

nature, a simplification of a complex reality. In practice, the separate elements of midwifery care are interwoven in biomedical and psychosocial spheres (Figure 8–1). These spheres are both integrated and overlapping and can strengthen (or weaken) each other. The biomedical element is highly evident in "obstetric technical care" and "risk selection." The psychosocial element is present in the "social environment of the client" and "relational care" and plays an important role in decision-making during "risk selection." In the case studies in this chapter many different elements of midwifery care are visible, although we highlight only one in each particular case.

Midwifery case studies are not descriptions of isolated obstetric events. They are embodied in a specific environment and cannot be separated from the way maternity care is organized. Because organizations, structures, and relations of power influence the quality and nature of the care midwives provide, the structure and organization of maternity care must be included in any analysis of midwifery case studies.

The Value of Listening to the Stories of Midwives

When we assemble and listen to the stories of midwives we are mapping the variety of care practices offered by midwives. When midwives refer to the midwifery case studies model they are documenting their own way of providing maternity care, a process that will ultimately lead to a complementing and broadening of insight into the profession of midwifery and the specific nature of midwifery care. This exercise is particularly valuable because many aspects of midwifery care are "invisible" when looked at by other professionals.

Midwives' stories serve yet another purpose: They allow midwives all over the world to determine their position with respect to the medicalizing trend within childbirth. In Western Europe and North America the boundaries of normal childbirth seem to be shifting under the pressure of increasing technological development and medicalization (see Chapters 9 and 12). When many midwives write case studies from their own theoretical frame of reference the characteristics of midwifery are documented at the primary source, offering a complete picture of the case and care given from a midwifery perspective.

Seven Midwifery Case Studies

Van der Hulst (1999b) originally published twenty-seven case studies in Dutch; three of which have been translated here. Case studies from the United Kingdom and Canada highlight similarities and differences between midwifery in different countries.

"I SAT DOWN FOR IT"

By Myriam Haagmans-Cortenraad (the Netherlands)

(Our first case study is from the Netherlands and highlights the technical skills of the midwife.)

Ms. P's first pregnancy was uneventful. The labor was rather slow and the baby was delivered by vacuum extraction with episiotomy.[1] Postnatally, Ms. P. suffered terribly from the stitches; therefore I advised the use of cold packs. The wound healed well and there was nothing exceptional to see. After the stitches were removed, Ms. P. continued to suffer from the wound. External and internal examination did not indicate anything exceptional, but the complaint did not go away. One-year postpartum, she was still complaining of pain during intercourse, and the scar gave her trouble just before menstruation. The pelvic floor function was affected.

A year and a half later Ms. P. became pregnant again. She delivered very quickly and spontaneously during a short-stay hospital delivery[2] with a second stage lasting ten minutes. As discussed antenatally, it was decided to cut again along the scar of the previous episiotomy, in the hope that the complaint would disappear. Again the wound healed very well and Ms. P. suffered less with the stitches than the previous time, and at postnatal checks everything looked better than before. Indeed, the complaint was lessened, but Ms. P was still not completely satisfied. She still had vague complaints of pain during intercourse and sometimes she experienced a heavy feeling down below. One year after the birth of her second child Ms. P decided to have scar-correcting surgery; afterwards Ms. P. felt like a new woman.

When Ms. P. became pregnant for a third time, she hoped that the previous problems and pains would not return. Although she had not planned a home delivery, she delivered very rapidly at home. A second-degree tear occurred, which was superficial and reached the anal muscle tissue. I consulted the obstetrician who had done the scar correction and we agreed that I should stitch the tear. At first I was not too keen, but after some supportive words from the obstetrician "I sat down for it" and stitched the tear very securely. When stitching at home I use a headlamp of the type used by cavers, which is strapped over the head with elastic and shines brightly on the work area. With such a tool it is unnecessary to move lamps or the woman in order to have good light when stitching. Fortunately, the woman had few complaints during the lying-in period and at check-up the wound was well healed and no longer caused pain. She had good bladder control.

This case confirmed my feelings that a tear heals better than an episiotomy and also causes fewer side effects. This feeling is now scientifically proven.

RESPONDING TO THE INVISIBLE FETAL HEART MONITOR

By Betty-Anne Daviss (Canada)

(This case study and the next have as their main theme risk selection. The first case study from Canada highlights the importance of the midwife's assessment of risk and her subsequent decision to reduce risk.)

In the late hours of a busy day I received a not uncommon call from a worried woman in her thirties, whom I will call Stephanie, who was 36 weeks pregnant with her first baby. She said: "I really feel that the baby hasn't been moving as well as usual."

We're careful in our midwifery practice to inform mothers that monitoring by fetascopes, dopplers, blood pressure gauges, and ultrasounds does not provide a definitive assessment of how well their baby is doing. During our prenatal care, we try to gently nudge mothers into developing an understanding of the secret life of the unborn miracle inside them, of the normal rhythms of their baby's movements. We try to help them develop a trust that they are their baby's best fetal heart monitor and that they may be able to intuitively detect the unusual.

This has its drawbacks. For some it can dash the hope that the office visits are the ticket to the 100 percent security that they expect from a good health practitioner. Highly anxious mothers come up with inquiries about the availability of electric fetal heart monitors that they might tie to their beds at home. It can become a circle of regret, as we start to backpedal and suggest that according to the baby's fetal heart tones, their own blood pressure, and the latest ultrasound everything is fine, so why are they worrying? After an anxious call, we often ask ourselves, "Do we pacify the woman with assurances or follow up on what might just be an anxiety attack?" Usually we can sense when a woman is "crying wolf." With Stephanie, I hadn't developed this sense because I had never met her—her primary midwife was away and I was covering all calls in the practice.

I was going to try an oft-used first response—"Take a hot bath and drink some orange juice, and maybe you'll feel the baby's movement better . . . call me back in an hour or two"—but I stopped myself. Stephanie said she had told my colleague about decreased activity the day before and both had hoped it would resolve itself. Knowing this and deciding that Stephanie was not being overly alarmist, I became concerned that there was really something abnormal going on. I decided to take her in and put her on the fetal monitor.

We met at the hospital shortly afterwards. The tracing on the monitor registered a little beat-to-beat variability, not entirely uncommon when the baby is sleeping. But after apple juice, cookies, trying to slosh the baby from side to side, as well as sneaking up on him and poking him on the side—everything short of sitting on the mother—it became apparent that nothing was going to provoke much movement. I paged the obstetrician on call who happened to be a new recruit to the hospital. Because it was at night and our normal ultrasound units were not working, I asked her how she felt about an old machine we had in the back operating room. She said she had tried it, and it wasn't trustworthy. I told her we should consider the tertiary care center where a unit was available all night. And then the obstetrician said something that I simply hadn't expected. She said we could go there or we could wait until morning, and just keep monitoring the baby.

I blurted, "Well I don't think Stephanie is going to want to do that," surprising even myself about how brisk a retort I had delivered. As we have not had hospital privileges for long, midwives in Ontario are still trying to be polite when suggesting an obstetrician's judgment might be off. It was also unusual for me to speak for a mother in her presence, as if I knew what she was thinking. But I really thought the obstetrician's suggestion was risky. The obstetrician conceded quickly and agreed with me. I don't know why she was less concerned than I was, and I never bothered to find out.

In the larger hospital the ultrasound also showed little movement, little reactivity, but the heartbeat and the amount of fluid around the baby seemed fine. A decision was made to get the baby out. A small amount of oxytocin to try to induce resulted in deceleration of the heart tones, and a cesarean section was performed instead, resulting in a small but healthy baby. There in the umbilical cord, imperceptible on the ultrasound, but very apparent through the translucency of the cord when the baby emerged, was a large dark clot, blocking normal blood flow and oxygen. An umbilical thrombus is something the neonatologists at the tertiary care center told us they usually see only with stillborn babies. Few mothers perceive this kind of problem soon enough to alert someone to do something about it.

On reflection I asked: What if I had not read the mother accurately? What if I had not trusted my own skills and expertise and had listened to the obstetrician? And the major question, what if the mother had not realized that something was wrong? Whether it emerges in the woman or in the midwife, intuition seems inextricably linked with the midwifery discipline.

HOW THINGS CAN GO WRONG AND STILL HAVE A GOOD ENDING

By Marike Roos-Ploeger (the Netherlands)

(The next case study focuses care based on the risk selection process as conducted by a Dutch midwife.)

Mrs. D. was the healthy mother of one child and now pregnant for the second time. Her first child, a girl, was delivered after an unproblematic pregnancy at term by vacuum extraction. During her second pregnancy things went less well right from the start. The main complaints were tiredness and lack of energy. However, in midwifery terms all went well. Her blood pressure was normal and the child was growing well.

At 26 weeks Mrs. D. (a teacher) decided to stay a week at home. At the end of her holiday she phoned to say that she was retaining fluid—her hands and ankles were swollen. There were few further complaints and she intended to go back to work on Monday. I explained I was in the middle of a delivery and that I would try to come along later on. I "missed" her on several occasions. In the end, I dropped a note through her letterbox asking her to contact me if she was still retaining fluid. Since I didn't get a reaction I assumed all was well. Meanwhile the woman was thinking, "Come on, don't complain too much, that headache is part of it and for my stomach pains I'll get something from the pharmacist. Monday I'm going back to work, no moaning."

On Monday the pharmacist advised the woman to contact me when she bought her stomach tablets because she looked rather bloated. She decided to rest in bed instead. Her husband phoned the GP when she began seeing stars. The GP advised her to take paracetamol. When the headache got worse rather than better, her husband phoned the GP again. The GP found her blood pressure dangerously high and referred her to the neurology department in hospital suspecting a brain hemorrhage. After some time the neurologist alerted the obstetrician. Finally, the woman was admitted with HELLP syndrome[3] at 28 weeks gestation to an obstetric department. At 31 weeks a daughter was delivered by cesarean section. Mother and child are well.

Relational Care: "Alternative" Birth Is Not Just for "Alternative" Types!

By Jillian Ireland (UK)

(This case study focuses on how care is based on the care provider/care receiver relationship in a UK hospital.)

I had been qualified as a midwife for a few months and was working in a "midwives" unit within a maternity hospital. Jasmine, a teenager in established labor, came in with her mother as her birthing companion. I was able to spend almost all of my time with them, as the unit was quiet that day.

Jasmine had left school because of this (unplanned) pregnancy. She was looking forward to having the baby but admitted that she had not wanted to think about the labor. She was going to let her mother advise her on baby care in the early days as she was still living at home. Because this was the first time I had met her I wanted to find out what she wanted to do in labor. She said she wanted me to decide. It's nice to be trusted as a professional, but I was afraid that, having given me "carte blanche," she would not tell me if I was doing something she did not really want.

I asked Jasmine's mother how her own labors had been and if there had been anything she would like to have done differently. She said that she had not expected much information from her own midwives, let alone to be asked what she wanted. She thought that the labors would have been easier had she been allowed to move around. She was not able to offer any physical support to her daughter as she suffered from arthritis.

I was glad that Jasmine's mother had suggested that being mobile would help because it made my care of her laboring daughter more effective. Jasmine had walked around and had been for a shower and the labor progressed quite quickly. Within a few hours, she started to feel some pressure in her rectum. This feeling persisted and quickly became an urge to push. During contractions I encouraged Jasmine to lean forward on the raised bed. She was managing to breathe through the contractions without pushing and said that she was happy standing and "rocking" her hips during contractions. I described the "supported squat" position for delivery to Jasmine and her mother. I had seen it used on video but never at firsthand. I was pleased when she said she would "give it a go."

Once the baby's head was just visible at the height of contractions we started to use the supported squat position with me standing behind Jasmine, supporting her under her armpits. Jasmine was pushing instinctively and I could hear from her noises that the baby's head was descending. Eventually I suggested that Jasmine lower herself to a kneeling position onto a soft mat, which had been prepared for her. I lowered the bed so she could lean on her arms for support. After a further ten minutes or so of pushing, Jasmine delivered her baby into my hands. She turned around and I handed her newborn daughter to her.

It was lovely to see someone who had been a bit scared change into someone so proud and glowing as Jasmine marveled at how she had coped with the pain using very little for pain relief.

This experience reinforces the notion that "natural" birth using so-called "alternative" positions are not only for the stereotyped "earth mother" who is middle-class, educated, and who has prepared herself whole-heartedly and extensively for childbirth. However, I wondered if I influenced the decision too much and this teenage mother simply followed my advice. I had done what I could to empower Jasmine given the constraints of the hospital-based maternity services in which midwives and clients most often meet for the first time when the woman goes into labor.

"A Premature Delivery At Home: An Experience"

By Annie Heuts-Verstraten (the Netherlands)

(The next two case studies highlight the importance of taking the social environment into consideration. The first is a story from the Netherlands.)

This exceptional event for me began with a late night phone call. I was busy with another woman who had just delivered. The husband told me that his wife had severe pain in her sides, especially on the left. When I asked if she had lost mucus or blood he said no. In the background I heard someone moaning as if a baby was about to be born. Because I knew that this woman was more than twenty-four weeks pregnant, I promised to send someone along straight away. I also told him that his wife was not allowed to go to the toilet.

I immediately phoned the GP on call because my midwifery colleagues had to come from too far away. I told him my suspicion: premature labor at 24+ weeks, colicky pain probably due to kidney stones or infection. Half an hour later he phoned me back to report that a premature baby had been born, which had died immediately after birth. I promised to come along as soon as possible.

On arrival the GP caught me at the front door and said, "The baby is still alive and it is a girl. We have given her an emergency baptism at the request of the parents. He had also consulted the pediatrician in the hospital when the baby began to show signs of life to establish the best thing they could do. The advice was to let the baby die at home because: "A too young premature baby who is not—or barely—viable and who had a strong asphyxia at birth which possibly led to irreparable brain damage." The GP outlined how he had found the mother under the shower. The head was already born and he received the rest of the body. The baby was floppy and very blue, which is why he told me initially that she was stillborn.

The mother was on the couch with the baby lying across her chest, her arms around it. The father was sitting a bit further away on a chair, looking spaced out and did not seem to understand what had happened to them. The baby's cord was not yet cut and the baby was about half an hour old. I felt a sense of powerlessness after I had admired the child. It was hard to find the right things to say. Only: "What a shame, so early"; "She is so beautiful and perfect"; and "Keep her with you for as long as possible." Since the GP did not bring a delivery bag, I cut the cord. Some cord blood was taken for analysis since the mother was Rhesus negative. The placenta was delivered quickly and was complete, blood loss approximately 100ml. The placenta was sent to the pathologist for examination. Although the woman's pain in her left side had disappeared, we decided to have some urine examined. The test did not show up anything. The baby weighed 500 grams.

After I wrapped the baby in a tinfoil cape and a towel I gave her back to the mother. We discussed the things that had to be arranged. The GP, a deputy for the family's own GP, was going to inform his colleague. We decided that I would stay with the baby until it died, probably within the next few hours. The mother constantly stroked the baby's cheeks. The father repeatedly said he felt guilty about the premature birth. When I looked at him, obviously surprised, he started to tell that after ten years of planned childlessness he could still not accept his wife's pregnancy. He did not want the baby and they had constantly quarreled about it and only recently (after the fifth month) did he begin to accept the situation. And then this happened.

As a midwife you listen and try to react as positively as possible. I said that it could not be his fault because premature birth has other causes. The mother said little and tenderly adored her baby, in order not to miss anything of her. The baby moved well because we heard the tinfoil rustle, when we checked we saw the baby move. The father was very worried whether the baby needed feeding, because it was 7 a.m. by now. He was also getting uneasy about the rustling of the tinfoil, therefore we went to get some clothes. Because the mother wanted to shower before the family arrived and since the father did not want to hold the baby despite repeated encouragement we went to find somewhere to lie her down.

The baby, named Bianca, was dressed in a white jumper which was more a dress to her and in which she could also be buried. We had talked about the funeral, the registration, and related things during the night. Bianca was put in the cot they had bought only two days before.

We agreed that I would do my postnatal visits during the morning if nothing happened. Meanwhile the family had arrived and we had coffee together, after which I left. When I returned in the afternoon, Bianca was still nicely pink and did not feel cold, despite the fact that she did not have a hot water bottle. When I called her name she made little noises. These little "shouts of contact" have got a special meaning to me and I felt it as a wonderful experience. It raised questions for me such as: Is she not too cold? Perhaps a wee drop of water for her too dry mouth? Strange without oxygen she was still pink and without a hot water bottle she still did not feel cold. Should I have done more? To what extent does the baby feel these negative and positive stimulations?

The mother and older sister stayed, and they were excellent support for the parents. I stayed the rest of the evening because I had agreed that I would stay until the baby died. Just like in the afternoon, Bianca seemed to react to the calling of her name. I was surprised how strong her will to survive was. Meanwhile the father was still suffering from guilty feelings.

The postnatal check up of the mother, fundus, temperature, blood pressure and HB were good, and she was given anti-D. We worked together until 10:30 P.M. The parents were tired and we decided that everyone would go to bed, because what we were expecting was taking longer than anticipated. Bianca would go upstairs with the parents to their bedroom. If any changes occurred I would be called. After I left, the parents decided to stay downstairs. The father told me afterwards that he found it frightening to be alone with the baby upstairs.

At 2:00 A.M., precisely twenty-four hours after the birth, the telephone went. The father told me with relief: "Bianca died just five minutes ago in my arms." I had to search for words and I could only think of one thing to say: "Just as well." To me it seems as if Bianca finally got to rest through recognition of the father. I asked them if they wanted me to come along, but they did not think that it was necessary.

In the morning they told me that the father's mother had tried to convince him one more time to hold his child with the words: "You might regret it if you don't hold her in your arms." The new mother told me that he held the baby and this touched her deeply. The baby made a few squeaking sounds, which she described as "like a coffee pot squeaking." The father told me that he had a good look at the baby. Then the head fell sideways and the little mouth opened and she died. He had her barely three minutes in his arms.

I visited the couple every day for support and check-ups, Bianca stayed in her cot until the day the three of us went to bury her. I felt privileged that I was allowed to participate in this young life of nearly twenty-four hours. The cause of this premature birth was probably placental insufficiency. The placenta did not show any peculiarities and no infection was detected. The couple had a second child in 1991 born at term weighing 2,470 grams.

TIPTOEING INTO TRUST: A SPECIAL HOME BIRTH IN CANADA

By Betty-Anne Daviss (Canada)

(A case from Canada that highlights the importance of knowledge of the social environment for midwifery care.)

Pire was a self-confident woman. She thought carefully about everything I said. She engineered her life events in a way that would not compromise the ideals she had for herself and her family, and her plans for birth were no different.

I first met her on a typical "see the midwife day" in the Ottawa Valley. Before midwifery was licensed in Ontario in 1993 vanfuls of pregnant women would make regular visits to my little hobby farmhouse for antenatal care.

After having lunch together and using my bath with hot water (an unknown commodity for some women), mothers gathered together to check out each others' latest measurements, commenting on the location of their latest aches and pains and catching me up on the general gossip. On this occasion, Pire had come along because she had heard about me through the other women. She eyed me very cautiously: "I've come to you Betty-Anne, because I've never been so close to civilization before when I've been pregnant, and so I thought I'd better see someone who was connected to civilization." I was not often seen as one connected to civilization. My city clients saw me as removed from the modern world, a cute, traditional midwife trained in

Guatemala who knew little about Canada and its hospitals and government-funded care. Needless to say, I was delighted by her perception of my status.

For Pire "civilization" was living *near* a road. She still had no plumbing or electricity. In Nova Scotia, from where she had just moved, she homesteaded in a small cabin that was a four-mile walk into the bush. In this setting Pire had birthed her first four children, attended only by her husband—when he was there. As we began to check out Pire's size and shape, she commented that she had been trying to figure out why babies come out head first, rather than bottom first. This did not seem very sensible to her, but no doubt there was a reason, and did I know it? Before I could answer, I felt an unusually hard round ball some inches above her belly button. I informed her that her baby had decided to take the very position she thought made more sense. I asked if she was aware that a breech baby could pose some trouble at the birth. I suggested that if she was going to have her baby at home, it would probably be safer to have it turned. One of the physicians in her area had expressed an interest in learning how to turn breeches, a maneuver I had learned from the midwives in Central America. I told her it would be a good opportunity, if she was agreeable, to let the physician watch me do it. The physician was interested but a little nervous. My papers were questionable; in fact, I had no papers. And the procedure seemed questionable. I knew only two other practitioners in Eastern Ontario who did it at that time (the early 1980s)—a GP from Britain who wasn't sure about the legal repercussions and an obstetrician who did it only under ultrasound at the regional academic hospital. Most physicians did cesareans for breech delivery. To protect his reputation, the Killaloe physician asked whether or not I would consider coming to his house to show him the procedure. He wanted to keep the whole thing quiet, removed from both professional and public scrutiny.

The procedure was a success, but the event was not exactly kept quiet; the entire community knew about it within days. A few weeks later Pire went into labor. I heard about it through the other women. Pire called neither the doctor nor myself to the birth, which went fine. Her rationale: Birth is a normal event, and you only need an attendant if you've moved into civilization and it causes things to turn upside down from what's normal. She had intuitively realized she might be in trouble and had the problem corrected. Some of those who thought her actions irresponsible would be the ones who would have a breech by elective cesarean because their doctor "told them it was safer."

A few years later Pire was pregnant again, and this time she invited me to the birth, although she was a bit hesitant to have me there. There had been an unattended home birth in the area and the woman hemorrhaged, became scared, and went to the hospital. Pire and the other women in the home birth community wanted to avoid a repeat performance. They figured it wouldn't be good for the reputation of home birth for something to happen that could be easily avoided by a competent birth attendant. When I crept into Pire's candle-lit house, I felt presumptuous taking even my little pinard horn inside, but I told her it was my safety hang-up, and she agreed that I could. The birth was longer and harder than usual. I asked her afterwards if she thought it was because I was there. She gazed out at her clothesline and said, "Yes."

I realized that night that if I ever had another birth of my own, I would want Pire to be my attendant.

A PREMATURE DELIVERY: "FALSELY RAISING EXPECTATIONS"

By Jillian Ireland (United Kingdom)

I was a student midwife working with an experienced hospital midwife when a woman was admitted to hospital in premature labor at 26 weeks. The woman had had several admissions with bleeding in this second pregnancy. There had been no problems in her first pregnancy and she had a healthy daughter. This time she was prepared for the worst. A scan at 24 weeks had showed a large blood clot behind the placenta and now her membranes had ruptured and she was having contractions.

The midwife told me that the baby would "not be for resuscitation." She told me not to be alarmed as the parents agreed. She also informed me that baby might make some reflex movements and, again, not to be alarmed by this.

The baby literally "slipped out" soon after a vaginal examination revealed a dilation of 8cm. He gasped and started to breathe and the midwife, deciding that this was more than expected, cut the cord and removed the baby to the adjoining resuscitation room. I was asked to put out an emergency call to the pediatrician from the neonatal unit. The neonatal unit had not been informed before because we were not expecting to transfer a live baby for treatment. The labor ward sister and I stood by the baby while the midwife returned to care for the mother.

The baby was a very poor color, obviously small for its gestational age, and was making no further attempt to breathe. He seemed at peace. A few minutes later the pediatrician rushed into the scene yelling: "Are you just standing there watching this baby die?" He started to resuscitate him and placed him in a transfer incubator. He would not listen to the ward sister who was trying to explain the situation. He was clearly angry. Instead, he took the baby to the parents and told them there was strong hope of survival.

The poor couple was in absolute turmoil. I was still in the frame of mind that the baby was critical, and, having looked on the admission form for a religious affiliation, had seen an entry made. I offered to call either the parents' own minister or the hospital chaplain. They chose to see the latter. When he arrived, I explained the situation to him and he spoke to the parents. While he was with them I went to the neonatal unit to tell them that the minister would be there soon to attend to the baby. I was greeted with overt hostility by a sister who said: "I hope you haven't told them the baby is going to die." I was confused and hurt and left the unit feeling very upset, not only at the sad situation but also at the way it was being handled. The parents had been ready to accept a serene passing away of a very small, very premature, and compromised baby. Now they were being given hope, which seemed so much in opposition to both their preparation and to reality.

In fact, on returning to the labor ward I met the father, who was on his way to see the baby. I told him that the baby was being ventilated and to expect a lot of activity around the incubator with tests being conducted and he said: "Why? There's nothing wrong with the baby, is there?" This was heart-wrenching to me. What had we done to these people with our lack of communication (or barriers to the pediatrician listening)? The baby died less than twelve hours later, and when I came on duty the next day, the mother had already gone home. I wonder to this day how the sad tale was explained to the parents.

Conclusion

What do these stories of midwifery care tell us? The most striking feature of all seven case studies is their attention to context. When you give midwives the opportunity to write about their work they write about its nonmedical aspects and the larger setting in which it occurs.

In a more general sense, case studies reveal the key features of midwifery work. The first story (Haagmans-Cortenraad) described the technical and practical skills that midwives bring to bear in their work. In the second and third case studies we find examples of midwives doing risk selection. Daviss tells us how she had to assess risk *twice,* once to decide whether or not to take the women to the local hospital, and a second time to decide to transfer the women to a tertiary center. Roos-Ploeger describes a situation where several caregivers are involved in assessing symptoms and defining risk. Strictly speaking, risk selection is part of the obstetric-technical, but both of these case studies show how primary care midwifery focuses attention on the social environment of the woman when assessing risk.

The main message of the fourth case study (Ireland) is the relational care provided by the midwife. Ireland highlights this: "As this was the first time I had met her I wanted to find out what she wanted to do in labor." She also makes an effort to involve the birth partner: "I asked Jasmine's mother how her own labors had been." In this example trust is a main theme, namely the unspoken trust of the woman in labor and her birth companion.

The next two case studies—from the Netherlands (Heuts-Verstraten) and Canada (Daviss)—have as their central message the midwife's attention to the woman's social environment. In the Dutch case the midwife shows an appreciation of the social environment of the woman and her partner. Notice how the midwife assesses the situation, creates an atmosphere, and provides care that fits the situation and the needs and values of family. The Canadian midwife focuses on the special circumstances of Pire, "a self-confident woman . . . [who] would not compromise the ideals she had for herself and her family." Again in this case trust was an important issue: trust in the midwife and the midwife's trust of her own skills.

The last case (Ireland) highlights that care is always provided within a specific maternity care system. Here a hierarchical hospital setting created poor interprofessional communication. In turn, poor relationships between professionals led to a difficult situation for the childbearing woman and her partner.

Mitchell (1979, p. 24) offers a sociological definition of the *case study* method: "[a] holistic [and] detailed examination of one instance [that provides] information about a class of entities." Our seven cases fit this definition perfectly: They offer a detailed look at the work of midwives that help us refine our notions of the profession of midwifery. The case studies allow midwives the opportunity to reflect on the defining features of their work. Inductive analysis of these and other stories will help midwives—wherever they work—establish and defend the boundaries of their professional identity.

Notes

1. The vertex in an occipito-posterior position means the baby is facing the mother's front rather than her back, leading to a labor often complicated by back pain, slow progress, and instrumental delivery.
2. Dutch women can have a short-stay hospital, attended by their community midwife, and if all goes well they leave hospital within hours of the delivery.
3. HELLP (hemolysis, elevated liver enzymes and low platelet count) syndrome is a condition in which the functioning of the mother's liver is disturbed, red blood cells are damaged, and the blood is less able to clot.

References

Hulst, L. A. M. van der. 1999a. Dutch midwives: Relational care and birth location. *Health and Social Care in the Community* 7: 242–247.

———. 1999b. *Vroedvrouwencasuïstiek: Van casus naar methode. Innovatie binnen de eerstelijns verloskunde.* (Midwife Case Studies: From Cases to Method. Innovation in primary care midwifery.) Houten/Diegem: Buhn Stafleu Van Loghum. (In Dutch.)

Mitchell, G. D. 1979. *A New Dictionary of Sociology.* London: Routledge and Kegan Paul.

Teijlingen, E. van and R. Bryar. 1996. Selection guidelines for place of birth. *Modern Midwife* 6: 24–27.

CHAPTER 9

Spoiling the Pregnancy

PRENATAL DIAGNOSIS IN THE NETHERLANDS

Barbara Katz Rothman

The relationship between technological change and social change is one that has long fascinated social scientists. The questions are often phrased in a chicken-and-egg fashion: Which came first? In my work on procreative concerns and practices in the United States, I have argued that underlying ideology drives technological development. Looking specifically at the relationship of ideology and technology in prenatal diagnosis, it seems to me that certain ways of thinking about pregnancy, childbirth, and the relationship between parents and children made the development of prenatal diagnosis and selective abortion feasible in the United States at the end of the twentieth century. The increasing commodification of children (see Zelizar 1985), one might say, made this development of screening techniques all but inevitable.

Of course, not all sociologists share the view that ideology drives technology. Those with a Marxist orientation would claim that ideology is part of the superstructure, resting on a base of production, including the technology of a society. Alternatively, within that same frame, technology can be viewed as being developed in the interests of the ruling class, out of their values, their needs, their ideology. But all such arguments assume a single, bounded society or social system that develops its own technology, its own ideology, and its own power relationships, in whatever dependent order. What happens—and this is the key question of this chapter—if the technology truly does arrive from outside?

Technology, I have always said, does not fall from the sky. And then one day I found myself in the Netherlands at a conference convened to discuss the introduction of the "triple test," a maternal serum screening test for neural tube defects and chromosomal abnormalities. This technology *had,* I suddenly realized, fallen out of the sky, arriving at Schiphol airport in the cases of medical sales people.

180

So what happens when a technology that does not develop out of underlying ideology is introduced to a society? This is a question of increasing importance as we see the development of a world market in biotechnology. In asking this question we must remember that an international community of scientists, physicians, and reproductive technologists supports the international *market* in biotechnology. This is certainly true in the case discussed here: Several Dutch scientists have made noteworthy contributions to the scientific work underlying the developing reproductive technologies, including prenatal diagnosis and screening. Nonetheless, in terms of cultural acceptance, patterns of use and disbursement, and marketing, the United States is a "marketing country" and the Netherlands is a "recipient country."

As noted elsewhere, these two countries provide a striking contrast in maternal care. In the United States, pregnancy and childbirth are highly medicalized; in the Netherlands, midwifery and home birth remain the standard of care. In the United States, medical care is privatized; in the Netherlands it is available to all. In the United States, paid maternity leave is not available for most women; in the Netherlands, all women have maternity leave both for late pregnancy and for the first ten weeks of newborn care. In the United States, services for people with disabilities are poor and generally getting worse; in the Netherlands, services are getting better.

Each of these factors—the medicalization of pregnancy and birth, the privatization of medical care, the absence of support for mothering and for people with disabilities—is significant in the American use of prenatal diagnosis. In the Netherlands, under such very different circumstances, the introduction of this testing has different consequences, different meanings. This chapter explores these issues.

Comparing two nations is inevitably complicated. Any observer can attest to considerable variation within each country: There are, for example, a few U.S. obstetricians supportive of the home birth movement and concerned with overmedicalizing pregnancy. Others are involved in the "Right to Life" anti-abortion movement, and opposed to prenatal screening on that basis. In the Netherlands, there is a cohort of Dutch obstetricians who are far more sympathetic to the medicalized view of pregnancy and birth management than the Dutch policy reflects. No discussion of differences between the two societies' acceptance of prenatal screening technologies should be read to obscure the variations that exist within each.

The research reported here, based on a series of focus groups conducted with Dutch midwives about their experiences with prenatal diagnosis, demonstrates a world of shifting meanings, of changing ideas, as midwives and their clients struggle to make sense of the imported technologies. Most of the Dutch midwives in this study, like most in the country, are in independent practice. The 20 to 25 percent who work in large academic hospital settings are underrepresented in this study, and while few immediate differences between these midwives and those in independent practice were observed, the views presented here are probably best understood as representing independent community midwives.

Fourteen focus groups were conducted with a total of sixty midwives in 1995,[1] scattered throughout the whole of the Netherlands. Participants represented the full range of Dutch midwifery practice (urban and village, hospital and home, higher and lower socioeconomic status). Focus groups lasted approximately two hours and were tape-recorded and transcribed.[2] While the country is small, there is cultural and regional variation within its borders.

Prenatal Diagnosis Testing: A Note on Technologies

Prenatal diagnosis refers to any technique for learning something about the condition of the fetus in utero. Amniocentesis, the removal of a small amount of amniotic fluid, permits study of the metabolic status of the fetus and also permits the examination of fetal cells for chromosomal abnormalities, most specifically Down syndrome, the condition of most frequent concern. Chorionic villus sampling similarly permits diagnosis of chromosomal abnormalities.

The testing is designed to identify fetuses with conditions such that the women carrying them prefer abortions to continuing the pregnancy to birth. Dutch midwives do have clients who choose the testing, who do indeed learn of such conditions, and who abort, and that too is a part of the midwife's job: "Guidance, helping people. If they have an abortion, that also is a piece of my trade."

Giving women choice is very much part of the midwifery ethos, yet "choice" may not be understood in the American way. For example, it is standard to offer amniocentesis or chorionic villus sampling to women with prior risk conditions (such as a known hereditary disease) and for women over the age of thirty-six, reflecting the increased risk of Down syndrome with increasing maternal age. Dutch midwives repeatedly stated that it was very important that women over thirty-six have the choice, and they do offer all the information and access to testing. But women under thirty-six? Sometimes it felt to me, an American with a different understanding of choice, that they did not understand the question: No, they would remind me, women under thirty-six are not eligible for amniocentesis.

In the United States, where women's choices are structured by economics, Americans are very wary of any overt statement of control. In the Netherlands, the economic constraints are absent, but the society has made a decision that only women at a particular level of risk, women over but not under thirty-six, are eligible for testing.

Dividing women into high-risk and low-risk groups by age and then offering the higher-risk women diagnostic testing has to a large extent become normalized in the Netherlands. Many women there (as in the United States) refuse the testing, but all (unlike the United States) are given access to it. There (as in the United States) the availability of the testing has raised fundamental questions about disability. Perhaps because of their experience with Nazi occupation, it seems that people in the Netherlands are somewhat more conscious of the eugenic questions involved in trying to rid the world of a particular kind of people, and questions about that were raised in the focus groups. Nonetheless, with one exception of a focus group in a very traditional area, freedom of choice for women with regard to abortion was highly valued, whatever its potential eugenic consequences.

The real concern in the Netherlands at the time of my interviews was not so much prenatal diagnosis, but more accurately prenatal screening, the mass testing of pregnant women for fetal defects. This was being introduced in several ways. In recent years a variety of "kits" have been developed to use in screening maternal blood serum for the likelihood of fetal abnormalities. These screens are just that: They are not diagnostic in themselves but (like age) screen for risk. I found that much of the discussion of prenatal diagnosis in the Netherlands focused on the introduction of the "triple test," designed to be used on all pregnant women and introduced on a trial basis in some areas.

Ultrasound examination, imaging the fetus using high-frequency sound waves, is another form of prenatal testing, used both for screening and diagnostic purposes. In the United States, as in much of Europe, ultrasound examination has become routine in prenatal care. In the Netherlands, the procedure, called *echoscopie,* is not (yet) routine, and its use is a matter of considerable discussion among midwives.

Using screening tests—including the triple test and *echoscopie*—separates populations into higher- and lower-risk groups. Inevitably, some of the women so screened and told they are of lower risk go on to have babies with the conditions for which they were screened (false negatives), and most women who are told they are at higher risk are eventually reassured that their fetus/baby is normal (false positive). As with most medical screening, levels are set to minimize false negatives, considered failures of the screening programs, at the cost of maximizing false positives, dismissed as "false alarms," and not generally recognized as having serious consequences in themselves. More on this later.

For virtually all of the conditions for which fetuses can be screened and tested, there are no treatments. The only choices offered the pregnant women are the selective abortion of affected fetuses or maintaining the pregnancy knowing the conditions of the fetus and the prognosis for the child it might become.

The Place of the Midwife

In the Netherlands, midwives stand between technology on one side and women on the other. It is their clients who are to be screened: Mass screening means that specifically low-risk women, young women, and healthy women are to be tested. The testing occurs in medical settings and involves the use of ultrasound to "scientifically" date the pregnancy. For American women, pregnancy has been so profoundly medicalized for so long that the introduction of yet another screening test may not be immediately perceived as significant. For Dutch women, many of whom go through their reproductive lifetimes of pregnancies and births without seeing a physician or making a hospital visit, this is a dramatic change.

One question facing the Dutch midwives is, "What will the medicalization of pregnancy mean for the management of birth?" Dutch midwives very consciously see themselves as the guardians of normal, what they call "physiologic," birth. While they provide care in hospital births as well, home birth is understood as essentially, prototypically normal. Consequences of prenatal testing for the management of birth are entering into midwifery discussion, often in the form of stories about women lost to technology. For example, a midwife having seen a woman through two successful home births sent to her, in her third pregnancy and now over age thirty-six, for prenatal diagnosis. An unusually shaped uterus was discovered, the woman was reclassified as "high risk" and she was transferred to obstetric care. Such stories abound.

The Dutch case allows us to see that the effects of prenatal diagnosis extend beyond the management of birth to the lives of pregnant women and to societal understandings of pregnancy, birth, and motherhood.

Spoiling the Pregnancy [3]

While most midwifery care involves assisting healthy women give birth to healthy babies, that is not always the case. We begin by hearing from midwives about the times when a baby's death is inevitable.

Ethicists who evaluate prenatal diagnosis are most often comfortable with these situations in which the fetus is diagnosed as having a condition that is inevitably fatal: It might not survive the pregnancy, or even if brought to term and born alive, would die shortly thereafter. In such instances, prenatal diagnosis is generally understood to present no ethical dilemmas. An abortion simply brings the inevitable to a more rapid conclusion.

Such an approach, like the medical model of pregnancy itself, is both product oriented and fetocentric. The medical model of pregnancy is the model or understanding that is taken-for-granted in American life. The purpose of pregnancy is to make a (healthy) baby: The point of all prenatal and childbirth management is to achieve that goal.

Critics of the American way of birth have recognized that this overlooks the experiences and consequences of pregnancy and birth management for mothers. "Fetal outcome" is generally the only independent variable that counts: How the mother feels about her body, her husband or partner, her family, her child, her sexuality, her self—all escape measurement, except as they might affect fetal outcome (see De Vries 1984). Particularly, since nutritional improvements have taken care of rickets and asepsis has stopped iatrogenic infections—two of the chief causes of maternal mortality—the focus of obstetric care is on fetal outcome, with the women variously seen as the carrier, host, environment, or barrier.

Midwifery, in contrast, is focused on women. That inevitably includes, in the management of pregnancy and birth, trying to help the woman have the healthiest possible baby. But it also means trying to give her a "good birth," a pregnancy and birth that make her feel good about herself as a mother, as a woman. It is not just the making of babies, but the making of mothers that midwives see as the miracle of birth. There is a general preference for prenatal rather than postpartum visits: Helping the woman is what midwifery is about. And that might very well mean, in a situation where the death of a baby is absolutely inevitable, helping a woman—and her family—come to terms with that in the best possible way.

In the medical model, the job is to get a healthy baby delivered. If you cannot get that done, then why bother continuing? That is, in a nutshell, the rationale for prenatal diagnosis and is certainly the logic used for testing conditions that are incompatible with life. If the woman could have known that the baby is going to die anyway, but did not find out, then she has in some sense been duped, made a fool of, wasted her time. Midwives, in contrast, ask a question that simply makes no sense in the medical model. If the baby is going to die anyway, than ask, "why spoil the pregnancy?" Why indeed? I've been working with midwives for so long that I didn't even realize that it was a strange thing to say until I shared it with American friends and colleagues who weren't midwives.

You can't spoil something if it has no intrinsic worth. If pregnancy is only about making healthy babies, and the baby is going to die anyway, then the pregnancy is spoiled. But that's not the way the midwives saw it. In one group, considering the possibility of a bad outcome, a midwife said, "Well, do they have to know it? Let them first have an untroubled pregnancy." And in another, when that idea was being talked about, a midwife leaned over to me, the American, the outsider, touched my hand, looked into my eyes, and explained: "Some of us find a good pregnancy very important whatever the outcome."

There are at least two ways of understanding the midwives' valuing of pregnancy as "good" when the outcome is "bad." The first reflects their view of life. If life is about accomplishing things, then pregnancies resulting in dead babies are pointless. But if life is about living, if it is just there, and we have only a finite time to live, then days spent in joyous anticipation are good days, and days spent in grief are bad days, and prenatal diagnosis of conditions that inevitably cause death simply moves days from the good to the bad side of the ledger for women.

A second way of understanding this—closely related to the first—is to postulate that pregnancy itself has a meaning and a value in a woman's life, and that for women who want to become mothers, a good pregnancy and a good birth are good things to have. Consider the following:

> In our practice was a child with a disorder that was not compatible with life. It didn't have a *middenrif* (diaphragm). Intestines up, heart in the wrong place. This woman had a good pregnancy, a difficult delivery, but she looks back on it very positively. The child lived a couple of hours. Of course they are sad about the child, but also had very positive feelings toward the child. And I saw a couple of pregnant women talking about it, and they said, "You could have seen it on an echo" (i.e., an ultrasound), which is true. "They should have done an echo, then they could have known." And that is how other pregnant people talk about it, like it's nice to know in advance that something is wrong. Theoretically. But they did not know this woman. This woman is very satisfied that she did not know anything in advance because an echo wouldn't have changed it. Yes, she would probably have had a hospital birth and three thousand echoes and pressure, and now it is at least a nice pregnancy and a positive experience of her delivery. The outcome would have been the same in both cases.

The outcome to which she refers is the loss of a child, a loss that was inevitable whether by abortion in the first half of the pregnancy or the death of a born child. Not all abortions are felt as a loss of a child. But for a woman planning on having a child, a diagnosis of a fatal condition has to mean the loss of that planned-on child. She was pregnant, planning on a baby. There will be no live baby, no living child. The outcome, however achieved, is the same.

Because the midwives think about the needs of the mother, they see pregnancy and birth differently. This exchange took place in a discussion of a baby with severe heart disease:

FIRST MIDWIFE: The children's doctor looked at the baby, everything okay. At night, the baby's temperature fell down. It had no chance to live outside the uterus. If I had made an ultrasound the disablement was shown. What will be the profit for this woman? She was pregnant, very happy, had a very good delivery, was very happy. However the baby died twenty-four hours later. But it died in her arms. What if we saw it on the echo?

SECOND MIDWIFE: No profit, only much worse I think. This was human.

THIRD MIDWIFE: Once I made an ultrasound, the baby was anencephalic, the child had no head. During the pregnancy the woman said goodbye to the baby. That was very important to that woman, so what is profit or loss?

In a medical model, that is readily answered: Profit is time saved, loss is time wasted. Rather than waiting for an anencephalic baby to be born and to die, an abortion is an efficient solution. But between the lateness of the diagnosis, and the fact that these are wanted pregnancies, these abortions are not comparable to ordinary, early abortions to get "unpregnant," where the pregnancy itself was a mistake. For the woman these abortions are the death of her baby, without the saving grace of a good birth and a good death.

The midwives are considering the process and not just the product. Let me clarify the distinction with a mundane example. Suppose you have a video camera and are filming your kids. They are mugging for the camera, singing a song, playing, laughing, and having fun together, when you notice you have run out of tape. If what you are trying to do is make a tape, then there is no point in continuing—you should tell the kids and maybe try again another day when you have a fresh tape. On the other hand, maybe you should just continue to do what you were doing, let the fun go on, and forget about the camera. Partly this is a difference between product and process, but it is also a way of thinking about what the product is: When filming the family, you are also constructing the family, making those very ties between your children that you seek to capture on tape.

Pregnancy is about making a baby, but it is also about making a family, making relationships, making the woman a mother. Even if the pregnancy is not successful in producing a baby, it may very well be successful in other ways. Death and grief and sadness also make a family. By nurturing the woman, her relationships with her partner and her family and friends, her feelings about herself and her lost child, midwives can construct success, satisfaction, family, even out of death. In this approach, since nothing is going to make the baby any better, one has no reason to learn ahead of time and spoil the pregnancy, burden the woman with untimely grief and ghastly birth-unto-death.

The case of a fetus whose condition is incompatible with life is as simple as prenatal testing gets. Whether you start from our standard American notion—that the whole point of pregnancy is to make a healthy baby, and if you can't do that there is no point in continuing—or from the position of these midwives—that something good can come out of even these pregnancies—this is the simplest case. As we pick our way down the slope, things get more complicated.

On Disability

Prenatal testing is designed for women who are carrying fetuses with conditions for which they should choose an abortion. If babies were going to die, the testing either saves, or costs, depending on how you see this, a few months. But for women whose babies would live with disabling conditions that the woman believes would make life not worth living, what the testing spares is a lifetime.

There are some (very) rare, absolutely devastating, nightmarish genetic conditions. But mass screening is aimed a little ways further down the slope, at Down syndrome and neural tube defects, both of which are very broad diagnostic categories, with a wide range of associated disability. Particularly with Down syndrome, but to some extent with neural tube defects, the prognosis—just how badly the child would be affected—cannot be judged prenatally. And these are not, by any means, the only conditions that can damage a baby. As one midwife said, summarizing a conversation on the limits of the tests:

> I think it's a too, too small test, and it's only for syndrome of Downs and spina bifida and there are many, many other problems, and I think it's too, too less to put so big pressure on women when you are only checking these two things, and they are really waiting, scared, *echoscopie,* and maybe the amniocentesis, and until nineteen weeks they are not happy pregnant, and I think that's really bad.

But these are the things for which fetuses are tested, and so we must ask, "How well do Down syndrome and neural tube defects fit the criteria of being conditions that make life not worth living?" And what exactly is it about those conditions—their physical consequences, their social consequences—that makes them so devastating? These are not entirely answerable questions, and in the context of this paper, they are not even questions I will fully explore (for a fuller discussion see Katz Rothman 1986). But certainly the answers are not the same throughout the world, and here too the United States and the Netherlands present significant contrasts.

There is a widespread and profound revulsion for mental retardation in the United States. While such feelings are not absent in the Netherlands, I sensed a different tone there. An affectionate *mongeltje,* or "little mongol," was often used when people talked about children with Down syndrome, not only in the focus groups, but in general conversations with ordinary people. It lacked clinical or political correctness, but it was said warmly. People with Down syndrome—accurately or not—have a reputation for being happy, easy-going, "simple" in many ways.

Of course there are structural issues at work as well. In the Netherlands, unlike the United States, having one child with Down syndrome doesn't mean that your other one(s) won't have money to go to a good college. People do not lose their homes and their savings to the costs of the disabled child. Universal health care coverage and decent facilities and services for people with disabilities change the type of concerns one has.

One focus group discussed health and happiness:

FIRST MIDWIFE: People want their babies to be healthy; but they want their children to be happy. Unhealthy means unhappy, but that is not necessarily so and then if you see an unhealthy baby that looks very happy it is much easier to deal with. . . . I have a child, I just want it to be happy. I don't care if it has two legs or one leg so long as it is happy.

SECOND MIDWIFE: But you don't know at birth if the child will be happy of course.

FIRST MIDWIFE: No, you don't know, but maybe the child will be unhappy anyway, but bad health is connected with unhappiness and that is what you are afraid of.

THIRD MIDWIFE: Unhappiness means unhealthy. In Dutch you often say *een ongelukkig kindje* ("an unfortunate or unhappy child") when you mean a disabled child.

If the child's own happiness or unhappiness is the criteria, and much of the unhappiness of Down syndrome can be socially attended to, then it makes sense that there is more concern, both within the Netherlands generally and among the midwives specifically, about the various physical impairments caused by neural tube defects.

Whenever I have critiqued prenatal testing in talks in medical settings as being enormously burdensome for pregnant women, physicians have responded with some version of "If you'd seen what I've seen. . . ." The way the opening gapes at birth, those horrifying medical textbook pictures, the (repeated) surgeries, particularly the failures, the long term hospitalizations. I've never been at such a birth. I've never held the gore in my hands and tried to repair it, so maybe I don't know what I am talking about. Maybe it is worth any amount of grief and anxiety by any number of pregnant women to avoid that scene.

Yet years of listening to disability activists critiquing the medical approach to disability makes me wonder if medical reality—as brutal a reality as it is—is the most informed understanding of what it means to bear a child with a neural tube defect or other disability. Midwives too have seen a lot, been at such births, so one question that was raised in all of the focus groups was what the midwives themselves had seen, what disabilities, deformations, birth defects, and anomalies they had seen.

One very striking thing, very hard to remember but very important to bear in mind in discussions of mass screening programs, is just how rare these problems are. Among women in their twenties and early thirties, Down syndrome occurs in less than 1 in 1,000 births; neural tube defect is even rarer. When asked, midwives had no trouble remembering such bad outcomes. They are rare enough to be remembered, common enough so that in every group midwives had attended births with these or similar problems.

Bad outcomes were discussed, but they were always contextualized in the woman's life and experiences, and often contextualized over time as well. An older village midwife,[4] for example, recalled the two children with neural tube defects whose births she had attended: One went to _____ a special care center and went back and has a bicycle with three wheels. He's a terrible boy, and he's spoiled like his father. . . . The other one, the child of a teacher, he goes with his father to school on the bicycle. He gets special attention. They do everything. And really are well."

The description of the severity of the neural tube defect by the type of bicycle the child rides—his own three wheeler or as a passenger on his father's—was very apt, and very Dutch. In a flat country where everything rolls, where the mail gets delivered by bike, where old ladies with orthopedic shoes hang their canes on the back of their bikes, and people with disabilities chug along in the bike lane on a variety of adapted bikes including motorized tricycles, the wheelchair is somewhat less disruptive in public life than it is in the United States.

A village midwife sees the horror of the gaping hole at birth, but also sees the continuity of that life, the child in the supermarket, on the way to school, and that in turn shapes how she sees the next child with such a problem at its birth. Perhaps we can turn the medical "If you saw what I saw" to "If they saw what the midwives saw"— the context, the whole of life, the family, the community—they too might think somewhat differently.

The Fullness of Time

Some disabilities—neural tube defects, club foot, cleft lip and palate—are immediately apparent at birth, while some for which prenatal testing is now available will not show up until middle age. Down syndrome is apparent early, but what might be instantly recognizable to an experienced birth attendant might not be so obvious to parents.

Prenatal diagnosis never tells anything one wouldn't have found out later on anyway. It changes the timing. In having prenatal testing a woman seeks immediately the information she would have had eventually. The reason to seek that information early is that abortion is possible early on. In choosing not to have a prenatal diagnosis, a woman may be seen as burying her head in the sand. Several Dutch midwives told me about one particular woman obstetrician who tells her patients who hesitate about having testing that that is what they are doing: burying their heads in the sand. It is the picture of foolishness: turning away from knowledge while exposing oneself to pain. But, as one midwife said regarding not diagnosing inevitably fatal conditions, "Yes, it looks a bit like putting your head in the sand, but on the other side, that isn't it. It's letting nature take its course."

When I shared this research with American midwives and childbirth educators, one of them used a phrase that resonated for me: the fullness of time. "Let it come, let her learn what she needs to know, but all in the fullness of time." Dutch midwives said similar things, although they are less eloquent when rendered in English: "There's time enough to worry about it when the time is right."

Sounding very much like "burying her head in the sand," one midwife spoke about late diagnosis, information coming past the time when an abortion is possible, as happens occasionally with ultrasound:

> With the echoes at 25 weeks and they see something, the pregnancy is spoiled because she has to live with something till birth is coming, because you cannot do anything. Or they see the baby has something not with life *verenigbaar* (compatible), what should you do? So I think it is better not to know, just give birth and then you will see.

And a second midwife elaborated: "The pregnancy is very abstract, you don't make a decision about the child, and when you see the child, it is not so abstract anymore and you make a decision based on your emotions."

A decision made during pregnancy, they are saying, cannot be a fully informed decision because it remains an abstraction and the emotions are not there yet. It is an interesting twist on the more usual (American? medical? male?) notion that emotions muddle and get in the way of informed decisions, that emotions are themselves a pull toward irrationality.

Down syndrome can be absolutely, definitively diagnosed relatively early in pregnancy, as early as 10 to 12 weeks with early amniocentesis or chorionic villus sampling, closer to 18 weeks when diagnosed as part of a mass screening program beginning with maternal serum of the "triple test" screen and moving on to definitive amniocentesis. At birth, Down syndrome is readily diagnosable with chromosomal testing, but not always instantly recognizable, especially for parents. Most of the discussion of Down syndrome in midwifery care revolved around disclosure issues:

when and how do you tell? This is a discussion I have heard both in these focus groups and informally in the Netherlands and in the United States. Experienced midwives in the Netherlands described a kind of watchful hovering while realization dawned—sometimes over a period of days—on the family. One spoke of a family joking at birth about the baby's "Chinese eyes," seeing and yet not seeing what was obvious before them. Returning daily, probing gently, finally the parents turned to the midwife: "It's not right, Chinese eyes, is it?" And no, the midwives told them, it's not right that the baby has Chinese eyes, and what do you think that might mean? And so a family slowly learned about Down syndrome. Compare that with Micheal Berube's (1996) description of the U.S. birth of his son with Down syndrome: just, just-born, "his neck wreathed in his umbilical cord. 'He looks downsy around the eyes,' I heard." (p. 5)

The pacing the midwives value is particularly possible with home births, where the midwife can control the flow of information. In hospitals, nursing and medical personnel intervene, even in a midwifery-managed birth. Such situations have often been described as information thrust upon an unready mother or of someone "blurting it" too soon. I've also heard of inexperienced midwives telling too quickly and even, in one case, of being wrong.

But even when the midwife is right, as Berube's doctors were right, an instant appraisal may be actively discouraged. The slowness is itself valued, the unfolding of knowledge with time. That time, those minutes, hours, or days, serve a purpose, the midwives explained. One midwife, telling of a period of several days of confusion before a diagnosis was made and the mother informed of the baby's Down syndrome, said: "I talked later to this woman and she told me exactly these days it was for me to adore my baby. If they told it the first day because they thought immediately about it, I cannot adore her. But she is already in my heart, I adore her. I hear she is not okay but it does not matter anymore, she is already my daughter."

In the language of contemporary medicine and psychology, this is called "bonding," a period in which attachment between the mother and baby, and baby and family, is solidified. Pregnancy itself, and the birth process, the midwives claim, serve this purpose. Speaking generally of women bearing babies with problems, one midwife said:

> Some women say that when they discover during the delivery that something is wrong, they say, "Fortunately I had nine months to bind to the child and it's my child. It's shocking, but I've had nine months a very nice pregnancy which no one will take away from me." And if they would have discovered while they were still pregnant that the child was not healthy? . . . Indeed you never know: How unhealthy is not healthy? What can you expect? And then you have a lot of doubts and you're not enjoying your pregnancy anymore.

And another, in a different group, talked about a woman who gave birth to a surviving child with multiple handicaps:

> It was a baby with these defects and we talked about it later and she told me she was very happy that she did not have the echo and that she also during the birth did not know that something was wrong with the baby. . . . You make a bonding with the baby, during birth you have a lot of contact with the baby. If she know it during the pregnancy she would

have stand so different in giving birth. Then you have already a reaction like, that, maybe, it's not my baby, you make a distance. And if you have the process together, and it is only a feeling, my baby and I, then you have a closer bond, this is what she told me.

In the era in which prenatal testing was being developed, it was standard American medical practice when a damaged or "defective" baby was born to a knock the mother out with anesthesia. Doctors did not want hysterical mothers in the delivery room. If the woman was not already unconscious for the birth, anesthesia was used for social control. The woman was then informed later, without seeing her baby. It was an open secret that some babies were allowed to die of exposure and hunger in the back of American neonatal wards and that survivors with severe disabilities were warehoused in institutional settings, families encouraged to forget them and have other children. A disabled child was an unqualified tragedy from which women should be spared.

Midwives see women differently. I have been told a few tales of mothers crying and rejecting babies at birth and then coming around to acceptance. But mostly the tales are of women's strength, not hysteria. The midwives talk about the strength as being there in the women; I see midwives nurturing women to tap their strengths, playing more of a role in the way mothers handle this than perhaps midwives give themselves credit for.

But can the woman who is strong and accepting and loving at birth—the woman who says of her daughter, "Maybe she's not okay but it doesn't matter anymore"— have those feelings without the fullness of time? Without the pregnancy, without the child, without the emotions of birth, it is not the same. Prenatal testing, if offered early enough, attempts to bypass all of that and permits abortion before the child becomes a child. How does one counsel a woman about ending a pregnancy with a fetus that the midwife knows the woman will grow to love? This is the problem expressed clearly by two midwives in a discussion of counseling for prenatal screening:

> FIRST MIDWIFE: [I ask women], "Which deviations do you think you can handle and which not?" I think when push comes to shove you are stronger than you think you are. That's what I see: People who have a child with some kind of deviation are always very strong.
>
> SECOND MIDWIFE, INTERJECTING: Yes, but then they are facing a fact. I don't know how these people would react when they knew it in the twelfth week of pregnancy.

No Guarantees

Midwives know that birth, like life itself, comes with no guarantees. A belief in the health and normalcy of pregnancy and birth is not to be confused with a fantastical expectation of all jolly pregnancies, happy healthy babies, well-adjusted mothers, and eternal happiness. Critics of midwifery often fail to understand this, confusing the midwives' conviction about the "naturalness" and "physiological" and "healthy" nature of pregnancy with a naïve "Pollyannaish" expectation of happy endings. It is somewhat ironic, then, that the midwives themselves use the same accusation of the testing process.

The testing, they find, implies for many women a kind of guarantee. Women say they want the testing for reassurance, for security. One group discussed use of ultrasound and the search for security, and as one midwife concluded: "It gives security, 'I'm so glad I have seen the baby and the doctor said everything was okay. And you could see the kidneys and the heart. It was quite nice.' So I'm scared about that security."

In group after group midwives told stories of women reassured and then surprised. Consider this excerpt from a discussion of a woman who had a child with disabilities in her first pregnancy and then considerable testing in her second:

> FIRST MIDWIFE: Then she was pregnant again and she really went twenty times for an ultrasound as well in _____ as in here. This time it's a fantastic child and she wanted to give birth at home. So there comes some eight-pounder, and it has *one hand* and nobody noticed that before. Then you stay there, and you know, *met je mond vol tanden* ("with your mouth full of teeth," that is, "speechless") I felt it soft below my feet. I never felt worse.
>
> SECOND MIDWIFE: And she got the impression, everybody looked at it so many times, there will be no problem, that's what you expect, but then . . . .
>
> THIRD MIDWIFE: Yes, it's a kind of false protection.

I think midwives tell each other these stories—and there are a lot of them—not just to complain about inaccurate testing but also because it raises a fundamental issue about the meaning of testing. Testing is about control, as if information led to control. Several midwives mentioned women wanting early ultrasound to reassure them about miscarriage. But early ultrasound will only tell them what they already know: that they are at that moment carrying a fetus. That you can see it on Monday does not mean that it will be there on Tuesday.

That is why midwives aren't just irritated by these false negatives, these false reassurances, but, as one said, scared by that security. Some see this as a product of changing times: "But it suits in these times we live in, we want to arrange everything, we want to control." Some recognize it as very specifically an American way being exported to the Netherlands. Talking about people demanding more and more testing:

> FIRST MIDWIFE: Then you get American scenes. Because everything has to be checked, with every pregnancy, and the costs!
>
> SECOND MIDWIFE: Yes, but, all right, it's appearing in Dutch society. That people are getting the eye for a defect.

Midwives are finding their clients asking for more testing. Some say it is city women more than village women, or the ones who "read everything"; some say it is the media, the magazines pushing these stories. Some see the push as coming from some of the Dutch research centers. But all are aware of these winds of change, and it scares them because this isn't just about pregnancy. This is about motherhood and about life itself. In counseling people one midwife says:

> It has something to do with someone's personality, the way he copes with deformation in life, isn't it? Like he can accept, or not, a child with a handicap. I explain that it is not true

that you don't have to worry any more when the pregnancy is passed. You are eager to have a healthy child, but after a chorionic villus sampling, amnio, an ultrasound and birth, your worries are not over yet. When the child is there you still have your concerns. Can he walk along the street on his own, and ooh, near the water, I hope he gets no accident, and I hope he doesn't get some wrong friends. It is a process, all life long, isn't it? Somehow or somewhere you have to let it go, you cannot control everything, and maybe you have to start to let it go at the beginning. You should dare to leave some questions without an answer.

A Lot of Commotion

Most of the time, of course, babies are healthy. What has the midwives very concerned, and led to considerable discussion in all the focus groups, were the false positives, the pregnancies spoiled for no good reason at all: "If you do the ultrasound they screen you only roughly to see if there are any congenital defects and it is like opening a cesspool. . . . It is horrible. I heard so many awful stories: People have a terrible pregnancy and afterwards it turned out all right."

This is an inherent, inevitable problem in any screening program. If the test(s) used identified only those affected it would be a diagnosis, not a screen. A screening test is essentially a very poor diagnostic tool, one that has lots of false positives. Screening tests are used when they are safer, cheaper, easier—or all three—than diagnostic tests. Doing amniocentesis and other definitive prenatal diagnostic tests on every pregnant woman is not feasible—the tests are dangerous, expensive, and difficult. So ultrasound and maternal serum screens like the triple test are used to identify women at higher risk for more testing.

It follows then that very often a problem picked up on the screen will turn out to be nothing. Helping women through this difficult period occupies considerable time and energy for the midwives, and they consider it a serious disadvantage of screening women: "You can ruin a pregnancy with it, or an entire part of it." And in another group: "You take away an unconcerned pregnancy, that's what you remove." And yet again:

> FIRST MIDWIFE: It seems to be there is something wrong, it causes a lot of commotion, and finally it comes out nothing is wrong.
> SECOND MIDWIFE: But you have a spoiled pregnancy.

False positives are routine in triple test screening, but even those midwives who were in areas where that was not yet introduced have had similar experiences with ultrasound. In some countries, including the United States, ultrasound is used repeatedly during pregnancy to visualize the fetus and provide rough diagnostic information. In the Netherlands, routine ultrasound is not done, but the criteria for doing an ultrasound are quite loose. A woman who wants to "see" her baby, to have a picture for herself and her family, has only to claim that she "doesn't remember" her last menstrual period and needs an ultrasound to date the pregnancy. Such "memory" lapses are apparently not uncommon and are joked about by midwives.

One midwife had a deaf woman as a client, and felt badly for her that she couldn't hear the baby's heartbeat. As a treat, she sent her for an echo, an ultrasound. Some kind of hernia was found, and one set of doctors warned the woman about severe heart defects, while the pediatrician minimized the problem:

> FIRST MIDWIFE: So it was sent to _____ and (the doctors) say we want an abortion, and I say no, you don't do so because the pediatrician said it was not so bad . . . . And the baby was born in (University Hospital), kept there for eight or ten weeks. And that opening on the stomach is growing closed. And it is a perfect baby with no heart problems at all. They thought so but it wasn't.
>
> SECOND MIDWIFE: But she had a terrible pregnancy.
>
> FIRST MIDWIFE: (She could have had) a nice pregnancy without worries and going up and down to (University Hospital). She wanted an echo for fun and it turns out to this.

While some of these "false alarms" are inherent in the nature of screening itself, others come because a baseline for normal has not yet been established. Doctors are only now seeing the development of, say, fetal kidneys or fetal hearts. In every other area of life there are ranges of normality, and here too variations will be seen that are not pathological, but not immediately recognizable as normal.

Midwives are downwind of test developments and experience erratic gusts of diagnosis. At the time I was doing the focus groups, cysts on the fetal neck as a possible indicator of Down syndrome were a hot issue. One midwife, given her recent experiences with all of these false alarms, reassured a woman whose fetus had such a diagnosis at nine weeks: "I know they are keen on this cyst in the neck, it is really there. So I say, forget about it, and if you like you can have an echo if the restless comes to you at about 20 weeks and you feel more comfortable, then you can have an echo to look at it, but it is not necessary, just leave it." In a more complete discussion of the diagnosis of cysts on the fetal neck:

> FIRST MIDWIFE: It (echo) has really bad side effects too, because in the past two, three years, three times there was something found (cysts) at the ultrasound and nothing in the end was wrong, but it did ruin their pregnancy, that was really bad. It (echo) is only nice when it is good.
>
> SECOND MIDWIFE: They come in a circle of lots of investigations, and that takes a couple of weeks, and then after five, six weeks they tell you everything is normal, but it was hell of course those five weeks.

A similar pattern shows up with the positioning of the placenta. At the time of birth, the placenta must be high above the cervix—a low placenta, or one that blocks the cervical opening (placenta previae), can prevent vaginal birth and can threaten hemorrhage. But earlier in pregnancy, the placenta may very well be lower down, moving higher with time. How often is it how low at how many weeks of pregnancy? The data are only now being made available, as the position of the placenta is routinely noted on ultrasound. One midwife described a woman who had an ultrasound and was told at 20 weeks (with half the pregnancy still to go) that she had a placenta previae. There were general murmurs of recognition of the situation, and one midwife said, "Yes, what do you do with it, but the panic has started"; another added: "It takes an awful lot of time to turn the clock back, to reassure people. It takes a piece of joy out of the pregnancy."

As long as I have been studying midwifery and maternity care, for well over twenty years now, this is a theme that I have heard. Obstetric research produces some problematic diagnosis, often connected to the development of some new diagnostic tool or technique. Lots of women get the diagnosis, lots of panic, concern, commotion—and then it dies down and they move on to another diagnosis. With time, with more experience with each new technology, the problem will resolve itself—only to go on to the next new technology and new diagnosis. Such is the nature of progress.

Conclusions

Even when there are no "problems," even when the fetus appears normal and the pregnancy is not threatened by test results, the very fact of testing introduces uncertainty, presents a challenge to the presumed normalcy of pregnancy, to the jolly pregnancy. For people who are already deeply imbued with the medical understanding of pregnancy, who approach it in this typically American way, fear is already a deep part of pregnancy, fear that something can go wrong, fear that the woman cannot do this, fear that the child will be damaged, deformed, monstrous, unlovable. If fear is structured into the nature of the pregnancy experience, then testing holds out hope of reassurance.

American women, Dutch midwives tell me, have lost trust, trust in themselves, in their own strength, their own power. If that is true, maybe that is why Americans need and developed all of this testing. But what does it do for Dutch women, who, their midwives tell me, still have that trust in themselves?

FIRST MIDWIFE: I think everything you do for extra, there is always the risk of *onrust* (unrest, unease).

SECOND MIDWIFE: That you lose the trust, the power of pregnancy.

FIRST MIDWIFE: With all the tests you introduce more and more and you also give . . . . How (many) more tests, how (many) more reasons to feel uncomfortable about a lot of things. To feel guilty.

THIRD MIDWIFE: How many tests do you need to get a stamp that allows to be pregnant? That's how it sounds, how it feels.

Ideology may very well produce technology, but technology that enters from outside does challenge ideology. It was my hope that these Dutch midwives, situated differently, working with a very different understanding of pregnancy and a different view of women, might find some way to use this technology that solved some of its many problems. I had hopes that they might creatively turn it around somehow. They have had some success with the various technologies for hearing and amplifying fetal heart tones, using doptones in different ways than do American physicians, with some creativity, even playfulness.

But it may be that the technologies of prenatal diagnosis, specifically maternal serum screening, ultrasound imaging, chorionic villus sampling, and amniocentesis—technologies employed for use with selective abortion—raise such very different issues that midwives have not yet and may not ever find their own way of using them.

My first and foremost goal in this research was to let a new voice be heard, the voice of Dutch midwives. I want to empower the midwives as the midwives empower the birthing women with whom they work. And yet, midwives told me, there is no readily translatable word for "empowerment" in *Nederlands*: They most assuredly do it, but they cannot easily speak about it. What would it mean to empower Dutch midwives? In marked contrast to the situation in the United States, birth and midwifery are, in a sense, nonissues for the Dutch. As noted in previous chapters, midwives and home birth is very much part of the Dutch landscape. There are no social movements coalesced around these issues and, consequently, no coalition building with other movements. To the eyes of American midwives, childbirth activists, home birth activists and feminists, Dutch midwives are surprisingly apolitical. That is of course not universally true: Over the years I have had many conversations with midwives, especially those who represent the Netherlands internationally, about the complacency they see in their colleagues. We can no longer afford their silence.

At a national conference in the Netherlands on the introduction of the triple test in 1989 various experts spoke: physicians, sociologists, ethicists, and psychologists. No midwives were invited as speakers or even attendees. The only midwives who were present were those who had learned about the conference from me and invited themselves. It was, the organizers assured the midwives later, only an oversight.

It is a significant oversight, and one that is repeated over and over again. While I lived in the Netherlands doing the research reported here, there were public debates on prenatal diagnosis. Again, the standard experts were heard from, including disability activists. I was impressed with all of those voices, the rich discussion, so much more open and public and concerned a discussion than goes on in the United States, where new technologies in medical and maternity care get introduced and disseminated with very little public debate. But I noticed that one voice was always absent: the midwife's.

Midwives cannot speak *for* women, but they can speak as midwives, as women themselves, as—translating from the *Nederlands* word for midwives, *vroedvrouwen*—wise women. These wise women have centuries of experience behind them. As one village midwife told me, dating the known history of midwifery in her village to 1559 "Don't we build up authority in all those centuries?"

Maybe we need more of this testing, maybe ultimately it spares more grief than it causes and is worth its costs. But something is being lost, and Dutch midwives can see that:

> FIRST MIDWIFE: Precisely there is a lot of commotion now and it is hard to solve this problem. This is a very important and negative aspect of this test, but . . .
> SECOND MIDWIFE: You don't have a happy pregnancy anymore.
> FIRST MIDWIFE: And those people who develop this test, they don't see this problem.
> THIRD MIDWIFE: No, they just like to do their research.

When we do our research within the confines of a single society, we see only the lurching along of social and technological change, each pushing and pulling the other, the chicken and the egg seeming to materialize together. When we cross boundaries and look both ways, we can more readily disentangle the relationship.

The introduction of prenatal testing has costs. In the United States we have focused on the benefits, and the reason we don't see the costs is because we paid up front: The medicalization of pregnancy, with the loss of trust, the introduction of fear and anxiety, the American "eye for a defect," all came first and made the development of the testing feasible. That may well be the pattern. An ideology, a way of thinking within a culture, sets the limits and boundaries for individuals. Technologies are developed to make life better within those constraints. But when the technology— with all of its benefits—is exported, so too are the limits and constraints that led to its development.

A Final Word

I sat at a conference in January, 1999, with an American home-birth midwife and a Dutch midwife. The subject of maternal serum screening and the "triple test" came up. "It's a bad test," the Dutch midwife said. "We're not using it any more. I am no longer permitted even to offer it to women." The American sighed, "And I have to—I can't not offer it."

Americans cannot see the costs of ruining a pregnancy, of taking out a piece of the joy, because we have already spoiled the pregnancy.

Acknowledgments

Many people, including the midwives, made this research possible. I particularly want to thank the Fulbright Program; the PSC-CUNY awards of the City University of New York; and, for their creative, unstinting generosity and help in countless ways, Tjeerd Tymstra, Linda G. Katz, and Annemiek Cuppen, to whose memory this chapter is dedicated.

Notes

1. I was chief investigator on this project, which was part of a Fulbright Research Fellowship at the University of Groningen. I was assisted by two Dutch colleagues who have been studying midwifery issues in the Netherlands, Eva Roelofsen and Inge Kamerbeek; we worked with a group of medical sociology students who participated as part of a research seminar I ran in Qualitative Methods. Roelofsen and Kamerbeek set up all of the groups. In twelve of the groups Roelofsen, Kamerbeek, or I moderated with a student assistant; two were moderated by students who had assisted at previous groups.
2. Medical sociology students did the transcribing and, where necessary, translations into English. Eleven of the focus groups were conducted in *Nederlands*; three were in English (for my benefit). All of the material quoted from the groups in this chapter is presented in English as the midwife spoke it, or in English as the student translated it. In either case, there is a recognizable English-as-a-second language sound. It is tempting to make the English smoother—but then one loses some of the idiosyncrasy of the underlying Dutch. The tangled relationship between language, grammar, and the very meanings I seek make that a dangerous strategy.

3. Portions of this section are drawn from my book, *Genetic Maps and Human Imaginations: The Limits of Science in Understanding Who We Are* New York: W.W. Norton, 1998, pp. 180–186.
4. A village midwife works in the community in which she lives.

References

Berube, M. 1996. *Life As We Know It: A Father, a Family and an Exceptional Child.* New York: Pantheon Books.

DeVries, R. 1984. "Humanizing" childbirth: The discovery and implementation of bonding theory. *International Journal of Health Services* 14: 89–104.

Rothman, B.K. 1986. *The Tentative Pregnancy: Prenatal Diagnosis and the Future of Motherhood.* New York: Viking Press.

———. 1998. *Genetic Maps and Human Imaginations: The Limits of Science in Understanding Who We Are.* New York: W.W. Norton.

Zelizar, V. 1985. *Pricing the Priceless Child.* New York: Basic Books.

PART III

Society, Technology, and Practice

Introduction to Part III

Cecilia Benoit

Part I approached the study of birth from the *macro* level, discussing the role of the state and a collection of other groups involved in designing maternal health services. Part II focused the social scientific eye on the *meso* level, analyzing the complex nature of professional group formation and competition within maternal health systems. The third and final part of the book takes the reader to the *micro* level, shedding light on two central themes: (1) the views of maternity clients on their access to and utilization of maternal health services and (2) the varied ways technology shapes the work of midwives and the experiences of birthing women.

The authors of Part III address the following questions: In what ways are intranational differences in women's experiences of maternity care policy marked by culture and history? How do women come to internalize, and act on, different notions of "risk" in childbirth? What role does technology play in "training" women's bodies for birth? What do women really *want* in the provision of maternity care?

Taken collectively, the four chapters in this final part of the book argue that society and culture shape birthing women's desires about what they *want* and the maternity care they *receive*. Evidence offered here also suggests significant variation in the use of obstetrical technologies in different societal settings.

The first chapter of Part III, Chapter 10, presents a fascinating study of how vestiges of the former East and West Germany influence attitudes about, and the use of, prenatal diagnostic technology. Erikson shows that policies in and of themselves do not dictate women's experiences of maternity care. The nearly parallel development of maternity care policies in East and West Germany had very varying impacts on the women (and men) living in these two nation-states, due in large measure to the value placed on women's work.

Chapter 11 focuses on the convergence of three topics that run throughout the maternity care literature: risk, technology, and medical malpractice litigation. Cartwright and Thomas examine the concept of "risk" within obstetrics, using the anthropological understanding of risk as an idea that is culturally constituted and reflective of particular social institutions in a particular historical and political context. The authors look at the interplay between obstetrical "risks" and the technologies that discover, verify, and ultimately strive to control these risks. Finally, they discuss one of the driving forces behind such mandates—medical malpractice. The U.S. malpractice system is compared to those in Sweden and the Netherlands, where the employment of obstetrical technologies *and* malpractice litigation are far less commonplace.

Obstetric technologies and maternity care in the Netherlands and France are the focus of Chapter 12. Three related themes emerge from the comparison of birth in these two countries by Pasveer and Akrich. The first is that a series of *trajectories* emerge through pregnancy and birth and relate women to obstetrics through a network of relationships and markers. The second theme concerns how obstetrical technologies work in practice: The authors claim that medical technologies are neither good nor bad a priori, rather, it is the way such technologies are employed (or not) that make maternity care practices (un)desirable. The authors' third theme concerns the way women's bodies come to be constituted by the trajectories and apparatus that define pregnancy and birth.

Fittingly, the last chapter of the section, Chapter 13, explores women's desires for particular maternity care services. What, in fact, *do* women want? De Vries et al. pose this question in four very different national contexts—the United States, Norway, the Netherlands, and the United Kingdom. In its own way, each story illustrates how maternity care systems shape the desires of women and how such systems also change to accommodate new demands. The authors claim it is difficult to know what women "really" want because their wishes are so closely intertwined with what their society makes available to them. Chapter 13 underscores the most important message of the book: Those who would like to see maternity care become more woman- (and family-) "friendly" must consider the all the social, historical, and cultural contingencies that design care at birth.

CHAPTER 10

Maternity Care Policies and Maternity Care Practices

A TALE OF TWO GERMANYS

Susan L. Erikson

Introduction

If there is a weakness of comparative maternity policy studies, it is that they sacrifice depth for breadth. The sheer amount of material generated in comparative research makes it difficult to do careful analyses of the history and culture of the societies being studied. Although this is an understandable omission, failure to dive into culture and history leaves a gap in our understanding of how maternity policies come to be—of how ideas *about* care are transformed into policies that *determine* care.

To correct this oversight, I have done what might be termed a "limited" comparative study of maternity policy in *one* country—Germany. Germany's history—with its long tradition of social welfare–oriented public health policy, its postwar division, and its now reunified national status—provides a rare opportunity to examine how the trajectory of maternity policy is influenced by historical and cultural contingencies. My analysis of maternity care in Germany allows us to see how public health care policies, specifically maternity care policies, are products of place-specific ideologies developed over time. My point is not to present each and every maternity care policy decision made throughout a century as part of an inevitable overdetermined march toward contemporary policy. Rather, I aim to demonstrate how contemporary policy is the most recent point on a trajectory of policy developed over time. Such a trajectory reflects the stresses and influences exerted in a particular place at particular historical moments and shows how current policies are dependent on those policies that have (or have not) come before. My "one-country comparison" also demonstrates how intranational differences in women's experiences of contemporary maternity care policy are marked by culture and history. The data used in this study are drawn from an ethnographic study conducted in 1998 and 1999 at two women's clinics, one in former East Germany and one in former West Germany.[1]

A History of "Maternity Protection" in Germany

As a legal concept and social welfare tradition, *Mutterschutz* (maternity protection) has existed in Germany for over a century. First introduced in 1878 as one of many regulations aimed at improving working conditions for female factory workers, *Mutterschutzgesetz* (maternity protection law) has evolved into a comprehensive set of laws regulating working hours, prenatal care, work breaks for women breastfeeding children, and financial support for unemployed pregnant women. The 1878 law, an outgrowth of an ambitious German Women's Movement agenda that sought to legislate the economic worth of women's work in both the factory and the home, made three weeks of maternity leave mandatory. The leave, however, was unpaid. The first of many revisions to *Mutterschutzgesetz* came in 1883 as part of Chancellor Otto von Bismarck's revolutionary social welfare reforms. Bismarck's reforms were notable for introducing a model of government-mandated-but-nongovernment-administered health care insurance, a cornerstone of contemporary German health care policy today. But the new law with regard to *Mutterschutz* mandated paid maternity leave only for self-insured workers—a fraction of employed women. German feminists criticized the reforms for not being far-reaching enough (Stoehr 1991). It wasn't until 1911 that a universal—for all working women, at least—maternity insurance law was legislated. The 1911 law legislated that obligatory insurance premium payments be made by employers and extended coverage to include domestic servants and agricultural workers. These payments to insurance companies on behalf of working women were for the coverage of physician and midwifery care, hospital births, and postpartum homecare and household help. In 1924 an extension of benefits to nonworking relatives of the insured (the insured usually being male), a breastfeeding allowance, and special benefits for poor women were legislated, leading up to one of the most significant labor laws of the Weimar Republic, the 1927 Maternity Protection Act. However, recurring economic crises in the late Weimar Republic, the political precursor to the Third Reich, turned back many of the gains of 1924 and 1927.

Although many of the late-nineteenth-century German feminists advocating *Mutterschutz* were promoting what they viewed as an emancipatory politicization of women's work (Stoehr 1991), some German historians (Evans 1997; Koonz 1987) have argued that the intent of the original *Mutterschutz* legislation was actually much more than that: "In the early years of the *Mutterschutz* movement, it clearly provided support for the [Social Darwinist] movement's radical ideas about marriage, contraception and abortion . . . [and] contained a strong element of authoritarianism" (Evans 1997, p. 61). Although the more radical types of Social Darwinists supporting *Mutterschutz* legislation were a relatively ineffectual political minority in the early 1900s, their power and popularity increased during the shaping of pre–World War I social welfare policy in Germany. Evans (1976, p. 138) has gone so far as to say, "All Mutterschutz enthusiasts believed to some extent in some form of racial hygiene," and *Mutterschutz* legislation was a step toward achieving this. Although the larger point of Evans's work is to illustrate the diversity of Social Darwinian thought in pre–World War II Germany, not only in relation to *Mutterschutz,* he concedes that without the emergence of Social Darwinian thought and language undergirding social policy, "Nazi ideology would not have been able to develop as it did" (Evans 1997, p. 78).

Today, with the advantage of hindsight, the "birth-by-design" intentions of *Mutterschutz* in Germany have an ominous ring. But using social policy to achieve particular types of people and particular configurations of the family, motherhood, and paternity was not unique to Germany in the 1920s and 1930s. For much of the first half of the twentieth century, "wellborn" science and eugenic policies were being established throughout the world. Countries as diverse as the United States, Brazil, Russia, and Sweden all had state-supported eugenic programs (Adams 1990). In keeping with the overall theme of this chapter it is important to note that only in Germany did the eugenic sciences manifest in systematic murder of Holocaust proportions (Goldhagen 1997). Economic crisis, maniacal leadership, unchecked anti-Semitism, and much more contributed to the eventual development of Nazi *Mutterschutz* policy. A historical accounting of *Mutterschutz* would be remiss without an acknowledgment of the way a policy originally intended to support women's work in the home and factory served as a foundation upon which Nazi family policy was built twenty years later.

When the National Socialists came to power in 1933, they took birth-by-design to its most grotesque limits. Historians have documented the National Socialist co-optation of family policies to (re)produce an Aryan populace (Koonz 1987; Mueller 1993; Pine 1997). But National Socialist pronatalist policies—the banning of birth control and abortion, interest-free marriage loans to encourage early single-income marriage and the dismissal of women from civil service jobs in a drive against *Doppelverdiener,* the two-income family, freeing women up for the responsibilities of motherhood and the home, financial support and housing for unwed but "hereditarily-biologically valuable" mothers (Pine 1997)—pale in significance when juxtaposed with the antinatalist policies of forced abortion, involuntary sterilization, and murder of Jewish, Roma (Gypsy), and "biologically unfit" mothers (Bock 1991). Forced sterilization of "unfit" women was also carried out in other countries, the United States, Finland, and Canada among them. But as Benoit (2000) points out in her book about Swedish maternity policies, pronatalist developments under Swedish social democrats were different and less devastating for women and marginalized groups.

Because the National Socialists so grossly violated human rights, the eradication of women's working rights for a comparatively privileged group of German women seems trivial. Yet in the context of this chapter it is worth noting that National Socialist policy was detrimental to the steady progressive acquisition of economic and political rights German women had been making from the mid- to late-1900s. Non-Jewish, non-Gypsy German women were relegated via policy incentives almost exclusively to the care of children. Bock (1991) points out that National Socialist maternity policy was not only discriminatory but also inherently sexist.

> The "duty" of begetting was considered more valuable than that of bearing and rearing children, women's contribution to procreation inferior to men's. This was not an old-fashioned cult of motherhood, but a modern cult of fatherhood. . . . the cult of motherhood was to some extent propaganda and ritual, the cult of fatherhood was propaganda and tough state policy. (pp. 243–244).

It was husbands who received marriage loans and tax rebates. And despite what on paper looked like compensation to women for the economic value of their work in the home—a point late-nineteenth-century German feminists fought for with great diligence (Stoehr 1991)—it was men as heads of households who were being paid by the state for their wives' housework. Family allowances, money paid for families with three or more children, were paid to fathers—unlike in Britain, Sweden, Norway, and France (Bock 1991, p. 243) where women received the benefits. Often, even when policy *appeared* to be advancing gender equity, a "cult of fatherhood" prevailed as an organizing principle. Such paternalism contributes to Kofman et al. (1996) labeling Germany a "strong male breadwinner state" and Esping-Anderson (1990) categorizing Germany as a *conservative welfare regime,* where "the preservation of status differences is central to social policy . . . and states intervene in a highly regulatory, although essentially conservative, way" (Duncan 1996, pp. 89–90). Still, despite the patricentric orientation of public health care policy surrounding the two world wars, late nineteenth- and early twentieth-century efforts of German feminists promoting policies supporting working mothers were not totally forgotten, and they would be picked up again by the communists in postwar East Germany.

The Post-World War II German Policy Divide

Two post–World War II Germanys took up the issue of "maternity protection," each with selective renderings of womanhood from Germany's past:

> In both East and West Germany the state drew on selective aspects of the shared historical legacy and represented these aspects as the "true" representation of German womanhood. In the East it was the ideological inheritance of the proletarian women's movements that figured in the party elite's claim that socialism would lead to the emancipation of women. In contrast, the West German leaders emphasized the role of the mother of the nineteenth century and idealized this interpretation as the true nature of women. (Young 1999, p. 43).

In the German Democratic Republic (GDR, East Germany), with the country's need for labor and families' need for material goods, the majority of women had little choice but to seek work in the formal economy. Drawing on communist theories of women's emancipation through paid labor, state media promoted an ideal of the working mother. Immediately after the war, in 1946, a Soviet decree gave women equal rights in all spheres and equal pay for equal work. *Mutterschutz* laws were officially reintroduced in 1950 as part of the Act for the Protection of Mother and Child and the Rights of Women, regulating working hours and workplace conditions for pregnant and postpartum women. Although, as Einhorn (1993) points out, the act promulgated expectations of women's dual role as worker and mother, a move that had no legal equivalent for men, it also served as the basis for attendant women's rights legislation in the years to come.

The Federal Republic of Germany (FRG, West Germany) put similar *Mutterschutz* laws into place in 1952 and passed an Equal Pay Act in 1955. But it was not until a sexual equality law was passed in 1957 that West German women were able to seek employment without their husbands' consent. The nuclear male-breadwinner/female-housewife family was not only assumed to be the cultural norm (Budde 1995; Fagnani 1996; Lobodzinska 1995), but was also the organizational gender arrangement upon which West German maternity policy was dependent from the 1950s until reunification.

In East Germany, the legal recognition of an increased need for male participation in family and household life was gradual: The Family Law in 1965, for example, espoused that both spouses share in the education and care of the children and the conduct of the household so that each partner might develop his or her potential (Einhorn 1993). A 1977 revision of the Labor Code declared that the state would ensure social conditions enabling women equal status at work and in the pursuit of education. This code specified state efforts for a successful reconciliation of work and family (Einhorn 1993, p. 23). In practice, women were still somewhat disadvantaged for the time they took off from work for the care of their small children. Still, and even though the roles of men as workers and fathers remained unexamined, East Germany went further than any other Eastern European and many Western European states in successfully providing state-supported policies that enabled women to work in the formal economy. Because the availability of childcare was considered essential for the predictability of female laborers, childcare centers were well established throughout East Germany by the late 1970s and early 1980s. *Krippenplatz* (literally, crib place) beginning six weeks after the child's birth, as well as *Kindergarten* (preschool) placements were guaranteed. In 1989, 80 percent of children under three years of age were in state-sponsored childcare. Ninety-five percent of children between ages three and six were attending nursery school (Schmude 1996, p. 175).

Conversely in West Germany, out-of-home care for small children was extremely difficult to find, prompting, from 1986 to1988, for example, almost 98 percent of working women to take maternity leave (Lobodzinska 1995). In the early 1990s, 64 percent of West German women stopped work during their first child's preschool period because (1) there were few childcare possibilities until age three, (2) there was an assumption that women should and would want to stay at home to look after small children, and (3) public opinion was that a young child needs its mother at all times and that mother-child separation is traumatic for the child (Fagnani 1996). Only 3 percent of children under three were (and are) cared for in public daycare centers, and fewer than 40 percent of three-year-olds attended nursery school (Fagnani 1996, p. 134). Out-of-home childcare beginning for children at age three was (and is) paid for privately. Women's part-time employment, an employment strategy normally reserved in East Germany for the transition of older women into retirement (Schmude 1996), was a common employment strategy for women combining work and family in West Germany.

Mutterschutz Today

Before 1989, few people in either East or West Germany anticipated reunification of the two nation-states. The sequence of events—beginning with the relaxation of border restrictions in East Germany's communist sister states in mid-1989, leading up to the momentous fall of the Berlin Wall in November 1989 and Germany's official reunification in 1990 after forty-five years of separation—parlayed into the collapse of the Soviet Union and brought a decisive if unexpectedly peaceful and rapid end to the Cold War. In Germany, fall-of-the-Wall euphoria was quickly replaced, however, with complex and sometimes contentious renegotiations about what the "New Germany" should look like. Political, economic, and social policy debates devolved not infrequently into ideological struggles and symbolic contests between two very different Germanys. The post-unification negotiation of women's reproductive rights and "duties" proved no exception, one of the most publicly contested examples being the reconciliation of the East's liberal and the West's conservative abortion policies (Grossmann 1997; Mushaben 1997). As in the case of abortion law, the "reconciliation" of East and West *Mutterschutz* policies meant a reduction of entitlements and state-paid services for formerly East German women.

In reunified Germany, *Mutterschutz* is a comprehensive set of laws intended to regulate (1) safe working environments for pregnant women, (2) work protection before and after the baby's birth, (3) work pauses specifically for women who want to pump breastmilk, and (4) payments for time off before and after delivery (approximately US $40/day, up to US $1400/month). General information and the law itself is detailed in a fifty-six-page booklet entitled *Mutterschutzgesetz: Lietfaden zum Mutterschutz* (Maternity Protection Law: A Guide to Maternity Protection), published in 1997 by the Federal Ministry for Families, Seniors, Women and Youth, and widely available in doctors' offices and women's clinics.

In Germany today, "maternity protection" begins six weeks before a woman's due date and officially lasts eight weeks after delivery. Women who had difficult deliveries are allowed twelve weeks of recovery time, as prescribed by a doctor. At the end of this time, working women must inform employers as to how much longer they will be at home with their baby, a leave known as *Mutterpause* (Mother pause) or *Mutterurlaub* (Mother vacation) for between one to three years. Women's jobs are held for them until they return to the formal economy after termination of their *Mutterpause*. Women who return to work while continuing to breastfeed their babies are guaranteed a *Stillenpause* (breastfeeding pause) at least forty-five minutes twice daily to pump.

No discussion of *Mutterschutz* would be complete without mention of the *Mutterpass* (Mother passport). Approximately the same size as a travel passport verifying citizenship, the *Mutterpass* is a small booklet pregnant woman must carry with them during pregnancy. Prominently printed on the back cover and inside front cover are reminders: "Do not forget to bring this pass to every doctor's examination during the pregnancy, delivery, and child's examination!" "During the pregnancy you should always have your Motherpass with you and bring it to every doctor's examination, especially to the delivery. Your Motherpass belongs with those documents which you should always keep in a secure place."[2] The pregnant woman presents the *Mutterpass* to each and every prenatal care provider, from a woman's own personal obstetrician to, if a woman needs more intense care, clinic personnel. During prenatal exams, the *Mutterpass,* along with computer-filed information, are the two most important sources of health information a doctor has about a patient. In one of the clinics where I conducted research, of the over 200 prenatal ultrasound exams I witnessed there, only one woman forgot to bring her *Mutterpass*. She was not examined until she returned the next day with her *Mutterpass* in hand. "Pregnant women who turn up without *Mutterpass*" is even a category deemed worthy of documentation in state prenatal statistics: In 1998 at my east German clinic site, only 8 of the 1,077 women (.7 percent) who gave birth there did not have a *Mutterpass;* at my west German site the statistics for 1997 were slightly higher, where 16 of 1093 women (1.6 percent) birthed and received care without having a *Mutterpass.*

Introduced in West Germany in the 1970s as a way to better educate women about their pregnancies (Künzel 1994) and not adopted in booklet form in East Germany until unification, the *Mutterpass* is now used by all German women to record their reproductive histories. Its sixteen pages contain charts for tracking fetal growth and compulsory prenatal care practices (e.g., ultrasound exams), and provide spaces for optional tests such as amniocentesis and cardiotachography. Without question, the role the *Mutterpass* plays in establishing prenatal care expectations cannot be underestimated. In comparison to many health care situations in North America where women often have a difficult time seeing and accessing their health care records, the German *Mutterpass* places an element of responsible pregnancy care literally in the hands of German women. But while the *Mutterpass* clearly fulfills the intended goal of educating women about pregnancy—it is given to women immediately following a positive pregnancy test and for first-time mothers often serves as the official blueprint for how to have a responsible pregnancy—some women's health care advocates have argued that the *Mutterpass* "normalizes" high-tech hospital birth and contributes to unwarranted evaluations of high-risk pregnancy. This point was taken up during a meeting I attended in Berlin in October 1999; the meeting was organized by women health care advocates from throughout Germany in order to organize their opposition to prenatal diagnostic testing. They spoke passionately about the need to revise the official "motherhood guidelines" (*Mutterschafts-Richtlinien*), a move that would have the trickle-down effect of changing the contents of the *Mutterpass,* thereby altering women's expectations about what constitutes appropriate prenatal care.

A closer look at German policy on prenatal diagnostic technologies—in particular the ultrasound examination—offers a more complete understanding of how maternity care is organized in Germany. Prenatal diagnostic, or, as they are otherwise known, "screening" programs have become routine throughout Northern Europe and North America.[3] Ultrasound exams are part of prenatal care for approximately 98 percent of all pregnant women in Europe (Levi 1998). But national policies for the most common prenatal diagnostic exam, ultrasound, vary widely. The Netherlands and Denmark do not routinely offer ultrasound exams during prenatal care, but Germany, Belgium, France, Italy, Luxembourg, and Spain offer three or more (Santalahti 1998). In Finland, two ultrasound exams per pregnancy are recommended (STAKES 1999). Sweden recently reduced the number of exams "officially" recommended from two to one after much public debate raising questions about both the reported innocuousness of ultrasound (e.g., Salvesen 1993) and the lack of evidence that ultrasound improves either infant or maternal outcomes (e.g., Ewigman et al. 1993). Such widespread use of ultrasound in Northern Europe and North America has resulted in, as Wrede (1997) points out for the Finnish case, a privileging of science- and technology-oriented obstetrics. This trend marks a turn away from family-education, midwifery-centered, and/or psychologically supportive prenatal care policies and a turn toward prenatal care policies that emphasize the management of risk, both maternal and fetal. As a result, identifying risky maternal behavior and physical anomalies, literally embodied by the mother or fetus as detected by technology, has recently become part and parcel of contemporary maternity care policy throughout Northern Europe and North America (see Chapters 9 and 12).

Indisputably, ultrasound has become routinely used and a standard of prenatal care throughout Northern Europe and North America in a relatively short period of time. But even by North American standards and despite serious competition from France for the highest usage rates in the world, Germany has very high average rates of ultrasound use per pregnancy, in part because insurance offers reimbursement for three ultrasounds per pregnancy and in part because of universal prenatal care. An exact average number of prenatal ultrasound exams is difficult to pin down because data on ultrasound use in Germany are not centrally collected. Statistics are collected individually by several of the sixteen *Länder* (states). In the two clinics where I conducted research, the rates of ultrasound use were comparable (see Table 10–1), although probably a bit low, as they are based only on the number of ultrasounds *recorded* in the *Mutterpass*. Because ultrasound has become a standard of care, many obstetricians use ultrasound during every prenatal exam, often at their own expense. Frequently, these "extra" exams are not recorded in the *Mutterpass* unless a pathological development is detected, thus accounting for the discrepancies between "official" and "unofficial" reports of ultrasound exam frequency. Women generally report having had several more ultrasounds than are recorded in their *Mutterpass,* usually one during each prenatal checkup.

Much of Germany's high rate of prenatal ultrasound use can be attributed to the law dictating doctor reimbursement for three ultrasounds per pregnancy. Obstetricians, in private practice *and* in clinics, are reimbursed by *Krankenkassen* (literally, "sickness funds," or the medical insurance paid for jointly by employer and employee) for three ultrasound exams per pregnancy, one per trimester. Although many Germans point to the *Krankenkassen* as the "official" body recommending multiple ultrasounds, the insurance companies base their reimbursement schedule on the *Muttershafts-Richtlinien.* Introduced in West Germany in 1966, the "motherhood

TABLE 10–1
Characteristics of Clients and Care at East and West Clinics

	East Clinic (N = 1077)	West Clinic (N = 1093)
German-born	93.80%	73.60%
Not German-born	6.00%	23.40%
Working during pregnancy	29.20%	42.50%
First exam during first trimester	79%	82%
10–14 prenatal exams	51.20%	60.20%
Over 14 prenatal exams	26.60%	11%
Median number of ultrasound exams	6	4.6
Average number of ultrasound exams over 5	49.50	29.7
Electronic fetal monitoring antepartum	98.10%	76.10%

guidelines," as they are commonly known, are forged by the Bundesausschuss der *Ärzte und Krankenkassen,* the national committee of doctors and insurance company representatives that determines the medical procedures insurance companies are obliged to reimburse. It is the *Bundesausschuss* that has determined that obstetricians are reimbursed a fixed sum (*Pauschale*) for a package of prenatal care that includes an ultrasound exam each trimester. An obstetrician who fails to provide ultrasound exams forfeits reimbursement of all prenatal care.

In Germany today, then, the creation, maintenance, and implementation of prenatal care policy in general and ultrasound screenings in particular are dependent on a complex of relationships between the *Bundesausschuss,* insurance companies, employers, employees, and prenatal care practitioners. As contemporary policy, this government-regulated, nongovernment-administered configuration has historical roots in Bismark's social reforms of the 1880s. As contemporary politics in a free-market economy, it leaves policy development to "experts" who set both the fees and the conditions for compulsory prenatal care, a process not immune to the pressures of market capitalism and special interest groups.

The *Mauer im Kopf* (Wall in the Mind)[4]

Because policies shape but do not determine women's experience, I turn now to differences between women's experiences of maternity policy in former East Germany and those in former West Germany. Differences are most evident among women between thirty and fifty years of age and generally depreciate with each year under age thirty. While little has changed for women in former West Germany since *die Wende* (literally, the Change, or reunification), the lives of their East German sisters are markedly different.

In 1990, when East and West Germany officially reunited after forty-five years, people expected demonstrable differences in the work and reproductive lives of women living in East and West Germany. They found them. Ninety percent of East German women were employed outside the home, compared to approximately 50 percent of West German women (Budde 1995; Einhorn 1993). In addition, East German women were more likely to be employed in jobs requiring higher levels of education. In 1950, for example, women made up 15 percent of all obstetrician-gynecologists in both East and West Germany. By 1989, the percentage had increased to 54 percent in the East and only 23 percent in the West (Arabin et al. 1999). East German women had their first child at twenty-four years of age compared with their West German counterparts, who had their first child on average at twenty-seven years of age (Fordert . . . 1999), a fact, no doubt, facilitated in East Germany by housing subsidies specifically for parents and children, but not for single or childless adults.

Other differences between East and West German women became evident more slowly. Employment rates fell in former Eastern Germany soon after reunification, and by 1993, female unemployment there was 21.5 percent, compared to 8.8 in former West states (Engelbrech 1994). The birth rate, which was about the same in the East and West per 100,000 inhabitants in 1989, plummeted in the East, from 1,197 per 100,000 inhabitants in 1989 to approximately 500 per 100,000 inhabitants in 1994. Abortion rates in the East increased by 30 percent in 1990, a fact a United

Nations report attributes to fear of both unemployment and revocation of maternity benefits (United Nations 1993).

Several of the more notable differences I found for women receiving care at the two clinics where I conducted research are presented in Table 10–1.[5] Foreign-born patients were more often found in the West Clinic population, at a ratio of almost one in every four patients. In the west, foreign-born patients tended to be Turkish women, although there was also a sizeable Russian population. In the east, foreign-born patients tended to be Vietnamese. With regard to women who worked during pregnancy, the numbers in the table are misleading, as the postunification employment figures for eastern women as a whole dropped precipitously, from 90 percent (Rueschemeyer 1993) to regionally variable figures such as the 29.2 percent reflected in the table. More than twice as many pregnant women in the former East had over 14 prenatal exams during the course of their pregnancy, as did women in the former West, and eastern women also more frequently recorded more than five ultrasounds per pregnancy. Almost 100 percent of the eastern women had electronic fetal monitoring at some point in their prenatal and delivery care, compared to just over three-quarters of the western women. One interpretation that explains the higher use of prenatal and birthing technologies in the east is that of symbolic parity: The technologies have taken on meaning beyond their diagnostic value and now simultaneously represent eastern parity with the west.

The different experiences created by maternity policies east and west of the former Wall were most clearly visible in women's attitudes about the (in)compatibility of motherhood and career:

> Conditioned by the constraints and opportunities afforded by two ideologically opposed systems after 1945, the personal qua social identities of eastern and western women had diverged considerably by 1989. The roles and rights of GDR [East German] women were framed by their simultaneous functions as mothers and wage-earners. West German women fell into three distinctive categories: those who defined their primary roles in terms of children and household; those who pursued the two roles sequentially; and those who identified themselves as career women (Mushaben et al. 1997, p. 147).

The difference between *simultaneous* and *sequential* pursuits of work and motherhood proved enormous. Whereas childcare in East Germany was designed to support employed mothers, childcare in West Germany functioned "more as a support for homemaker mothers. Mothers can better devote a short amount of time, free from children, to domestic tasks and services" (Duncan 1996, p. 83). After reunification, this difference in emphasis turned contentious. Media promoted the image of children in childcare as children neglected by their working mothers, disparaging working women with the label *Rabenmutter* (mother crow)—women who leave their children with other people to raise. It was a media campaign that both fed and reflected an ideology of motherhood prevalent in West Germany, and it was used to justify the preservation of the traditional maternal role that predominated there.

Despite nearly parallel development of *Mutterschutz* policies in East and West Germany, the resulting ideologies of work and motherhood were demonstratively different, in large part because concomitant labor laws supporting women's work in the East were also actively enforced. One of the ways the ideological difference has played out in contemporary practice is in ethical discourses about selective abortion after a positive diagnosis for fetal disability. Ultrasound and amniocentesis diagnoses result in what German doctors call pathological results in about 2 percent of all cases. Over 90 percent of these fetuses are aborted (Klinkhammer 1997); prior to 1994 the rate was 98 percent for pregnancies with Down syndrome diagnoses (Mushaben et al. 1997, p. 160). Various sectors of the German public in both the east and west are actively asking and attempting to answer difficult questions about what the issue of postdiagnostic abortion *means* for women, disabled people, and German society over time. Is selective abortion eugenics? Is abortion of a fetus diagnosed prenatally as disabled an insult to people living with the disability? Is it morally wrong to prefer giving birth to a non-disabled child?

Public engagement with these questions has varied in eastern and western Germany. Public discourses in former West Germany almost always include references to selective abortion practices and medical experiments conducted by the National Socialists. Such references are nearly nonexistent in East Germany. Several of the doctors with whom I spoke in both the former East and West explained the difference in terms of the narratives promoted by the respective postwar governments. In the years following World War II, West Germany embraced educational and political policies that acknowledged culpability for the Holocaust. This culpability translates today into a fairly widespread self-consciousness about Nazi war crimes, which is often just beneath the surface of political, economic, and social discourse. In the 1980s, it fueled a surge of legislative, scholarly, and activist opposition to postdiagnostic selective abortion. Then and today, as diagnostic technologies become more commonplace, well-organized opponents of these technologies call up images of *Nazizeit* (Nazi time) when staking out public positions. As one activist said to me, "It is where we get our power."

Conversely, in the former East, analogies to Nazi medical crimes wield little of the censorious, incriminating power that they possess in the former West. East German postwar narratives emphasized a redemptive, exculpatory Soviet victory over fascism that effectively acquitted East Germans of responsibility for the Holocaust (Herf 1997; Welsh 1997). Laws and curricula were revised in keeping with communist priorities. Communism was promoted as a fresh start, a clean sweep—politically, economically, and morally. In the mid- to late-1980s, as ultrasound machines were slowly introduced in clinics and later in doctors' offices, there was virtually no public debate about their use. This was because their use was not yet widespread and because debates regarding medical technologies fell within the purview of the medical community, not the public. Diagnostic technologies, when available, were generally welcomed by women. And since reunification, diagnostic technologies have come to possess meaning beyond their clinical function: They represent a coming of age, a symbol of parity with the west. Although the maternity policy promoting ultrasound use in prenatal care is now the same in eastern and western Germany, both the machine and the exam mean different things to women depending on their location.

Conclusion

This brief review of maternity policies in the two Germanys illustrates that women's experiences of maternity care are shaped by more than just state decisions about maternal health. The nearly parallel development of maternity care policies in former East and former West Germany had extremely varying impacts on the women (and men) living in these two nation-states because of great differences in the way women's work was valued.

I conclude this chapter on public policy with a personal and slightly polemical note. While I was in Germany conducting research, whenever I had discussions with Germans about health care policy, I repeatedly experienced something I came to privately label "The Gap." The Gap is that gap in comprehension that happens cross-culturally even when both sides are conversing with the best of intentions. The Gap happened when I, in an attempt to illustrate how easy it is for middle-class Americans to go without health insurance, spoke of the fact that while in graduate school I had gone for four years without medical insurance. Those four years also happened to coincide with the births of my two children. The fact that I had gone without medical insurance for a single moment, not to mention my pregnant moments, struck people dumb—literally. They were speechless, incredulous. And while it is true that some Americans would be horrified as well, Americans would be much more likely to blame the individual than would former East and West Germans, who tended to locate their dismay in the failings of the U.S. health care system.

When Northern Europeans and Canadians talk policy with Americans, they often use the same words, but they are speaking about very different things. Former East and West Germany organized their societies around a social welfare model that provides for all its citizens. The "New" Germany continues in that tradition. Likewise, for most Northern Europeans and Canadians, social (and) welfare are not dirty words. Welfare is something that everyone benefits from, not just the poor, as is the case in the United States. More often than not, welfare is viewed by European nations and Canada as something society just does, an obligation of the more well-endowed members of society to provide care for all, something necessary for living with other people, some of whom are privileged, some of whom are not. Europeans and Canadians, by virtue of their longstanding social welfare systems, assume access to health care rights and services which, if not government administered, are at least government regulated. These same rights and services in the United States are left to the individual to acquire. The importance of this difference cannot be underestimated.

The peculiar histories of social welfare in democratic societies make a tremendous difference in how public opinion and culture drive, support, and contest contemporary public policy development. Maternity policy history explains, for example, why German women assume they will receive prenatal care regardless of their employment or socioeconomic status, while most American women expect that they will not. It explains why German women from every socioeconomic level *expect* the government to provide ways and means to their having a baby, while most American women do not. It explains why women in the former West Germany are more likely to feel social pressure to personally care for their children under age three in their own homes than are either their former East German or French counterparts, who regularly send their children to state-organized childcare facilities (Fagnani 1996). On a much larger scale, history and culture explain why in Northern European countries social welfare connotes a widely supported and accepted *noblesse oblige* approach to social policy, while in the United States social welfare connotes parsimoniously allocated moneys for poor people trying to take advantage of "the system." All of this evidence reaffirms the message of *Birth by Design*: Maternity care systems cannot be understood without locating them in place and time, without an understanding of the societal, historical, and cultural setting in which they operate.

Notes

1. Throughout the text, a capitalized East and West refers to the two countries before unification, and a lowercase east and west refers to these sections of Germany after unification.
2. *"Vergessen Sie nicht, dieses Heft zu jeder ärztlichen Untersuchung wärend der Schwangerschaft, zur Entbindung und zur Untersuchung des Kindes mitzubringen!" "Wärend der Schwangerschaft sollten Sie Ihren Mutterpass immer bei sich haben und zu jeder ärztlichen Untersuchung mitbringen, insbesondere auch zur Entbindung. Ihr Mutterpass gehört zu den Dokumenten, die Sie immer sorgfältig aufbewahren sollten."*
3. In the early days of their development, prenatal diagnostic technologies were explicitly intended for use by medical practitioners to "avert" the births of disabled infants (see Kuppermann et al. 1999). Today, although averting the births of disabled infants is often implicit in use, the need for prenatal diagnostic testing is more often justified in terms of having more information so that parents can make better decisions and/or be better informed about the child that will be born to them.
4. This phrase refers to the cognitive distance still existing between some East and West Germans, as used by Klingmann and Hofferbert 1994.
5. East Clinic and West Clinic are pseudonyms. East Clinic data are from 1998; West Clinic data are from 1997.

References

Adams, M. B. (ed). 1990. *The Wellborn Science: Eugenics in Germany, France, Brazil, and Russia*. New York: Oxford University Press.

Arabin, B., Raum, E., Mohnhaupt, A., and F. W. Schwartz. 1999. "Entwicklung der Qualität und subjektiven Einschätzung der Perinatalmedizin in Ost- und West-Berlin zwischen 1950 und 1990. (The development of the quality and subjective evaluation of perinatal medicine in East and West Berlin between 1950 and 1990). *Frauenheilkunde plus* (*Gynecology plus*) 11: 508–509.

Benoit, C. 2000. *Women, Work and Social Rights: Canada in Historical and Comparative Perspective*. Scarborough, Ontario: Prentice Hall Canada.

Bock, G. 1984. Racism and sexism in Nazi Germany: Motherhood, compulsory sterilization, and the state. In *When Biology Became Destiny: Women in Weimar and Nazi Germany*, ed. Renate Bridenthal, Atina Grossman, and Marion Kaplan. New York: Monthly Press, pp. 271–296.

———. 1991. Antinatalism, maternity and paternity in National Socialist racism. In *Maternity and Gender Policies: Women and the Rise of the European Welfare States, 1880s–1950s*, ed. Gisela Bock and Pat Thane. New York: Routledge, pp. 233–255.

Budde, G-F. 1995. How long did "women's finest hour" last? German women's situation and experiences between 1945 and 1995. In *Women and Political Change: Perspectives from East-Central Europe* (Selected Papers from the Fifth World Congress of Central and East European Studies, Warsaw, 1995), ed. Sue Bridger. London: St. Martin's Press.

Bundesministerium für Familie, Senioren, Frauen und Jugend (Government Ministry for Family, Seniors, Women and Youth). 1997. *Mutterschutzgesetz: Leitfaden zum Mutterschutz* (Maternity Protection Law: A Guide to Maternity Protection.) Bonn. (In German.)

Clinic Data East (pseudonym). 1998. Yearly data.

Clinic Data West (pseudonym. 1997. Yearly report.

Duncan, S. 1996. The diverse worlds of European patriarchy. In *Women of the European Union: The Politics of Work and Daily Life,* ed. by Maria Dolors Garcia-Ramon and Janice Monk. New York: Routledge, pp. 74–110.

Einhorn, B. 1993. *Cinderella Goes to Market: Citizenship, Gender and Women's Movements in East Central Europe.* London: Verso.

Engelbrech, G. 1994. Frauen nur Reservearmee für den Arbeitsmarkt? (Are women only a reserve army for the labor market?) *Die Frau in unserer Zeit (The Woman in Our Time)* 1: 14–23. (In German.)

Esping-Anderson, G. 1990. *The Three Worlds of Welfare Capitalism.* London: Polity.

Evans, R. J. 1976. *The Feminist Movement in Germany, 1894–1933.* London: Sage.

———. 1997. In search of German Social Darwinism: The history and historiography of a concept" In *Medicine and Modernity: Public Health and Medical Care in Nineteenth- and Twentieth-Century Germany,* eds. M. Berg and G. Cocks. Cambridge: University Press, pp. 55–80.

Ewigman, B., J. Crane, F., Frigoletto, M., LeFevre, R., Bain, D., McNellis, D., and the Radius Study Group. 1993. Effect of prenatal ultrasound screen on perinatal outcome. *New England Journal of Medicine* Vol. 329: 821–827.

Fagnani, J. 1996. Family policies and working mothers: A comparison of France and West Germany. In *Women of the European Union: The Politics of Work and Daily Life,* ed. Maria Dolors Garcia-Ramon and Janice Monk. New York: Routledge, pp. 126–137.

Fordert, was ihr kriegen könnt. 1999. *Der Spiegel* 47: 84–89.

Goldhagen, D. J. 1997. *Hitler's Willing Executioners: Ordinary Germans and the Holocaust* New York: Vintage Books.

Grossmann, A. 1997. The debate that will not end: The politics of abortion in Germany from Weimar to National Socialism to the postwar period. In *Medicine and Modernity: Public Health and Medical Care in Nineteenth- and Twentieth-Century Germany,* eds. Manfred Berg and Geoffrey Cocks. Cambridge: Cambridge University Press, pp. 193–212.

Herf, J. 1997. *Divided Memory: The Nazi Past in the Two Germanys.* Cambridge, MA: Harvard University Press.

Klinkhammer, G. 1997. Entschieden gegen eugenische Tendenzen. (Decisively against eugenic tendencies) *Deutsches Ärzteblatt* (German Physicians' Paper) 94, Heft 22, 30. Mai (33): A-1485. (In German.)

Klingmann, H-D., and R. J. Hofferbert. 1994. Germany: A New "Wall in the Mind?" *Journal of Democracy* 5: 30–44.

Kofman, E., and R. Sales. 1996. The geography of gender and welfare in Europe. In *Women of the European Union: The Politics of Work and Daily Life,* ed. Maria Dolors Garcia-Ramon and Janice Monk. New York: Routledge, pp. 31–60.

Koonz, C. 1987. *Mothers in the Fatherland: Women, The Family and Nazi Politics.* New York: St. Martin's Press.

Künzel, W. 1994. The birth survey in Germany: Education and quality control in perinatalogy. *European Journal of Obstetrics, Gynecology and Reproductive Biology* 54(1): 13–20.

Kuppermann, M., J. D. Goldberg, R. F. Nease, Jr., and A. E. Washington. 1999. Who should be offered prenatal diagnosis? The 35-year-old question. *American Journal of Public Health* 89(2)(Feb):160–163.

Levi, S. 1998. Routine ultrasound screening of congenital anomalies: An overview of the European experience. *Annals of the New York Academy of Science* 847: 86–98.

Lobodzinska, B. 1995. "Part IV: Germany (former German Democratic Republic). In *Family, Women, and Employment in Central-European Europe,* ed. by Barbara Lobodzinska. London: Greenwood Press, pp. 101–110.

Moeller, R. 1993. *Protecting Motherhood and the Family in the Politics of Postwar Germany.* Berkeley, CA: University of California Press.

Mushaben, J., Giles, G., and S. Lennox. 1997. Women, men and unification: Gender politics and the abortion struggle since 1989. In *After Unity: Reconfiguring German Identities,* ed. K. Jarausch. Oxford: Berghahn Books, pp. 137–172.

Pine, N. 1997. *Nazi Family Policy: 1933–1945.* New York: Berg.

Rueschemeyer, M. 1993. Women in East Germany: From state socialism to capitalist welfare state. In *Democratic Reform and the Position of Women in Transitional Economies,* ed. Valentine M. Moghadam. Oxford: Clarendon Press, pp. 75–91.

Salvesen, K. A., Vatten, L. J., Eik-Nes, S. H., Hugdahl, K., and L.S. Bakketeig. 1993. Routine ultrasonography in utero and subsequent handedness and neurological development. *British Medical Journal* 307: 159–164.

Santalahti, P. 1998. *Prenatal Screening in Finland: Availability and Women's Decision-Making and Experiences.* Turku: STAKES, National Research and Development Centre for Welfare and Health, University of Turku.

Schmude, J. 1996. Contrasting developments in female labour force participation in East and West Germany since 1945. In *Women of the European Union: The Politics of Work and Daily Life,* eds. Maria Dolors Garcia-Ramon and Janice Monk. New York: Routledge, pp. 156–185.

STAKES (National Research and Development Centre For Welfare and Health). 1999. *Perhe-suunnittelun ja äitiyshuollon asiantuntijaryhmä. Seulonnot ja yhteistyöäitiyshuollossa, suositukset 1999.* (Screening and Collaboration in Maternity Care. Guidelines 1999.) Jyväskylä: STAKES Oppaita 34. (In Finnish.)

Stoehr, I. 1991. Housework and motherhood: Debates and policies in the women's movement in imperial Germany and the Weimar Republic. In *Maternity and Gender Policies: Women and the Rise of the European Welfare States, 1880s–1950s,* ed. Gisela Bock and Pat Thane. New York: Routledge, pp. 213–232.

United Nations. 1993. *Abortion Policies: A Global Review, Vol. II: Gabon to Norway.* New York: United Nations.

Welsh, H. A., Pickel, A., and D. Rosenberg. 1997. East and West German identities: United and divided? In *After Unity: Reconfiguring German Identities.* ed. K. Jarausch. Oxford: Berghahn Books, pp. 103–136.

Wrede, S. 1997. The notion of risk in Finnish prenatal care: Managing risk mothers and risk pregnancies. In *Images of Women's Health: The Social Construction of Gendered Health,* ed. Elianne Riska. Åbo, Finland: The Institute of Women's Studies, Abo Akademi University, pp. 133–180.

Young, B. 1999. *Triumph of the Fatherland: German Unification and the Marginalization of Women.* Ann Arbor: The University of Michigan Press.

CHAPTER 11

Constructing Risk

MATERNITY CARE, LAW, AND MALPRACTICE

Elizabeth Cartwright and Jan Thomas

Danger has always attended childbirth. Among the many complications of pregnancy and delivery are hemorrhages, obstructed labor, infection, toxemia, and unsafe abortions (Adeyi & Morrow 1997). Fetal/neonatal problems include asphyxia, neurological problems, infections, and prematurity (Stalnaker et al. 1997). Before maternity care was moved into medical institutions, pregnancy and birth were widely regarded as dangerous events. Midwives and other women attended births at home and did what they could to alleviate the laboring woman's pain and ease the passage of the baby, but morbidity and mortality were a pregnant woman's constant companions (Arney & Neill 1982).

By the early twentieth century, obstetricians had replaced midwives as birth attendants in the United States, and a new view of the dangers of birth was emerging. As childbirth moved from a domestic to a medical event, obstetrical dangers became institutionalized within a growing body of medical knowledge. Danger was transformed into biomedically constructed and sanctioned notions of *risk*. This was more than a mere semantic shift: "Danger" implies a fatalistic outlook on birth, "risk" implies an activist stance. New medical definitions of risk require that childbirth be accompanied by medical technology, monitoring, and oftentimes intervention (DeVries, 1996).

In this chapter we explore how modern medical systems turned the "normal" complications of birth into quantifiable "risks" measured by diagnostic technologies. In addition, we examine how the new vocabulary of risk creates the possibility of legal actions against care providers in the form of medical malpractice suits. Our main focus is obstetrics in the United States—where these developments have been most visible—but to place notions of risk and malpractice in a larger social and cultural context we also consider the situation in Sweden and the Netherlands, two high-income countries with different ideas about birth and technology.

The Construction of Obstetrical Risks from Childbirth Dangers: The Case of the United States

Contrary to common belief, risk is not a value-free assessment of the possibility that certain dangers will occur (see Douglas 1992; Hall 1989; Skolbekken 1995). Rather, risks are specific dangers that a particular society chooses from among all possible dangers that exist. Risks may not represent the most likely dangers or even the most fearsome dangers faced by a society. Risks are dangers believed to be most immediate or—as in the case of obstetrics—dangers that practitioners believe that they can or must control. How is an obstetrical danger transformed into an obstetrical risk?

The first step in the social construction of obstetrical risk is the selection of a particular danger from among the many dangers that attend birth. Most often a danger becomes visible or measurable through the development of a new technology. Once captured by the biomedical gaze, the problem lies under the purview of obstetrical practice and ways are found to quantify and treat it.

The danger must be made visible (through technologies of visualization) or quantifiable (through technologies of measurement) so that the effects of treatment can be assessed. The presence of an obstetrical risk must be verified by output from a diagnostic technology that can register both the normal and the abnormal and show progress between the two states. When the numbers fluctuate outside the more or less arbitrarily defined limits of "statistical norms," practitioners must either treat the condition or be able to justify why they are withholding treatment. The power of medicine is thus enacted: Risks are identified and can be controlled only through medical surveillance and treatment.

Skolbekken (1995, p. 298) argues that preoccupation with medical risk as a statistical and scientific construct emerged from the development of computer technology that allowed large-scale data analysis. Statistically represented possibilities generated by these analyses created an ideological background that supported the use of more and more biomedical technologies. Measurable risks implied the need for risk reduction and gave practitioners a way to assess their success in doing so.

When practitioners accept a particular risk discourse they must convince their patients that the dangers seen and measured by technology are real. In the United States most women unquestioningly accept this medical point of view. The few birthing women who refuse to believe that birth is fraught with risk—who break medical protocols and sign themselves out of hospitals, "against medical advice"—are seen as challenging the authority of medicine and medical institutions. Douglas (1992, p. 29) comments: "[risk is not about] the reality of the dangers, but about how they are politicized. The debate always links some real danger and some disapproved behavior, coding the danger in terms of a threat to valued institutions." Birthing women who resist institutional values are often forced to comply in the name of the "welfare of the infant." When a mother shows a reluctance to accept official protocols, she is often reminded about the "risk" to her baby. When a practitioner states that an intervention needs to be done "for the baby," it is extremely difficult for the mother to disagree. (Browner & Press 1997).

We must note that medical personnel in the United States do not always accept standard notions of obstetrical risk. Like their fellow citizens, American physicians value their independence: Rather than practicing along the lines of institutionally set protocols, they tend to practice with their own styles—styles based on their training, their years of experience, their intuition, and what "feels comfortable." The recent call for practitioners to engage in "evidence-based practice" challenges this "medical individualism." Evidence-based practice asks practitioners to operate at "proven" levels of competency (and social conformity), rather than at their "comfort levels."

The call to be more "scientific"—to use the latest protocols and to purchase the newest equipment—suggests the existence of fundamental disagreements in obstetrical "standards of care." King and Kovac (1996) discuss the example of practice standards for vaginal birth after a cesarean section (VBAC). When a woman with a scar from a previous cesarean section is laboring, there is always the risk, although very small, that the old incision will split apart during contractions or during the pushing effort. This is a very rare but devastating occurrence for the mother, the baby, and often for the physician, especially if he/she is subsequently called into court for the resulting death(s) or disabilities. The Prevention Task Force (King & Kovac 1996, p. 232) states that a "trial of labor" should be given despite these practitioner fears:

> Because of its proven safety and efficacy, trial of labor (in women with previous cesarean sections) has been supported by many third-party payers, preferred provider organizations, and health maintenance organizations. This approach attempts not only to control spiraling health care costs but also to increase corporate profitability. Recently obstetricians have begun to be graded with regard to their clinical performance, cesarean section rate, trial of labor attempts, and successful vaginal births. It is anticipated that insurance plan participation and credentialing will soon be based on some of these factors.

This new standard of care is driven by third-party payers and health maintenance organizations and is mainly aimed at cost-containment and corporate profit. Here we find practice standards based not just on (perceived) safety, but on cost and conformity to the (more or less informally established) notions of acceptable ways of practicing obstetrics.

This discussion demonstrates that obstetrical risks in the United States are produced in a complicated environment that includes biomedical technologies, corporate interests, and an amalgamation of fears and feelings of vulnerability among both patients and practitioners. In the United States, with its highly medicalized views of birth and a competition-based health care system, "risk surrounds practice, it is in the background, there is an atmosphere; it is always there" (Annadale 1996, p. 420). Providers practice in a climate of risk, institutional demands, and—as we discuss in the next section—a threat of malpractice suits. The most common response to this situation is the creation of protocols and hospital rituals designed to reduce risk, *even in the absence of data supporting their routine use.*

Risk and the U.S. Legal System

The transformation of the "dangers" of birth into "risks" has given the medical profession control over maternity care, but it has also had at least one important negative consequence: the rise of malpractice suits. "Risk" implies the possibility of control. A woman who is encouraged to give over the management of her birth to obstetrical supervision to minimize risk is bound to be upset when these risks are not controlled. A physician who promised to manage risks is seen as a failure when the outcome of birth is poor; the response to this broken promise is often legal action. Malpractice suits are the shadow side of risk control.

When a medical malpractice lawsuit is filed in the United States, the practitioners' behavior is measured against a legal yardstick known as the "standard of care." The standard of care is defined by statute or by case law. In either event, the test is relatively uniform throughout the fifty states. The following excerpt, taken from the statutes of the state of Florida, is typical:

> Medical Negligence; Standards of Recovery (1) In any action for recovery of damages based on the death or personal injury of any person in which it is alleged that such death or injury resulted from the negligence of a health care provider as defined in n1 s. 768.50(2)(b), the claimant shall have the burden of proving by the greater weight of evidence that the alleged actions of the health care provider represented a breach of the prevailing professional standard of care for that health care provider. The prevailing professional standard of care for a given health care provider shall be that level of care, skill, and treatment which, in light of all relevant surrounding circumstances, is recognized as acceptable and appropriate by reasonably prudent similar health care providers. (www.floridamalpractice.com, accessed May 24, 1999).

The statute establishes the test as care judged to be "appropriate by reasonably prudent similar health care providers." In reality this standard tends to demand that the practitioner employ the most sophisticated technology and the most recent advances of medical science. Anything less can be made to look shoddy in a courtroom by a seasoned medical malpractice lawyer.

In the 1980s, the United States experienced a large increase in the number of liability cases. A study of sixteen states found that there was a 58 percent increase in such cases between 1975 and 1997 (Glaberson 1999, p. 6).[1] The medical specialty that was hit the hardest by the increase in liability suits was obstetrics. In the early 1970s, obstetrics was the source of only 2 percent of all medical malpractice claims in the United States; by 1985, the number had jumped to 10 percent (DeVille, 1998, p. 206). The combination of increased medical malpractice lawsuits, increased insurance premiums, and a few excessive jury verdicts converged in a perceived "crisis" in tort (negligence) liability suits. There are those who challenge the notion that the United States is plagued by a malpractice crisis. It is fashionable to claim that the high cost of health care in the United States is the result of malpractice suits. But, in fact, medical malpractice suits are not that common. Only a small portion of the money paid out on malpractice claims ends up in the plaintiff's pocket. Most of the settlement goes to insurance companies and lawyers (Starr 1992, p. 21).

These findings suggest the costs of medical malpractice are borne by patients rather than by practitioners or insurance companies. These facts demonstrate that malpractice litigation is *not* a major source of the cost problem in the American health care system. However, fear of lawsuits (even if unfounded) *does* impact practitioners' use of technology and diagnostic testing as protective devices (Annadale 1996, p. 434).

U.S. obstetricians can expect to be sued eight times during their careers for "less than optimal" outcomes (Schifrin et al. 1985). Not surprisingly, practitioners fear those few times when something *does* go wrong with the mother or baby, a fear that is compounded by the "statute of limitations" in the United States that allows cases to be litigated anytime during the twenty-one years following the birth of the baby. For U.S. practitioners, then, the issue of safety in childbirth is enmeshed in a legal system looking to blame someone for a "bad outcome." In an effort to protect themselves, care providers practice "defensive medicine"—that is, they use all available technology.

Technology and Risk

The activism implied by the view of birth as "risky" has led to the routine use of sophisticated technologies in U.S. hospital births. Obstetrical risks and legal fears are kept at bay by a plethora of technologies whose presence is ever-more-standard and ever-less-questioned on hospital labor and delivery wards. Most U.S. women have their labor monitored by electronic fetal monitors, are given epidurals to reduce pain, and have episiotomies to aid in the delivery of their child. They have come to believe that the use of these technologies is necessary to reduce the risk of harm to themselves and their babies. Once technology becomes available and widely used, it is difficult to move backward to less technology and intervention (Bortin et al. 1994, p. 46). However, as DeVille (1998, p. 201) has noted, there is an irony here: Once a "particular technology is performed frequently and both the profession and the public believe that it generates predictable results and substantial benefit" the rate of lawsuits increases. The fastest growing area of medical malpractice allegations in the United States is the failure to diagnose an existing illness or injury. Further, failure to diagnose and promptly treat fetal distress is the most common claim in obstetrical malpractice cases (Mackauf & Tessel 1997).

The routine use of electronic fetal monitors (EFMs) in the United States is a visible reminder of this situation. In order to try to decrease the chances of something going wrong during the labor and delivery, the woman's contractions and the baby's heartbeats are continually monitored and displayed. Practitioners watch the fetal monitors and comment on the woman's progress and on possible interpretations of the EFM tracings. Based on interpretations of the fetal heart tracings, delivery is expedited with the use of vacuum extractions, forceps deliveries and cesarean deliveries. In the United States, fetal monitoring is required by hospital protocol in certain situations, such as pitocin inductions. Women are required to maintain uncomfortable positions so that the machine can monitor the baby's heartbeat and assess if it is being stressed by the pitocin-induced contractions. In a recent study by Howell-White (1999, p. 74), 92 percent of women who chose a hospital birth attended by an obstetrician had intermittent EFM, and 69 percent had continuous monitoring. Interestingly, studies of EFM have shown that "neonatal outcome has not been improved in low-risk populations" and that the EFM "seems to be of no benefit in the general population" (Benson 1994, p. 55).

"Sitting on a bad strip" (holding off on any clinical action) can be a nerve-wracking situation where a practitioner's credibility can be called into question. The course of action or inaction chosen may result in criticism by other practitioners or in future litigation on the part of the patient or her family in the event of problems surrounding the birth. The threat of litigation is sometimes described by doctors, nurses, and midwives as constantly "hanging over our heads" (Annadale 1996). As one nurse-midwife interviewed for this project reflected:

> My fetal monitor assessment and my level of concern is so different than most of the people here (at a large teaching hospital) because after sixteen years of seeing "worrisome strips" and babies with Apgars of 8, 9 (sign of a healthy baby) I understand very well the problems with fetal monitoring. But what sends chills up my spine is sitting on a strip and knowing that other practitioners are peeking at the strip in the doctor's lounge and saying "What's goin' on here? What is she doin' here?" (personal communication with a certified nurse-midwife)

Practitioners' fears are reinforced by biomedical technologies that are sometimes ambiguous, but accepted as indicative (with varying degrees of confidence), of serious or even life-threatening problems.

From the consumer's viewpoint, new drugs and technologies carry with them new hopes and expectations. In many U.S. hospitals epidurals are used in more than 90 percent of births (Romm 1998, p. 84), attesting to the cultural acceptance of medicalized pain management and the belief of women and practitioners that the pain will be too much for women to bear. Glass (1998, p. 46) has noted that the desire to be "numb" during childbirth seems to cut across race, class, and age. It seems that labor pain is nearly too overwhelming an experience, one to be avoided at all costs. However, heightened expectations often lead to frustration and resentment when technology fails or "bad outcomes" occur. Any intervention carries with it associated risk. For example, the use of epidurals to reduce the pain of childbirth can lead to complications ranging from failure to relieve pain to cardiac arrest and fetal distress (Cunningham et al. 1996). Each of these complications brings with it its own unique "corrective scenarios," each requiring the use of additional technology. The following is a description of one such scenario that could be triggered by the placement of an epidural:

> A "severe" deceleration of the fetal heart rate is noted (on the monitor screen). Immediately several practitioners rush towards the patient's room. The door flies open. Doctors and nurses begin treatments based on previously established protocols. Adrenaline pumping, they perform vaginal exams to check for a possible prolapsed umbilical cord, change the mother's position to maximize blood flow to the uterus, place internal monitors for increased accuracy of pick-up as well as a host of other actions. If none of these measures is effective at restoring a normal fetal heart rate, an emergency surgical delivery is performed (Cartwright 1998, p. 246).

U.S. women expect epidurals to work and, when they do not, it is especially difficult for women to cope with the pain that they trusted the anesthesiologist would be able to "cure." In reality, this technology, like all other technologies, is not infallible. Initially convinced that only the epidural can cure the pain of contractions, it is very difficult to get a woman to take control over her own pain when the epidural fails. In addition to these risks, recent research implicates epidural analgesia with prolonged labors that may lead to increased rates of cesarean deliveries. Alexander et al. (1998) compared the progress of labor in a homogenous cohort of women and found that first and second stages of labor were prolonged in those women who received epidurals, in comparison to the control group that received the intravenous drug meperidine (Demerol). For this latter group of women, time from their hospital admission to the point of delivery of their baby was, on average, two hours shorter than for the women that received epidural anesthesia. When labors are prolonged there is, of course, more time for the practitioner to feel the need to intervene: "When poor progress in labor is combined with nonspecific though nonreassuring FHR (fetal heart rate) tracings, there is additional motivation to choose cesarean birth" (Porreco & Thorp 1996, p. 372). Thus, the technology of fetal monitoring interacts with the technology of epidural anesthesia, sometimes providing safety and comfort for the woman, but other times creating more physiological problems and even increased operative deliveries. While generally deriding the common use of fetal monitoring, U.S. obstetrician Michael Benson (1994, pp. 55–56) points to the need for monitoring *because* of the increased use of labor interventions and the absence of current knowledge about how to monitor the fetus *without* technology.

As we point out in the next section, the relationship between technology and risk must be understood in its social and cultural setting. In the United States, where practitioners, insurers, and hospitals are all competing for patients and profit, "choices" in childbirth are often illusory. Physicians have so convincingly sold themselves and their services as the only "safe" choice that consumers blindly believe that medical science will do no harm: "Technology encourages us to think differently about pregnancy" (Katz Rothman 1993, p. vii). Once certain diagnostic tests (such as ultrasound and EFM) become widely used, refusal of such technology implies a lack of responsibility and caring on the part of the mother (Browner & Press 1997, p. 127; Corea 1985). Such a belief system about safety and technology is manifested in malpractice suits when things go wrong.

Although the malpractice "crisis" in the United States is exaggerated, it is clear that malpractice litigation—especially against maternity care providers—is more common there than in other high-income countries. We can better understand the U.S. case by examining maternity care and malpractice litigation in Sweden and the Netherlands, two high-income countries with procedures for accomplishing birth that are quite different from those found in America.

Obstetrical Care and Malpractice in Sweden and the Netherlands

We begin our comparison by looking at maternity care in Sweden. The underlying philosophy in Sweden is that "[health] care is of prime importance in a modern welfare state and should be accessible to everyone regardless of his or her economic situation" (Giesen 1988, p. 541). The twenty-six County Councils of Sweden are responsible for public health care services for the inhabitants of their region. Virtually all Swedish women deliver their babies in hospitals but are attended by nurse-midwives rather than family physicians or obstetricians. Swedish women usually see the same midwife during the pregnancy and then are attended in the hospital by staff midwives (McKay 1993, p. 117). Intervention occurs, but at a lower rate than in the United States. In 1997, about 25 percent of Swedish women had epidurals, and 25–50 percent of women had their labors augmented by oxytocin (Rooks 1997, p. 409). In Sweden, the episiotomy rate was approximately 9–10 percent, with about 11 percent of women having cesarean sections (Gaskin 1999, p. 32).

The Swedish National Board of Health and Welfare supervises and evaluates the clinical work of health providers, midwives, and physicians (Wennstrom 1997). In 1975 a "no-fault" system was put into place by the National Board to handle malpractice claims. In general, no-fault systems offer providers liability insurance, without regard to fault. Patients are compensated for any and all injuries that may arise during their health care, regardless of whether the cause is deemed to be negligence of the provider or an "unavoidable" result of receiving care. Thus, health complication, rather than perceived provider negligence, is the main criterion for compensation in the Swedish system (Danzon 1985, pp. 213–214). Each Swedish county government pays insurance premiums, and patient claims are submitted to the Patient Compensation Insurance Fund. If patients demonstrate that their health has been harmed, they are compensated, without proof of negligence required. The Medical Responsibility Board (Lassey, Lassey, & Jinks 1997, p. 201) handles disciplinary action against providers. In short, the Swedish system removes the burden of fear about malpractice from providers and puts responsibility for compensation into the hands of a neutral third party—the Patient Compensation Fund.

The Netherlands uses a mix of public and private health care financing to provide care to its population. Approximately two-thirds of the Dutch population are publicly insured. Those with income above a certain level obtain their own insurance (Hingtsman 1994, p. 380). The government encourages home birth for all women with low-risk pregnancies but offers them a choice of home or short-stay hospital for delivery (Hingstman 1994, p. 384; Wiegers et al. 1998, p. 193). Virtually all pregnant women have access to prenatal care (Lassey, Lassey, & Jinks 1997, p. 199) and, as in Sweden, Dutch women are entrusted to carry their own health records with them.

Perceived "risk" in Dutch maternity care delivery is assessed through a three-tiered screening system. Midwives in the Netherlands are designated by the government as the providers of maternity care during normal pregnancies. If a midwife is available, mothers must use her services in order to have the full cost of care covered by the state insurance program. If a midwife is not available in a particular area, then a general practitioner provides maternity care. In the 1950s, a screening system was introduced that provided a list of indicators/criteria to clarify which pregnancies fall under a "high-risk" category and need the care of an obstetrician (Hingstman 1994).

Providing these guidelines are followed, the cost of the delivery is fully covered by Dutch health insurance. As a result of this system, the number of home births in the Netherlands—approximately 30 percent—is high when compared to other high-income countries. Dutch care providers, like their counterparts in Sweden, use obstetrical technology less often than do their counterparts in the United States. For example, only 11.2 percent of pregnant Dutch women had cesarean sections in 1997 (CBS, 1999).

Virtually all (99 percent) the inhabitants of the Netherlands are insured, and thus there is no need to litigate to cover additional or anticipated medical costs associated with malpractice. The Dutch legal system limits the amount of compensation awarded for everything from medical mistakes to plane crashes, effectively eliminating large financial rewards as an incentive for legal claims (van Teijlingen 1998).

"Bad outcomes" of pregnancy may occur in Sweden and the Netherlands just as they do in the United States. However, technological intervention is less expected and less accepted in these countries. Belief in the "technological imperative"—that any available technological intervention should be used—does not have the same cultural support in Europe that it has in the United States. In the United States, the value placed on medical intervention is interwoven with a distrust of natural processes. In countries where childbirth is viewed as "a natural process that should be subjected to as little intervention as possible" (Hingstman 1994, p. 37), the notions of risk and liability are less meaningful. Little technological intervention is the norm, not a sign of "negligence."

Conclusion

In this chapter, we have attempted to illustrate the linkages between cultural beliefs about childbirth, social constructions of risk, the use of technology, and malpractice litigation. In contrast to its general medicalization in the United States, childbirth in Sweden and the Netherlands is considered a "safe" and "normal" physiological process. Birth attendants and health care providers in these latter two countries hold the general belief that women are capable of birthing babies without technological intervention and that that the process of birth is a personal and family event (McKay 1993, p. 120).

The American fondness for malpractice suits can be attributed to many factors. We have focused on the link between malpractice and culturally constructed notions of risk. Future work in this area could profitably examine structural features of different societies only hinted at here, including the number of practicing lawyers, the use of contingency fees (where the plaintiff's lawyers are paid a percentage of the settlement), and health care payment systems.

Our analysis calls attention to the fact that, in the realm of childbirth, decisions about care made by health practitioners and women are not freely made. Obstetrical technology must be understood in the context of how and why it is implemented—not only from a biological perspective but also from a larger social critique of its symbolic meanings and uses. The diversity that exists in high-income countries, both in maternity care practices and in configurations of malpractice litigation, gives us a view of alternate possible futures.

Acknowledgment

We would like to thank the editors of this volume for their excellent support and encouragement, especially the section editor, Cecilia Benoit. Also, our thanks to Gary Doernhoefer and Kathleen Williamson, who gave helpful advice on this manuscript.

Notes

1. It should be noted that this same study showed that there were 9 percent *fewer* cases filed in 1997 than in 1986, suggesting that the rise in malpractice cases occurred between the mid-1970s and the mid-1980s (Glaberson 1999, p. 6).

References

Adeyi, O., and R. Morrow. 1997. Essential obstetric care: Assessment and determinants of quality. *Social Science and Medicine* 45(11): 1631–1639.

Alexander, J., et al. 1998. The course of labor with and without epidural analgesia. *American Journal of Obstetrics and Gynecology* 178(3): 516–520.

Annadale, E. 1996. Working on the front-line: Risk culture and nursing in the new NHS. *Sociological Review* 33: 416–451.

Arney, W. J. and J. Neill. 1982. The location of pain in childbirth: Natural childbirth and the transformation of obstetrics. *Sociology of Health and Illness* 4: 1–24.

Benson, M. 1994. *Obstetrical Pearls*. Philadelphia: F.A. Davis Company.

Bortin, S., Alzugaray, M., Dowd, J., and J. Kalman. 1994. A feminist perspective on the study of home birth: Application of a midwifery care framework. *Journal of Nurse-Midwifery* 39: 142–149.

Browner, C., and N. Press. 1997. The production of authoritative knowledge in American prenatal care. In *Childbirth and Authoritative Knowledge,* eds. R. Davis-Floyd and C. Sargent. Berkeley: University of California Press, pp. 113–131.

Cartwright, E. 1998. The logic of heartbeats: Electronic fetal monitoring and biomedically constructed birth. In *Cyborg Babies: From Techno-Sex to Techno-Tots,* eds. R. David-Floyd and J. Dumit. New York: Routledge.

CBS (*Centraal Bureau voor de Statistiek*). 1999. *Verloskunde Vademecum* (Obstetric Vademecum). Rijswijk, the Netherlands: CBS. (In Dutch.)

Corea, G. 1985. *The Hidden Malpractice: How American Medicine Mistreats Women.* New York: Harper & Row.

Cunningham, G., et al. 1996. *Williams Obstetrics*. New York: McGraw-Hill.

Danzon, M. 1985. *Medical Malpractice: Theory, Evidence, and Public Policy*. Cambridge, MA: Harvard University.

DeVille, K. 1998. Medical malpractice in twentieth century United States: The interaction of technology, law and culture. *International Journal of Technology Assessment in Health Care* 14: 197–211.

DeVries, R. 1996. *Making Midwives Legal*. Columbus: Ohio State University Press.

Douglas, M. 1992. *Risk and Blame: Essays in Cultural Theory*. New York: Routledge.

Gaskin, I. M. 1999. Review of *The Risks of Lowering the Cesarean Delivery Rate* by B.P. Sachs et al. In the *New England Journal of Medicine,* Jan 7, 1999. *Birth Gazette* 15(2): 32.

Giesen, D. 1988. *International Medical Malpractice Law: A Comparative Law Study of Civil Liability Arising from Medical Care*. Dodrecht: Martinus Nijhoff Publishers.

Glaberson, W. 1999. When the verdict is just a fantasy. *New York Times,* June 6, Section 4, pp. 1, 6.

Glass S. (1998) The epidural: A ritual of relief. *Midwifery Today* 14: 22–48.

Hall, W. 1989. The logic of a controversy: The case of agent orange in Australia. *Social Science and Medicine* 29(4): 537–544.

Hingstman, L. 1994. Primary care obstetrics and perinatal health in the Netherlands. *Journal of Nurse-Midwifery* 39(6): 379–386.

Howell-White, S. 1999. *Birth Alternatives: How Women Select Childbirth Care.* Westport, CT: Greenwood Press.

King, J. C., and S. R. Kovac. 1996. Evidence-based practice in obstetrics and gynecology: Its time has come [letters to the editor]. *American Journal of Obstetrics and Gynecology* 175(1): 232–233.

Lassey, M. L., Lassey, W. R., and M. J. Jinks. 1997. *Health Care Systems around the World: Characteristics, Issues, Reforms.* Upper Saddle River, NJ: Prentice Hall.

Mackauf, S. and S. Tessel. 1997. *Obstetrical Malpractice: Failure to Diagnose Fetal Distress.* New York: Law Journal Seminars Press.

McKay, S. 1993. Models of midwifery care: Denmark, Sweden, and the Netherlands. *Journal of Nurse-Midwifery* 38(2): 114–120.

Porreco, R. P., and J. A. Thorp. 1996. The cesarean birth epidemic: Trends, causes, and solutions. *American Journal of Obstetrics and Gynecology* 175 (2): 369–374.

Romm, A. 1998. *Pocket Guide to Midwifery Care.* Freedom, CA: Crossing Press.

Rooks, J. 1997. *Midwifery & Childbirth in America.* Philadelphia: Temple University Press.

Rothman, B. Katz. 1993. Going Dutch: Lessons for Americans. In *Successful Home Birth and Midwifery: The Dutch Model,* ed. E. Abraham-Van der Mark. Westport, CT: Bergin and Garvey, pp. 201–211.

Schifrin, B. S., Weissman, H., and J. Wiley. 1985. Electronic fetal monitoring and obstetrical malpractice. *Law, Medicine, and Health Care* 13(3): 100–105.

Skolbekken, J. 1995. The risk epidemic in medical journals. *Social Science and Medicine* 40(3): 291–305.

Stalnaker, B. L., et al. 1997. Characteristics of successful claims for payment by the Florida Neurologic Injury Compensation Association Fund. *American Journal of Obstetrics and Gynecology* 177(2): 268–273.

Starr, P. 1992. *The Logic of Health Care Reform.* New York: Peguin Books.

Wennstrom, G. 1997. *The Swedish Health Care System and Its Problems.* Presentation at the National Health Board, June 10, Stockholm, Sweden.

Wiegers, T. A., van der Zee, J., and M. Keirse. 1998. Maternity care in the Netherlands: The changing home birth rate. *Birth* 25(3): 190–197.227

CHAPTER 12

Obstetrical Trajectories

ON TRAINING WOMEN/BODIES FOR (HOME) BIRTH

Bernike Pasveer and Madeleine Akrich

Birth—Introduction

Mrs. Borst, the Dutch minister of health affairs, thinks Dutch women should birth their babies at home more often, and she has provided quite a sum of money to encourage the practice. In the Netherlands, health insurance companies, midwives, and spokespersons of women's rights tend to favor home birth. As noted in earlier chapters, the Dutch maternity care system rests on the assumption that pregnancy and birth are normal life events. This means that during pregnancy and birth, women are attended by a primary care provider: a midwife or general practitioner (GP).[1] These "first-line" caregivers assess their clients continuously on the basis of a list of obstetric indications. This list places women in one of three categories: low risk, medium risk and high risk. Women in the first category need not see any other medical professional but their midwife, and they may choose to give birth at home or in hospital. Women in the third category are handed over to a gynecologist[2] and hospital right away and usually stay under specialist care until after their child is born. Women in the second category—meaningfully coined the "gray area" by midwives—are affected by some medical or other problem (or the suspicion thereof) that is not quite grave enough to hand them over to a gynecologist and a hospital (the so-called "second line"). A specialist must examine these women, and, depending on the diagnosis, they go back to midwife care or stay under the specialist's supervision.[3]

Thus the Dutch system functions on the basis of a continuous and prescribed selection of its clients, according to which everyone is assumed to get a unique and appropriate combination of professional care, technologies, and place (of birth). Because Dutch obstetrics assumes that pregnancy and birth are considered normal until there is evidence of the contrary, midwives and gynecologists practice an appropriate kind of "expectant" care: One tries to interfere/intervene in the birth process as little as possible, and midwives try to keep women out of the second line as long as possible. Interestingly, research shows that the ways in which this expectant obstetrics is practiced vary widely both among midwives and among hospitals/gynecologists (Pel & Heres 1995; Wiegers 1997).

Dutch obstetrics, both in theory and in practice, has something of a hard time surviving in the midst of new prenatal technologies, women's "demands" for hospital birth and epidurals,[4] and the shortage of practicing midwives and maternity nurses. Dutch women tend to have their first pregnancy later in life, which statistically implies more complications, and according to the Obstetric Indications List (referred to as the "VIL" in Dutch), midwives are to refer a primipara older than thirty-eight years to a specialist obstetrician.[5] Another reason for the gradual decrease in the percentage of home births in the Netherlands[6] is the increased diagnosis and treatment of fertility problems. An in vitro fertilization (IVF) pregnancy is classified as high risk and is usually taken care of by a gynecologist from beginning to end.

But there is more. The percentage of women referred during labor is going up. As Figure 12–1 shows, almost all percentages of referrals increased between 1989 and 1993, but two reasons for this increase are particularly interesting: insufficient progress of first stage and second stage.

It must also be noted that many more "low risk" women are choosing a hospital delivery with their midwife for reasons of comfort, safety, or because many of their peers have done the same (Wiegers & Berghs 1994). Research tends to show that the place of delivery influences its medical and obstetrical outcomes (Pel & Heres 1995).[7] This means that low-risk women's safety seems not to improve in a hospital. The nearness of obstetricians and medical apparatus, and perhaps the atmosphere of the hospital, too, change the delivery more than the slogan "a policlinic delivery is simply a relocated home birth" suggests.[8]

But why do women want to give birth in hospital with their midwife? And how is it that the percentage of referrals during planned home births has increased steadily?[9] Is the best strategy to promote home birth a campaign to make women conscious of the value and safety of home birth? How safe is it for women who want to give birth at home? Can midwives still "stand by with their hands on their back and wait quietly?" (Croon 1998a, p. 245).

In this chapter we examine why it is that women plan to deliver in a hospital and why they are increasingly referred to specialist care during labor. Our hypothesis is that a *marked* rupture tends to occur in the obstetrical trajectory designed for women, and that this rupture inscribes itself in the ways women (and midwives) (fail to) trust the working of an unassisted body during labor. During pregnancy, (Dutch) women's bodies are increasingly educated in trajectories in which markers of their pregnancy are produced outside and separated from their bodies, while no obvious efforts are made to reconnect these markers to the embodied pregnancy. Increasingly, women's obstetrical trajectories are marked by ultrasound, triple test, and amniocentesis, all of which inform a woman about her body, its health, and the growth and well-being of its little inhabitant. Women and midwives experience the pregnancy at least partly through these markers.

FIGURE 12–1

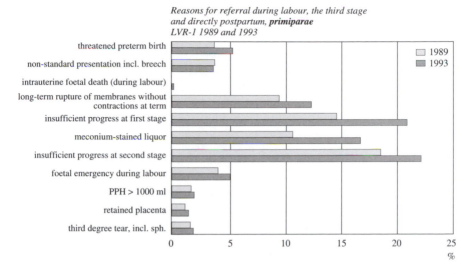

*Reasons for referral during labour, the third stage
and directly postpartum, **primiparae**
LVR-1 1989 and 1993*

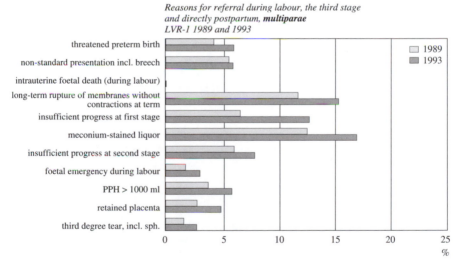

*Reasons for referral during labour, the third stage
and directly postpartum, **multiparae**
LVR-1 1989 and 1993*

SOURCE: *Obstetrics in the Netherlands, Trends 1989–1993*. Utrecht: SIG Health Care Information, p. 75.

During home birth, however, these and other excorporate traces of how someone is doing are principally absent. We insist that these markers, these prenatal technologies, are not neutral: Like other medical technologies, they produce a specific distribution of competencies, potentialities, and trusts among those who participate in their functioning. Thus during pregnancy, a regime of visual and graphic surveillance is increasingly installed, whereas during home birth the woman has just her body and the midwife to inform her of where she is going. It is this disjuncture on the level of the body-knowledge that might be responsible to some extent for the difficulties of home birth.

Of course, our hypothesis is not meant to do away with other explanations of the threats to Dutch obstetrics. However, by setting up our thesis, we do wish to be critical of some views of medical technologies and we are trying to work on a different conceptualization of the pregnant body/the body in labor, one that sees the body as an entity that is "learning to be affected"[10] by a specific, defined trajectory and the markers thereof. Medical technologies—used or unused, prenatal or antenatal—are not neutral providers of insight into a stable body. Using recent work from the sociology of technology, we argue that medical technologies inform what is diagnosed, changing the body by the act of diagnosis. In that sense, machines are never neutral, nor are they simply manifestations of underlying ideologies. Similarly, bodies are never "given." For any medical technology to work, those who participate in the performance of that technology—physicians, patients, bodies, professionals, institutions— are brought in line with the apparatus and vice versa. In every medical setting—be it of a midwife and her client at a home birth or of a gynecologist and a patient at a cesarean section with an epidural—specific definitions and distributions of competencies occur between the various participants.[11] We examine how this process works in present-day Dutch obstetric practices.

Our argument elaborates on three related themes. The first is that of *trajectories* that emerge through pregnancy and birth and that relate a woman to obstetrics through a series of associations and markers. Here we suggest that what is designed for women tends to become ambiguous in the Dutch context. The second theme is that of how *technologies* work: We claim that medical technologies are neither good nor bad a priori, but that it is through their specific use that practices are established that are, or are not, desired. For example, ultrasound has become a very "normalizing" technology during pregnancy for a number of reasons; this process may happen with other prenatal diagnostics depending on the infrastructure that construes a technology's working. Our third theme concerns women's bodies. We wish to claim that bodies, and the way the processes of pregnancy and birth occur, are not *given and ready to be discovered,* but are constituted by, and constitutive of, the trajectories and apparatus that mark them. Bodies are trained, or educated, and during that process they become "loaded" with experiences and competencies that match the trajectories designed for them. They "learn to be affected"—and in contemporary Dutch obstetrics this happens in an ambiguous manner. Using comparative data from French obstetrics, we suggest this particular rupture is not produced there. With regard to what women and bodies learn and are affected by, French obstetrics is more coherent. We do not suggest that French obstetrics is therefore the preferred system. We offer our trilogy of trajectories, technologies, and bodily affections as a "grid" of diagnosis, analysis, and precaution for those who wish to change their country's obstetrics. Would-be reformers of maternity care must pay attention to competencies and the ways they are affected through specific and situated technological trajectories.

Home Birth in the Netherlands—A Description

The start of a delivery can take a long time. "Looking back, I have had contractions for days, I was dilating when I was doing the shopping!"[12] Dutch women are told by their midwife that "as long as you are in doubt, real contractions have not yet started.

Real contractions are so unambiguous and painful, you cannot miss them" (Smulders & Croon 1996, p. 21). When a woman has regular contractions, when there are signs or feelings of unease, or when her water breaks, a woman who has planned home birth is to call her midwife. "My midwife said she would be there at five o'clock. But it hurt so much that I called her again and I said 'if this continues like this for another 15 minutes, you *have to come.*' But she got there before I could call her again. I had dilated eight centimeters in half an hour." "I had contractions every half-hour and only in my back. I thought it was strange that I only had contractions in my back and none in my belly. I called R and she told me that this could happen. I was to call her again if I had contractions every four minutes. She said that could take a while and that the baby might come only after the weekend." "It started at night when the waters broke. The midwife had said we need not call at night if the waters were clear. They were, but there was blood in it, so we called her. She said there was nothing to be worried about, and we should go back to bed."

Between the onset of labor and the nearing of full dilation, the midwife may visit her client just once or a number of times. Upon visiting, her work consists of doing an internal examination to check upon the progress of labor, listening to the baby's heartbeat with a "doptone,"[13] and getting an impression of the situation: Is her client at ease or very upset, is she managing labor well or is she panicking? She might also suggest that her client try another position for labor. "When she arrived I was taking a shower. She sent me back to bed because she could see I was in much pain and could not walk anymore. The two of them (partner and midwife) helped me from the shower to bed." "No sooner had the midwife gone than I got ill, really ill, fever, throwing up. I had to go to the bathroom, to sit on the loo, and that was a good position. So when she came later on, she saw me there, and she saw that was okay for me. I asked whether it was not dangerous, could the baby not be born with me sitting there on the loo, and she said, no, we'll get you up on a birthchair when it's time."

Upon the nearing of full dilation, the midwife stays. This means that during labor, the woman is assumed to be able to do without the midwife's presence and interventions. None of the others present during those hours can assist her physically with managing contractions. The environment (including the partner and material objects like the shower, the bed, and furniture) can be mobilized only to afford the woman-in-the-body the power to concentrate upon what happens. This can mean different things. Most women follow preparation courses, where they learn specific breathing techniques, positions and "things to say" to manage labor. "I went to yoga and to pregnancy gym. The things we had learned during yoga were of more use than the gym. We did more exercises for breathing 'low.' The pregnancy gym was more talking about your feelings and that was fine too. During gym we had put a few exercises on paper, like what to do. So I had those papers next to me during labor, and I tried out these things. Like breathing thoroughly, or like choosing a position so that my husband could massage my back." "During labor, I did a sort of a yoga or anyway a number of basic yoga things. There were other things too. Things like that. It is not that you do exercises during labor, but that you pay attention to your breathing."

It is our contention that these preparation courses are an important chain in the "normality trajectory" as it is designed for pregnant women, as they prepare for mobilizing assistance, as it were, from the body and the environment that is present: the partner, the shower, the breathing, a variety of positions. Yet they do so more in terms of setting up a disposition in which the woman and the body and their environment learn to be affected by labor and birth and to manage, rather than in terms of giving them concrete information that can be "applied" to get through labor.

When a woman has reached full dilation, she is informed by her midwife who tells her that she can start pushing. Yet this phase—called the transition stage by professionals—is quite intricate. Women feel things changing, they have more difficulty in "puffing away" contractions, pressure on the perineum increases, and often they tell the midwife they are unable to manage contractions at this point, that they "need to go to the bathroom." Some women report that the stage of expulsion, in which they must push with contractions instead of puff through them, is a relief; others find it the worst of all. "I did not want to go on with it. It hurt. But on the other hand, it was okay. R encouraged me. She told me she could see the head. I wanted to touch it and I asked her if I could. I touched the baby's head. Then at a certain point I couldn't take the contractions anymore and I could start pushing."

> Q: Didn't she first have a look whether you had full dilation?
> A: No, she said that the last time it had also gone so fast that she could see that I could just start pushing. Let it go. . . . And it did indeed go very fast.
> Q: Didn't she do an internal at all? Only once when you hadn't dilated fully yet?
> A: No, but she said that the birth was so nice that she didn't need to do anything.

During the last stage, the midwife is present, and she is referred to a lot in women's stories. Women hardly notice that the midwife unpacks her bag with instruments. "You know, it was only afterwards that I saw this sheet with the instruments, for cutting, and sewing and things. She had put it up behind a bedcover or so." It is the midwife's ways of going about and her actions that are remembered: her encouragement, the fact that after most pushing contractions she listens to the baby's heart, the hurt of the baby's head "standing," and the period just after the baby is born.

> Q: Can you remember any of the things K. had brought with her?
> A: No idea. I don't think she had that many things in the room. I cannot remember her having displayed a whole "tool kit." Anyway she had the things for suturing and that thing she used to listen to the child's heartbeat.
> Q: Could you listen as well?
> A: No. I actually found her doing that rather annoying.
> Q: Why?
> A: I felt that it only distracted me.
> Q: That it disturbed you?
> A: Yes. "Let's just get on with it quickly because. . . ." But I didn't say that to her.
> Q: Do you know when she did that? During the pushing?
> A: I'm not sure. Anyway, she did it a couple of times. Especially in the beginning and then towards the end when the head was already out. By then the contraction came quite quickly one after another, so then it was a question of . . . I believe she did it during the first half an hour of the pushing. She left the umbilical cord attached for a while. She even put the baby to have a bath with the cord still attached. She makes it walk on your belly. You see that it was still attached to the cord. She was between my legs and I had to take her myself. I think that just the feet were still inside and I had to pull her.

Q: Did K. tell you to do that?
A: She encouraged me but I didn't *have to* do it.
Q: But you didn't intuitively want to do it?
A: Well, I was just glad that she was born.

We see here a delivery with a number of participants, some temporarily present, some who stay for the whole thing. Markedly, the midwife only stays for the last part, which implies that labor, during home birth (as well as during hospital birth), is something that must be accomplished by the woman. The "disposition" within which she and her body are afforded this, is not empty of obstetrical markers, but neither is it filled only with obstetrics. The woman is expected to work in an environment that deliberately carries no permanent obstetrical markers that tell her how she is doing and into which every now and then the midwife appears and produces obstetrics. Yet the manner in which she does this, and the temporary nature of the explicit obstetrical information she provides, is meant to be continuous with the embodied work of labor rather than to lift things out of that body and make them into an external reference for the woman to look at. Home birth stories recount both the markers produced by the midwife:

> She did an internal and it appeared that I was at 1 cm only!

> Within an hour I had gone from 2 to 9 cm!

and the markers present or made present in the setting itself:

> The teapot too worked good: at every of its rounds I was to say while puffing which color it was, so M. was surprised when he heard me puff "yellow," "blue," "orange."

> I chatted, laughed, sighed and puffed the time away, which at some points went very fast and at others seemed to stand still. I had no idea, in fact, of time. M. was sitting next to my bed on the floor and did his best to sigh and chat and laugh with me. Sometimes he'd squeeze my hand to keep me with the right breathing, for I'd loose the rhythm at some points.

Home birth is "alone birth"—it proceeds and must proceed in/as an obstetrical setting in which obstetrical markers are hardly explicit, and if they are, this is only temporarily so. Women are expected to be able to "manage" that situation, to be able to produce, with the mobilization of anything useful in their environment and in their bodies, a setting that confirms and produces a "normal" delivery. The obstetrical markers—the breaking of the water, the onset and progress of labor, the midwife's presence, and the examinations she is required to do in order to check upon the assumption of normality—are both explicit and implicit: They are known to happen and they are also known to be part of "normality."

We would like to suggest that the possibility of such an event is not just a matter of organizing the right care and the right "consciousness" of a woman and her environment, but is also a matter of organizing a setting in which a woman and her body have learned exactly this: to be able to be affected by a process that is at once new, painful, surprising (certainly if it concerns a woman's first delivery), maybe frightening, and at the same time, "doable," normal, no need to worry. A woman must work through labor with her trained body, her trained partner, her trained midwife—yet it is only through her ways of doing and through acquiring temporal access to the body that the midwife can inform herself about the situation. As soon as she stops listening to the baby's heart, it returns back into the body. At no point, as long as normality is guaranteed through these very same markers, are traces of the delivery taken out of the body and, as it were, put on the wall to look at. The concentration on/in the body is crucial and is constituted by the environment, the work of the midwife and also her absence during long periods of labor, the instruments she can use, and the work of the other participants.

Dutch birth assumes and organizes a woman-and-a-body who is able to deliver a baby on her own. And women embody this ability for being affected by the event, we argue, as an effect of the obstetrical trajectory that is designed for that. "Natural" birth is not something that occurs all by itself—it is (or has become) just as much an obstetrical arrangement as the "technical" deliveries elsewhere. There is nothing wrong or "unnatural" with that—we have long stopped treating the natural as self-evident and the cultural as in need of explanation. But it is precisely because the natural, or the normal, has become "equipped" that we need to study that equipment in order to find out what goes wrong and what can be done better.

We believe that the current concern over Dutch obstetrics has to do with the fact that no one has paid attention to the ways the body as an entity "learns" and becomes "loaded" with experiences, expectancies, and abilities. Most people assume that learning is done by the brains, the consciousness—hence efforts in Dutch obstetrics to render women "conscious" of the values of home birth. But it is also the body that must be able to be "affected" by home birth, that must be trained to do so. Thus it is crucial to take a look at the training the bodies of Dutch women receive. What does the trajectory leading up to a possible home birth look like? Does it (still) lead up to the ability of normal and "incorporated" birth?

Pregnancy in the Netherlands—Part of a Trajectory of Associations

A pregnant woman visits a midwife some twelve to fifteen times during pregnancy, with visits increasing in frequency toward the end of pregnancy. At the first visit, the midwife takes an extended anamnesis. Some blood is taken (by the midwife or in hospital) for the determination of specific values. At later visits, a similar series of examinations is done. The woman is weighed, the belly is measured and palpated, the position of the baby is determined, its heartbeat is listened to with a doptone, the woman's blood pressure is taken, often her urine is checked for glucose, and at particular points her blood is checked for anemia. Usually at all visits, time is taken for asking questions and reporting worries and experiences. "She did the normal things. You know, weighing, feeling my belly, getting my pressure, asking how 'we' are doing, things like that."

Most women follow pregnancy gym or yoga, but not all do. "I am a professional singer, so I thought I could do without breathing techniques, and I really was not looking forward to the chatty stuff at pregnancy gym." "I've done it the first time, so I know what it's about." Women also tend to read a lot about pregnancy and birth. "I have read everything that I could get my hands on, really everything." And, of course, they have their mothers and friends with whom to share experiences.[14] Thus, women's world of information, expectations, and training consists of various sources—of which the midwife is an important one.

The explicitly obstetrical part of the trajectory of a low-risk pregnancy passes through the midwife and the instruments she uses to check up on health and growth. So here, like in the home birth, the knowledge of what is happening circulates in a tiny circuit. Hardly any lasting signs of someone's pregnancy are produced that can travel without the woman's body. Thus the midwife keeps record on a standard form about the markers of the pregnancy; sometimes she keeps a written memory of things that require special attention—and that is all. The woman carries a copy of the form so that in an emergency any medical person is able to see her trajectory thus far.

This minimal version appears to be rather continuous—at least in terms of what happens to the body—with the event of home birth. In both situations, knowledge circulates between midwife and woman/body, and in neither situation are obstetrical articulations produced that come to lead a life as an external referent of the pregnancy. The dispositive is thus small: Midwife and client are related and interdependent for their information. Moreover, this configuration is practically identical to the obstetrical one in which home birth takes place: There, too, we find a woman, her partner, her home environment, and the midwife with apparatus that cannot produce traces of the delivery by taking them out of her client's body.

Yet this small circuit of bodies of knowledge tends to become extended in ways that may disrupt this continuity.[15] Over the last decade, the fetal ultrasound has become a very popular marker of pregnancy in the Netherlands. Women will often pay for an echo as a souvenir of the pregnancy, and one or two "official" ultrasounds per pregnancy are becoming a part of "normal" practice. In the Netherlands, health insurance companies pay for two ultrasound scans per pregnancy. Some midwifery practices have acquired their own ultrasound apparatus. Most, however, refer their clients to a nearby hospital to have a scan made. It also appears that whereas some midwives take the first blood sample themselves and send it in to a laboratory, most others have this done in hospital. In addition, an impressive body of new prenatal diagnostic technologies has (recently) made an appearance as a possible articulator of any pregnancy.

It is here that we see a possible rupture of the trajectory that performs pregnancy and birth in the Netherlands. Our analysis offers a slightly different reading of the threat that is indicated by others (Wiegers 1997): If medical technologies tend to colonize normal pregnancy and childbirth it is because the very use of these technologies redefines the experience as a high-risk event. A technology like amniocentesis, for example, is used to examine pregnancies of women over thirty-six years of age. Without suggesting that this should not be done, it is good to know that the very presence of this prenatal diagnostic turns some women's pregnancies into the category of "increased risk." Research has shown that the mere belonging to such a category changes the experience of the body as a safe place to be (Popkema, Pieters, & Harbers 1997). Many new prenatal technologies that produce new articulations on risk during pregnancy or birth appear to be so complex or unregulated that they tend to become owned by obstetrical specialists (De Vries, Horstman, & Haveman 1997).

These new technologies do much more than offer a better view of given and unchanging processes. They change the very ontology of pregnancy: They change trajectories, they change pregnancies and their markers, and they change the content and the distribution of competencies. Prenatal trajectories that consist of visits to a series of caregivers, of examinations by a variety of people and apparatuses residing in different and rather unconnected places, and of a number of dossiers that contain crucial information about the pregnancy but that are not "owned" by the pregnant woman are different from trajectories that consist of visits to a midwife, examinations within her practice, and a dossier that is carried around by the woman herself. The first kind of trajectory makes for a referent—the pregnancy—which is distributed over a number of actors who are related, but not physically attached, to the woman. The second kind of trajectory makes for a pregnancy that remains in the body, that loads the body with abilities, knowledge, and confidences that come in handy at home birth. In this trajectory the midwife is the (only) external informant, and she is present at the birth.

We suggest that as Dutch obstetrics tends to allow more and more pregancies to become informed by the first trajectory, it also feeds into a woman-body and a midwife that/who is less and less able or prepared to have a home birth that must do without all these external and unembodied points of reference.

It is not our intention to say that new prenatal technologies in and of themselves are bad and should not be used. We rather suggest that their use will in all cases reorder the pregnant body. What is more, we think that the increasing excorporation of the pregnancy, combined with the enlargement of the circuit within which knowledge of a specific pregnancy travels, and with the differences in kind between markers that can travel without a body and markers that cannot, will produce a woman-and-a-body that are increasingly unprepared, quite literally, to be able to be surprised by the event of home birth in which they must get along without this circuit of excorporated information about their bodies.

Here other obstetrical organizations come to mind. In France, for example, almost all women deliver in a hospital. Although there is quite some variety within the country and between hospitals/clinics, a large percentage of births take place in large hospitals, the woman lying on her back or side on a (small) bed, connected to a monitor that registers fetal heartbeat and contractions, an infusion that regulates the strength and rhythm of contractions, and an epidural that takes away labor pain and usually remains at work until after the delivery —requiring a woman to push the baby out on command of the midwife.

Birth is thus a highly distributed event with a lot of excorporal markers: Contractions are sensed by the monitor and regulated through the oxytocin administered by the infusion instead of through the oxytocin produced in the body; pain is "unsensed" through the epidural. Birth is not performed without the woman or/and her body, however. Rather, they are partners in a collective that cannot function when she is unwilling or unable to participate.

Pregnancy in France is also excoporated, distributing the pregnancy over a series of participants. Three ultrasounds are routine, as is a triple test. Amniocentesis was once reserved for women over thirty-eight years old, but now it is standard for every woman whose triple test is "positive." Women see gynecologists as well as midwives and general practitioners for different "aspects" of their pregnancies. Preparation courses always contain one or more information sessions with an anesthetist about the pros and cons of the epidural and training sessions for learning to push without sensing contractions.

This quick summary is not meant to make us sigh or be horrified by French obstetrics. It is meant to indicate that the excorporating trajectories that are becoming more common in Dutch obstetrics create assisted and distributed pregnancies that "fit" better in the French obstetric system. As the Dutch rearrange pregnancy, as they reorganize its referent (before the woman as well as before the midwife) from something in the body to something in many places and forms (an ultrasound, a DNA-code, a microscopic image, a heart beating, a belly growing), women will come to have different bodies, and they will have bodies that are experienced differently, both by them and by midwives. A distributed pregnancy is less apt to lead up to the more simple and centered event of a home birth.

Conclusions

Although it may seem an evident conclusion, we do not wish to conclude that medical technologies must to stay out of pregnancy and childbirth. Rather, our argument is a plea to evaluate the ways in which the "minimal" care provided for low risk-pregnancies and deliveries co-constitute a coherent trajectory and trained body that is prepared for home birth. And it is an argument to include the question of the trained body in our evaluations or prospective studies of the implantation of new prenatal diagnostic technologies: If one expects women to be able to (desire to) deliver "alone," and if one expects to be able to guard birth "alone" as a midwife, how must one use the procedures and the apparatuses with which a woman's and a baby's health are monitored? How can one prevent women from needing all kinds of external referents and informants by the time she is to be loaded with referents and informants herself? We argue that it matters who, how, and with what means pregnancy and birth are monitored. Specific diagnostic settings make for specific articulations and distributions of potentialities and competencies. Thus a French woman who gives birth in hospital under an epidural watched by electronic monitoring must be able to lie still and push on command, whereas a Dutch woman who gives birth at home must be able and trained to have a body that can give birth on instinct, to work on the basis of a "body that knows exactly what it must do and when" (Smulders & Croon 1996, p. 15). Note that we do not assume that having such a body comes "naturally." On the contrary, we argue that it comes through deliberately training a woman and a body, and those who are with her, for the power to have an instinct and to know what the body does, to be prepared to be affected and surprised by the setting in which a baby is born.

Our approach is not anti-technological: The example of ultrasound shows that disembodied markers, to use Duden's (1993) terminology, are very much able to become embodied. Of course, in the process, the body changes—but it does not (necessarily) go from "natural" to "colonized by technology." The popularity of ultrasound images, their association with the normality of pregnancy rather than with the search for pathologies, with seeing into one's own body rather than in a strange, abstract, and unreadable reduction, shows that knowledge can be taken out and put back into the embodied experience.

If the Dutch wish to rescue home birth, they need more ways of analyzing the workings of those who monitor pregnancy and birth—midwives, obstetricians, and the apparatuses they employ. To try to make women conscious of the safety and value of home birth may be a good strategy (Schoon 1996), but we cannot overlook the "fact" that bodies too have a consciousness, a memory.[16] To be cautious, as midwives, about new prenatal diagnostics is the best thing to do (see Croon 1998b)—but more is at stake than the question of whether the information such technologies provide is necessary. For this is not what technologies do: They *do* inform, but in so doing they require the cartography of the body to change in order to be informative, and they change that body's owner and the one who cares for her.

Notes

1. Eight percent of all women who are attended in the "first line" of care, are seen by their GP. We use "midwife" for both midwives and GPs. See SIG 1996.
2. In the United States the physician specialist who provides care at birth is referred to as an obstetrician or an obstetrician-gynecologist. In the Netherlands this person is typically called a gynecologist. Several words in the Dutch language can be used to denote an obstetrician: *obstetricus, vrouwenarts,* and *gynecoloog,* but the latter is most common. When referring to the Dutch physician specialist in childbirth we follow the Dutch convention and use the term gynecologist.
3. In the Dutch maternity care system midwives are specialists of physiology and gynecologists are specialists of pathology.
4. For those who read Dutch, an interesting and shifting discussion about labor pain and epidural can be followed on http://www.ouders.nl. In the 1998 archive of the site, women discuss the epidural mainly in connection with other interventions: If I must have a cesarean, is it better to have an epidural or a complete anesthesia? In the 1999 discussion the focus had shifted: women wrote to say they wanted an epidural and asked where they can get it, and complained about their midwife being not enthusiastic about their desire for pain suppression. Someone even accused midwives of being motivated by economic reasons in their hesitation to send clients in for an epidural-on-demand, but Croon (1999) adequately replied to that accusation: "Midwives surely have other things on their mind than to guard their income. Our greatest worry is the enormous shortage of midwives and the enormous work-pressure."
5. No one can be held to follow that rule, however, and it is not always practiced. See, for example, Verstegen 1997; Iedema-Kuiper 1996.
6. Between 1965 and 1978, the percentage went from 68.5 to 35.8 percent and declined further to 31.6 percent in 1992. From the group of 81,592 women who were attended by midwives from pregnancy to puerperium, including referrals during labor, after which care during puerperium was taken over by the midwife, 58,239 never were referred to the second echelon (SIG 1996). Of this group, 55.3 percent of the primiparae and 66.3 percent of the multiparae delivered at home. The others delivered in hospital with their midwife (Wiegers 1997).
7. "[W]omen having their first baby increasingly appear to prefer a hospital birth. . . . [M]ost women are inclined to repeat that first choice, regardless of whether the birth was free of complications or not. . . . [F]or women at low risk of obstetrical complications, the outcome of planned home birth is at least as good as the outcome of planned hospital births for first time mothers, and that for other mothers the outcome of planned home birth is significantly better than that of planned hospital birth" (Wiegers 1997, p. 101).
8. The idea that a delivery in a hospital with one's midwife and, if all goes well, without use of the apparatus and personnel that "belong" to the second echelon was for some time said to be simply a home birth in a different place—a relocated home birth.

9. In 1988, 35 percent were referred (16.9 percent during pregnancy and 18.1 percent during labor); in 1993, 42 percent were referred (19.6 percent during pregnancy, 22.4 percent during labor). See: SIG 1996. Between 1969 and 1991, the percentage of nulliparous women who started labor with a midwife and were referred to an obstetrician increased from 10 percent to 39.1 percent, for parous women this percentage increased from 2.7 percent in 1969 to 11.8 percent in 1991. See Wiegers 1997, p. 82.
10. See also Gomart and Hennion 1999; Latour (forthcoming).
11. For examples of this kind of reasoning, see Berg 1997; Akrich and Pasveer 1996; Pasveer and Akrich 1996; Berg and Mol 1998.
12. Unless otherwise indicated, all quotes are derived from interviews performed in the course of our research.
13. A doptone is a handheld sonar device for listening to a baby's heartbeat.
14. Wiegers and Berghs (1994) note that "low risk" women tend to base their decisions about where and how to give birth mostly on their communication with their "peers": i.e., family, best friends.
15. Elsewhere we have analyzed two midwives' practices to show that what appear to be only personal and subjective ways of working also perform different obstetrical agendas. See Akrich and Pasveer (2000).
16. An extremely rich language of bodies as entities with a proper experience of their own is developed, perhaps accidentally, by Shalev 1999.

References

Akrich, M., and B. Pasveer. 1996. *Comment la Naissance Vient aux Femmes* (How Birth Comes to Women). Paris: Les Empêcheurs du Penser en Rond. (In French.)
———. 2000. Multiplying obstetrics. Techniques of surveillance and forms of coordination. *Theoretical Medicine* (in press).
Berg, M. 1997. *Rationalizing Medical Work. Decision Support Techniques and Medical Practices.* Cambridge, MA: MIT Press.
Berg, M., and A. Mol. 1998. *Differences in Medicine. Unraveling Practices, Techniques, and Bodies.* Durham, NC: Duke University Press.
Croon, M. 1998a. De maakbaarheid van de mens. (The makeability of man.) *Tijdschrift voor Verloskundigen* (Journal for Midwives) 22(4): 245. (In Dutch.)
———. 1998b. Prenatale zorg op de helling. (Prenatal care in danger.) *Tijdschrift voor Verloskundigen,* 23(11): 757.
———. (1999. Routinematige ruggenprik is onverantwoord. (Routine epidural is irresponsible.) *NRC Handelsblad* May 4, 1999.
Duden, B. 1993. *Disembodying Women.* Cambridge, MA: Harvard University Press.
Gomart, E., and Hennion, A. 1999. A sociology of attachment. In *Actor Network Theory and After,* eds. J. Law and J. Hassart. Oxford: Blackwell Publishers/The Sociological Review, pp. 220–247.
Iedema-Kuiper, H. R. 1996. *Geïntegreerde Thuiszorg bij Risico-Zwangeren—Een Gerandomiseerd Onderzoek* (Integrated Home-Based Care for High-Risk Pregnancies). Utrecht: Ph.D. Dissertation. University of Utrecht. (In Dutch.)
Latour, B. Forthcoming. Learning to be affected. In *Theorizing Bodies,* eds. M. Akrich and M. Berg. Durham, NC: Duke University Press.
Pasveer, B., and M. Akrich. 1996. Hoe kinderen geboren worden. (How children are born.) *Kennis en Methode,* (Knowledge and Method) 20(1): 116–145.
Pel, M., and M. H. B. Heres. 1995. *OBINT. A Study of Obstetric Intervention.* Amsterdam: Thesis Publishers.

Popkema, M., Pieters, T., and H. Harbers. 1997. Technologie en zwangerschap. De politiek van een prenatale screeningstest. (Technology and pregnancy. The politics of prenatal screening.) *Kennis en Methode,* (Knowledge and Method) 21(2): 97–123.

Schoon, L. 1996. Haalt de thuisbevalling het jaar 2000? (Will home birth survive the year 2000?) *Tijdschrift voor Vrouwenstudies,* (Journal for Women's Studies) 17(1): 65–74.

Shalev, M. 1999. *The Loves of Judith.* New York: Ecco Press.

SIG. 1996. *Obstetrics in the Netherlands, Trends 1989–1993.* The Hague: SIG Health Care Information.

Smulders, B., and M. Croon. 1996. *Veilig Bevallen.* (Safe Birthing.) Utrecht and Antwerpen: Kosmos–ZandK Uitgevers. (In Dutch.)

Verstegen, A. 1997. Drie casus over 'oudere nulli-para' van de Vroedvrouwenpraktijk Breedstraat. (Three cases on "older nulli-para" of Midwifery Practice Breedstraat.) *Tijdschrift voor Verloskundigen* (Journal for Midwives) 22(7/8): 36–38. (In Dutch.)

Vries, G. H. de, Horstman, K., and O. Haveman. 1997. *Politiek van Preventie* (Politics of Prevention). The Hague: Rathenau Institute. (In Dutch.)

Wiegers, T. 1997. *Home or Hospital Birth?* Utrecht: NIVEL.

Wiegers, T., and G. Berghs. 1994. *Bevallen . . . Thuis of Poliklinisch?* (Giving Birth . . . at Home or in Hospital?) Utrecht: NIVEL. (In Dutch.)

CHAPTER 13

What (and Why) Do Women Want?

THE DESIRES OF WOMEN AND THE DESIGN OF MATERNITY CARE

Raymond DeVries, Helga B. Salvesen,
Therese A. Wiegers, and A. Susan Williams

We were well along in the planning of this book when it occurred to us that we had overlooked the most important actors in the drama of birth: mothers (to-be) and their families. In our effort to explain the variation in maternity care systems we had set to work examining the influences of state policy, educational institutions, the professions, medical systems, and technological developments. In the midst of this flurry of academic research we somehow failed to ask how the preferences of pregnant women affected the delivery of care at birth.

Our immediate response to this omission was embarrassment: How could we organize a book on the design of maternity care without exploring the desires of clients? We scolded ourselves and set about outlining a chapter on what women want in their maternity care. However, after further reflection we are no longer sure that our oversight is cause for embarrassment. The question, "What do women want?" is much more complex than it appears. Consider this letter to the editor of the *British Medical Journal* (Johnson et al. 1992):

> Editor, We have been following with interest the mixed response to the recent report of the House of Commons Select Committee on Maternity Services advocating more home births in British obstetric practice. The report had a frosty reception from the Royal College of Obstetricians and Gynaecologists, while the Royal College of Midwives and others welcomed its proposals.

The views of pregnant women have not been heard in this exchange of opinion. As part of our course on public health medicine we surveyed 299 women at varying stages of pregnancy in antenatal clinics at two hospitals in Leeds, asking them where they would prefer their baby to be born and why. We started the survey in the expectation that, as the select committee suggested, there would be considerable unmet demand for home births. We were therefore surprised that only 8% of the women (95% confidence interval 4.8% to 10.6%) indicated they would prefer to have their labor at home. The most commonly given reason for preferring hospital birth was that skill and technology are available should any unforeseen complication arise (50%).

Later in the letter the authors acknowledge that theirs was a biased sample (a hospital population); nevertheless, they conclude that efforts on the part of the British government to encourage birth at home might be misguided because "a large proportion of women with completely normal pregnancies prefer to deliver in a hospital."

Like us, the authors of this letter are anxious to let the voices of women—the clients of the system—be heard ("The views of pregnant women have not been heard . . . "). But their method of soliciting the opinions of their clients is sociologically naïve; indeed, their letter is an apt illustration of the difficulty of asking women what they want. Clients' knowledge of "appropriate care" at birth is shaped almost entirely by the existing maternity system; if you ask women what kind of care they prefer, it is *no* surprise to learn they favor the type of care they are offered. Seen in this light, the fact that 8 percent of their sample is interested in birth at home *is* surprising: not because the number is so small, but because it is rather large for a country where just over 2 percent of births occur at home.[1]

Our initial failure to include a chapter on the desires of women is now more understandable. Unlike lay persons or "birth activists," we are inclined to see the desires of women as dependent, rather than independent, variables. We do not wish to discount the role of clients in the creation of maternity care systems, but we are keenly aware that opinions about health care are as much a *product* as a *cause* of that care. This insight makes problematic the oft-cited need for more "woman-centered" care. What does such care look like? Is it more or less technological, or both, depending on the individual wishes of each woman? The idea of woman-centered maternity care is quite empty if it requires eschewing all drugs and technology for some births while scheduling epidurals and cesarean sections for others.

This truth about the desires of women—that they are created by, and are creators of, existing arrangements—is not the end of the story, however. If it were, you would not be reading this chapter, there would be nothing more to say. We recognize—as earlier chapters attest—that maternity care systems *do* change and that some of that change can be attributed to the voices of women asking for "better" care. Thus, we acknowledge that the design of birth is the result of the desires of women, but hasten to add that these desires are the product of larger social currents and medical ideas.

To highlight the socially situated nature of women's wishes in maternity care, we take a closer look at women's preferences in the United States, Norway, the Netherlands, and the United Kingdom. In its own way, each story illustrates how maternity care systems shape the desires of women and how maternity systems change to accommodate new demands. In the United States we pick up on a theme introduced in Chapter 4, looking at the efforts of a small but vocal group intent on changing a system of care they found costly and demeaning. In Norway we look at a similar movement, but one that had a different effect as a result of different organizational and professional arrangements. The high rate of birth at home in the Netherlands leads us to ask whether the continued use of home birth is a product of women's wishes or some other force in society. And the British case allows us to illustrate the complicated ways women's desires interact with the interests of professionals, consumer groups, and government agencies—in the context of a nationalized health service. We conclude by reviewing what these case studies teach us about how women's desires shape, and are shaped by, professional advice, interest groups, the state, and the media. In these case studies our goal is to identify the influence exerted by the clients of maternity care in the struggle to shape maternity policy. We are not concerned with the intrinsic *value* of different kinds of maternity policy or their impact on health, but with the conflicts and negotiation that led to the *development* of policy—in other words, the relationship between policy and politics.

The United States: The Alternative Birth Movement and the Authority of Obstetrics

In the mid-1970s several important social movements—including the civil rights movement, the women's liberation movement, the anti-war movement—emerged in the United States. These organized efforts to change society gave birth to a variety of smaller social movements, one of which was the "alternative birth movement" (ABM). A brief look at the successes and failures of the U.S. alternative birth movement affords us the opportunity to see how the wishes of maternity care clients were expressed, received, and translated by American obstetrics.

The ABM brought together an interesting collection of people—feminists, members of the religious right, "back to nature" types, pro-family crusaders, peace activists, and libertarians—all of whom wanted to see U.S. obstetrics made more "humane," more "woman-centered." Theirs was a campaign to "demedicalize" pregnancy and childbirth, making a place for birth at home and for midwife-assisted birth. The climate of the times—this was the era where the major institutions of society, including medicine, were seen as part of an oppressive "power structure"—and the "obvious" need for change made the goal seemed easy to attain. Birth in the United States was costly, inefficient, and subjected women to needless, often painful, medical interventions.

The movement employed a twofold strategy. On the *local* level, members of the ABM pressured hospitals to revise their policies, making room for more natural, less technological birth. Practices that had become routine were condemned—shaving of the pubic area, mandatory IVs, electronic fetal monitoring, episiotomies, drugs to speed (or slow) labor, separation of moms and babies, the use of infant formula. Alternative practices were encouraged—the creation of home-like birthing rooms, fathers and siblings at birth, "bonding," and breastfeeding. On the *state* level, the ABM organized and lobbied for the rewriting of medical practice acts to (re-)create an independent profession of midwifery.[2]

The task of changing American birth practices proved more daunting than the ABM assumed. Members of the movement were well aware that the American view of birth was shaped by an obstetric science convinced that birth is fraught with risk—according to American obstetricians, birth can be seen as "normal" only in retrospect, after technology guides a birthing woman around the dangers of deformed fetuses, prolonged labor, decelerating heart tones, excessive bleeding, difficult presentations, torn perinea, retained placentas, and the like—but they assumed the spirit of the times favored their reform effort. Surely women of the 1970s would require little argument to see American obstetrics as a patriarchal vestige.

However, what seemed "obvious" to members of the movement seemed exotic and dangerous to nearly everyone else, including the vast majority of childbearing women. The anti-institutional bias of the times did not extend to the "obstetric" view of birth. The energy and enthusiasm of the movement was met by apathy or resistance among the very women it sought to help. By the 1980s the movement was dissipated with little to show for its efforts. Hospitals had made cosmetic changes in their policies: Most had "birth centers," allowed (selected) family members to be present at birth, and encouraged women to develop "birth plans." But midwives remained marginal, cesarean sections continued at a dizzying pace, birth at home was seen as dangerous and weird, and women were encouraged to use new and improved pain medications.

How did American obstetrics deflect the challenge of the ABM? Analysis of the fate of the ABM in the United States reveals how medicine responds to—and accommodates—changing social and cultural conditions.

Admittedly, the ABM was a small, ragtag movement lacking political power. It did not threaten organized medicine the way the civil rights movement threatened the power structures of the American South. But, at a deeper level, the critique of American obstetrics offered by the ABM was connected to changes in society that *did* pose a significant challenge to the medical establishment. In the 1970s the American medical citadel was under assault on several fronts. The feminist movement exposed the sexism of medicine, the "back to nature" movement called attention to the overuse of technology by doctors, a renewed interest in the spiritual dimension of life revealed medicine's dualism, and concern about the runaway costs of medical care showed the fiscal irresponsibility of caregivers and medical institutions.

In the 1930s women demanded "modern" maternity care—care that was scientific, hospital-based, dependent on surgical skill and pharmaceutical knowledge.[3] Now, less than a half-century later, this same care was regarded as sexist, costly, overly technological, dangerous, and ignorant of the social, psychological, and spiritual needs of women and their families.

The providers of maternity care had to find a way to respond to this critique. Perhaps most challenging for obstetricians and hospital personnel was the need to go outside of what they saw as their legitimate jurisdiction—the health of mother and baby—and show concern for the "experience" of birth. Up until this point, the primary concern at birth was only with its outcome. "Activist" obstetrics was the logical response to this concern: Better births were assured by new and better technologies. But as birth became less dangerous and yielded "better results" (i.e., less mortality and morbidity) concern shifted from the "product" to the experience of birth. Birth was no longer just a way to produce an heir (or a laborer), but an opportunity for personal growth (see Levesque-Lopman 1983). In large part, the demands of the ABM were the incarnation of this shift from product to experience.

Not surprisingly, the initial response of doctors to this emphasis on experience was to insist on the primacy of outcomes. Writing in the *Journal of the American Medical Association* in 1980, two physicians noted (Adamson & Gare 1980, emphasis added), "We believe that certain priorities in the birthing process must be maintained if rational decisions regarding birth environments are to be made. The first priority is a live and healthy mother; the second, a live and healthy baby; and *third,* a psychologically rewarding experience for the parents and the baby" (p. 1736). Caregivers found it difficult to give in to the wishes of women. And the ABM might well have been ignored if it were not for two factors. First, there was an increasing amount of scientific evidence suggesting that concern with the quality of birth influenced its outcome. American obstetrics was hoist on its own scientific petard as study after study showed that the well-being of mother and baby was influenced by the setting of birth (see, for example, Kennell et al. 1974; Klaus & Kennell 1976, 1981; Klaus et al. 1972). Second, the 1970s "birth dearth" in the United States lead to increased competition for obstetric patients (National Center for Health Statistics 1980). In the American free market health care system, it was in the economic interest of medical institutions to listen to the demands of clients.

The ABM's critique could not be ignored. American obstetrics needed to find a way to reverse the small but worrisome trend toward home birth (see Yankauer 1983) and to respond to the ABM without undermining its authority. Salvation came from an unexpected quarter: study of the bonding process—early attachment between parent and infant. It was research on bonding that allowed the ABM to *challenge* American obstetrics; nearly all of this research led to the conclusion that there were important reasons to focus on the experiential aspects of birth. But, ironically, this same research allowed American obstetrics to control and deflect pressure for change. The work of Klaus and Kennell (1976, 1981) was indeed critical of standard obstetric care, but it also gave medical organizations acceptable scientific grounds for restructuring hospital birth. In their "Statement on Parent and Newborn Interaction," the American Medical Association (1977) said:. "[I]ncreasing evidence has accumulated to support the concept of an 'attachment and bonding' process in the human race. It is timely to review all hospital procedures and professional practices for their appropriateness and thereby encourage the hospitals to reassess their policy in support of the bonding principle." The sentiments of the American Medical Association were mirrored in a 1978 report, "The Development of Family Centered Maternity/ Newborn Care in Hospitals," prepared by an Interprofessional Task Force comprised of obstetricians, pediatricians, hospital representatives, and nurses.

As a result of these reassessments, hospitals and obstetricians across the country created "alternative birth centers." In contrast to the cool efficiency of a "modern" labor and delivery suite—where women labor in semi-private rooms and are rotated through a central delivery room arranged for the convenience of the physician or midwife—alternative birth rooms were assigned to only one woman and allowed family members and friends (i.e., nonmedical personnel) to be present. The typical alternative birth room of this era was furnished to create a "homey look" with a queen-sized bed, carpeting, hanging plants, pictures, overstuffed chairs, and perhaps a dining table. These new birth centers were simultaneously a way to respond to client demand and retain control over maternity care. The birth center promised enhanced parental control over birth but functioned to increase caregiver control of the experience. Those who wished to use the birth center had to be screened and monitored, conforming to medical definitions of "low risk" (see De Vries 1980, 1983, 1984). And with their newly found expertise, physicians and midwives took control of the experiential dimension, "helping mothers to love their babies" (*British Medical Journal* 1977, Jenkins & Westhus 1981; Ounsted et al. 1982; Rising 1974). Criticized for not allowing parents and babies the time or place for attachment, medical organizations now became marketers of "bonding."

A vocal group of women came to obstetrics wanting to enhance the experience of birth, demanding less use of technology, more contact with their infant, and more emphasis on the relational aspects of the event. Obstetrics responded by "scientizing" experience, treating experience as one among several variables that influences the outcome of birth, a suitable object of study in new randomized trials (see Chalmers 1986). Yes, the desires of women were accommodated in the design of maternity care—small adjustments were made—but in the United States of the 1970s obstetrical assumptions about birth remained dominant and the authority of obstetrics remained unchallenged. The digestion of the ABM by obstetrics offers evidence of the cultural dominance of science. Experience may be an important dimension of the birth process, but it must be certified and approved by science.

Women's Choices in Norway

Like their sisters in the United States, feminist groups in Norway also began advocating for change in Norwegian maternity care in the 1970s. They emphasized that birth is a normal event, important for the whole family, and they insisted that mothers and fathers have the opportunity to participate in the birth of their children. Unlike the United States, however, this pressure resulted in more than cosmetic changes. Over the last thirty years there has been a gradual but significant change in attitudes within maternity wards, with a notable shift from strict hygienic routines to cozier settings that combine medical safety with a tolerance for simple human needs. Over the last ten years some hospitals have also built separate "Alternative Birth Care" units within their maternity wards. In appearance these units are somewhat similar to hospital birth centers in the United States—they are located near traditional delivery units, they have a less hospital-like atmosphere, and they include bathtubs, double beds, and rooming-in for the whole family (Bergsjø 1988; Nylander 1995). However, compared to the United States, these units have promoted more widespread change in Norwegian birth care. The fact that breastfeeding rates increased from less than 30 percent at twelve weeks in 1968 to more than 80 percent in 1991 is widely attributed to these changes (Endresen & Helsing 1995). Those monitoring breastfeeding routines in maternity wards during this period noticed an increase in undisturbed and prolonged contact between mother and baby and more individualized care in line with the international recommendations in the joint statement by WHO/UNICEF: "Ten Steps to Successful Breast Feeding" (WHO 1989).

Another change that emerged at the same time as the creation of alternative birth units is the development of postnatal care in separate patient hotels in the vicinity of the hospital. For a healthy mother and child there is an option to stay in these "hotels" with their spouse or other family members after the delivery rather than in the traditional postnatal wards within hospitals.

How have the desires of Norwegian women led to changes in care? A brief history of changes in one hospital is instructive. In the 1990s, a new maternity unit was being planned in Bergen, a city with about 230,000 inhabitants on the west coast of Norway. At that time there was only one delivery unit available, located in the Haukeland University Hospital; this maternity care service managed approximately 5,000 deliveries a year. Hearing of planned changes in the maternity unit, influential women's groups argued that an alternative unit should be built. These groups were in favor of a care center located away from the traditional hospital environment, one that would allow women a real choice between a traditional birth in a hospital and a delivery in a setting that was less medical and more family-friendly.

Several groups claimed to represent the opinion of women in the region, but it was apparent to those planning the unit that there was no systematic study of women's wishes with regard to maternity care. Wishing to respond to the desires of clients, a survey was done: 792 women answered a questionnaire during their pregnancy or postnatal period concerning their view of the obstetric care (Trovik et al. 1995).

This survey revealed that the large majority of Norwegian women expect a high level of medical response. To feel secure during their labor, 94 percent of the women wanted a midwife available immediately; an additional 3 percent said they wanted midwife care available within thirty minutes, and 3 percent had no opinion regarding this. Further, the majority (72 percent) wanted an obstetrician, a pediatrician, and an anesthesia-team to be immediately available; 15 percent were content to have those services available within thirty minutes. Only 2 percent of the women said that they did not consider it necessary to have these health professionals available during labor, and 11 percent expressed no opinion. Most women (91 percent) reported that they consider investigations by ultrasound and electronic fetal heart rate monitoring to be reassuring, but a minority answered that they found these investigations frightening, disturbing, or unnecessary. Routine visits by the obstetrician team when in labor were regarded as reassuring by 86 percent of the women, while the rest found these visits disturbing, unnecessary or had no opinion. Seventy-four percent wanted epidural anesthesia available to them during labor: There was no significant difference in the answers given by women before or after their delivery. Women with at least one previous delivery were more anxious to have this service available when compared to women with no previous deliveries.

Regarding the structure of the planned new maternity unit, one-fourth of the women answered that they did not know what they preferred. Among the women with an opinion on this issue, the majority (76 percent) wished to see the structure of the unit reorganized to have combined labor and postnatal wards, while the rest (24 percent) preferred the traditional model with separate units for delivery and postnatal care. The arguments given by the first group were that a combined unit would give better continuity in their contact with the staff; women in favor of the separated units argued that this would give them a quieter environment after delivery.

Interestingly, nearly 10 percent of the respondents claimed that they would like the possibility for home deliveries to be improved in the region.[4] In Norway, the proportion of planned home deliveries is less than 1 percent (Birth Registry of Norway

1998); here we find, as was found in Britain (see Chapter 1), a small but significant percent that want the option of home birth to be available, even though few women birth at home. This pattern is also found in Denmark, a country where women have a legal right to birth care at home. A Danish study showed that while between 13 and 15 percent of the women plan a home delivery, only 1.3 percent actually gave birth at home—and this is in a country where the geographical conditions allow quick transportation to a hospital if needed during labor (Kamper-Jørgensen et al. 1985).

The results from the Norwegian study, presented in the *Journal for the Norwegian Medical Association,* led to a lot of discussions on television, the radio, and in newspapers. Some groups interpreted the results in favor of the model with hospital deliveries, while others drew attention to the fact that there were many women who expressed a desire for an alternative to current services. The authors of the study called for caution in the interpretation since the difficulties in assessing what women *really* want is well known. It might well be that the survey of preferences in maternity care is more like a mirror image of the existing system and that the opinions of health professionals influence women to a large extent. However, the study reinforces the existence of real differences in women's preferences regarding the type of maternity care available. This puts health professionals in the challenging situation of having to respond to the desires of women while developing models of care that they, the caregivers, consider medically safe.

In 1995, after considering the responses to this survey, the Haukeland University Hospital built a separate ABC unit—named *"Storken"* (after the bird that brings babies through the chimney)—adjacent to the existing delivery unit. The unit was designed to handle about 1,500 selected low-risk deliveries per year. Development of the alternative model of care was mainly the responsibility of a midwife. In addition to the normal amenities—bathtubs, double beds, and rooming-in for the whole family—the ABC features the use of alternative methods for pain relief and a variety of positions during delivery. In fact, epidural anaesthesia and electronic monitoring of the fetus are not allowed within the unit. A panel of health professionals including midwives, obstetricians, pediatricians, politicians, and women representing users concluded that the new alternative birth unit was medically safe. They also concluded that the positive experience with alternative approaches to normal deliveries should be extended to the more traditional units.

Women's satisfaction with the unit was also evaluated by means of a survey. Women who delivered in the alternative unit ($N = 120$) and women who delivered in the traditional unit (but who were eligible to deliver at the alternative birth unit, $N = 96$) completed questionnaires. In general, both groups were very content. This is no surprise given the fact that all of the women had healthy babies and had chosen the unit in which they delivered. There were a *few* interesting differences between the groups, however. Women delivering in the traditional unit were more satisfied with the pain relief they received; women delivering in the alternative unit seemed more focused on the improved food, the availability of the phone, and the room facilities than on the difference in delivery philosophy at the alternative unit.

In which direction is the maternity care moving in Norway today? The importance of the individual woman's needs and the opportunity for mothers and fathers to participate in decision-making regarding the birth of their children seem to be relatively well integrated in all maternity care units in Norway. However, the scattered population, the great (and rugged) distances between cities, and the relative isolation of communities—especially during winter—provide an additional challenge in planning and organizing maternity wards. Continuing debates focus on the issues of safety and risk. A recent governmental review of women's health in Norway (NOU 1999, pp. 8, 13) defines the different types of risk that apply in this discussion: the objective risk that can be calculated and the subjective risk that deals with a "sense of safety." Recent studies indicate that even after thorough selection, the large specialized units still seem to be safer in terms of perinatal outcomes (NOU 1999, pp. 8, 15). However, low-risk multiparous women might *feel* safer in local maternity wards than they would in centralized units that require long travel. Interestingly, this report also notes the lack of systematic studies on how and where women want to give birth, even though many groups, including physicians, midwives, and women's interest groups, claim—at least to some extent—to act on the behalf of women in general. The national report calls for further studies regarding women's wishes, as well as further investigations to elucidate the selection criteria that combine safety with the continued use of smaller maternity wards. The conclusion of the review is that Norway also in the future will need a local preparedness to provide childbirth services (NOU 1999, pp. 8, 15).

For the time being, the Norwegian Board of Health (1997) recommends keeping three levels of maternity care in Norway (see Chapter 1) and the issue of safety in the few remaining small maternity homes in rural areas is heavily discussed (*Jordmorbladet* 1998; Lund et al. 1999; Øian 1998; Schmidt et al. 1997). Caregivers in Norway continue to work to find a way to accommodate women's wishes while preserving safety for mother and child.

What Do Dutch Women Want?

Given the high percentage of home births in the Netherlands, it seems logical to conclude that Dutch women want to give birth at home. But is this a demand Dutch women put on the health system or a demand the Dutch health system puts on women?

Three professional groups are involved in maternity care in the Netherlands: general practitioners, midwives, and obstetrician-gynecologists.[5] General practitioners and midwives are both primary caregivers, qualified to provide care during normal pregnancy and childbirth. In case of pathology or (threatening) complications they will refer their client to a specialist gynecologist. High- and low-risk pregnancies are distinguished by means of an extensive list of indications for specialist care. Underlying the Dutch system is a conviction that pregnancy and childbirth are natural, physiological processes that do not need medical intervention or a medical environment when there are no specific risks. Home birth is regarded as safe and preferable for births that are expected to progress normally (*Adviescommissie Kloosterman* 1989).

In 1965 the majority of all births in the Netherlands (68.5 percent) took place at home, without referral to specialist care. But over the last three decades this started to change as a result of a variety of factors, such as the increasing numbers of obstetrician-gynecologists, rapid developments in medical technology, increasing use of referrals to specialist obstetricians—before and during labor—demographic changes, and changes in health care policy (Wiegers 1997; Wiegers, van der Zee, and Kierse 1998). Developments in other countries, where childbirth was rapidly shifting from home to hospital, did not go unnoticed in the Netherlands, and more women began asking for hospital birth. Gradually hospitals opened their doors for midwives and general practitioners to use the hospital labor and delivery suites for their own clients, without first referring them to a specialist obstetrician. This was called a *poliklinische bevalling* (a short-stay hospital birth) or *verplaatste thuisbevalling* (a home birth away from home). Since then women with low-risk pregnancies have been allowed to make their own choice where to give birth, at home or in a hospital, assisted by their own midwife or general practitioner. These births are referred to as planned home and planned hospital births. But not every planned home birth results in an actual home birth: When complications during labor need specialist attention, transfer to the hospital and referral to the obstetrician will take place. Therefore, the actual home birth rate is always lower than the preferred or planned home birth rate.

As a result of these developments, the actual home birth rate declined rapidly from 68.5 percent in 1965 to 35.4 percent in 1980 and, more slowly, to 30.7 percent in 1993.[6] It is often assumed that the decline in home birth was caused by a change in the preferences of women. Studies about consumer wishes in maternity care are scarce, however. One of the first studies in which women's preferences for home or hospital birth were described (Laprè 1972) showed that in the early 1970s almost 70 percent of the women surveyed preferred to give birth at home. In that year the actual home birth rate was 57 percent. In 1985 a study was conducted among 170 first-time mothers (to-be) with initially uncomplicated pregnancies, living in an urban area. This study showed that most women had already decided early in their pregnancy where they wanted to give birth: 59 percent of the women preferred to give birth at home, 26 percent preferred to go to hospital, while 15 percent remained undecided (Kleiverda 1990; Kleiverda et al. 1990). A small number of women changed their mind later in pregnancy and shifted from a preference for the hospital to a choice for a home birth. Of those who were in doubt early in pregnancy, the majority (80 percent) decided to give birth at home. There were some distinct differences between the groups: When compared to women who planned a hospital birth, women who wanted to give birth at home were older, better educated, had better jobs, were less traditional, and more often planned to continue their work following their maternity leave.

In 1987–1988 a survey was done among 5,500 men and women in the age group of twenty to forty-four years. This study, which included many different health care issues, showed that the majority of people, men and women, have a clear opinion about maternity care and place of birth. Almost 40 percent of the respondents expressed a preference for home birth, 36 percent preferred a hospital birth, while 25 percent had no preference. Prior experiences are known to be important in shaping the preference for a future birth location. Of the women in this study who had experienced a home birth the majority (57 percent) preferred a home birth again next time and only 9 percent expressed an interest in a hospital birth. Of the women who previously had given birth in hospital, a minority, approximately 45 percent, desired a hospital birth again and 25 percent preferred a home birth next time. This research also found that women with a lower education more often prefer a hospital birth, while highly educated women more often prefer a home birth (Hingstman et al. 1993).[7]

A study conducted in 1991–1992 among 1,720 pregnant women receiving midwifery care showed 63 percent favoring birth at home and 37 percent choosing hospital birth (with less than 1 percent in doubt). Of the first-time mothers-to-be 57 percent preferred a home birth, while of the women who had given birth before 69 percent preferred to give birth at home (Wiegers & Berghs 1994; Wiegers, van der Zee, Kerssens & Kierse 1998).

Three studies have moved beyond simply measuring the preferences themselves to exploration of the reason for one preference or another (Damstra-Wijmenga 1982; Kleiverda 1990; Wiegers 1994, 1997). Damstra-Wijmenga (1982) studied 1,692 births in one of the northern provinces (Groningen). She found that the most important reason to want to give birth at home was the "familiar surroundings" (89 percent) and the "dislike of the hospital" (6 percent). Reasons to prefer a hospital birth were "feelings of security" (64 percent) and the "rest and care received at the hospital" (20 percent).

According to Kleiverda's (1990) study, preferences for home birth can be classified in two categories: advantages related to the home environment and disadvantages related to the hospital environment. Advantages of the home environment were described as a relaxed atmosphere with more privacy and greater intimacy. Disadvantages of the hospital environment included restrictions imposed on the woman and her partner, a lack of privacy, and a dislike of hospitals in general. The preference for a hospital birth can be similarly classified by listing the advantages of the hospital and disadvantages of the home environment. The most mentioned advantage of the hospital was its greater perceived safety. Disadvantages of giving birth at home included having to clean up the mess it creates and fear of having to go to the hospital while in full labor.

In the Wiegers study (1994) comparable reasons were found for choosing a home or a hospital birth. The women preferring a home birth mentioned as the most important reason that home was the natural environment for giving birth after a normal pregnancy. The most important reason to opt for a hospital birth was the aspect of safety for mother and child. Feeling comfortable and at ease was mentioned as reason for choosing a home birth as well as for choosing a hospital birth.

The influence of "significant others" was found to be important in these studies. The choice was often made in accordance with the preference of significant others, such as partner, family (in-laws), and close friends.

The most recent study about preferences for birth location and reasons for that choice is from Manshanden (1997). Of 112 first-time mothers-to-be, with uncomplicated pregnancies, 79 percent preferred to give birth at home and 21 percent preferred a hospital birth. The majority of them had made their choice before getting pregnant, and they indicated that their choice was strongly influenced by their partner and, to a lesser extent, close friends. Women preferring a home birth rated the influence of the midwife higher than those preferring a hospital birth. Safety aspects were the most important reasons to choose a hospital birth, while for the women preferring a home birth privacy aspects were the most important ones mentioned. They felt safe enough knowing that, in case of complications, they would always be able to go to the hospital.

Although these data are from different studies, with different study populations, and are therefore not comparable, they all show that a majority of people in the

Netherlands still prefers home birth over hospital birth. This may create the misleading impression that there is no discussion about maternity care issues in the Netherlands. Currently there is an extensive discussion about the use of technology and its beneficial and harmful effects, not only on the birth process itself, but on the whole system of maternity care in the Netherlands (see Chapter 12). In a mirror image of the United States—where a small group of women prefer home birth despite the highly medicalized maternity care system—there is a small but growing movement in the Netherlands demanding easier access to epidurals and elective cesarean sections. They feel that the Dutch system is restrictive and is forcing women to suffer, denying them routine access to anesthesia and surgery (see Manschot 1993).

Recently a member of parliament made a casual remark suggesting that the "midwife Mafia" denied laboring women pain relief because they fear it will interfere with the bonding of mother and child (Vuijsje 1999). The comment evoked a lot of protest, especially from midwives (see Croon 1999). But the underlying thought—that pain is no longer acceptable and that all women should be given an epidural on request—is gaining ground. If in the future enough people support these views, the Dutch system of maternity care will change because not only do women want what is offered to them, but—if they are strong enough—they can also make sure that they will be offered what they want.

What Do Women Want in Britain? A Story of Maternity Policy

At this point we can safely say that all those who play a part in the design of maternity care seek the same goal: a healthy outcome for baby and mother and the satisfaction of childbearing women. But, as we have seen, not all agree on the means to achieving this goal.

As in other countries, the design of maternity care in the United Kingdom has been largely dominated by the politics of various competing interest groups, of which mothers are just one—the others include obstetricians, midwives, general practitioners (GPs), the government, and political parties. The power and alliances of each group have shifted over time, and some groups—or at least subgroups, such as poor women or unqualified midwives—have had very little power and been unable to protect their own interests. The struggle between these various groups has operated within a changing social and economic context that gives added weight at different times to the influence of a particular group—through economic growth, say, or the sudden lack or availability of beds within the National Health Service (NHS). To understand recent policy developments in maternity care in the United Kingdom, we look at key historical moments in the latter half of the twentieth century. We begin by looking at the postwar shift from home confinement to virtually 100 percent hospital delivery. This was a period when everyone, women as well as men, was entitled to health care on the basis of need, so that struggles over policy were about access and control; the maternal death rate had fallen dramatically, but the perinatal death and morbidity rate was high relative to similar countries. We move on to scrutinize the development—in the last few decades of the twentieth century—of a consensus to promote woman-centered care. This period is difficult to investigate, since all the relevant government records are not yet available to the public.

THE POSTWAR SHIFT FROM HOME TO HOSPITAL DELIVERY

In 1944, the Royal College of Obstetricians and Gynaecologists (RCOG) advocated that 70 percent of confinements take place in a hospital. Then, after the war and the creation of the NHS, the college shifted away from its earlier alliance with midwives to consolidate its own position. In 1954, in a *Report on the Obstetric Service under the National Health Service,* it advocated that all births should take place in an institution. It said that this would provide "the maximum safety for mother and child and, therefore, the ultimate aim should be to provide obstetric beds for all women who need or will accept institutional confinement." The report also recommended that GPs should not be permitted to give obstetric care unless they had received special training to do this (RCOG 1954, pp. 16, 17). This was a strike at GPs and Local Authority medical officers.

Mothers themselves were now making demands for hospital delivery. The numbers of women giving birth in a hospital increased dramatically during the war because the Emergency Medical Services had arranged for women in cities to be taken to maternity homes in safer areas. Then, after the inception of the NHS in July 1948, the attraction of a hospital birth was enhanced. Not only was it free under the NHS, but it also spared a family the extra expenses of giving birth at home, like food, bedclothes, sanitary towels, extra washing, and adequate fuel (Barnes to the Technical Advisory Sub-Committee 1951). Confinement in a hospital also gave women the chance of a rest away from housework and the demands of a family. Before the war, the rate of death in childbirth had been higher in hospitals because of the high rate of puerperal infection on a maternity ward. But now, the risk was greatly reduced by antibiotics and the margin of safety was further increased by the development of other medical techniques, like blood transfusions. But in any case, C. P. Snow's "New Men" were rapidly developing an influence over national life at this time and the public had enormous confidence in scientific experts and expertise. A number of factors militated against mothers' demands for hospital birth. There was a shortage of maternity beds, which was aggravated by the increase in the birth rate. There was also an *overall* shortage of beds, which led hospital boards in the early 1950s "to divert beds now used for obstetric cases to other patients in greater need of hospital treatment" (Grigson to NBTF 1953). This was met with outrage. The Women's Cooperative Guild passed a motion at their 1951 Annual Congress deploring "the lack of accommodation and facilities for maternity cases in our nationalized hospitals" (Women's Cooperative Guild Annual Report for 1951, p. 32). In early 1954, the Labour MP Barbara Castle asked the Minister of Health during Question Time in the House of Commons if he was aware that many women in her constituency of Blackburn were being "compelled to have their babies at home against their will owing to the shortage of the maternity beds?"(*Hansard,* 21 January and 4 March 1954). In 1960, an organization called AIMS—Association for the Improvement of the Maternity Services—was set up by mothers to campaign for hospital beds.

However, the government was unable to offer more beds, and so defended home delivery. "Confinement which is expected to be normal," it insisted, "is as safe at home as in hospital" (MH Minute 1954; see also Webster 1988, p. 379). Its position was defensive: Although the maternal mortality rate had fallen dramatically, the perinatal mortality rate was high relative to other countries. It sought to prioritize needs in order to determine who should be allocated a bed: The second confidential enquiry into maternal deaths advised "better selection of cases for hospital confinement based on the 'priority' classes" (Ministry of Health 1960).

Because of the controversy at this time between the relevant professional groups over methods of care, the Guillebaud inquiry into the NHS identified in its 1956 report "a state of some confusion" in the maternity services and recommended a thorough review (cmd. 9663, 1956, para 733, p. 263). This led to the appointment by the government of the Cranbrook Committee, which was chaired by the Earl of Cranbrook (Ministry of Health 1959, p. 1). The eventual report devoted a whole chapter to "The Place of Confinement: Home or Hospital?," presenting arguments for both; it recommended the maintenance of a good domiciliary service and hospital beds for 70 per cent of all deliveries (Ministry of Health 1959, Chapter 5). When the report was published in 1959, the rate of hospital birth was 64.2 percent. This meant that 70 percent was a realistic target, so it was welcomed by the Ministry of Health; however, it disappointed the obstetricians.

Negotiations over beds and between doctors and consultants have taken place, of course, within the larger context of the NHS. Sir George Godber, who was then Chief Medical Officer, recalls "the tremendous change that took place in the 50s. Planned development of specialist staff in hospitals was produced and the quality of specialist care and the amount of work done in hospitals was immensely improved" (ASW interview with Sir George Godber, November 4, 1994). This was followed by the Hospital Plan of 1962, which laid out a long-term capital program for hospital rebuilding in order to provide "the most advanced diagnostic and treatment facilities for the entire population" (Berridge, Webster, & Walt 1993, p.110). The cornerstone of the Hospital Plan was the idea of the district general hospital, with a maternity unit where full consultant cover would be at hand for all beds. Godber was driven by a dream of social equality—and was supported by a period of economic growth.

By 1965, the Cranbrook Report's target of 70 percent hospital delivery had been reached, and by 1968, the national figure (although concealing regional variations) was over 80 percent. One important reason for this was the availability of beds following the decline in the birth rate, which had not been anticipated by the Hospital Plan of 1962. Filling these empty beds was more cost-effective for the government than developing the domiciliary midwifery service. This was a pragmatic approach to the question of health care delivery, on the basis of the resources that were available. However, it also gave implicit government support to the view of hospital confinement as safer than a home delivery. A government committee was set up in 1967 to consider the future of the domiciliary midwifery service and the question of bed needs for maternity patients. Chaired by the consultant obstetrician John Peel, it was known as the Peel Committee. In 1970, it produced a report that has been described as "an important watershed in policy on the place of birth" (Campbell & Macfarlane, 1990, p. 218) because it recommended that "*sufficient facilities should be provided to allow for 100% hospital delivery. The greater safety of hospital confinement for mother and child justifies this objective*" (Department of Health and Social Security 1970, p. 60; emphasis added).[8] The Peel Report drew heavily on the data of the 1958 national survey into the maternity services, the Perinatal Mortality Survey, which had been conducted by the National Birthday Trust Fund. The Birthday Trust, of which Peel was a member, had lost its prewar association with midwives and was now largely run by obstetricians. Common to both the Peel Report and the report of the 1958 survey is the assumption of the greater safety of hospital confinement for mother and child, although neither actually establishes that this greater safety exists or even compares the relative risks of home and hospital delivery.

The message of the Peel Report was confirmed by the 1980 Report of the House of Commons Social Services Committee on Perinatal and Neonatal Mortality, the Short Report. Just as the Peel Report had drawn on the conclusions of the 1958 national survey, this drew on the report of the 1970 national survey, *British Births,* which also assumed—but did not actually establish—the increased safety of hospital over home delivery. The higher perinatal mortality rate in consultant beds was simply accounted for by the fact that the births with greatest risk take place in hospitals. Like the 1958 survey, the 1970 survey had been led and conducted for the most part by obstetricians.

Titmuss had pointed out in 1958 that behind the development of the social services known as "The Welfare State" lay a kind of social inequality in which the better-off, who had most power and occupational success, were still rewarded by much better services (Titmuss, 1958/1960, pp. 53–55). The Short Report recognized this and linked it to the growing evidence of inequalities in health, with a steep social class gradient in perinatal mortality rates. It aimed "to secure more equality between mothers of different socio-economic classes" and hoped to achieve this by advising that an increasing number of mothers should be delivered in large units and that selection of patients should be improved for smaller consultant units and isolated GP units. "Home delivery," it added, "*should be phased out further*" (Social Services Committee, 1979–1980, pp. 52, 160, 161; emphasis added). A decade later, 98 percent of women in the United Kingdom gave birth in NHS hospitals.

PROMOTING WOMAN-CENTERED CARE

From the mid-1970s, a new set of issues arose—the NHS was not meeting the needs and wishes of pregnant women. By now, the maternal and perinatal death and morbidity rates had fallen dramatically and the earlier demands by women for beds had been fully met. This created a new opportunity for resistance to the kind of care that was available. In particular, there was concern at the shift away from home to hospital delivery and suspicion of the increased medical intervention in labor, such as the sharp rise in cesarean sections (in 1984, one woman in nine having a baby had a cesarean section, which was more than twice the number in 1972). A consumer movement sprang up, organized by women and for women, which soon became a formidable interest group in the struggle over the maternity services. It was spearheaded by AIMS, the National Childbirth Trust (NCT), and The Maternity Alliance. AIMS and the NCT were largely run by middle-class women who objected in particular to the virtual disappearance of home delivery. Supporting policies to help poor women was the chief aim of The Maternity Alliance, an umbrella organization closely linked to the trades unions and other interested organizations.

In the early 1990s, a government committee (called the Winterton after its chairman) was set up to reexamine the maternity services, with a particular focus on the management of normal pregnancy and birth. In the evidence that was presented to the Winterton Committee, a widespread view emerged that was deeply critical of the maternity services, especially of the massive shift to hospital delivery. The Minister of Health, Virginia Bottomley, stated in her own evidence that "there was no reliable statistical evidence which established the superior safety of birth in consultant obstetric units as against home births and those in GP units" (Department of Health 1992, pp. x, xi). In the government camp, therefore, there were women speaking out on behalf of women's interests. This was also the case in the camp of the RCOG: Wendy Savage, a London obstetrician, was suspended from medical practice in 1985 for allegedly being a danger to her patients; in fact, as she was able to demonstrate, she was being persecuted for adopting a different, woman-centered, approach to obstetrics. She successfully fought the suspension with massive support from the public. Her reinstatement can be seen as a reflection of growing public concern about issues of medical power and practice and, also, of the increasing influence of her approach to care.

The Royal College of Midwives (RCM) and the RCOG presented conflicting arguments when they gave their evidence. The RCM, along with other midwifery groups, proposed the restoration of "a normal approach rather than a pathological approach to childbirth," which paid greater attention to the needs and wishes of the mother. It advocated a move away from 100 percent hospital delivery and an increase in home births, attended by midwives (Health Committee 1991, p. 130). To support this argument, it drew on reports of recent research (in particular, see Chalmers, Enkin, & Keirse, 1989). The RCM had made efforts from the mid-1970s to draw on new research to inform and to improve its practice and to make the profession a research-based movement (Allison 1992, pp. 167–174).[9] This introduced a new interest group in the debate over maternity services—the growing army of researchers working in the area of maternal health.

The president of the RCOG, Stanley C. Simmons, warned *against* giving birth at home in his evidence to the Winterton Committee, on the grounds that such a delivery would be too far from the emergency facilities of a consultant unit. The RCOG had not prepared as carefully as the midwives for the evidence session and did not draw on recent research data to support its argument.

The eventual *Winterton Report* concluded that improving the maternity services "requires an affirmation that the needs of mothers and babies are placed at the centre, from which it follows that the maternity services must be fashioned around them and not the other way round" (Department of Health 1992, p. xciii). This was a triumph for midwifery groups and the maternity consumer movement. During the session at which the RCOG and the RCM both gave evidence to the Winterton Committee, the public area was packed with supporters of midwives and home delivery (personal communication by Ruth Ashton to ASW, October 23, 1995). In 1993 the Department of Health issued *Changing Childbirth,* the report of the Expert Maternity Group that was chaired by Baroness Julia Cumberlege. This took the conclusions of the *Winterton Report* even further. It rejected the argument for 100 percent hospital births, concluding that, "On the basis of what we have heard, this Committee must draw the conclusion that the policy of encouraging all women to give birth in hospitals cannot be justified on grounds of safety." Purchasers and providers in the NHS, it said, must ensure that home birth is a real option for the women who wish it. The shift to hospital birth, it added, had been based on presumptions based on unproven assertion. As part of its support for home delivery, it recommended the improvement of midwives' pay and conditions and of the means whereby they might take on greater responsibility (Department of Health 1993, pp. 16, 25). This can be seen as a triumph for mid-wives and for those women who were lobbying for home birth and for choice (an interest group that is mostly middle class).

But the concerns of *Changing Childbirth* were very narrow: Whereas Winterton had identified the health and weight of the baby as a key factor in maternity care, this was entirely absent from Cumberlege. Indeed, the word "baby" is not even used in the report. This absence of concern with the baby's health is a serious one from the point of view of those families who are least well off.[10] The "inescapable" conclusion of the 1980 Black Report, produced by the Working Group of Inequalities in Health, was that "occupational class differences are *real* sources of difference in the risk of infant mortality" (Townsend & Davidson 1982, rpt. 1992, p. 115), and research shows an increase in the unequal distribution in infant death and in the proportion of low birthweight babies. Poverty is increasing more sharply in the United Kingdom than in any other Western countries (see Atkinson 1996), and it has grown so rapidly that by the mid-1990s, one in three babies is born into families that depend in whole or in part on welfare benefits or have earnings less than half the average wage (Rowntree Foundation, 1995). A report produced by the Joseph Rowntree Foundation in July 1997 reveals that one in twenty mothers goes without food to meet the needs of her child: If they are pregnant, these women will not only be depriving themselves but may also be putting at risk the future health of their babies.

CHANGING CHILDBIRTH?

In effect, then, the recent changes in childbirth in the United Kingdom do not represent a move toward greater equality. Despite the challenge of clients to the entrenched interests of professionals, it is still the more powerful and articulate interest groups—such as better-off women, doctors, and midwives—who struggle over policy, while the least powerful—poor women and their families—have inadequate access to care. Their neglect today is possibly more shocking because it takes place within the context of a huge overall improvement in maternal and perinatal maternity and morbidity rates in Britain. The story of maternity service provision in twentieth-century Britain is not a simple one of ideology or good and evil: of men against women, consultants against doctors, or doctors against midwives. Rather, it is a story with many different strands, in which the various interest groups have changed sides and shifted alliances—and in which some interest groups have very little power or influence on the evolution of care.

Conclusion: Desiring Change and Changing Desire

Our brief look at maternity care and the desires of women in four countries brings us back to where we began. We have seen how the desires of women closely track the care they are offered *and* we have seen that collective action by concerned groups can influence the content and style of care. Thus we are left with a paradox: Women desire (only) what they are offered, but what they are offered is influenced by their desires. Reviewing the data from our case studies and from research done by others allows us to offer at least a partial explanation for this observed contradiction. Our (partial) explanation considers the way professionals, the state, and the media influence care systems.

First, our case studies offer ample evidence of the critical role professionals and professional associations play in shaping the desires of women. The opinions of individual professionals hold great sway in the clinical setting, a point well illustrated in the case of prenatal testing. Press and Browner (1997) have shown how providers of care direct women's understanding of the meaning and purpose of maternal serum alpha fetoprotein screening and, consequently, their desire for the test. Santalahti et al. (1998) illustrate the tendency for such professionally sanctioned tests to become "self-evident" in the minds of most women. The power of professionals to shape the desires of women is well described by Porter and Macintyre in their 1984 research note: "What is, must be best." Today we might rephrase that, "What my caregiver offers must be best," an attitude that reflects a strong trust in individual caregivers and in the science that is presumed to support clinical practice. Noticing this trend, childbirth reformers have learned to couch their demands in the language of science.

If "what is, must be best," it is important for professionals to maintain control of the maternity care system and any changes that occur there. Our case studies show that professionals have largely succeeded in this task. Note that the childbirth reform movements that have had success have found a way to ally their interests with those of professional groups. Physicians and anesthesiologists supported women in their efforts to promote Twilight Sleep and, much later, epidurals (see Chapter 1); midwives have played a key role in movements that are seeking to make birth a less medical experience (see Chapters 3 and 4). Professional involvement and support is a necessary component of maternity care reform.

The effectiveness of professional groups in controlling maternity care policy is related to their level of organization. Compared to client groups—which come in great variety, have little monetary support, and are often racked with internal divisions and squabbles—professional associations are better organized, well funded, and able to speak (publicly) with one voice. Furthermore, their command of resources (e.g., hospital admissions, educational systems, prescription drugs) gives them greater power with influential policymakers and administrators.

Our case studies also highlight the influence of the state on the relationship between women's desires and the maternity care system. The role of the state in the provision of maternity care is discussed in Part I of this book, but we would like to make a few further comments on the way the state manages professional and client interests and directs change in maternity care. In our case studies the most striking comparison is between the United States and the three European countries. In the European countries the state plays a stronger role in health policy, steering decisions about maternity care. This is not to say that professional and consumer interest groups have no influence there, but—unlike in the United States—larger state interests are brought to bear in maternity care policy. Thus we see the Dutch government making a concerted effort to reverse a trend away from home birth in the interest of reducing unneeded obstetrical interventions and saving money. In the United States, state involvement is limited to allowing interest groups to bring their concerns to the appropriate legislative and legal bodies. Because health care is a largely private matter in the United States, the decisions made about these concerns are not influenced by budgetary constraints or the desire to see care provided equally to all.

A third important factor in shaping the desires of women—one that is little discussed here or elsewhere—is the media. The media—particularly television—plays a significant role in defining a good and desirable birth. In one of the few studies of the way maternity care is represented on television, Kutulas (1998) makes interesting observations about the way the desires of women are channeled. Although her focus is on the connections between television stories of maternity care and the goals of the feminist movement, her conclusions are quite similar to the ones we make here (pp. 15, 30):

> [W]omen's stories [of pregnancy and birth] are . . . told against a larger social backdrop. They are necessarily about how society contextualizes women's events, how men receive and react to babies, and how the culture talks about men's and women's responsibilities vis-a-vis babies. Maternity stories are a perfect example of the hegemonic dialectic between culture and ideology, reinforcing culturally dominant ideas about motherhood while allowing the safe exploration of other possibilities. Stories about pregnant women titillate viewers with subversive gender acts, but finally contain that behavior in socially acceptable ways. . . . Television both echoes and contributes to a female experience where pervasive social guilt about never being good enough turns liberation back onto women and makes its limitations their fault.

Kutulas's research is limited to U.S. television, but we must remember that the United States produces many of the most popular television shows in Europe.

If nothing else, our case studies have illustrated the complexity of the relationship between women's desires and maternity care. We have noted that women's wishes are heterogeneous—women have been involved in efforts to promote both *more* and *less* medical birth environments—and that the wishes that end up making a difference in maternity care are those that are carried by larger social themes.

We have also seen that the best-articulated opinions about needed change in maternity care are found when care systems are in transition. For women's wishes to do more than mirror existing arrangements ("What is, must be best"), true choice must be possible. As Porter and Macintyre (1984, p. 1200) point out: "[I]f women tend to say they like whatever care they receive, then uncontrolled studies which assess preferences for a particular pattern of care at a single point in time are difficult to interpret and cannot be validly construed as indicating 'real' levels of satisfaction with prevailing modes of care." Studies that discover *dis*satisfaction with existing care (see for example, Kojo-Austin et al. 1993; Viisainen et al. 1998) are those that are done in situations where real choice exists or believable hypothetical choices are constructed. If we want "what is *best* to be what *is*" we must find a way to present real and safe choices to women and their families.

Notes

1. Contrast this number—8 percent interested in birth at home—with the number given by the Expert Maternity Group of the Department of Health (UK). That group cites a study showing 22 percent of women in the United Kingdom desiring a *choice* of home birth (Expert Maternity Group 1993, p. 23).

2. In the United States each of the fifty states has a separate "medical practice act" defining the practice of medicine and acceptable practices for different types of caregivers.
3. Several historians have noted the same women who organized to gain the vote also demanded, and won, the right to "Twilight Sleep" during childbirth (see Wertz & Wertz 1977).
4. This is in contrast to the answers that suggested women wished to have a high level of medical response. This discrepancy could be the result of the way the question was posed: Women were not asked what they wanted for themselves at the time of delivery; they were asked what services they wished to see available.
5. See Chapters 1 and 6 for a more detailed description of maternity care in the Netherlands.
6. More recent data are not comparable with the older ones, but the latest survey results show an increase of the home birth rate from 34 percent in 1992/1993 to 36 percent in 1996/1997 (CBS 1998).
7. Campbell and Macfarlane 1994 (pp. 115–116) report on similar studies done in the United Kingdom. A 1946 study showed that 50.2 percent of women who gave birth at home indicated that it was their first choice, while 16.6 percent of women giving birth in the hospital indicated that the hospital was their first choice. A study done in England and Wales in 1975 showed 92 percent of women who had a home birth and a previous hospital birth preferred home delivery, while 23 percent of women who had a hospital birth and a previous home birth preferred hospital delivery.
8. The Peel Report has been widely regarded as the natural development of the 1959 Cranbrook Report, which had recommended a 70 percent hospital delivery rate. In fact, however, these reports were not related: The Cranbrook Committee was set up by the Minister of Health and produced an official government report. The Peel Committee, on the other hand, as a Sub-Committee of the Standing Maternity and Midwifery Advisory Committee of the Central Health Services Council, was a relatively low-status committee of the independent advisory machinery. The Peel Report was not, therefore, an expression of government policy, like the Cranbrook Report. The author is grateful to Charles Webster for pointing out this difference.
9. A leading figure in this process was Julia Allison, Head of Midwifery Studies at the Norfolk College of Nursing and Midwifery. Concerned that midwifery practice and policy were governed by medical rather than midwifery research, she reviewed community midwives' records for 1948–1972 on more than 35,000 home births in Nottingham; this retrospective study showed that babies of all weights survived at a greater rate if born at home.
10. This reflects the tendency we saw in the United States, with emphasis shifting from the "product" of birth (i.e., the health of the baby and mother) to the experience of birth.

References

Adamson, G., and D. Gare. 1980. Home or hospital births? *JAMA,* 243: 1732–1736.
Adviescommissie Kloosterman. 1989. *Regeringsstandpunt Adviescommissie Kloosterman.* (Government Standpoint on the Kloosterman Advice Commission). Ministerie van Welzijn, Volksgezondheid en Cultuur, SDU-uitgeverij: 's Gravenhage, the Netherlands. (In Dutch.)
Allison, Julia. 1992. Midwives Step out of the Shadows. 1991 Sir William Power Memorial Lecture. *Midwives Chronicle and Nursing Notes* 105: 1254.
American Medical Association. 1977. *Statement on Parent-Newborn interaction.* Chicago: American Medical Association.
Atkinson, Tony. 1996. *Incomes and the Welfare State.* Cambridge: Cambridge University Press.

Barnes to the Technical Advisory Sub-Committee, April 26, 1951. Contemporary Medical Archives Centre, London, National Birthday Trust Fund archives (hereafter NBTF). NBTF/ A1/5/2.

Bergsjø, P. 1998. A perspective on childbirth at home and in hospital. *Nordic Medicine* 103: 97–101.

Bell, B. 1931. Summary of a National Maternity Scheme as outlined by Professor Blair Bell in the Ingleby Lecture at the University of Birmingham, June 4 1931. *The Lancet.*

Berridge, V., Webster, C., and G. Walt. 1993. Mobilisation for total welfare, 1948 to 1974. In *Caring for Health: History and Diversity,* ed. C. Webster. Buckingham: Open University Press, pp. XX.

Birth Registry of Norway. 1998. *Medical Birth Registry of Norway, Annual Report 1997.* Bergen, Norway: University of Bergen.

Campbell, R. and A. Macfarlane. 1990. Recent debate on the place of birth. In *The Politics of Maternity Care,* eds. J. Garcia, R. Kilpatrick, and M. Richards. Oxford: Oxford University Press.

Campbell, R., and A. Macfarlane. 1994. *Where to Be Born?,* 2nd ed. Oxford: National Perinatal Epidemiology Unit.

CBS. 1998. V*ademecum Gezondheidsstatistiek 1998.* (Vademecum of Health Statistics of the Netherlands 1998.) 's-Gravenhage: Sdu/uitgeverij / CBS-publicaties. (In Dutch.)

Chalmers, I. 1986. Minimizing harm and maximizing benefit during innovation in health care: Controlled or uncontrolled experimentation? *Birth* 13: 155–164.

Chalmers, I., Enkin, M., and M. J. N. C. Keirse (eds.). 1989. *Effective Care in Pregnancy and Childbirth.* Oxford: Oxford University Press.

Croon, M. 1999. Routinematige ruggenprik is onverantwoord. (Routine epidurals are irresponsible.) *NRC Handelsblad* May 4, p. 9. (In Dutch.)

Damstra-Wijmenga, S. M. I. 1982. *Veilig bevallen: een vergelijkende studie tussen thuis- en de klinische bevalling* (Safe birthing: A comparative study of home and hospital birth). Doctoral Thesis, Groningen University, Groningen, the Netherlands. (In Dutch.)

Department of Health. 1992. *Health Committee Second Report, Maternity Services,* Vol. 1 (Winterton Report). London: HMSO.

Department of Health. 1993. *Changing Childbirth.* London: HMSO.

Department of Health and Social Security. 1970. *Domiciliary Midwifery and Maternity Bed Needs* (Peel Report). London: HMSO.

DeVries, R. 1980. The alternative birth center: Option or cooptation? *Women and Health* 5(3): 47–60.

———. 1983. Image and reality: An evaluation of hospital alternative birth centers. *Journal of Nurse Midwifery* 28(3): 3–10.

———. 1984. "Humanizing" childbirth: The discovery and implementation of bonding theory. *International Journal of Health Services Research* 14: 89–104.

Endresen, E. H., and E. Helsing. 1995. Changes in breast feeding practice in Norwegian maternity wards: National survey 1973, 1982 and 1991. *Acta Paediatrica,* 84: 719–724.

Expert Maternity Group (Department of Health, UK). 1993. *Changing Childbirth,* Vol. 1. London: HSMO.

Grigson, Secretary of Regional Hospital Boards, Ministry of Health, to NBTF. September 25, 1953. NBTF/ F7/1/2.

Hansard (21 January and 4 March 1954)

Health Committee: Examination of witnesses (Miss Margaret Brain, Miss Ruth Ashton, Miss Beverley Bryans, Miss Anne Rider and Ms Lesley Page) by Health Committee. June 12, 1991. PRO/ HC430II 1990-91.

Hingstman, L., Foets, M., and J. Riteco. 1993. Thuis of in het ziekenhuis bevallen. Meningen van de consument (Home or hospital birth. Opinions of consumers). *Tijdschrift voor Verloskundigen,* 18: 66–73.

Jenkins, R., and N. Westhus. 1981. The nurse role in parent-infant bonding. *Journal of Obstetric, Gynecological, and Neonatal Nursing* 5: 114–118.

Johnson, M., Smith, J., Haddad, S., Walker, J., and A. Wong. 1992. Women prefer hospital births. *British Medical Journal* 305: 255.

Jordmorbladet. 1998. Flere fødestuer og større ansvar til jordmødrene. (An increasing number of small maternity homes with more responsibility for the midwives.) *Jordmorbladet* (Midwife Journal). 8: 14–15. (In Norwegian.)

Kamper-Jørgensen, F., Madsen, M., and T. Sørensen. 1985. *Graviditet, fødøsel og valg av fødested. Kvindernær oplevelser, ønsker og meninger.* (Pregnancy, Deliveries and Choice of Place to Deliver. The Women's Experiences, Wishes and Opinions.) Copenhagen: Dansk institutt for klinisk epidemiologi. (In Norwegian.)

Kennel, J., Wolfe, H., Jerauld, R., Chesler, D., Kreger, N., McAlpine, W., Steffa, M., and M. Klaus. 1974. Maternal behavior one year after early and extended post-partum contact. *Developmental Medicine and Child Neurology,* 16: 174.

Klaus, M., and J. Kennel. 1976. *Maternal-Infant Bonding.* St. Louis: Mosby.

———. 1981. *Parent-Infant Bonding.* St. Louis: Mosby.

Klaus, M., Jerauld, R., Kreger, N., McAlpine, W., Steffa, M., and J. Kennel. 1972. The importance of the first post-partum days. *New England Journal of Medicine,* 286: 460–463.

Kleiverda, G. 1990. Transition to parenthood, women's experiences of 'labour.' Doctoral thesis, University of Amsterdam, the Netherlands.

Kleiverda, G., Steen, A. M., Andersen, I., Treffers, P. E., and W. Everaerd. 1990. Place of delivery in the Netherlands: Maternal motives and background variables related to preferences for home or hospital confinement. *European Journal of Obstetrics, Gynecology, and Reproductive Biology* 36: 1–9.

Kojo-Austin, H., Malin, M., and E. Hemminki. 1993. Women's satisfaction with maternity health care services in Finland. *Social Science and Medicine* 37(5): 633–638.

Kutulas, J. 1998. "Do I look like a chick?" Men, women, and babies on sitcom maternity stories. *American Studies* 39(2): 13–32.

Laprè, R. M. 1972. *Aspecten van marktanalyse met betrekking tot verloskundige diensten in Nederland.* (Aspects of market analysis with regard to obstetric services in the Netherlands.) Nijmegen, Dekker en Van de Vegt. Doctoral thesis, Catholic University of Nijmegen, the Netherlands. (In Dutch.)

Levesque-Lopman, L. 1983. Decision and experience: A phenomenological analysis of pregnancy and childbirth. *Human Studies* 6: 247–277.

Lewis, J. 1980. *The Politics of Motherhood.* London: Croom Helm.

Loudon, I. 1992. *Death in Childbirth.* Oxford: Clarendon Press.

Lund, E., and M. Kumle. 1999. Riktig fødsel på riktig sted? (The right delivery at the right place?) *Tidsskrift For Den norske laege Forening* (Journal of the Norwegian Medical Association) 119: 1869, 1999.

Maclean, Sir Ewen. 1936. Maternity services. *British Medical Journal.*

Manschot, A. 1993. December. Is al dat lijden nog wel nodig? (Is all that suffering still needed?) *Opzij,* pp. 28–31. (In Dutch.)

Manshanden, J. C. P. 1997. De keuze van nulliparae; wanneer, waarom? (The choice of nulliparous women: When, why?) *Tijdschrift voor Verloskundigen* (Journal for Midwives) 22: 34–40.

MH Minute. September 4, 1954. DHSS 94524/2/19; quoted in Charles Webster, *The Health Services since the War* (London: HMSO, 1988)

Ministry of Health. 1959. *Report of the Maternity Services Committee* (Cranbrook Report).

Ministry of Health. 1960. *Report on Confidential Enquiries into Maternal Deaths in England and Wales 1955–57.*

National Center for Health Statistics. 1980. *Monthly Vital Statistics Report* 29 (1, Supplement), April 28, 1980.

Norwegian Board of Health. 1997. *Faglige krav til fødeinstitusjoner.* (Professional Require-ments in Maternity Wards.) Oslo, Norway: Statens helsetilsyn. Utredningsserie. (In Norwe-gian.)

NOU. 1999. *Kvinners helse i Norge. Norges offentlige utredninger NOU 1999:13.* (Women's Health in Norway. Official Reports of Norway.) http://www.odin.dep.no/nou/1999-13, ISSN 0806-2633 (NOU Computerfile). Sosial- og helsedepartementet, Oslo. Accessed December 22, 1999. (In Norwegian.)

Nylander, G. 1995. Medisinsk og emosjonelt trygge fødsler i sykehus. (Medically and emo-tionally safe deliveries within hospitals.) *Tidsskrift For Den norske LaegeForening* (Journal for the Norwegian Medical Association) 814–814. (In Norwegian.)

Øian, P. 1998. Fødeinstitusjoner i endring - kan risikofødsler selekteres? (Changes in the maternity wards—can high risk deliveries be identified?) *Tidsskrift For Den norske Laege-Forening* (Journal for the Norwegian Medical Association) 118: 1174. (In Norwegian.)

Ounsted, C., Roberts, J., Gordon, M., and B. Milligan. 1982. Fourth goal of perinatal medi-cine. *British Medical Journal* 284: 879–882.

Porter, M., and S. Macintyre. 1984. What is, must be best. *Social Science and Medicine* 19(11): 1197–1200.

Press, N., and C. Browner. 1997. Why women say yes to prenatal diagnosis. *Social Science and Medicine* 45(7): 979–989.

RCOG. 1954, July. *Report on the Obstetric Service under the National Health Service.* Private papers.

Rising, S. 1974. "The fourth stage of labor: Family integration. *American Journal of Nursing* 74: 870–874.

Rowntree (Joseph) Foundation. 1995. *Inquiry into Income and Wealth.* York: Joseph Rowntree Foundation.

Santalahti, P., Hemminki, E., Latikka, A., and M. Ryynanen. 1998. Women's decision making in prenatal screening. *Social Science and Medicine* 46(8): 1067–1076.

Schmidt, N., Abelsen, B., Eide, B., and P. Øian. 1997. Fødestuer i Norge. (Small maternity homes in Norway.) *Tidsskrift For Den norske laegeForening* (Journal for the Norwegian Medical Association) 117: 823–826. (In Norwegian.)

Social Services Committee, Session 1979–1980. *Second Report. Perinatal and Neonatal Mor-tality,* Vol. 1 (Short Report).

Titmuss, Richard M. 1958/1960. The social division of welfare. In *Essays on "The Welfare State."* (reprint ed.) London: George Allen & Unwin.

Townsend, P., and N. Davidson. 1982/1992. *The Black Report.* In *Inequalities in Health* Har-mondsworth: Penguin.

Trovik, J., Salvesen, H. B., Marøy, M., and K. Dalaker. 1995. If the woman giving birth had her choice . . . Results of a consumer study in the region of Bergen. *Tidsskrift for Den norske LaegeForening* (Journal for the Norwegian Medical Association) 115: 838–841. (In Norwegian.)

Viisainen, K., Gissler, M., Raikkonen, O., Perala, M., and E. Hemminki. 1998. Interest in alternative birth settings in Finland. *Acta Obstetrica et Gynecologica Scandinavica* 77: 729–735.

Vuijsje, M. 1999, April. Hilda Verwy-Jonker en Marjet van Zuijlen over grote en kleine vrouwenzaken. (Hilda Verwey-Jonker and Marjet van Zuijlen on large and small women's issues.) *Opzij,* pp. 60–63. (In Dutch.)

Wertz, R., and D. Wertz. 1977. *Lying-in: A History of Childbirth in America.* New York: Free Press.

WHO. 1989. *Protecting, Promoting and Supporting Breast Feeding. The Special Role of Maternity Services* (A joint WHO/UNICEF statement). Geneva: WHO.

Wiegers, T. A. 1997. *Home or Hospital Birth. A Prospective Study of Midwifery Care in the Netherlands.* Doctoral thesis, Leiden University, the Netherlands.

Wiegers, T. A., and G. A. H. Berghs. 1994. De keuze voor de plaats van bevallen. (The choice for the place of birth.) *Tijdschrift voor Verloskundigen* (Journal for Midwives) 19: 392–400. (In Dutch.)

Wiegers, T. A., Zee, J. van der, Kerssens, J. J., and M. J. N. C.. Keirse. 1998. Home birth or short-stay hospital birth in a low risk population in the Netherlands. *Social Science and Medicine* 46: 1505–1511.

Wiegers, T. A., Zee, J. van der, and M. J. N. C. Keirse. 1998. Maternity care in the Netherlands: The changing home birth rate. *Birth* 25: 190–197.

Women's Cooperative Guild Annual Report for 1951. CWG/BI.

Yankauer, Alfred. 1983. The valley of the shadow of birth. *American Journal of Public Health* 73: 635–638.

Appendix

The Politics of Numbers

THE PROMISE AND FRUSTRATION OF CROSS-NATIONAL ANALYSIS

Eugene Declercq and Kirsi Viisainen

Few would argue with the basic premise of this book—that comparative inquiry enhances our understanding of maternity care practice. Indeed, the comparative method is a cornerstone of social science research; when comparative research is challenged the criticisms focus on inconsistencies in the measurement of the variables being compared, not on the method itself. In this chapter we focus on the difficulties faced by researchers looking for comparative data in maternity care. Given the natural inclination of researchers to compare (e.g., which country has the highest and which the lowest cesarean rate?) and their inherent curiosity to know what is going on in different countries (e.g., what is the home birth rate in the Netherlands?), good comparative data are precious commodities. But can we find maternity care statistics that are truly comparable? The answer is a confident yes . . . sort of, more or less, in some cases, under the right conditions. Comparisons are possible, but rarely ideal and never simple.

This chapter presents data from two general sources. The first is the database developed by the Organization for Economic Co-operation and Development (OECD): From this collection of information we present data on twenty countries that are OECD members. The second data source is reports generated by individual countries and collected by various authors in this book. The OECD data have the considerable advantage of being collected by a single agency. The OECD provides documentation of the standards used in measurement and takes responsibility for providing consistency of data, although all OECD reports caution users about the limits on cross-national comparisons. Equally important, it is relatively current (most data presented here will be from 1995 or later) and readily available in a format (CD-ROM) that allows researchers to manipulate the data to better address the questions of interest to them. Unfortunately, the OECD health data set does not contain complete information on many of the variables of interest to students of maternity care practice. This is a classic difficulty in secondary analysis: the "good" data that are widely available do not include the variables of greatest interest (in this case, for example, cesarean births) to researchers. The other source of data used here, individual country reports, has the kind of data maternity care researchers want: e.g., gestational age, use of epidural anesthesia, forceps use. However, these separate data sets present problems with access (is there a national report?), language barriers, and use of different protocols concerning measurement and reporting.

This presents a somewhat bleak picture, but there are developments that suggest that the potential for comparative data analysis will improve in the future. The most important of these is the growth of the Internet. Data sets are now available that just a decade ago would have required travel to a given country or relentless letters and phone calls to local authorities pleading for access to their data. There is also an increasing number of research institutes, particularly in Europe, collecting regional and national health data in registries. Data collection is also abetted by the growing number of cooperative agreements between countries, especially within the European Union (EU). More recently, United Nations agencies have taken greater interest in compiling such data, while the OECD, in addition to their data archives, periodically commissions studies of health-related topics that include comparative health data (OECD 1994).

The Use of Birth Registries

Most countries have some form of a birth registry as a component of their vital statistics system. A study by the U.S. Department of Health and Human Services (1998) examined the systems for health data collection used by forty industrialized countries. Most of the countries maintained a birth registry, which has a major advantage over aggregated statistics since a register contains data on individuals (Scheuch 1966). These administrative registers are collected for national planning, follow-up, monitoring, evaluation, management, legislative tasks, and research (Gissler 1999). The USDHHS study found that virtually all countries studied collected the following data: births and birth rates by maternal age, length of gestation and mother's marital status, infant birthweight, infant death by age, gender and cause, length of hospital stay, diagnosis, and surgical procedures, numbers of doctors and midwives. On average these data were available within two to three years of the date of collection. Of course, the fact that countries may collect such data does not necessarily mean researchers have access or that the data are comparable. One promising development in the mid 1990s was the issuance by the U.S. National Center for Health Statistics of national natality data on CD-ROMs. They could be purchased at a minimal cost (less than $20) and contained individual level data on over 100 variables for all (approximately 4 million) U.S. births for a given year.

Many countries conduct periodic national health interview surveys, with several countries—including France, the Netherlands, Sweden, and the United States—implementing an annual national survey. Of course maternity care is only a small part of these surveys; the focus in these studies is primarily on questions about health (USDHHS 1998).

Differing patterns of national data collection and storage create problems for researchers. The nature of these problems is best illustrated by looking at procedures in the Nordic countries and the United States. In the Nordic countries data collection on newborns' health started in the 1960s with the formation of separate "malformation registers" after the discovery of birth defects caused by thalidomide. Norway was the first country to widen its malformation register to include all newborns by introducing a nationwide Medical Birth Register (MBR) in 1967. The other Nordic countries followed, with Finland being the last to set up a registry in 1987 (Gissler et al. 1996). Outside the Nordic countries, the pattern is mixed with many countries using regional rather than national registries. In the United States, collection of birth data is typically the responsibility of each state working with local hospitals and city and town clerks. All fifty states have their own birth certificate, with states agreeing to collect a core set of measures that will be provided to the National Center for Health Statistics. The result is the National Certificate of a Live Birth. The measures that constitute the "core set" are reviewed every ten to fifteen years. The last change was in 1989 when, for example, the birth certificate was expanded to include dozens of new items including questions on prenatal behavior (e.g., smoking and alcohol use); medical interventions (e.g., use of ultrasound, inductions); birth attendant (distinguishing nurse and other midwives); and outcomes such as congenital anomalies. The next change is planned for 2002 or 2003 with some proposed changes including better specification of length of stay, identification of the use of epidural anesthesia, and several measures of maternal morbidity. Also, items added in 1989 that appear to have been poorly measured will be dropped. There has also been a movement in the United States toward an electronic birth certificate that will help shorten the time between data collection and publication of the results, which, for national data, is now approximately twenty-two months after the end of a calendar year. Despite these promising developments, the greatest limitation for cross-national comparisons remains a paucity of comparable registers and a lack of interest in funding agencies to sponsor such research.

The Challenges to Comparative Data Analysis

The number and breadth of content of national registers have been increasing in recent years because of the rapid progress of computer technology. Despite the likelihood of future improvements in cross-national data analysis, several serious problems remain.

SELECTIVE DEPOSIT AND SURVIVAL

The data a country chooses to collect systematically, retain, and make available to researchers itself suggest something of the values of that society, as well as the nature of care in that country. For example, in countries where vaginal births after cesareans (VBACs) are thought to be very rare, there may seem little need to collect the data necessary to document rates that may be used either as a baseline for a longitudinal study in that country or a comparative study of the practice. However, the fact that a country does not generally report a practice does not mean it does not exist. For example, in the United States, as the popularity of epidural anesthesia began to rise in the 1980s and 1990s, there was no population-based data to document its growing use. The use of epidurals has been added to the revisions on the next birth certificate, but that will not be in place until 2002 at the earliest. The problem for a book that focuses on maternity care is that most of the variables of greatest interest that present more than a surface picture of maternity care are not published. So while we have data on fertility rates, birthweight, and infant mortality, little data on the nature and content of prenatal care, anesthesia use in labor, and practices (e.g., VBAC) related to cesarean birth are published.

USING SOMEONE ELSE'S DATA

Countries collect and publish data for their own purposes; these may not correspond to researchers' hypotheses. For those involved in cross-national research, the barriers to collecting original data from multiple countries make it easy to be drawn to existing rather than ideal measurements. Data can drive hypothesis development rather than the reverse. As Øyen (1990, p. 15) suggests, researchers may be "guided by the principles of least resistance or invitation by opportunity." Typically data are available only in published form, either in print or electronically. If these publications report rates and not the actual data, the researcher cannot do the manipulations necessary to allow comparisons. For example, some countries (e.g., the United States and Norway) report births to teens broken into three groups (<15; 16–17, 18–19) while others simply group all births to adolescent mothers together; unless one has access to the original data, the category cannot be disaggregated and the researcher is forced to make comparisons on what is comparatively available, in this case, births to mothers age nineteen or younger.

Timing of Data Collection and Publication

One of the devices used in the tables presented here is the designation of year as "1994–1996." This does not mean that the data presented are an average of that three-year period but reflects the fact that countries publish their data at different time periods. The researcher is then faced with a dilemma. Ideally, exactly the same year should be used for comparison, but what if one country out of twenty has not published the particular rate since 1990 and data on other countries are from 1996 or 1997? There is no simple answer. For purposes of description (rather than analysis) it is best to present the most recent figure available for that country. The problem is exacerbated if one tries to examine trend data and has to deal with different starting and end points.

The Problem of Equivalence

As Teune (1990, pp. 53–54) notes, "In order to compare something across systems it is necessary to have confidence that the components and their properties being compared are the 'same', or indicate something equivalent." Even in cases of vital statistics measuring what appear to be straightforward concepts, differences abound in specific definitions used. Perinatal or infant mortality rates are the most widely used cross-national measures of the quality of a country's perinatal system. They are also used in some cases as an overall measure of health system performance. Their popularity rests largely on their availability: Virtually all countries report one or both of these rates. One might expect that widespread use would lead to uniformity of measurement. Progress in this direction is being made, but problems remain (Congressional Budget Office 1992; Office of Technology Assessment 1993).

The standard measure of infant mortality is based on the annual number of deaths before one year of life divided by total live births for the same period. Because infant deaths are relatively rare events, it is presented as deaths per 1,000 live births per year. Putting aside (but not forgetting) the possibility of poor record-keeping and deaths and/or births not being recorded by the system, there is the larger issue of how countries define a live birth. Is a fetus born at 21 weeks who dies within a few hours of birth a live birth? In France and Japan it may not be. These countries are more likely to record these as stillbirths, which are not included in the infant mortality rate. In the United States it is more likely to be entered as both a live birth and an infant death, thus inflating the infant mortality rate. There is also the question of the timing of the infant death. The death of an eleven-month-old infant may be a stronger indicator of a country's child health system than its maternity care system. It is for this reason that many analysts prefer the perinatal mortality rate, which combines late fetal and early neonatal (within seven days) infant deaths and divides the total by all births (stillbirths plus live births).

However, countries differ on what they include as a "late fetal death" (Keirse 1984). Adding to the confusion, different data sources use different definitions of perinatal mortality. The OECD rates reported here use "fetal deaths of 28 weeks of gestation or more." The ICD-9 definition, which is promoted by the WHO, recommends including fetuses and infants delivered weighing at least 500 grams or, if the birthweight is missing, delivered at 22 completed weeks of gestation, in national statistics. WHO recommends the weight limit of 1,000 grams to be used in statistics for international comparison (WHO 1977). The effect of differing definitions is highlighted by the example of the Finnish rates: In the 1998 MBR data perinatal mortality was 5.66 per 1,000 using the ICD-9 definition, 4.96 per 1,000 using the OECD definition, and 3.91 per 1,000 using the WHO definition for international comparison (Finnish MBR, unpublished data). The rate published in national statistics was 6.47 per 1,000 (STAKES 1999). There is a difference between the ICD-9 based rate and the national published rate because Finland is using a national definition of perinatal death including (1) births showing any signs of life despite their birthweight or gestation length and (2) stillbirths weighing less than 500 grams but having a gestation length of 22 weeks or more (Gissler et al. 1994).

Because of its widespread use, the infant mortality rate has also been the subject of considerable cross-national analysis concerning measurement and data quality. A major source of this research is the United States. Over the past three decades the United States has ranked poorly in international comparisons, and some analysts suggest that measurement issues account for the discrepancy. However, while measurement differences may account for some of the variation, by virtually any standard the United States still fares poorly in these comparisons (Congressional Budget Office 1992).

THE PROBLEM OF AGGREGATION

There is an implicit assumption in cross-national presentation of data that there is greater variation across countries than there is *within* countries. There is little evidence to support such an assumption. As the authors of Chapter 5 note in their examination of the relationship of social class differences to outcomes within the United States and Sweden, considerable intracountry variation also exists. The differences noted go beyond social class, since in many countries health services are themselves decentralized and financed, implemented and evaluated at the local level. For example, when the United States was in the midst of debate over postpartum length of stay, one study found that average lengths of stay varied by 2.5 times across different regions of the United States, differences in many cases as large as those between countries (Declercq & Simmes 1997). Of course, the sheer difference in the size of different countries suggests the potential for greater homogeneity in some smaller countries. For example, Finland's 60,000 yearly births would place it twenty-fourth among the individual states of the United States, while California's 526,000 births in 1997 ranks only behind Germany, France, and the United Kingdom among the countries studied in the book.

THE PROBLEM OF DENOMINATORS

Since countries collect data for their own purposes, they may carefully measure the prevalence of a particular practice, but not collect an associated measure needed to calculate a rate that can be compared cross-nationally. There is interest, for example, in the apparent growing number of VBACs. There are two problems in trying to examine this cross-nationally. First is the lack of reliability in measures that involve retrospective examinations of past births (Green 1998). In other words, while most systems accurately report that the current birth was a vaginal birth, to report it as a VBAC means linking this birth to information that the past birth was a cesarean, since the denominator in a VBAC rate is number of cesareans. Likewise, even when the number of VBACs is known, one might question if a better measure should use number of women who had a trial of labor as a denominator, a figure rarely reported nationally on a population basis.

THE PROBLEM OF CONTEXT

The same variable measured in precisely the same way may still have a different meaning in different countries. The proportion of births to unmarried mothers varies widely across countries with rates highest in Sweden, Denmark, and Norway. However, it has been the United States, ranking fifth among the countries studied in this chapter, that has focused the greatest attention on the "problem" of unmarried motherhood, and perhaps for good reason. Compared to the Nordic countries with higher rates, unwed mothers in the United States are considerably younger, much less established financially, and do not have the social and health service supports available in European countries. Therefore, even when a measure is calculated in the same way in each country studied, it does not have the same meaning for analysis. True comparability would require a better understanding of the nature of the health system and social norms within which the maternity system operates. This is a daunting task. Studies have attempted with mixed success to identify common features of systems that might be codified into models for analysis (Basch 1999; OECD 1992, 1994).

The Comparative Data

The tables that follow illustrate one of the primary challenges of cross-national research—deciding who and what to compare. This book has focused on industrialized countries in Northern Europe and North America. However, to provide a slightly broader context for comparison, and succumbing to the lure of existing information, data from twenty countries are presented Tables A–1, A–2, and A–4. We have chosen countries that are members of OECD from Western Europe as well as Canada, the United States, Japan, Australia, and New Zealand. The OECD, as described earlier, publishes a wide range of demographic and health status data on member countries, and selected measures are presented in this section.

HEALTH SYSTEM CONTEXT

The data presented in Table A–1 remind us that even when looking at a comparatively limited range of wealthier countries, profound differences exist in the geographic and financial contexts in which the maternity care systems operate. For example, the chapter on place of birth suggests that a necessary—but not sufficient—condition for the continued reliance on home birth in the Netherlands is the country's high population density. This hypothesis is supported by the data in Table A–1. The Netherlands has a population density more than twenty-five times greater than Norway or Finland, two of the countries with near complete hospitalization of birth. However, the danger of oversimplification is also apparent since home birth has virtually disappeared in the Netherlands' densely populated neighbor Belgium.

Since health outcomes are generally a function of both the health system and the existing economic and social structure, Table A–1 presents both general economic and health spending data. Countries adopt different patterns, with some having substantial wealth and large health expenditures both in terms of absolute spending and proportionally (e.g., United States and Switzerland), while others have lower expenditures in proportional and absolute terms (e.g., the United Kingdom and Spain). This suggests that as countries reach a certain level of wealth they devote more of their resources to health care. Of course there are pronounced exceptions to these patterns. Canada, for example, has the fourth lowest level of per capita GDP but is tied for fourth highest on proportional spending (9.2 percent) on health. As we have discovered throughout this book, there are no simple answers in comparing countries. These data simply describe a context in which to understand the potential for different patterns of behavior to occur with socio-cultural factors explaining the remaining variance in practices and outcomes.

TABLE A–1
Context of the Health System

Country	Population 2000 (millions)	Population per Square Mile	Per Capita GDP 1999 in U.S. Dollars	Per Capita Total Health Spending, U.S. $, 1999	Percent GDP Spent on Health, 1998
Australia	19.2	6	$21,248	$1,691	8.5
Austria	8.1	250	$25,853	$2,148	†8.3
Belgium	10.2	869	$24,200	*$2,169	8.8
Canada	30.8	8	$19,967	$1,893	9.5
Denmark	5.3	320	$32,748	$2,729	8.3
Finland	5.2	40	$24,891	*$1,724	6.9
France	59.4	279	$24,292	$2,304	†9.5
Germany	82.1	596	$25,810	$2,706	†10.5
Ireland	3.8	140	$23,765	$1,447	6.4
Italy	57.8	497	$20,166	$1,698	†8.4
Japan	126.9	870	$34,644	*$2,283	7.6
Netherlands	15.9	1010	$25,040	*$2,143	8.6
New Zealand	3.8	37	$14,297	*$1,127	8.1
Norway	4.5	36	$34,043	$2,912	†8.6
Portugal	10.0	282	$11,096	*$859	7.8
Spain	39.5	202	$15,126	*$1,044	7.1
Sweden	8.9	51	$25,753	*$2,146	8.4
Switzerland	7.1	448	$35,995	*$3,834	10.4
United Kingdom	59.8	632	$23,908	$1,685	†7.0
United States	275.6	74	$31,935	$4,390	†13.7

SOURCES: Population and population per square mile from the Population Reference Bureau, *2000 World Population Data Sheet;* economic data from OECD Health Data, 2000.
*1998
†1999

THE CONTEXT FOR MATERNITY CARE

Table A–2 reflects the problem of timing of data collection and publication. The most recent data from the respective countries come from several different years. Since the purpose of these tables is descriptive rather than analytical, we made the decision to sacrifice some comparability in order to present the most recent data available. In the case of births, the variance in time frames is remarkable, since this is one of the most essential vital statistics recorded by countries. As with the population data, birth data remind us of the vast size differences between the countries examined here with more births in the United States in a month than the annual birth total for all the Nordic countries combined. The relatively low fertility rates of these more developed countries are apparent when compared to the world rate of 2.9 or the rate for less developed (excluding China) countries of 3.7 (Population Reference Bureau 2000). Patterns of postpartum hospitalization also vary widely, with French, Japanese, and

Swiss mothers on average staying in the hospital three times longer postpartum than U.S. mothers. Ironically, while the United States has the shortest postpartum length of stay among the countries in Table A–2, it also has one of the least developed systems for postpartum home-based care. Births to unmarried mothers also vary widely, although as discussed earlier, the meaning of this measure is highly varied. The relatively high rates in Sweden, Norway and Denmark reflect large numbers of older unmarried women in stable relationships as opposed to the younger, unmarried mothers found in the United States. For example, in 84 percent of the births to unmarried mothers in Norway in 1996, the mother was listed as "cohabiting" (Medical Birth Registry of Norway 1997). While comparable data do not exist for the United States, it is noteworthy that almost one in three births (30 percent) to unmarried mothers in the United States in 1998 was to a teenager and almost two-thirds (66 percent) were to mothers younger than twenty-five (Ventura 2000).

TABLE A–2
Context of Maternity Care System

Country	Total Births, 1997	Fertility Rate, 1998	Postpartum Length of Stay, 1997 (days)	Percentage of Births to Unmarried Mothers
Australia	253,834[a]	1.80[b]	3[a]	19
Austria	81,233[b]	1.34	6.1[a]	29
Belgium	116,513[d]	1.53	5.2	15
Canada	348,598	1.62[c]	2.1[a]	NA
Denmark	67,638[a]	1.72	3.3	46
Finland	60,723[a]	1.70	3.9	37
France	725,000	1.75	5.3[a]	39
Germany	812,173	1.34	5.6[a]	18
Ireland	50,655[a]	1.93	3.5	27
Italy	526,064[c]	1.19	4.2	8
Japan	1,191,665	1.44[a]	6.4[c]	NA
Netherlands	192,443	1.62	2.7	19
New Zealand	58,100	2.00[c]	2.9	NA
Norway	61,314	1.81	4.2	49
Portugal	113,510[b]	1.46	3.1	20
Spain	363,469[d]	1.15	3.4[a]	11
Sweden	95,158[a]	1.51	2.9	54
Switzerland	83,000[a]	1.44	6.2[c]	8
United Kingdom	725,810	1.72	NA	37
United States	3,941,553[b]	2.06[a]	1.8[a]	33[c]

SOURCE: Births, fertility rate and postpartum length of stay from OECD data 2000; percentage of births to unmarried women from *Eurostat Yearbook 1999*.
NA; data not available.
[a]1996; [b]1998; [c]1995; [d]1994.

Maternity Care Practices

Earlier we noted that the data one is most interested in are often unavailable. This problem is evident in Table A–3. Even using a more limited list of countries there are numerous empty cells in the table, and in one case (i.e., Germany) the data are drawn from only part of the country. Nevertheless, these data remain of interest. Given the ease with which information concerning clinical practices can move across borders and the growing emphasis on evidence-based medicine, we expect increasing uniformity in data on practices such as cesarean section and use of induction. Obviously there is great variation in these practices. Table A–3 shows the cesarean rates in the United States and Canada to be more than 50 percent higher than those of the Netherlands, Sweden, or Norway. The variance concerning cesarean births is mirrored in the other practices in Table A–3: Countries with the highest rates of a given practice often double the same rate found in the country that is least likely to use that practice. Interestingly, different countries have the highest rate for each of the practices identified, although partial data suggest the epidural rate in the United States might be as high or higher than that of Sweden. Overall, Table A–3 demonstrates the challenge and fascination of cross-national analysis: The data are interesting and suggestive, but remain partial and inconsistent.

Table A–3
Birth Practices (in Percentages)

Country	Induction	Epidural[a]	Episiotomy	Instrumental Delivery[b]	Cesarean Section
Canada	–	–	–	–	20.5
England (1994–95)	20	–	19	10.8	15.5
Finland (1998)	15.1	29.4	34.8	5.2	15.5
Germany (1996–98)[c]	16.3	17.3	53.0	7.2	18.9
Netherlands (1997/98)	–	–	–	–	11.2
Norway (1998)	12.4	13.9	NA	8.0	13.6
Scotland (1997)	24.3	NA	NA	11.3	17.1
Sweden (1997)	9.1	27.9	2.3	7.3	12.9
United States (1998)	19.2	–	43.0[d]	9.0[e]	22.0[f]

Sources: Data from Nordic countries from Medical Birth Registry of Norway 1999, STAKES 1999 of Finland, and unpublished data from Medical Birth Registry of Sweden; U.S. from Ventura et al. 2000, Martin et al. 1999, and Curtin 1999; German data supplied by Susan Erikson from individual state reports; Scottish data from Information and Statistics Division 1998; Dutch data from *Central Bureau voor de Statistiek* 1999; English data from Macfarlane et al. (2000).
[a]Includes pain relief and anesthesia for cesarean.
[b]Forceps and vacuum extraction.
[c]Four states in Germany (Thuringen, Bayern, Hessen, Nordrhein-Westfalen) with a total population equal to 47 percent of the national total.
[d]1996
[e]1997
[f]1999

BIRTH OUTCOMES

The outcomes presented in Table A–4 are familiar to many who examine cross-national maternity care data. The poor ranking of the United States (last among the twenty countries in Table A–4 on infant mortality, third worst in perinatal mortality, second worst in rate of low birthweight babies and fourth worst perinatal mortality) is frequently noted. Of some interest is the strong performance of Spain—a country not studied in this book—which does well on all outcomes presented in Table A–4. The countries in which women are at greatest lifetime risk for maternal mortality are France, the Netherlands, Denmark, and the U.S., while risk is lowest (and on average

TABLE A–4
Birth Outcomes

Country	Percent Low Birth Weight Babies (< 2,500gm) 1998	Infant Mortality Rate (IMR), 1998	Percent Positive Change in in IMR, 1960–97	Perinatal Mortality Rate, 1998	Average Maternal Deaths per 100,000 Live Births 1995–98[g]
Australia	6.1[a]	5.0	73.8	5.8	5.3
Austria	6.1	4.9	87.5	6.6	3.2
Belgium	NA	6.0[b]	80.8[a]	7.8[d]	NA
Canada	5.8[a]	5.5[a]	79.9	6.6[a]	4.9[e]
Denmark	5.5[b]	4.7	75.4	8.0[b]	8.7[f]
Finland	4.2	4.2	81.4	5.1[a]	3.3[e]
France	6.2[a]	4.7[a]	82.9	7.0[a]	10.8[f]
Germany	6.2[a]	4.7	85.8	6.2	5.9
Ireland	NA	6.2	78.8	9.0[d]	NA
Italy	NA	6.2[b]	85.9[a]	7.6[b]	3.5[f]
Japan	8.1	3.6	88.0	6.0	6.7
Netherlands	4.8[b]	5.2	72.1	7.9[a]	9.7
New Zealand	6.3	6.8[a]	69.9	6.5[a]	5.2[e]
Norway	4.7	4.0	78.3	6.2	4.1[e]
Portugal	6.7	6.0	91.7	6.8	6.5
Spain	5.9[a]	5.0[a]	88.6	6.3[a]	2.7[e]
Sweden	4.1	3.5	78.3	5.4[a]	4.2[e]
Switzerland	5.6[a]	4.8	77.3	6.8	5.3[e]
United Kingdom	7.5	5.7	73.8	8.3	6.8
United States	7.6	7.2	72.3	7.5[a]	7.6

SOURCE: OECD data 2000.
[a]1996; [b]1996; [c]1960–1996; [d]1995; [e]1995–97; [f]1995–96

[g]The relative infrequency of infant mortality in industrialized countries results in considerable annual variation, therefore the ratios represent the average of the most recent years available between 1995 and 1998.

one-third that of the four worst countries) in Spain, Austria, Finland, and Italy. The different rankings by countries on maternal and infant mortality may reflect both variances in measurement and differing approaches to protecting the lives of infants and mothers.

Conclusion

In summary, using cross-national data for comparative purposes is not for the faint-hearted. One must engage in what Øyen (1990) calls the "art of methodological compromise" and make hard decisions about the limits on analysis. The more one delves into the nature of the measures used in the respective countries, the more one realizes how little of what they thought they knew was true. Nonetheless, this is precisely one of the benefits of comparative research, moving us beyond parochial perceptions of the nature of problems. As Etzioni and Dubow (1970, p. 2) note:

> If we approach the data with an open mind, we quickly discover the habits and beliefs which we consider fundamental may be viewed by others as marginal, and vice versa. Institutions we consider natural turn out to be only our particular way of doing things, and we may see other routes by which our problems have been approached.

Acknowledgments

Data from the Nordic Medical Birth Registries was received from Dr. Lorentz M. Irgens, Norway; Ms. Milla Pakkanen, Sweden; and Ms. Riitta Koskinen, Finland.

References

Basch, P. 1999. *Textbook of International Health,* 2nd ed. New York: Oxford University Press.
Central Bureau voor de Statistiek. 1999. *Vademecum Health Statistics.* Rijswijk, Netherlands: Central Bureau vour de Statistick.
Curtin, S. 1999. Recent changes in birth attendant, place of birth and the use of obstetric interventions, United States, 1989–1997. *Journal of Nurse Midwifery* 44: 349–354.
Declercq, E., and D. Simmes. The politics of drive-through deliveries: Putting early postpartum discharge on the legislative agenda. *Milbank Quarterly* 75(2):175–202.
Dogan, M., and D. Pelassy. 1990. *How to Compare Nations: Strategies in Comparative Politics,* 2nd ed. Chatham, NJ: Chatham House.
Etzioni, A., and F. Dubow (eds.). 1970. *Comparative Perspectives.* Boston: Little and Brown.
European Commission. 1999. *Eurostal Yearbook 1999.* Luxembourg: European Commission.
Gissler, M. 1999. *Administrative Registers in Health Research. A Cohort Study of Finnish Children Born 1987* (STAKES, Research Report 97). Helsinki: STAKES.
Gissler, M., Louhiala, P., and E. Hemminki. 1996. Nordic Medical Birth registers in epidemiological research. *European Journal of Epidemiology* 13: 169–175.
Gissler, M., Ollila, E., Teperi, J., and E. Hemminki. 1994. Impact of induced abortions and statistical definitions on perinatal mortality figures. *Paediatric and Perinatal Epidemiology* 8: 391–400.

Green, D., Moore, J., Adams, M., Berg, C., Wilcox, L., and B. McCarthy. 1998. Are we under-estimating rates of vaginal births after previous cesarean birth? The validity of delivery methods from birth certificates. *American Journal of Epidemiology* 147: 581–586.

Information and Statistics Division. 1998. *Scottish Health Statistics 1997.* Edinburgh: National Health Services in Scotland.

Keirse, M. J. 1984. Perinatal mortality rates do not contain what they purport to contain. *Lancet* 26: 1166–1169.

Macfarlane, A., Mugford, M., Henderson, J., Furtado, A., Stevens, J., and A. Dunne. 2000. *Birth Counts: Statistics of Pregnancy and Childbirth.* Vol. 2: Tables. Norwich, England: The Stationery Office.

Martin, J., Smith, B., Mathews, T., and S. Ventura. 1999. Births and deaths: Preliminary data for 1998. *National Vital Statistics Reports,* Vol. 47, (No. 25). Hyattsville, MD: National Center for Health Statistics.

Medical Birth Registry of Norway. 1997. *Births in Norway through 30 years.* Bergen: Medical Birth Registry of Norway.

———. 1999. *Annual Report 1998.* Bergen: Medical Birth Registry of Norway.

Organisation for Economic Co-operation and Development. 1992. *The Reform of Health Care Systems: A Comparative Analysis of Seven OECD Countries.* Paris: OECD.

———. 1994. *The Reform of Health Care Systems: A Review of Seventeen OECD Countries.* Paris: OECD.

———. 1999. OECD health data 99: A comparative analysis of 29 countries. Paris: OECD.

———. 2000. Health Data (CD-ROM). OECD: Paris.

Øyen, E. 1990. *Comparative Methodology: Theory and Practice in International Social Research.* Newbury Park, CA: Sage Publishers.

Population Reference Bureau. 2000. *2000 World Population Data Sheet.* Washington DC: Population Reference Bureau.

Scheuch, E. K. 1966. Cross-national comparisons using aggregate data: Some substantive and methodological problems. In *Comparing Nations: The Use of Quantitative Data in Cross-National Research,* eds. R. Merritt and S. Rokkan. New Haven, CT: Yale University Press.

STAKES. 1999. *Finnish Perinatal Statistics 1997–1998* (Statistical report 4/1/1999). Helsinki: STAKES.

Teune, H. 1990. Comparing countries: Lessons learned. In *Comparative Methodology: Theory and Practice in International Social Research,* ed. E. Øyen. London: Sage, pp. 38–62

U.S. Congress Congressional Budget Office. 1992. *Factors Contributing to the Infant Mortality Ranking of the United States.* Washington, DC: Congressional Budget Office.

U.S. Congress Office of Technology Assessment. 1993. *International Health Statistics: What the Numbers Mean for the United States* (OTA-BP-H-116). Washington, DC: U.S. Government Printing Office.

U.S. Department of Health and Human Services. 1998. *International Health Data Reference Guide, 1997* (DHHS Publ. No. [PHS] 98-1007). Hyattsville, MD: USDHHS.

Ventura, S., Martin, J., Curtin, S., Mathews, T., and M. Park. 2000. Births: Final data for 1998 (*National Vital Statistics Reports* Vol. 48, No. 3). Hyattsville, MD: National Center for Health Statistics.

WHO. 1977. *International Classification of Disease. Manual of the International Statistical Classification of Disease, Injury and Cause of Death,* 9th revision. Geneva: WHO.

Contributors

Madeleine Akrich (akrich@csi.ensmp.fr) is *maître de recherche* at the *Centre de Sociologie de l'Innovation, Ecole des Mines de Paris.* Her work is mainly devoted to the sociology of technology, with a special interest in the users of technology. Her recent research is in the area of obstetrics—looking at the way technology influences the experiences of women and the relationships and practices of professionals—and in the area of new information technologies in biomedicine—examining their influence on the constitution of new professional and patient collectives. The work reported on here was supported by MIRE (*Mission Interministérielle de Recherche et d'Expérimentation*) and INSERM (*Institut National Supérieur d'Expérimentation et de Recherche Médicale*).

Cecilia Benoit, Ph.D. (cbenoit@uvic.ca) holds two jobs at the University of Victoria, British Columbia, Canada. She is Professor in the Department of Sociology and Assistant Director of the Office of International Affairs. Her primary teaching and research interests are in women's work and social rights, occupations and professions, comparative health care systems, gender, and health. She is author of *Midwives in Passage* (1991) and *Women, Work and Social Rights* (2000) and coeditor of *Reconceiving Midwifery: The New Canadian Model of Care in Childbirth* (forthcoming).

Ivy Lynn Bourgeault, Ph.D. (ivyb@julian.uwo.ca) is Assistant Professor in Sociology and Health Sciences at the University of Western Ontario in London, Ontario, Canada. She presently heads a major study funded by the Social Sciences and Humanities Research Council of Canada on the impact of the integration of midwifery into the Canadian health care system. She has been active within the midwifery and alternative childbirth movement in Ontario for over ten years, most recently as a Director of the Toronto Free Standing Birth Centre. Her research interests include alternative medicine, patient consumerism, and the relations between health professions and the state.

Elizabeth Cartwright, Ph.D. (carteliz@isu.edu) is Assistant Professor in the Department of Anthropology at Idaho State University in Pocatello, Idaho. Her current work is focused on two topics: comparative studies of obstetrics, risk and malpractice law in the United States and Western Europe, and migration and health among farmworker populations in the United States and Mexico, with a special focus on the ethnogynecology of cervical uterine cancer and menopause.

Robbie Davis-Floyd, PhD. (davis-floyd@mail.utexas.edu) is Research Fellow in the Department of Anthropology at the University of Texas at Austin. The research she reports on here was funded by the Wenner-Gren Foundation (Grants #6015 and #6427). She specializes in medical anthropology and the anthropology of reproduction and is the author of *Birth as an American Rite of Passage,* coauthor of *From Doctor to Healer: The Transformative Journey,* and coeditor of *Childbirth and Authoritative Knowledge: Cross-Cultural Perspectives, Cyborg Babies: From Techno-Sex to Techno-Tots and Intuition: The Inside Story.* She is at work coediting books on midwifery in Mexico, Canada, and the United States, as well as a special issue of *Medical Anthropology* entitled "Daughters of Time: The Shifting Identities of Postmodern Midwives."

Betty-Anne Daviss, RM, CPM, MA (midwife@istar.ca) is a registered midwife in Ontario and Quebec, Canada; Chair of the Statistics and Research Committee of the Midwives' Alliance of North America (MANA); Preceptor for Midwifery Education Program in Ontario; skills evaluator for Manitoba midwives; and a regular guest lecturer at Women's Studies at Carleton University, Ottawa. Her current academic work centers on understanding the collision course between social movements and health professions and on the creation (with epidemiologist Ken Johnson) of a home/hospital birth database.

Eugene Declercq, Ph.D. (declercq@bu.edu) is Associate Chair of the Maternal and Child Health Department at the Boston University School of Public Health. He was a childbirth educator for almost twenty years and combines his interest in maternity care issues with his training as a political scientist to examine maternal and child health policy both in the United States and in international settings. His research on the United Kingdom was supported by grants from the Nuffield Foundation and the British Foundation.

Raymond DeVries, Ph.D. (devries@stolaf.edu) is Professor of Sociology at St. Olaf College in Northfield, Minnesota. He has done a great deal of research on maternity care and midwifery and is completing a book on the maternity care system of the Netherlands. He has also edited *Bioethics and Society: Constructing the Ethical Enterprise* (Prentice-Hall, 1998) and continues to do research in the sociology of medical ethics.

Susan L. Erikson (erikson@ucsu.colorado.edu) is a Ph.D. candidate in the Department of Anthropology, University of Colorado, Boulder. She is currently conducting research on prenatal diagnostic technology use in Germany with financial support from the National Science Foundation and the Wenner-Gren Foundation. Her primary academic interests include the politics and ethics of reproductive technologies and the social implications of the Human Genome Project.

Myriam Haagmans-Cortenraad is an independently practicing midwife in the Netherlands. She serves as a supervisor for student midwives on placement and is a yoga tutor.

Annie Heuts-Verstraten is an independently practicing midwife, working for more than twenty-five years in a small Dutch village. She serves as a supervisor for student midwives and is interested in echoscopy in primary care midwifery practice. She also facilitates workshops at a Belgium midwifery college.

Jillian Ireland, RGN, RM, B.A., M.Sc. (jillian@nmdu3.swinternet.co.uk) is a midwife at Grampian University Hospitals & Grampian Primary Health Care Trusts, Aberdeen, Scotland. She trained as a midwife in Scotland and later worked for a year in Zimbabwe and Botswana. Jillian has researched several aspects of midwifery; she is currently interested in social and attitudinal dimensions of the promotion of breastfeeding.

Barbara Katz Rothman, Ph. D., is Professor of Sociology at the City University of New York, Baruch College and the Graduate School. The work presented here was funded in part by a Fulbright Fellowship of the Council for the International Exchange of Scholars and by the Professional Staff Congress of the City University of New York. Her research examines midwifery, maternity care, and issues in new technologies of procreation and genetics. Her most recent book is *Genetic Maps and Human Imaginations: The Limits of Science in Understanding Who We Are* (W.W. Norton, 1998).

Wouter J. Meijer, M.D. (w.meijer@fed.knmg.nl) is a staff member at the Royal Dutch Medical Association in the field of appropriate use of information and communication technology in health care. His research on cooperation between midwives, obstetricians, and general practitioners was done when he was at the Netherlands Institute for Health Care Research (NIVEL) in Utrecht; the study was funded by the Dutch Ministry of Health, Welfare and Sport.

Janneli F. Miller (janneli@u.arizona.edu; jannelim@hotmail.com) is a licensed midwife and a Ph.D. Candidate at the University of Arizona in Tucson. She is conducting fieldwork in Chihuahua, Mexico, on the birthing practices of the Tarahumara. As a licensed midwife with over twenty years of experience, her research interests in anthropology extend to all facets of maternal child health practices and services in cross-cultural contexts, as well as ethnomedicine, ethnobotany, ritual healing, and phenomenological research methodologies.

Margaret K. Nelson, Ph.D. (mnelson@jaguar.middlebury.edu) is Hepburn Professor of Sociology, Middlebury College, Middlebury Vermont. She has written about social class differences in childbirth, women's work of caregiving (*Circles of Care: Work and Identity in Women's Lives* [with Emily Abel], SUNY Press, 1990; *Negotiated Care: The Experiences of Family Day Care Providers,* Temple University Press, 1999), and family survival strategies in an era of economic restructuring (*Working Hard and Making Do: Surviving in Small Town America* [with Joan Smith]. University of California Press, 1999). She is currently conducting research on the support system available to, and created by, single mothers.

Bernike Pasveer (b.pasveer@tss.unimaas.nl) is Assistant Professor in the Faculty of Arts and Culture, University of Maastricht, the Netherlands. Since 1994, she has been working with Madeleine Akrich on a study of obstetrical mediators (machines, hospitals/homes, partners, books, midwives, etc.) in pregnancy and birth, their role in the definitions of "normal" birth, the configuration of bodies, the distribution of competencies and agency, and women's experience of birth. She is also working on a study of the presence/presentation/constitution of illness, death, and disability in everyday family photography.

Rebecca Popenoe, Ph.D. (popenoe@swipnet.se) is Assistant Professor of Anthropology at Linköping University (Sweden). She did her Ph.D. research among Arabs in Niger, West Africa, exploring their female aesthetic of fattened bodies and its embeddedness in their concepts of sexuality, gender, health and illness, and Islam. She has been living in Sweden for three years and is interested in gender roles and the welfare state.

Marike Roos-Ploeger is an independently practicing midwife in the Netherlands. In her twenty-five year career she has worked in a variety of practice settings—solo, duo, and group. She serves as a supervisor for student midwives and is interested in the use of homeopathy in midwifery.

Helga B. Salvesen, M.D. (hesa@haukeland.no) is associated with the Department of Obstetrics and Gynecology at Haukeland University Hospital in Bergen, Norway. She is currently doing research on women's wishes regarding maternity care and genetic alterations in tumors associated with gynecologic cancer. Support for the research discussed in this volume was provided by the Ella and Kaare Nygaard Foundation (St. Olaf College, Northfield, Minnesota).

Jane Sandall, Ph.D. (j.sandall@city.ac.uk) is Reader in Midwifery at City University, London, England. Her Ph.D. in sociology was on the impact of the changing organization of midwifery care on midwifery work and the personal lives of midwives in the United Kingdom. Her current research examines the changing roles of maternal health professions in the United Kingdom and the implications of the new genetics on maternity care.

Beate A. Schüecking, M.D. (Beate.Schuecking@rz.uni-osnabrueck.de) is Professor in the faculty of Health Sciences and Psychology at the University of Osnabrueck (Germany). She is interested in establishing a place for midwifery studies in the German academic system and is doing quantitative and qualitative research in the field of reproductive health. Professor Schüecking acknowledges the assistance of the Association of German Midwives (BDH), who chose her as their counselor.

Jan Thomas, Ph.D. (jthomasphd@cs.com) is a Visiting Assistant Professor at Georgetown University. Her current work focuses on the politics of midwifery and the social construction of pain in childbirth. Her teaching interests include health and illness, women's health, social movements, and gender.

Leonie van der Hulst (L.A.vanderHulst@amc.uva.nl) is a midwife and research sociologist at the Amsterdam Medical Centre in the Netherlands. She trained and worked as an independent midwife, is currently working on a Ph.D. in midwifery, and has published widely on aspects of Dutch midwifery.

Edwin R. van Teijlingen, Ph.D. (van.teijlingen@abdn.ac.uk) is lecturer at the Dugald Baird Centre for Research on Women's Health and the Department of Public Health, University of Aberdeen, Scotland. His Ph.D. in sociology was on the organization of maternity care in Scotland and the Netherlands, and his current research includes health promotion evaluation and many different aspects of midwifery and maternity care. He is coeditor of *Midwifery and the Medicalization of Childbirth: Comparative Perspectives* (Nova Science, 2000).

Kirsi Viisainen, M.D., M.A. (kirsi.viisainen@stakes.fi) works as a researcher at the National Research and Development Centre for Welfare and Health (STAKES) in Helsinki, Finland. Her research is currently centered on evaluating maternity care practices in Finland and in developing countries from both health system and client perspectives and on evaluating the effectiveness of specialized hospital care.

Therese A. Wiegers, Ph.D. (t.wiegers@nivel.nl) is a Research Fellow at the NIVEL (Netherlands Institute for Health Care Research). She uses her training in psychology and epidemiology to study the social and professional context of maternity care, including midwives, general practitioners, gynecologists/obstetricians, and maternity home care.

A. Susan Williams, Ph.D. (s.williams@ioe.ac.uk) is Lecturer in History at the Institute of Education University of London. She has written on a wide range of issues related to women's lives and work. Her most recent books include *Ladies of Influence: Women of the Elite in Interwar Britain* (Penguin, 2000) and *Women and Childbirth in the Twentieth Century* (Sutton, 1997). She has edited and coedited several books, including Penguin anthologies of writing by women, *The Politics of the Welfare State* (UCL Press, 1995), and *Mother Courage: Letters from Mothers in Poverty at the End of the Century* (Penguin, 1997).

Sirpa Wrede (sirpa.wrede@abo.fi) is a Ph.D. candidate and researcher in the Department of Sociology at Åbo Akademi University, Turku, Finland. She is presently finishing her Ph.D. thesis on Finnish maternity care services and Finnish midwives. Her future work will include participation in a Nordic study of woman-dominated professional groups.

Index